Law, Governance and Technology Series

Volume 42

Series Editors
Pompeu Casanovas, Barcelona, Spain
Giovanni Sartor, Florence, Italy

The *Law-Governance and Technology Series* is intended to attract manuscripts arising from an interdisciplinary approach in law, artificial intelligence and information technologies. The idea is to bridge the gap between research in IT law and IT-applications for lawyers developing a unifying techno-legal perspective. The series will welcome proposals that have a fairly specific focus on problems or projects that will lead to innovative research charting the course for new interdisciplinary developments in law, legal theory, and law and society research as well as in computer technologies, artificial intelligence and cognitive sciences. In broad strokes, manuscripts for this series may be mainly located in the fields of the Internet law (data protection, intellectual property, Internet rights, etc.), Computational models of the legal contents and legal reasoning, Legal Information Retrieval, Electronic Data Discovery, Collaborative Tools (e.g. Online Dispute Resolution platforms), Metadata and XML Technologies (for Semantic Web Services), Technologies in Courtrooms and Judicial Offices (E-Court), Technologies for Governments and Administrations (E-Government), Legal Multimedia, and Legal Electronic Institutions (Multi-Agent Systems and Artificial Societies).

More information about this series at http://www.springer.com/series/8808

Romain Boulet • Claire Lajaunie • Pierre Mazzega
Editors

Law, Public Policies and Complex Systems: Networks in Action

 Springer

Editors
Romain Boulet
Univ Lyon, Jean Moulin, iaelyon,
Magellan
Lyon, France

Claire Lajaunie
DICE International, Comparative and European
Laws
INSERM
Aix en Provence, France

Pierre Mazzega
Geosciences Environment Toulouse
CNRS
Toulouse, France

ISSN 2352-1902   ISSN 2352-1910   (electronic)
Law, Governance and Technology Series
ISBN 978-3-030-11505-0   ISBN 978-3-030-11506-7   (eBook)
https://doi.org/10.1007/978-3-030-11506-7

This Springer imprint is published by the registered company Springer Nature Switzerland AG.
The registered company address is: Gewerbestrasse 11, 6330 Cham, Switzerland

Foreword

A Significant Contribution to Sustainability Science

On 25 September 2015, in the year it turned 70, the United Nations succeeded in agreeing on a new, comprehensive global development framework, when the delegates of the 193 member states approved the resolution entitled "Transforming our World – the 2030 Agenda for Sustainable Development". A few months later, in December of the same year, the COP 21 Paris Agreement on climate change was a spectacular operationalisation of multilateral determination to effectively reach the Sustainable Development Goal on climate action (SDG number 13). The 2030 Agenda is the fruit of long and intensive labour and a key step forward for a process which has held over the past decades [UN-DESA (2012) Back to our common Saez E, Zucman G Future. Sustainable Development in the 21st century (SD21) project].

At the UN Stockholm Conference in 1972, which marked the beginning of international environmental policy, the thematic focus was still on environmental protection. The subsequent conference, the 1992 Earth Summit in Rio de Janeiro, already used a much broader definition of sustainable development, thanks to the preparatory report of the Brundtland Commission [World Commission on Sustainable Development (1987) Our common future]. This report established the groundbreaking premises of sustainable development that are still valid today: that, in addition to economic growth that has been central in development policies since the end of World War II, we should take into account the societal and ecological dimension of sustainability and ensure justice and fairness within today's generations and between them and future generations (inter- and intra-generational equity) (Wissenschaftlicher Beirat der Bundesregierung Globale Umweltveränderungen 2011. Welt im Wandel – Gesellschaftsvertrag für eine Große Transformation – Zusammenfassung für Entscheidungsträger). The 1990s saw the adoption of the crucial global Rio conventions on climate change, biological diversity and desertification, as well as countless other binding multilateral and bilateral environmental agreements. Efforts however remained largely sectoral, and the sobering assessment of outcomes at the turn of the millennium finally led to the first agreed multilateral agenda for sustainable development, the UN Millennium Development Goals (MDGs 2000–2015).

The MDGs reflected the global community's high expectations of finally calling a halt to poverty and to the destruction of the natural and social environment of our planet, even though they were focused on developing countries, the rich OECD ones being only concerned in the area of development assistance. Recent advances in scientific knowledge have played a major role in influencing the subsequent *SDGs 2030 Agenda* to express a deeper understanding of sustainable development which includes all countries and all of society in each country. The core message, *"leave no one behind"*, of the 2030 Agenda comes from research that has shown that despite growing overall prosperity, progress in absolute poverty eradication and some reduction of inter-countries inequality, a large part of the world's population is still experiencing critical human deprivations and thus lacks dignified living conditions [World Bank (2016) Poverty and shared prosperity 2016: taking on inequality], and the last 40 years have seen an unprecedented rise in intra-country inequalities in most parts of the world [Alvaredo et al (eds) (2018) World inequality report 2018]. In Agenda 2030, the principle of equity is now becoming an essential means of implementation that links sustainable development with other overarching normative systems, such as basic human rights, gender equality, social inclusion and democracy [Waas et al (2011) Sustainable development: a bird's eye view. Sustainability 3:1637–1661; UNDP (2011) Human Development Report 2011 sustainability and equity: towards a better future for all].

In parallel, our improved understanding of dynamic processes within the Earth system has demonstrated that profound changes affecting this system are no longer largely caused by natural forces: they comprise human-made global change, which has accelerated sharply since the middle of the twentieth century [Steffen et al (2006) Global change and the earth system: a planet under pressure]. Scientists today refer to the Anthropocene [Crutzen (2006) The "anthropocene." In: Earth system science in the anthropocene. pp 13–18] as a new geological epoch in which the multiple ecological pressures acting upon Earth are too high to guarantee a safe habitat for all living species, including mankind [Rockström et al (2009) A safe operating space for humanity. Nature 461:472–475], some authors explicitly relating this threat to the specific economic and technological developments of an international capitalist system since the beginning of the industrial revolution [Malm (2016) Fossil capital: the rise of steam power and the roots of global warming; Bonneuil and Fressoz (2017) The shock of the anthropocene: the earth, history and us]. Due to the Earth system's complexity, even small changes can lead to major events with unforeseeable and irreversible consequences. We are bound to reach so-called *tipping points*, for example in the climate system, with increasing global warming [IPCC (2015) Climate change 2014: synthesis report. Contribution of Working group I, II and III to the Fifth Assessment Report of the Intergovernmental Panel on Climate Change] and in ecosystems with irreparable loss of biodiversity. Regarding climate change, the window of opportunity is currently estimated at less than a decade [Figueres et al (2017) Three years to safeguard our climate. Nature 546:593–595]. This underlines the urgency of finding solutions to these environmental problems while keep on improving the living conditions of the most vulnerable and poorest sectors of the world's population.

Quite interestingly, the contribution of science has not only been fuelled by the growing awareness of many scientists in various disciplines that they should take into account the potential contribution of their results for transformations towards a more sustainable development. This is of course a positive step, but it would have remained similar to some sectors of finance deploying sincere efforts for "green washing" and including "social responsibility" in their business activities that have been accelerated in response to the 2008 world economic major recession. Most of the major scientific advances for sustainable development have rather been the outcome of the emergence of a new field of research that has been called "*sustainability science*" by the National Academy of Sciences of the USA, as early as 2001 [Kates et al (2001) Sustainability science. Science 292(5517):641–642]. The NAAS [Clark (2007) Sustainability science: a room of its own. PNAS 104(6):1737–1738] defined sustainability science as the attempt to "un*derstand the integrated "whole" of planetary and human systems* [which] *requires cooperation between scientific, social and economic disciplines, public and private sectors, academia and government* [and] *a massive global cooperative effort*". As a direct consequence, "*one major task of sustainability science is to assist integrated cross-disciplinary coordination*".

Because most real systems consist of a large number of interacting, multi-typed components, with heterogeneous behaviours and information networks, the focus of sustainability science is on interdisciplinary investigation of complex causal chains affecting societal and ecological systems as a whole. Because globalisation in our twenty-first-century world is so full of close systemic interlinkages, sustainability science gives special attention to minimising negative interactions between sectors, and between global and local, and today and tomorrow as well as maximising positive synergies between the different dimensions of sustainability [International Council for Science (2017) A guide to SDG interactions: from science to implementation; Abson et al (2017) Leverage points for sustainability transformation. Ambio 46:30–39]. Three other key features distinguish sustainability science from "conventional" disciplinary research. First, it transfers scientific results to technologies and societal change beyond the classical "technology-push" and "demand-pull" approaches in order to promote innovations which take into account the "*3F's*" challenges of sustainable development: finitude (or planetary boundaries), fragility (growing vulnerability of eco-socio systems) and fairness (in access to technologies as well as natural resources). Second, it gives more emphasis to scientific cooperation between developed and developing countries' academic communities, since "*the limited Western view of sustainability is stifling progress*", by underestimating that "*the global south is rich of sustainability lessons*" [Nagendra (2018) The global south is rich in sustainability lessons that students deserve to hear. Nature 557:485–488]. Last but not least, sustainability science needs to be more "participatory" since communities and population groups should not be considered as end users of scientific and technological results but be actively involved, as much as needed, in the elaboration and implementation of research programmes on the ground.

Beyond the specific contributions it contains in both fields of health and water management in direct connections with SDG3 ("Good health and well-being") and 6 ("Clean water and sanitation"), which themselves interact with most of the other 15 SDGs, this book edited by Romain Boulet, Claire Lajaunie and Pierre Mazzega appears to be a significant and original triple contribution to sustainability science.

First, Francophone scientific communities have been less influential in the emergence of sustainability science than their Anglo-Saxon counterparts, and as already mentioned, their colleagues from developing countries. By dealing in depth with some interdisciplinary issues that are crucial for transformations towards sustainable development, this book will be a strong incentive for French and Francophone researchers to become explicitly involved in the specific field of sustainability science and in international debates about the Agenda 2030.

Second, and more importantly, it emphasises the actual and potential contributions of network analysis to the progress of sustainability science. Originally applied to brain network analysis [Fornito et al (2016) Fundamentals of brain network analysis], the paradigm of these innovative approaches has quickly diffused to other domains including investigation of social networks by social scientists [Scott (2016) Social network analysis]. In my own field of economics, early attempts to introduce direct and local interactions between heterogeneous individuals go back to the pioneering work of Föllmer (1974. Random economies with many interacting agents. J Math Econ 1(1):51–62). However, the relaxation of the traditional assumption of the "representative rational agent" which is key in neoclassical orthodox economics met with little response until the influence of other disciplines, such as physics and biology, in which analysis of interactive complex systems plays a central role, has helped challenge economists' vision of individual behaviours [Kirman and Zimmerman (2001) Economics with heterogeneous interacting agents. Lecture Noyes in Economic & Mathematical Systems 503]. Network analysis implies that economics must abandon the notion that agents act anonymously through market mechanisms and recognise the importance of direct relations between individuals and the role of the networks through which these interactions are mediated. Such evolution also leads to increasing mutual interest between economics, sociology and psychology. This book makes another complementary contribution by showing how network analysis can be very useful to deal with legal issues which are often key barriers to implementation of SDGs at international, national and local levels and how creative thinking may help identify practical and politically feasible pathways for transformation.

This leads to the third remarkable contribution of this book: its pertinence for bridging the intrinsic gap between science and public policies. One of the main reasons of this gap is that even the most undisputable scientific results do not easily and mechanistically translate into effective societal changes if some mediation is not found to influence public policies and modify behaviours of economic, political and social actors. In the process itself of the adoption of the 2030 agenda [Dodds et al (2016) Negotiating the sustainable development goals. A transformational agenda for an insecure world], doubts were voiced about the extent to which such an exhaustive multilateral framework, with its 17 goals and 169 targets, has the necessary transformative power to guide decision-makers from politics, business and civil society. Concerns have been raised that it may indeed be too comprehensive and imprecise, leading instead to arbitrary and fragmented policies. At a time when some major players on the international scene tend to contest multilateral agreements as a way to solve conflicts and find solutions to global problems, these concerns may appear even more legitimate. Of course, a successful implementation of the SDGs would mean a profound modification of current trends in the economic, societal and environmental affairs and very brave public policies ready to limit the influence of highly powerful lobbies and interests, which go far beyond the sole responsibility of the international scientific community. However, as many examples in this book also suggest, a sharper and more evidence-based focus and better scientific measurability of the SDGs are certainly part of the solution [ICSU and ISSC (2015) Review of targets for the sustainable development goals: the science perspective].

As the CEO of IRD, whose mandate is to promote fair scientific partnerships with developing countries, as well as one of the 15 members of the Independent Group of Scientists (IGS) appointed by the United Nations to produce the first four-year critical of the SDGs (2015–2019, https://sustainabledevelopment.un.org/globalsdreport/2019), and as the President of the French National Alliance for Research on the Environment (ALLENVI) whose mission is to ensure strategic coordination of the French research institutions in the field of the environment, I strongly welcome this book as a fruitful contribution to sustainability science and to its capacity to impact policies towards sustainable development. I am convinced that it would serve as a benchmark and an example to follow, notably in the francophone world.

Aix-Marseille University, Marseille   Jean-Paul Moatti
France

French National Research Institute for
Sustainable Development (IRD)
Marseille, France

French National Alliance for Research
on the Environment (ALLENVI)
Marseille, France

Scientific Committee of the Publication

- **Barreteau Olivier**—IRSTEA Institut National de Recherche en Sciences et Technologies pour l'Environnement et l'Agriculture, UMR G-EAU Gestion de l'Eau, Acteurs et Usages, Montpellier, France
- **Boëte Christophe**—IRD Institut de Recherche pour le Développement, ISEM UMR5554 Institut des Sciences de l'Evolution de Montpellier, France
- **Boulet Romain**—IAE Institut d'Administration des Entreprises Lyon – Ecole universitaire de management, Lyon, France
- **Bourcier Danièle**—CNRS, CERSA UMR7106 Centre d'Études et de Recherches de Science Administrative, Université Panthéon-Assas – Paris 2, Paris, France
- **Casanovas Pompeu**—Autonomous University of Barcelona, Department of Political Science and Public Law, Faculty of Law, IDT Institute of Law and Technology, Barcelona, Spain
- **Castets-Renard Céline**—Université Toulouse Capitole, Faculté de Droit, Toulouse, France
- **Drobenko Bernard**—Centre de Gestion Universitaire Boulogne-sur-Mer, Université du Littoral Côté d'Opale, Département de Droit, Boulogne-sur-Mer, France
- **Fernandez-Barrera Meritxell**—OECD Directorate for Education and Skills, Paris, France
- **Lajaunie Claire**—INSERM – DICE UMR7318 Droit International Comparé et Européen, Université Aix-Marseille, Aix en Provence, France; Affiliate researcher SCELG *Strathclyde* Centre for Environmental Law & Governance, University of Strathclyde, Glasgow, Scotland
- **Leblet Jimmy**—IAE Institut d'Administration des Entreprises Lyon – Ecole universitaire de management, Lyon, France
- **Mazzega Pierre**—CNRS, GET UMR5563 Géosciences Environnement Toulouse, France; Affiliate researcher SCELG *Strathclyde* Centre for Environmental Law & Governance, University of Strathclyde, Glasgow, Scotland
- **Morand Serge**—CNRS ISEM UMR5554/CIRAD ASTRE, Faculty of Veterinary Technology, Kasetsart University, Bangkok, Thailand

Contents

Editors and Contributors

About the Editors

Romain Boulet is Doctor in mathematics and associate professor at the iaelyon School of Management and is a member of the Magellan Research Center in Lyon, France. His research areas include graph theory (especially algebraic graph theory) and network analysis, with a particular interest in interdisciplinary collaboration. He has focused on the analysis of legal networks and organised workshops on complexity and public policy. https://www.researchgate.net/scientific-contributions/13021519_Romain_Boulet

Claire Lajaunie is Doctor of Law, HDR (accreditation to supervise research, Aix-Marseille University, France) and researcher at Inserm, in the Centre of European and International Research and Studies, within the International, Comparative and European Law research unit (CERIC, UMR DICE 7318, CNRS, Aix-Marseille Univ., Université de Toulon, Univ. Pau & Pays Adour, France). She is affiliate researcher at the Strathclyde Centre for Environmental Law and Governance, Law School (University of Strathclyde, Scotland). She is a Board Member of the International Multidisciplinary Thematic Network "Biodiversity,

Health and Societies in Southeast Asia" (Thailand). She is working on Global Environmental Law and public policies, their links with regulation regarding health (infectious diseases) and ethical issues. She is currently involved in research projects focusing on Southeast Asia, and she is particularly interested in the relationship between environmental law, ecology and rural development. https://www.researchgate.net/profile/Claire_Lajaunie

Pierre Mazzega is Doctor in earth observation from space, Engineer in geophysics and HDR (accreditation to supervise research, Toulouse University, France). Senior scientist at CNRS in the "Geosciences Environment Toulouse" research unit (GET UMR5563, France), he is affiliate researcher at the Strathclyde Centre for Environmental Law and Governance, Law School (University of Strathclyde, Scotland). He is developing research on the modelling of environmental law, policy and governance as complex systems. He has various experiences, in different research contexts, on environmental modelling and on nonlinear data analysis and assimilation in models. https://www.researchgate.net/profile/Pierre_Mazzega

Contributors

Ana Flávia Barros-Platiau IREL, Institute of International Relations, University of Brasilia, Brasilia DF, Brazil

Romain Boulet Univ Lyon, Jean Moulin, iaelyon, Magellan, Lyon, France

Élisabeth Catta Commission Supérieure de Codification, Paris, France

Charles Chansardon UMR5563 GET Geosciences Environment Toulouse, CNRS/University of Toulouse, Toulouse, France

Ricardo De Gainza Pertina SA, Paris, France

Alexandre Delliaux KRILL Company, Deuil-La Barre, France

Claire Lajaunie INSERM, CERIC, UMR DICE 7318, CNRS, Aix Marseille University, University of Toulon, University of Pau and Pays Adour, Aix-en-Provence, France

Strathclyde Centre for Environmental Law and Governance (SCELG), University of Strathclyde, Glasgow, UK

Fiona Larkan Centre for Global Health, Trinity College Dublin, Dublin, Ireland

Jimmy Leblet University of Lyon, Jean Moulin, iaelyon, Magellan Research Center, Lyon, France

Dominique Le Queau Aeronautics and Space Science and Technology Foundation, Toulouse, France

Pierre Mazzega UMR5563 GET Geosciences Environment Toulouse, CNRS/University of Toulouse, Toulouse, France

Strathclyde Centre for Environmental Law and Governance (SCELG), University of Strathclyde, Glasgow, UK

Claude Monteil DYNAFOR, Université de Toulouse, INRA, Castanet-Tolosan, France

Serge Morand CNRS ISEM/CIRAD ASTRE, Faculty of Veterinary Technology, Kasetsart University, Bangkok, Thailand

Jarlath E. Nally Bacterial Diseases of Livestock Research Unit, National Animal Disease Center, Agricultural Research Services, United States Department of Agriculture, Ames, IA, USA

Ugo Pagallo Torino Law School, University of Torino, Torino, Italy

Armand Purwati Dr. Soetomo Regional General Hospital, Institute of Tropical Diseases, Airlangga University, Surabaya, East Java, Indonesia

Christine A. Romana UFR of Medicine, University of Paris Descartes, Paris, France

University Sorbonne Paris Cité, Paris, France

Daniel Sant'Ana University of Brasilia, LACAM, Faculty of Architecture and Urbanism, Brasilia DF, Brazil

Christophe Sibertin-Blanc Institute of Research in Computer Science of Toulouse, IRIT, Université de Toulouse, CNRS, UT1, Toulouse, France

Olivier Therond AGIR, Université de Toulouse, INRA, Castanet-Tolosan, France

Bianca van Bavel Centre for Global Health, Trinity College Dublin, Dublin, Ireland

Priestley International Centre for Climate, University of Leeds, Leeds, United Kingdom

Radboud Winkels Leibniz Center for Law, University of Amsterdam, Amsterdam, Netherlands

Chapter 1
Public Policies, Law, Complexities and Networks

Pierre Mazzega, Claire Lajaunie, and Romain Boulet

Abstract Whatever the sector—codification and management of legal norms, climate change regime, governance and multilateralism, social-ecological interactions, health, natural resource management—law and public policies form complex systems resulting from the diversity of agents, resources, norms and principles they imply, and from the multiplicity of processes and activities that contribute to the evolution of the state of affairs. The complexity is also demonstrated by the poor control that stakeholders and decision-makers have over the impacts of the instruments deployed and over the responses to their implementation. In such a context, as evidenced by the studies gathered in this volume, the methods deployed to interpret, understand or explain the law or the public policies in action multiply the types of approaches and the means solicited for their study. However, an emerging trend not only provides analytical tools, but also inspires several approaches to phenomena related to law and public policy. It consists in apprehending these phenomena in terms of various networks, supports for change, intricate exchanges, knowledge and innovation, management, but besides essential ingredients of the incessant, sometimes labile, interactions between the systemic components.

P. Mazzega (✉)
UMR5563 GET Geosciences Environment Toulouse, CNRS/University of Toulouse, Toulouse, France

Strathclyde Centre for Environmental Law and Governance (SCELG), University of Strathclyde, Glasgow, UK
e-mail: pierre.mazzegaciamp@get.omp.eu

C. Lajaunie
INSERM, CERIC, UMR DICE 7318, CNRS, Aix Marseille University, University of Toulon, University of Pau and Pays Adour, Aix-en-Provence, France

Strathclyde Centre for Environmental Law and Governance (SCELG), University of Strathclyde, Glasgow, UK
e-mail: claire.lajaunie@inserm.fr

R. Boulet
Univ Lyon, Jean Moulin, iaelyon, Magellan, Lyon, France
e-mail: romain.boulet@univ-lyon3.fr

© Springer Nature Switzerland AG 2019
R. Boulet et al. (eds.), *Law, Public Policies and Complex Systems: Networks in Action*, Law, Governance and Technology Series 42,
https://doi.org/10.1007/978-3-030-11506-7_1

1.1 Introduction

Practice considers it inoperable to use theoretical insights of the systems that it constructs and manages, without any prior assured plan, by interactions of numerous agents or actors according to changing configurations and more or less explicit consultation processes. Formally, theory finds no foundation in the way public policies and law constantly inventing and renewing their modes of action (and inaction), are implemented in practice. These are the ranges of tension that each of the chapters of this collective work undertakes to express. The emerging global vision could be conceived as an analysis—among many other possibilities—of the policy of public policy, of the normativity of normative legal systems, but seen through concrete applications, located in many specific contexts.

The approaches to law and public policy presented here are the result of works conducted from a perspective that is often strongly interdisciplinary,[1] the dialogue between various scientific cultures and the mixing of methods leading to new perspectives on complex objects of study taken in their empirical reality.[2] They do not reduce the relevance of more traditional approaches—highlighting the links between public policy and administration (Henry 2004), the public policy cycle (Howlett and Ramesh 2003), the sociological approach to public action—but they preferentially exploit other concepts—such as complexity (Gilbert and Bullock 2014), ontology (Sartor et al. 2011), networks, partial order—and implement other methods (like formal models, object-oriented analysis) and tools (social simulation, scenarios, etc.).

The following chapters are part of a field of research that is evolving very rapidly, as we see in a certain distance already taken with, for example, a reference manual published only 10 years ago, which takes stock of the methodologies of political analysis (Box-Steffensmeier et al. 2008). As far as the present work can testify, this movement is explained by a shift of the centres of interests towards questions related to the increasing importance of the tangled governance dynamics (which goes beyond a cyclical vision of the life of the public policies, standards and organizations, and transgress a pyramidal organization of legal norms).

Nowadays, research on law and public policies, considered as complex systems are developing at the international level, relying strongly on modelling (see e. g. Ghose et al. 2015; Aldewereld et al. 2016) following innovative methods for

---

[1]If, unsurprisingly, there is no consensus on what inter-disciplinarity is, measures have been proposed for a decade or so, based on bibliometric data and network analysis. For example, Rafols and Meyer (2010) suggest combining two concepts: "disciplinary diversity indicates the large-scale breadth of the knowledge base of a publication; network coherence reflects the novelty of its knowledge integration". For examples of mapping of inter-disciplinarity in academic research, cf: http://idr.gatech.edu/concept.php. Accessed 25 Feb 2018.

[2]In this sense we converge on one of the conclusions put forward by Szostak et al. (2016, p. v) in their book on the organization of interdisciplinary knowledge: "A novel approach to classification, grounded in the phenomena studied rather than disciplines, would serve interdisciplinary scholarship much better. It would also prove advantageous for disciplinary scholarship."

concrete implementation. Among the featured areas, law as network of evolutive and interactive norms is now a prominent sphere of study.[3] In a similar way, public policies are now a topic on their own due to the fact that policy can no longer be examined as a linear process, but its study should encompass the complexity of networks of actors, norms and resources involved (Nguyen and Snasel 2016; Wierzbicki et al. 2016); the interdependency of their application domain, the uncertainty or the weak predictability of their direct or indirect impacts.

This volume results from the Second research workshop on "Complexity and Public Policies" jointly organised by the IAE Lyon School of Management (Jean Moulin-Lyon 3 University), by the Center for Studies and Research of Administrative and Political Sciences (CERSA UMR7106, CNRS and University Panthéon-Assas—Paris 2) and Geosciences Environment Toulouse (GET UMR5563, CNRS and University of Toulouse). This workshop aimed at assessing how law and public policies, taken as complex systems, are studied by various scientific communities (legal scientists, politists, sociologists, mathematicians, computer scientists . . .). The main themes examined concern codification, governance, climate change, norms networks, health, water management, conflicts of use, legal regimes conflicts, use of indicators or prospective scenarios.

1.2 Complexity Faced by Jurists

This book is divided into three parts. The first part "Complexity faced by jurists" intends to illustrate the different paths taken by the jurists when it comes to deal with the complexity of law and a variety of public policies and even to cope with their unexpected effects. It suggests ways and methods to simplify and rationalise the law (Chap. 2), to understand the functioning of institutional organisations involved into the development of public policies and related rules (Chap. 3) or to allow gathering a variety of knowledge and points of view in order to improve decision-making (Chap. 4). Few articles highlight new approaches of law in relation to networks (Chaps. 2, 3).

The Chap. 2 by E. Catta and A. Delliaux demonstrates how public authorities have adopted public policies in order to reduce the complexity of the law by rationalising and simplifying it. Facing a dense and always increasing network of legal norms, itself resulting from the multiplication of distinct public authorities, various public policies of law rationalisation have been adopted to codify the law. It led to the creation in 1999 of the High Commission for codification in order to simplify the law and facilitate the accessibility and the understanding of the law by the citizens in respect of the principle "ignorance of the law excuses not". Thanks to a systemic approach using computer science, and the Agil method, the purpose is to

---

[3]See the Springer books entitled "AI approaches to the complexity of legal systems" published these last years (for ex. Casanovas et al. 2010).

look for relevance rather than exhaustiveness and to allow a coherent codification. The reticular law, form of the modelling of law is also presented, as it offers a new dimension of legal science increasing altogether the flexibility and security of the legal system.

C. Lajaunie and P Mazzega invite us to examine the capacity of an informal network of organizations to produce answers in response to complex tasks requiring the integration of masses of information designed as a high-level cognitive and collective activity (Chap. 3). Studying how networks dedicated to health or environment in Southeast Asia interact, produce and share information and particularly how they integrate international law in relation to health and the environment at the regional level, through the definition of public policies and rules). Thus, they evaluate the ability to integrate information within a network of networks of organizations by assessing effective (e. g. through the composition of governing boards, the institutionalised partnerships) or potential governance (partial recoveries of roles, missions, or training offers) of themes offered by a group of organizations. For that purpose, they present a method inspired by the Information Integration Theory issued from the modelling of consciousness. They use the analogy between artificial consciousness and a potential organizational consciousness to determine if some network configurations are more favourable than others to accomplish specific tasks.

The Chap. 4 by C. Sibertin-Blanc, O. Thérond, C. Monteil et P. Mazzega presents a conceptual framework for integrated agent-based modeling and simulation of socio-ecological systems (SESs) in the form of a formal "entity-process meta-model". The MAELIA project developed an agent-based simulation platform to study environmental, economic and social impacts of scenarios of land use and water management in combination with climate change. The platform is dedicated to support decision-making processes of organizations involved in managing water scarcity in the Adour-Garonne basin (south-western France). The purpose of such a framework is to allow building an integrated representation of a system of reference that is agreed upon, and thus well-understood, by everyone on a project involving people with a variety of theoretical or empirical knowledge, viewpoints, concerns and duties. It also considers stakes in project outcomes. The complexity is dealt thanks to the model modularity allowing taking into account different dynamics into the various components of the meta-model and to present them to the decision-makers and the variety of stakeholders involved into land use and water management.

1.3   Complexity in Action and Policy Analysis

The second part of the book "Complexity in action and policy analysis" is focusing on different field situations mainly in relation with health and water management and draw lessons from field study to improve policy analysis. It shows the necessity of interdisciplinary settings and of the consideration of the different dynamics at play for a better policy response.

In Chap. 5, B. Van Bavel, F. Larkan, J.E. Nally and A. Pruwati present a field study based on 275 household surveys in pilot sites located in three different Regencies of East Java, Indonesia. The sites have been chosen because they had the highest rate of reported cases of leptospirosis within the Province. This study intends to identify environmental and social risk determinants of cases of leptospirosis, a zoonosis of public health importance in Southeast Asia where most countries are endemic for leptospirosis. It highlights two new key factors attributable to changes in the distribution of leptospirosis. In addition to socio-economic and sanitation deprivation, the study insists on the lack of integrated surveillance and mandated notification system. This research reinforces the success of local and adaptive surveillance initiatives and calls for wider integration of efforts and resources across communities, institutions, and sectors. The results of this study can be used to communicate associated impacts of poor domestic environments and demand for healthier circumstances in such deprived communities. Interdisciplinary dialogue is recommended to inform leptospirosis research, strengthen surveillance, and affect public health action.

In the Chap. 6, C. Lajaunie, S. Morand and P. Mazzega are showing, thanks to insights gained from research projects in the area, the necessity to develop process-based scenarios of future health in Southeast Asia Indeed, the results underlined that biodiversity changes, notably land use changes at regional to local scales are factors of health risks and of emergence of zoonotic diseases. It also confirmed the importance of the spatio-temporal dynamics of the land use land cover in determining the diversity of wildlife and their parasites (using network analyses), with implications for human risk of zoonotic diseases. It appeared necessary to understand the various dynamics at stake and to develop scenarios of future health that are embedded in the socio-ecosystems and integrating the effects of policies and law as factors of change. The purpose is to develop indicators for decision-makers from local to regional (ASEAN) level, along with their uncertainty and caveats about the limitations of their use, including ethical, and prospective proposals of strategic directions for evidence-based policies linked with the possible mitigation of outbreaks and spread of infectious diseases in the ASEAN economic corridors.

In order to determine and detail the complex activities of monitoring, surveillance and warning of the French Institute for Public Health Surveillance (InVS, French Public Health Agency), R. De Gainza and C. Romana design an architectural pattern for a surveillance and early warning system based on the description contained in three InVS reports (2005, 2006 and 2011) as requirements for a Public Health Surveillance and Early Warning System. The conceptual framework of this modelling work implies studying risk exposure situation to environmental health threats of human, animal or vegetal populations and responsibilities of the system in charge of monitoring, reporting and warning in case of unacceptable risks. Based on examples of three environmental health threats, the architectural pattern proposed is a meta-model that can be applied to any case of environmental health threat. The architectural pattern presented in Chap. 7 aims to enable seamless information sharing between institutional actors in charge of surveillance and early warning. It also acts as an interface between expert's knowledge and operational tasks. The application of this tool to forecast, develop and manage health surveillance and early warning systems could deliver better information and resource sharing, more precise characterization of surveillance and early warning target exposure situations and clearer management options when forecasting risks.

Chapter 8 presented by P. Mazzega, D. Le Queau, C. Sibertin-Blanc and D. Sant'Ana advocates for the need for an explicit and assumed strengthening of the coordination of water stakeholders at all levels of governance in order to reach the expectations of a comprehensive policy in the field of water management and development. For this purpose they propose to develop interdisciplinary and intersectoral collaboration using new hybrid modelling approaches (coupling multi-agent system, geographic information system, equation models, cellular automata, etc.), allows to precisely simulate the scenarios of evolution of water resource management and development, to assess ex ante their social, economic and environmental impacts and to anticipate the contribution of an increased coordination of water stakeholders in a logic of development-friendly actions.

C. Sibertin-Blanc comes back to the dramatic event which led to the death of an opponent to the construction of a dam in Sivens, Tarn (France) insisting on the fact that the violence of the means deployed for the realization of this work and the determination of the opponents presaged the possibility of such a drama whose circumstances are woven by the play of all the actors of this project. Using a formal analytical grid based on the sociology of organized action and on the basis of interviews with actors and the important documentation available, this Chap. 9 proposes an analysis of actors' conflict through model and simulations of this actors' game. This model highlights the over-determined character of the conflict. As such, it could be used, in the case of the realization of a public equipment, in the determination of strategies leading to an acceptable compromise by the actors.

1.4 Complexity and Networks

The third part of the book is considering complexity and networks through different perspectives. One chapter invite to use the web of law to exploit new relevant sources of law on the internet (Chap. 10) while another one uses the hypergraph theory in order to show the level of connectivity between the environmental and trade regimes using the modelling of ratification of United Nations multilateral treaties (Chap. 11). The partial order set theory allows the comparison between national sets of indicators of environment and development the analysis, notably for countries with economies having a strong impact on climate change (Chap. 12) while Chap. 13 relies on network theory to study how scholars approach the law as a matter of information.

In Chap. 10, R. Winkels presents a project developing a platform that enables users to find legal information more easily, organize it the way they want and share it with others. The OpenLaws platform is an open source and open data platform designed and operated by legal communities and IT communities. It focuses first on legal professionals, but it is open to anyone. Its goal is to enable users to find legal information more easily, organise it the way they want and share it with others. The project is to create the web of law if it is not available in machine readable form, or extend it use. It uses network analysis of both legislation and case law to recommend potentially interesting new sources of law. The chapter presents results of experiments using analysis of the network of references or citations to suggest new documents. The aim is to allow automatic suggestions based on analysis of existing data and in the future, it could also be based on user-generated data.

Thanks to hypergraph modelling, R. Boulet, A.F. Barros-Platiau and P. Mazzega compare and analyse (Chap. 11) the trend of ratifications of Multilateral Environmental Agreements (MEAs) and United Nations-based trade agreements. Indeed, the hypergraph-based analysis of the temporal successions of ratifications allows highlighting informal and emerging communities of countries that tends to ratify these types of agreements in the same period of time. The chapter gives insights about the interest to use hypergraph analysis in a legal context. The comparison of the dynamics of ratifications of two regimes—environment and trade—within the United Nations framework shows that they follow parallel evolution, in spite of the strengthening of their intertwining since the 1990s, notably from an institutional point of view. The UN has a central role in the environmental agenda while for the trade agenda, on the contrary, the role of the United Nations is becoming less and less important, and the multilateral summits had a very limited impact.

Another type of comparison, using the partial order set theory, is presented by P. Mazzega, C. Lajaunie, J. Leblet, A. F. Barros-Platiau and C. Chansardon. Chapter 12 analyses the relative positions (partial order) of a set of countries with consideration for environmental and development indicators. Using data from 2013 on three integrative environmental indicators and two development indicators (human development index and GDP per capita), the analysis mainly covers the countries with economies having a strong impact on climate change—China, the USA, the European Union (member States), India, Russian Federation, Japan, Brazil, Canada, and Mexico. Global findings show that there are two groups of states, the EU and the BRICS, that matter in global environmental politics and related issues, like energy, climate change, health and ocean governance. The analysis of indicators tends to trigger the introduction of new measures to improve a particular situation in a specific field. As such the composition of a variety of indicators followed by the analysis of the comparability of countries can be useful in making international or national decision, or even for the involvement of a growing number of state or non-state actors in solving societal or environmental issues.

Finally, U. Pagallo concentrates on network theory and the law and focuses on the analysis of the law conceived as a set of rules or instructions for the determination of other informational objects, or in other terms, legal information for reality and distinguishes distinguishing three different levels of analysis on legal information "as" reality, "about" reality, and "for" reality. It stresses that network theory can be fruitful either as a support for the deliberation and decisions made by legislators and policy makers, or as a support for scholars and experts about what should be deemed as legally relevant.

1.5 A Reticular Vision of the Volume

On another scale, a reticular vision of the book gives a taste of its content. The choice of keywords has not been guided by any particular principle, has not followed any guideline. Thus, each group of authors is likely to use identical words but whose connotations, or the network of neighbouring concepts is not identical and depends on the culture and sensitivity of each one. Conversely, different names can refer to the same notion, and the same idea can be expressed in numerous and various ways. These observations affect any use of a natural language, as is the case in the description of public policies or regulations, although in the latter case, especially, certain concepts are included in a definition of a normative nature. Thus, the content of this book can be both synthesized and mapped by first gathering the keywords under main topics—in this case conceived as classes of concepts or lists of expressions (the "bags of words" in text mining) here chosen by the editors—then representing how these topics are distributed between the chapters of the book and reciprocally how the chapters cover the topics. This double organization is shown in Fig. 1.1 as a Galois lattice, a mathematical structure that is widely used in knowledge representation (Ganter and Wille 1999; Codocedo and Napoli 2015).

Apart from its use for reading the book, we present the construction of this lattice because it illustrates some of the key difficulties that arise in the analysis of public policy and law, the provision of methods of knowledge representation, the flexibility of natural language and the need to explain the categories and concepts used (even if other choices can be made). We propose to bring together the topics under two meta-classes: the first, whose label could be "knowledge-oriented keywords" includes the classes "data analysis", "methodology", "governance" and "risk"; the second with the label "resource (and goods)-oriented keywords" includes "global change", "water", "biological diversity", "health" and "knowledge".

Of course, each article produces knowledge on public policies or on the legal norms analyzed, but here "knowledge" is considered as a resource, a component of the studied systems, with specific characteristics (legal complexity, collective consciousness) and requiring specific methods of management (science- policy dialogue, monitoring or warning systems, data management, actors' games, case law, legal order). Under the term "methodology" we group codification, dematerialization of the law, networks (and graphs) analysis, ontologies, constructions of models, scenarios, questionnaires, object-oriented analysis, social simulation, natural language processing or machine learning. We proceeded in the same way for the other classes of key words or expressions. Reading the chapters which follow should assure the reader of the consistency of this categorization.

The authors and editors of the chapters that follow are grateful to the members of the scientific committee of this book (see its composition at the beginning of the

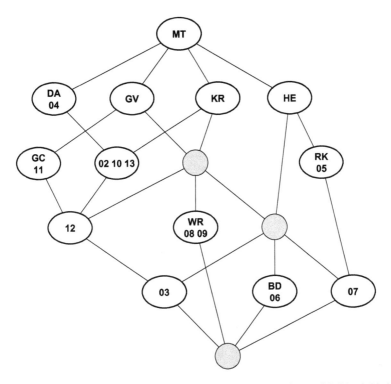

Fig. 1.1 Lattice of the main topics (letter labels) and chapters (number as labels) of this book. Topics' labels are as follow: *GV* governance, *MT* method, *GC* global change, *HE* health, *DA* data analysis, *KR* knowledge resource, *RK* risk, *WR* water resource, *BD* biological diversity (see text). Each chapter (identified by its number) addresses the topics with which it is attached by an ascending path. Each theme is addressed by all the chapters with which it is bound by a descending path of the lattice

book) as well as to the anonymous referees that greatly contributed to the overall quality of this collective work.

References

Aldewereld H, Boisier O, Dignum V, Noriega P, Padget J (eds) (2016) Social coordination frameworks for social technical systems. Law, governance and technology series 30. Springer, Basel

Box-Steffensmeier JM, Brady HE, Collier D (2008) The Oxford handbook of political methodology. Oxford University Press, Oxford

Casanovas P, Pagallo U, Sartor G, Gianmaria A (eds) (2010) AI approaches to the complexity of legal systems complex systems, the semantic web, ontologies, argumentation, and dialogue. International workshops AICOL-I/IVR-XXIV Beijing, China, September 19, 2009 and AICOL-

II/JURIX 2009, Rotterdam, The Netherlands, December 16, 2009. Revised Selected Papers. LNAI 6237. Springer, Switzerland

Codocedo V, Napoli A (2015) Formal concept analysis and information retrieval - a survey. In: Baixeries J, Sacarea C, Ojeda-Aciego M (eds) Formal concept analysis. Proceedings of the 13th International Conference on ICFCA 2015, Nerja, Spain, June 2015, LNCS 9113. Springer, Berlin, pp 61–77

Ganter B, Wille R (1999) Formal concept analysis. Mathematical foundations. Springer, Berlin

Ghose A, Oren N, Telang P, Thangarajah J (eds) (2015) Coordination, organizations, institutions, and norms in agent systems X. COIN 2014 International Workshops, COIN@AAMAS, Paris, France, May 6, 2014, COIN@PRICAI, Gold Coast, QLD, Australia, December 4, 2014 Revised Selected Papers. LNAI 9312. Springer, Switzerland

Gilbert N, Bullock S (2014) Complexity at the social science interface. Complexity 19:1–4. https://doi.org/10.1002/cplx.21550

Henry N (2004) Public administration and public affairs, 9th edn. Prentice-Hall Inc, Upper Saddle River

Howlett M, Ramesh M (2003) Studying public policy – policy cycles and policy sub-systems. Oxford University Press, Oxford

Nguyen HT, Snasel V (eds) (2016) Computational social networks. 5th International Conference, CSoNet 2016 Ho Chi Minh City, Vietnam, August 2–4, 2016 Proceedings. LNCS 9795. Springer, Switzerland

Rafols I, Meyer M (2010) Diversity and network coherence as indicators of interdisciplinarity: case studies in bionanoscience. Scientometrics 82:263–287. https://doi.org/10.1007/s11192-009-0041-y

Sartor G, Casanovas P, Biasiotti MA, Fernandez-Barrera M (eds) (2011) Approaches to legal ontologies. Theories, domains, methodologies. Law, governance and technology series 1. Springer, Dordrecht

Szostak R, Gnoli C, Lopez-Huertas M (2016) Interdisciplinary knowledge organization. Springer, Basel

Wierzbicki A, Brandes U, Schweitzer F, Dino Pedreschi D (eds) (2016) Advances in network science. 12th International Conference and School, NetSci-X 2016 Wroclaw, Poland, January 11–13, 2016 Proceedings. LNCS 9564. Springer, Switzerland

Part I
Complexity Faced by Jurists

Chapter 2
Codification, Between Legal Complexity and Computer Science Agility

Élisabeth Catta and Alexandre Delliaux

Abstract Complexity of law, although regularly denounced by both the authorities and the citizens, is a growing phenomenon. There are many reasons for this: the proliferation of norms, the multiplication of different normative sources of law or the regulations required by the evolution of our society. Under all regimes, governments have sought to reduce complexity by implementing simplification policies, one of the most effective of which has been codification, which decreases complexity by using simplifying modes of logical thinking. The dematerialisation of the law has transformed the process of its knowledge by the memorisation and the manipulation of the signs and the computer tool allowed a modelling of the law by passing from an inaccessible concrete to a handleable abstraction. New concepts such as interaction, regulation, feedback or evolution can now be grasped. The systemic approach and its methodological extension, agility, alternate theory and practice and look for relevance rather than exhaustiveness. The reticular law, another form of the modelling of law this time in the form of graphs, integrates "nodality", or sporadic aggregations of legal relations, and offers itself as a new dimension of legal science. While it does not reduce the complexity of law, the pooling of legal and informatics knowledge opens perspectives that are only starting to be explored by proposing new configurations of the legal fields.

2.1 Opening Remarks

When going back to the reports and studies of the Conseil d'Etat (1991, 2006)—that remain relevant in the absence of substantial changes—complexity of law identifies with various phenomena of modern times such as: the proliferation of norms of all

É. Catta (✉)
Commission Supérieure de Codification, Paris, France

A. Delliaux
KRILL Company, Deuil-La Barre, France
e-mail: alexandre.delliaux@societekrill.com

© Springer Nature Switzerland AG 2019
R. Boulet et al. (eds.), *Law, Public Policies and Complex Systems: Networks in Action*, Law, Governance and Technology Series 42,
https://doi.org/10.1007/978-3-030-11506-7_2

13

categories,[1] the multiplication of internal or external sources of law, the emergence of new normative fields and the decline of the art of useful lawmaking.

This complexity, felt and denounced even by the highest state authorities, mightily attempting to initiate policies for accessibility and simplification of the law, impede knowledge and understanding of rules as well as their right interpretation and implementation. The rule steal away in front of a bewildered citizen and thus becomes *a major source of fragility for society and our economy*.[2] Complexity of law, described as characteristic of elements not completely explainable but understandable, raises numerous interrogations leading us to develop organisations and thinking tools, joining legal and informatics knowledge.

No matter how dismal is the conclusion of that complexity, it does not turn it into an operational concept. Truth is that the difficulty to agree on an indisputable or shared concept of complexity (Millard 2007), together *a problem word and not a solution word* to quote Morin (1990), gives back opportunities of multiple perspectives on law, law which complexity *would rather be the opposite of unidimensionality, unilaterality, monism* (Doat et al. 2007). Furthermore, even though the expected simplification can appear to mutilate or to reduce law as a result, complex thought encompasses, to its own good, some simplifying modes such as ordering, distinction, hierarchy, precision, coherence in order to facilitate knowledge. Relationship between simplicity and complexity are thus richer and more paradoxical than it appears.

Even so, we must admit that law—since it exists—has never been an easy thing to grasp nor to communicate as reflected by the history of its transmission. If we take apart the Roman precedents, Theodosian code in the Fifth Century or Justinian code a century later, the writing down of customs according to the ordinance of Montils-les-Tours in 1454 illustrates a first attempt of the sovereign to clarify legal texts and make them accessible. This effort will be followed up by the Henri III code, drawn up by Barnabé Brisson and printed in 1587, gathering in a single volume all the edicts and ordinances of the French Realm without ordering or classifying them. Couthon and Cambacérès are credited with the first plan of codification having the political ambition to write up and classify the entire legislation.[3] The project of legal codification made a major leap forward with the five codes elaborated at the request of Napoleon under the Consulate and the Empire. Following the long stream of the different French political regimes, we can notice that consistently, with more or less

---

[1]France breaks records in terms of normative inflation. Recently, the World Economic Forum ranked France 130th for a total of 144 countries relatively to the burden of government regulation, (cf. Schwab and Sala-i-Martín 2013). In 2015, the Official Journal of the French Republic published: 14758 bylaws, 3962 decrees, 109 laws and 69 ordinances.

[2]Report of the Government on simplification measures of the year 2003, quoted by the Public report of the Conseil d'Etat (2006).

[3]Decree of 11 Prairial of the Year II (30 May 1794). Lawyer at the Clermont bar then Avocat au barreau de Clermont puis Conventionnel, Couthon took an active part into the French Revolution. Sentenced to death with Saint-Just and Robespierre, he was guillotined on the 28th July 1794. Cambacérès, more discrete, will go on with its legist work.

method and success, public authorities have tried, following both their own interest and the interest of a good governance, to reduce the effects of legal complexity inherent to the structure of the various legal corpora constituting normative systems.

Writing, gathering, publishing, organising: this is how codification, techniques of organisation and transmission of law, become throughout centuries, a political and technical tool aiming, whatever the period, at improving the access to law by users. The relaunching of the political project of codification in 1989 benefited from the development of new technologies, as writing could have taken advantage of Gutenberg's invention but in transforming *writing in memory engineering* (Bourcier and Thomasset 1996) and in exploiting the infinite potential of numerisation, paving a new way in complexity spaces.

Agility, computer science approach, pragmatic and iterative, opened unexpected perspective in this area as it allows going from concept to practise and looking more for relevance than for exhaustivity. Computer science tool does not reduce the inevitable complexity of law but helps to *unfold* it, to explore ways of knowledge and understanding.

2.2 Complexity of Law: Outcomes and Prospects

2.2.1 Complexity, Result from a Norm Network of Increasing Density

Is it the arachnoidal spreading of social facts, or the law supposed to contain them, which is complex? Is the word helping to describe the feeling that law is impossible to seize, because it results from a multitude of fragments coming from various horizons we can only hardly connect to give them a meaning or to find concretely the right answer to the question?

Evidently, law has evolved, diversified, mutated and dug its objects to adapt itself to the transformations of the society and to its progress, going together with complexification of phenomena and of the means of their knowledge. Causes we observe every day are numerous: creation of new technologies, social challenges represented by employment or migrations, ideological changes, ecological requirements, collective effort or individual choice and all this at a global level. From this perspective, law is complicated because the analysis of a single question requires to gather more elements to address it such as the legal category identification, actors, jurisdiction or appropriate text designation, in an inter-normative and judicial, national and international setting, moving apart from a traditional unitary hierarchical system.

A more and more important number of elements are interacting within our legal systems and constitute dense and interdependent normative networks. This dependence between norms can be revealed by the use and mention of cross-references, numbered, or *references,* creating a grid and an interface between texts. The value of these references when they are readable (cf. Sect. 2.5.3. infra, notions of *reverse reference*) is not identical because they underline different levels of logic or interpretation; some are performed "horizontally" at equivalent legal norms and have *normative* implication (Commission supérieure de codification 2013) while others are only used to lead to related topics regulated by other texts and thus have an informative character, such as a road sign.[4]

These references included into norms are remaining us that if legal thought should distinguish or separate, it cannot isolate norms one from another.

The present challenge for a lawyer lies in its ability to reveal coherence and intelligibility from the complexity of those different networks and norms, constituted by disparate elements and to give a grasp to the user and allow him access to knowledge, or at least to knowledge fragments, that should not be the privilege of law specialists or experts.

2.2.2 Complexity, Product of the Multiplication of Normative Authorities

It might grieve us but the reality of globalisation and its pressure on our legal system is very much present. It is now mundane to name and describe, as an element of the normative mosaic and of complexity, the myriad of norms governing us from inside as well as the increase of international law sources that are linking our country to the rest of the world through conventions or treaties or even, the permanent infiltration of European Union law in our legal system. As stated by the Constitutional Council, it exists "*a Community legal order integrated to our internal legal order and distinct from the international legal order*".[5]

Thus, the citizen cannot invoke a national norm that would be conflicting with a Community norm. Relatively to the flow, integration of European Union directives into national law—more than a hundred in 2015[6]—inexorably increase the number of legislative or regulatory texts needed to adapt them into the most various areas as agriculture, transportation, health, etc.

Internal law is not really safe from these sources emitting norms. The multiplication of independent administrative authorities (IAA) since the creation in 1978 of the French Data Protection Authority (Commission nationale Informatique et Liberté, CNIL), first of its kind, raised concerns of the parliamentarians. The report of the Parliamentarian office of assessment of the legislation underlines the fact that *the multiplication of independent administrative authorities could lead to the questioning of the legitimacy of traditional administrative action*. This situation

---

[4]2014 Annual report of the Commission supérieure de codification p. 9: "*Like the civil code which contains a number of articles providing an outline, codes may include liaison or guidance articles*".

[5]Decision 2004-505 DC 19 November 2004.

[6]https://www.legifrance.gouv.fr/Droit-europeen/Actualite/Reglementation/Directives-2015.

had not considerably evolved in 2014 despite these recommendations. De facto, IAA produce regulation and decisions that jurisdictions must combine with the other norms previously mentioned.[7]

Closer to the citizen, territorial communities, being self-governing, have inherited competences previously exercised by the State but the entanglement of these different collectivities, of their territories, of their grouping, of their competences, or of their financing led to a flood of regulation whose legality and quality are hardly constrained by themselves or by the State. The latest law of 2010, 2013, 2014 and 2015 adding up to the previous, increased the complexity of the administration and the citizens get lost in an administrative maze more and more enigmatic.

Finally, more exotic, the multiple layer law from the *Overseas*—according to the formulation in use—(Guadeloupe, Guyane, Martinique, La Réunion, Mayotte, Saint-Barthélemy, Saint-Martin, Saint-Pierre-et-Miquelon, Wallis-et-Futuna Islands, Polynésie française, Nouvelle-Calédonie, Terres australes et antarctiques françaises and Clipperton) presents a kaleidoscope of competence sharing, from the state to local level, difficult to unknot between the laws of the Republic and the specific law of each entity, leading to conflicts of law and a very acrobatic reading of the law.[8]

Multiplication of norms finally led to more and more narrowed definition of law areas. We witness a scissiparity phenomenon, where the notion of the area of law does not stop subdividing itself over time to reach an arborescence difficult to convey to the final recipient of the rule of law: tourism law, NGO law, minor law, etc. For instance, where can we look for rules regarding fire arms? Numerous "legal fields" are competing, from criminal law to security law, to conclude to a new and autonomous field of law is needed.

Law is relentlessly trying to formalise reality and social facts complexity and to manage hazards and exceptions. The requirements of individuals, disseminated by the media, impel the legislator to insert into the norm elements bringing more protection and predictability. The rule thus loses its unity and its generality to scatter into the management of exceptions and the increase of rules automatically creates legal suborders (Molfessis 2006). In order to solve this complication, new concepts are emerging that in turn will create new specific regimes. Nevertheless, law has already many tools helping to assimilate reality complexity by integrating elements specifically designed to reduce hazards and unpredictability as the notion of force majeure or unpredictability theory. These uncertainties or fuzzy margins can be dealt by complexity, while simplification reject them.

---

[7]Report of information of M. Patrice Gélard for the Commission of laws—n° 216—"autorités administratives indépendantes 2006–2014: un bilan".

[8]Cf. Conseil d'Etat, public report 2016 p. 29 et s.: *Outre-mer*.

2.2.3   Other Perspectives on Law Coming from Complexity

As Colin (2012), we can think that it would be necessary to identify networks underlying legal systems and their interrelations in order to induce a change into law architecture, so it can be more *modular* and integrate links emerging from different areas of law. The different branches of law (public, private, criminal, etc.) are not isolated and their concepts may become converging points and sources of enrichment and inventions. Instead of bracing against rigid concepts confining an area of law, we should progress toward a systemic understanding of the law integrating various disciplines and use the network mechanic to give a new impetus to our thoughts.

In this regard, codification, considered from the sole point of view of a specific code or from the total of the 70 French codes structuring our legal information, appear as a new means of investigation about interactions, unknown until now, between norms with a corpus or norms from different corpora. This can be done thanks to computerised treatment of some tasks like the occurrence search of specific words, population thresholds, penalty scale, etc.

Even though these networks studies, suggesting a different way to build law, could add up to existing techniques leading more in disconnecting legal elements, they would obviously have to face public policies of rationalisation of the law which need to be simplifying to be efficient. This rationalisation entrenches the reality of law within a coherent system and everything contradicting this coherence (fuzziness, uncertainty, assessability, unpredictability) is set apart or delayed, as itching the system.

2.3   Public Policies of Simplification and Codification of the Law

2.3.1   The Variety of Political Solutions

Among the suggested solutions to reduce law complexity, public authorities have successively brought up elements of solutions briefly presented here and most of time they lead to:

- open access of the essential of legislation and jurisprudence on a public and official website (LEGIFRANCE[9]): legal databases increase both in terms of quantity—providing a more and more complete information—and quantity, due to their swift update. Nevertheless, legal information call for an adaptation by the user, and the need of legal knowledge is different for the lawyer or for the layman.

---

[9]https://www.legifrance.gouv.fr/.

It is doubtful that the non-specialist will find an answer to its questions only by searching on a database.

- The simplification of relationships between the administration and the citizens: the website "Service Public" has been created in 2000 (renovated in 2009 then 2015 in order to respond to the need of practical information and guide the user toward services allowing to know its rights and obligations and carry out formalities. This is the official website of the French administration,[10] the unique portal of administrative information and access to tele-procedures, in partnership with national and local administrations: a renewal of legal vocabulary better converging to daily or community language[11] and a start of legal language normalisation through writing rules of law tending to a more formal and manageable. This effort led to the elaboration of the *Guide of legislative drafting (Guide de légistique)*,[12] basic handbook for any text writer, it tends to provide rules of writing uniformisation, facilitation the management and the understanding of legal texts.

2.3.2   Simplification of Law as a Policy

The goal is to overhaul the existing law to adapt it to realities or aspirations of the society and notably to meet its expectations of administrative simplification. Nevertheless, there is some unpredictability regarding the effect of reforms and the aim of reducing complexity sometimes has opposite effects than those initially pursued because of human phenomena of reluctance to change or because of the difficulty to get used to a new complexity. If politically, simplification became a goal for the government, simplification shock[13] inevitably calls for the production of new texts supposed to reduce complexity. Thus, we cannot keep track any more of the various simplification laws,[14] some of them widely using the technique of accreditation

---

[10]The website service-public.fr is edited by the Direction of legal and administrative information (DILA). It got 260 million hits in 2014 (among them 40 millions on mobile phones).

[11]Thus, the car driver spontaneously looking for the term "voiture" (car) in the road code (960 articles i.e. 230 legislative articles and 730 regulatory articles) will find it quoted only 14 times including 3 times for "*voiture à bras*" (pushcart) and 1 time in the expression "voiture d'enfant" (pram). It is not even question to look for "auto".... The legal translation of "car" is "motorized (terrestrial) vehicle" (véhicule terrestre à moteur) which is quite far from the daily language. The term "vehicle" (véhicule) is quoted 2228 times (422 in the legislative part and 1806 times in the regulatory part).

[12]https://www.legifrance.gouv.fr/Droit-francais/Guide-de-legistique.

[13]http://www.gouvernement.fr/action/le-choc-de-simplification: the simplification shock has been announced by François Hollande, President of the French Republic during an interview on television on March 19th, 2013.

[14]Law n°2003-591 of 2 July 2003 giving habilitation to the government to simplify law; Law n° 2004-1343 of 9 December 2004 relative to law simplification; Law n° 2012-387 of 22 March 2012 relative to law simplification and streamlined administrative procedure; Law n° 2013-1005 of 12 November 2013 giving habilitation to the government to simplify relationships between the

allowing the government to adopt numerous ordinances or publish a code of relationships between the public and the administration.[15] Paradoxically, simplification of norms is thus a ... complex process.

2.3.3 Codification Policy

In 1995, in order to solve the issues linked to the complexity of norms and their proliferation, the Picq[16] report suggested codifying all the enforceable provisions *by the end of the century* and the Constitutional Council few years later[17] enshrined the principle of law codification as serving the general interest and allowing the respect of accessibility and understanding of the law. Despite the indisputable effort, the goal of the Picq report was not reached yet in 2010 where according to an assessment by the General Secretariat of the government, only 44% of the whole law (legislative and regulatory texts) was codified and the proportion of codified law represented 62% of the published laws.[18]

Such a programme requires a political will: during the last century, French codification has been presented and materialised has a public policy of law rationalisation first in 1948[19] and in 1989. Michel Rocard decides that the policy of codification is under the responsibility of the Prime Minister and set a High commission for codification[20] composed mainly of law professionals with the aim to rationalise the whole French law, in updating already codified law (public health code) or codifying law (code of education). This commission has an official

---

administration and the citizens; Law n° 2014-1545 of 20 December 2014 relative to the simplification of the life of companies and containing various provisions of simplification and clarification of law and administrative procedures; Law n° 2015-177 of 16 February 2015 relative to modernisation and simplification of law and procedures in the areas of justice and internal affairs.

[15]Ordonnance n° 2015-1341 of 23 October 2015 relative to legislative provisions of the code of relationships between the public and the administration and the decree n° 2015-1342 of 23 October 2015 relative to the regulatory provisions of the same code.

[16]J. Picq, Report to the Prime Minister: the State in France: serve a Nation open to the world (*L'État en France: servir une nation ouverte sur le monde*), La Documentation française, Collection des rapports officiels, 1995 (http://www.ladocumentationfrancaise.fr/rapports-publics/954026900/index.shtml).

[17]Decision n° 99-421 DC of the 16 December 1999.

[18]In 2008, Jean-Marc Sauve, director of the General Secretariat of the Government, organised a department of statistics and law quality, with a qualitative and quantitative assessment published on Legifrance Quality of Law but not on open access.

[19]The decree n° 48-800 of 10 May 1948 creating a commission in charge to study codification and simplification of legislative and regulatory texts: the presidency was ensured by the Secretary of State in charge of the public service and the administrative reform. This commission contributed to the publication of 23 codes and the elaboration of 25 other codes between 1948 and 1989.

[20]Decree n° 89-647 of 12 September 1989.

methodology, established by a circular in 1996 and publish every year a report on its work, presenting its advice and precising its doctrine.

2.3.4 Code, Between Complexity and Simplification of Law

Codification, even though it is not a panacea, allows de facto the reduction of law complexity. The code is a rational tool facilitating access to the system of norms within a legal corpus and translate the will to convey a coherent view of it. Facing the confusion coming from the number and diversity of rules, our intelligence needs logical structures and landmarks to better apprehend reality and give it a meaning. As written by Cambacérès *"each law has an infinity of relationships with other laws. It is a huge family where all is connected, and nothing looks alike."*[21] Norms having fuzzy or interfering boundaries, because of their codification, are contained by codes structuring various areas of law. It would nevertheless be a mistake to limit the definition of the area of a code in determining its boundaries. It would be better to look for its core, its epicentre, sometimes revealed by it sole title. Once again, the globality is more than the sum of its elements.

Codification, as every knowledge, proceeds by selection or rejection of norms by distinguishing or separating them, associating or unifying it, by ranking them according to the logic of organisation and of political perception of the world at a given time. Those operations are necessary to law intelligibility, but they should not eliminate other perceptions as those offered by uncertainty, contradiction or similarities between norms, that are precisely giving an overview of the complexity richness and allowing us to humanise knowledge.

Code is generally defined as a *set of rules of law, collected, structured and promulgated by a public authority.* Codification consists in creating a unique document, the code, within a specific area of law such as health or labour law, containing both legislative and regulatory norms. These norms are coordinated by a *plan* commanded by supra-logical principles of organisation of legal thought and adapted to a specific area, which simplifies reader search. Law, gathered as such, has beforehand been clarified and updated allowing the codifier to suggest the repeal of obsolete texts or of texts incompatible with the Constitution or international agreements.

Material process of codification (collect and actualisation of texts, code planning, numbering of articles, correlation tables, etc.) have been quickly facilitated par the emergence of new technologies and the creation of computer tools developed according to a systemic approach. Following a empirical and pragmatic process rather than a determinist one, we would say "agile"[22] today, and considering all the

---

[21]Cambacérès report for the decree of 11 Prairial year II.

[22]One of the precepts of *agile* development is the simplicity or the art of maximizing the amount of work not to do (Boisvert and Trudel 2011).

uncertainty factors, a specific software has been built using conventional office software, easily handleable.

The challenge of dematerialisation in relation to legal writing (and thus to codification) is double because, on the one hand, dematerialisation expands the writing potentialities par the summarisation of signs and one the other hand, it transforms the process of knowledge through memorisation and use of those signs.

With this sort of tools and the tasks to realise on legal material for codification, we should avoid the pitfall of a simplifying thought, isolating for instance an article of law from its context and environment, hiding the variety of sources, forgetting the implementation specificities in space and time, destroying the spirit of the text, losing the richness of observations or commentaries, etc. The main risk is to disconnect knowledge elements, in order to get a simplified object, the code, and to suppress all the interesting elements coming from its complexity.

Yet, from organised and structured elements, collected from computerised databases, the codification software allows to keep the richness of characteristics of law complexity and to avoid damaging it thanks to functionalities such as:

- conservation of information regarding the history of the provision to codify, *i.e.* reference of the *source text* and its subsequent modifications;
- indication of the territorial field of application of the provision (Overseas, Alsace, etc.);
- addition of a diacritical mark (L, R or D) associated to the numbering and defining the legal nature (legislative or regulatory) or codified articles;
- precise qualification of codification operations processed on articles, allowing their understanding and traceability from the source text to the codified text such as: *codification proposal, repeal proposal, scission or fusion of articles*, etc.;
- automatic management of numbered citations between articles according to modifications of the internal organisation of the subdivisions of the code (plan) as well as references from article to article;
- constitution of a working paper in five columns, ensuring, for each article scrutinised, the traceability and readability of the operations processed on it and with the necessary legal analysis and commentaries;
- automatic production of correlation tables between the source text and the codified article, or the opposite, facilitating the access of users to the new code and identification of articles from a same law[23];
- management and follow-up of the various steps of elaboration of the project: concertation between public services and ministries, examination by the High Commission of Codification, the Conseil d'Etat and the Parliament, publication

---

[23]We can note the creation of the software "déCODE" developed for the redesign of the consumption code, entered into force on July 1st 2016, by A. Delliaux, co-author of the present article. This software is freely downloadable on the website of the Directorate General for Competition Policy, Consumer Affairs and Fraud Control: http://www.economie.gouv.fr/dgccrf/nouveau-code-consommation-table-concordance-telechargeable.

in the French Official journal and diffusion through traditional paper or electronic form.

This is how the development of new technologies and the elaboration of an electronic tool designed to help the codifier in the necessary mastering of text complexity and its treatment, opened the way to an easier mode of knowledge regarding law.

2.4 Computer Science Agility: A New Analytical Approach

Until now, the Cartesian approach of the descriptive functioning of a system is determinist in the sense that it supposes that the individual understanding of each constitutive element can lead to the understanding of the whole system (Colin 2012). Regarding law we can wonder if knowing all the rules of certain area of law (consumption law for instance) is enough to know the whole system.

This quite static view is a first approach of law modelling from an inaccessible concrete to a handleable abstraction. It is a relevant answer to the definition of legal objects with all the pitfalls of the model:

- legal texts of different natures (Constitution, code, law, decree, etc.) and territoriality (local, national, international);
- the subdivisions aiming to organise hierarchically the material within a legal text (part, book, chapter, section, etc.);
- articles, only object with a normative value.[24]

Yet knowing an area of law cannot be reduced in enunciating all the articles being part of it. The full set of articles constituting a law would not anymore be a unitary, organised system, but the result of the conjunction of norms, coming from many different legal orders which have various types of relationships (Millard 2007). It is thus necessary to apprehend new concepts such as interaction, regulation, retroaction and evolution. This systemic approach reflects the shift from absolute science to science of rationality. It is the joint combination of knowledge and practice (see Fig. 2.1).

In a concrete way, the systemic approach and its methodological translation, agility, calls for an alternation between concepts (theory) and learning (practice), encourages progressing and decide without knowing everything and to look for pertinence rather than exhaustivity and stay open to possibilities of improvement.[25] This pragmatic and iterative way is also used in computer science: it complements

---

[24]The article is not an "atomic" legal entity: it is possible to define a structure infra-article (paragraph, sub-paragraph, etc.).

[25]The continuous improvement or kaizen (kai: *change* and zen: *better*) is one of the lean management actions: "When the issue is well understood, the improvement becomes possible" (Ohno 1989).

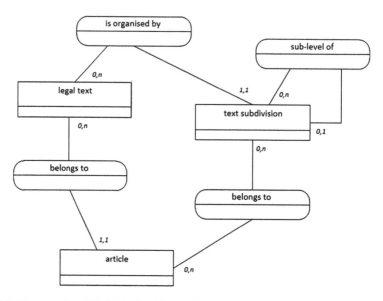

Fig. 2.1 Conceptual model of data for objects of law

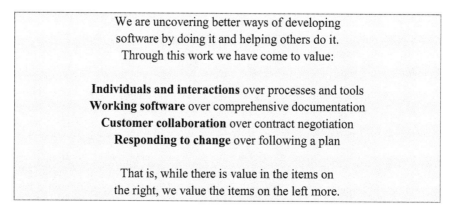

Fig. 2.2 Agile Manifesto

the traditional analytical approach and constrains the control of methodology over the goal pursued.

Historically, agility, in the software field, has been officially introduced in 2001 with the publication of the Agile Manifesto (AA 2016; see Fig. 2.2):

The construction here is ambitious but put individuals back to the core of the process, within the context of interdisciplinary collaboration, informatics and legal, command short and adapted circuits of communication and the adoption of a more relevant modelling method of law goes in line with agility.

It states a new perception of the reality of the world, taking into account, for the law area we consider, characteristics that were previously ignored such as instability, openness, fluctuations, chaos, disorder, fuzziness, creativity, contradiction, ambiguity, paradoxes (Donnadieu and Karsky 2002).

2.5   Reticular Law, Another Modelling of Law

2.5.1   Introduction

In this abstraction, objects of law are modelled following a more dynamic approach using networks (*graph* in mathematics). A network is defined by a set of vertices (or *node*) expressing the typology of objects of law (legal text, text subdivisions and article) and a set of links (or *edge*) (Fig. 2.3). Here links represent citations between legal elements, but various types of links exist such as abrogation, modification, transposition, jurisprudence, doctrine links, etc. the edge linking two vertices expresses a selected link (Boulet et al. 2012). The challenge of complexity management resides into the faculty of integration of these various links.

Network can be observed according to different scales whether we choose a macroscopic level (for instance, the legal text level) or microscopic (for instance, the level of the article). It is considered as an hypergraph insofar as network nodes bear additional information and granularity depends on the observation scale (Bouille 1977). Modeled as such, legal science should now integrate a new dimension: the nodality (legal system organisation based on occasional clustering of legal links (Colin 2012).

2.5.2   Identification of Law Resources: ELI

In order to describe an existing legal network, it is absolutely necessary to define objects identification methods. The use of such a method is recommended at the

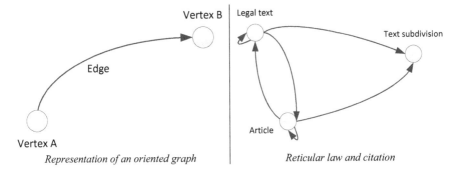

Representation of an oriented graph   *Reticular law and citation*

Fig. 2.3 Reticular law modelling

Table 2.1 Example of ELI's identifier (available on LEGIFRANCE website)

Legal text	URI identifier from ELI
Law n° 2015-990 of 6 August 2015 or economic growth, activity and equality of economic opportunities (known as *Macron Law*)	Identifier based on the n° NOR[a]: http://www.legifrance.gouv.fr/eli/loi/2015/8/6/EINX1426821L/jo Alias based on the legal text references (nature + date + number): http://www.legifrance.gouv.fr/eli/loi/2015/8/6/2015-990/jo

[a]The NOR system is a normalised system of official French texts: Circular of 8 December 1986 relative to the establishment of a normalized system of numbering (NOR) of official public texts

European Union level with the introduction of a European Legislation Identifier or ELI (European Union Official Journal 2012).

ELI's objective is to facilitate, thanks to a unique and perennial identification of legal documents, access to the legislation of member countries of the European Union, the sharing and inter-connection of legislative data contained into national, European or even global legal databases.

ELI norm is based on:

- Metadata describing the legal resource (topic, issuing authority, applicability, date of entry into force, transposed by, consolidation and date, need for an implementation text, etc.);
- Harmonised rules of identification, denomination and access to European and national legal texts thanks to URI[26] (cf. Table 2.1);
- One ontology—information exchange format—describing legal texts properties and their relations with other concepts or national and international acts.

2.5.3 The Big Diversity of Legal Links: Example of Reverse References

Currently, only citations are clearly expressed in legal texts (Catta and Delliaux 2010). Some are juxtaposing areas of law and are only used as signage for a unique rule which is enunciated into another corpus (here the Electoral code) as in this article L. 3121-2 in the General Local Authorities Code:

> Art. L. 3121-2: The composition of departmental councils of and the length of councillors mandates are regulated by the provision of the articles L. 191 and L. 192 of the Electoral code.

---

[26]An URI (Uniform Resource Identifier) s a string of characters used to identify a resource or a network. Its syntax follows the norm RFC 3986. For instance, an URL (Uniform Resource Locator) is an URI allowing access to a resource (a web page) from its representation (HTML file) obtained via a protocol (http for example: http://www.google.fr).

Others combine a principle and its conditions of implementation, propagating from article to article or from corpus to corpus. Thus, the article L. 151-2 states:

Art. L. 151-2: The territorial collectivities of the Republic take part into the freedom of education under the conditions stipulated by the articles L. 442-6 et L. 442-7.

The citation being undertaken, the article L. 442-6 stipulates:

Art. L. 442-6: Courses offered by private secondary school institutions under association contract benefit from an investment funding should be compatible with the orientations defined by the provisional training plan provided for in article L. 214-1.

Then, following this article citation, the article L. 214-1 details:

Art. L. 214-1: Given national orientations and upon agreement of the departmental councils for the educational institutions within its remit, the regional council adopts and transmit to the representative of the state in the region the provisional plan of trainings in secondary schools (junior high schools and high schools), professional high schools, professional maritime high schools and agricultural vocational schools mentioned in articles L. 811-8 and L. 813-1 of the Rural and maritime fisheries code.

. . .

Then, we have to open the Rural and maritime fisheries code . . .

This succession of citation does not ease text reading and can become a source of legal insecurity in case of a reform. The software tool MAGICODE[27] created a real law engineering by establishing hypertext links between citations[28] and the automatic and systematic use of *reverse citations*. Within the previous example, the article L. 214-1 has at least one reverse citation, the article L. 442-6 (which is not cited by the article L. 214-1). The reverse reference (or reverse citation) is the symmetric citation of the simple citation, so far limited to article numbers.[29]

The inverse reference, search for and integrated by the codifier, is used as a control tool at the text proposal stage as it establishes the link with other norms and highlights the compatibility or incoherence with them. That information is thus particularly efficient to assess the impact of the modification of an article over the

---

[27]Codification software created for the code for local authorities in 1994 and recommended by the Circular of 30 May 1996 relative to the codification of legislative and regulatory texts. It has been used for the elaboration of 35 French legal codes and has been adapted to the international context (Cambodia, Vietnam, Marocco).

[28]If this method is now widely use dit was innovative in 1994.

[29]The reverse citations at various levels within a code could be treated in the same way.

articles citing it in terms of legal coherence and also in terms of legal policy. Concretely, we can immediately check if the project of abrogation or re-numbering of an article needs the removal or adjustment of its citation (number) in the articles citing it, which prevent from errors or omissions. It is the same when a provision about to be modified is linked to specific conditions of time or territorial space for its implementation. In this view, it is obvious that being able to list reverse references of external corpora or at other subdivision levels would be particularly efficient. This kind of link, effective thus not clearly expressed, brings legal security to each operation on the cited article while being used as a control tool.

2.5.4   Application: Emergence of an Area of Law

Introduction

In the same vein, the use of modelled law through graphs allows thinking about new perspectives of complexity reduction. This purely empirical assertion, tends to demonstrate that law modelling, under a reticular form, gives an opportunity to consider law in another way. The experiment suggested here comes from the observation that legal practitioners have constant difficulties using the Code of criminal procedure: its legislative sedimentation made its reading particularly troublesome.

The hypothesis consisted in put the codified corpus back into its legal ecosystem thanks to citations between articles. The enumeration of citations, whether external (from or towards the code) and internal (between articles of the code), and their representation allow visualizing distinct corpora of rules, relatively coherent, autonomous and homogenous. The selection of one of these sets, identified as such, could enable the constitution of a new code (code of the public prison service) and thus see the emergence of a new area of law more accessible and less complex for the user.

Codified Legal Ecosystem of the Code of Criminal Procedure

The analysis of citations between articles of the code of criminal procedure with other codes ("incoming" links: articles of other codes citing an article of the code of criminal procedure and "outgoing" links: articles of the code of criminal procedure citing an article from another code) shows the distribution presented in Figs. 2.4 and 2.5.

Another perception, with a scale change within the code itself, allows the identification of subdivisions, structured according to the general architecture of the code, with the following distribution (Table 2.2):

We immediately notice that legal material is distributed in a heterogenous way as Book V (Execution procedures) represents in itself a third of all the articles of the criminal procedure code.

When analysing internal citations within the criminal procedure code (study of the links which articles are the nodes of a network) and their distribution by book, it

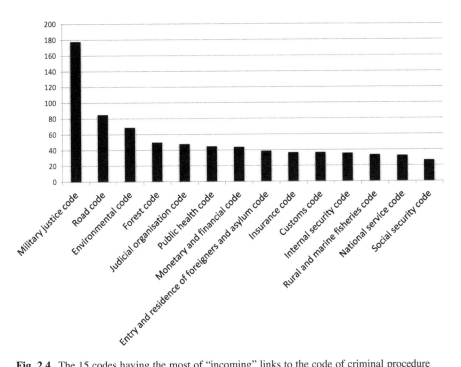

Fig. 2.4 The 15 codes having the most of "incoming" links to the code of criminal procedure

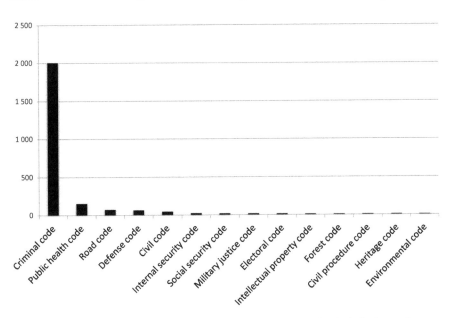

Fig. 2.5 The 15 codes having the most of "outgoing" links to the code of criminal procedure

Table 2.2 Distribution of the number of articles according to subdivisions of the criminal procedure code (book level)

Subdivisions	Title	Legislative	Regulatory	Order	Total
Preliminary title	General provisions	49	20	–	69
Book I	Exercise of public prosecution and judicial investigation	445	380	52	877
Book II	Trial courts	471	54	36	561
Book III	Special remedies	74	–	2	76
Book IV	Some specific proceedings	534	246	1	781
Book V	Execution procedures	359	1106	37	1502
Book V *bis*	General provisions	–	4	5	9
Book VI	Provisions applicable to overseas departments of Guadeloupe, French Guiana, Martinique and La Réunion	151	158	4	313
Book VII	Provisions applicable to new Caledonia	–	2	2	4
Book VIII	Provisions applicable to French Polynesia	–	–	4	4

Table 2.3 Distribution of internal citations to the code of criminal procedure by subdivision (book)

Subdivisions	"Incoming" links	"Outgoing" links	Internal links
Preliminary title	77	39	30
Book I	567	157	1280
Book II	409	105	890
Book III	25	42	16
Book IV	222	399	812
Book V	336	318	1532
Book V *bis*	1	4	6
Book VI	–	569	23
Book VII	–	4	–
Book VIII	–	–	–

is possible to distinguish three types of citations for each book: internal (articles of departure and at arrival are belonging to the same book), outgoing and incoming.

The distribution is as follows (see Table 2.3 and Fig. 2.6):

The analysis of citations targets leads to the following graph (Fig. 2.7):

Book V remains quite autonomous regarding its relations with other books. A conclusion, to demonstrate juridically, would be the emergence of a code of execution procedures which density of content and autonomy of links, mainly internal links,[30] strongly suggest the existence.

---

[30]If we put apart the links to the book VI, which are only transposing metropolitan law to overseas law.

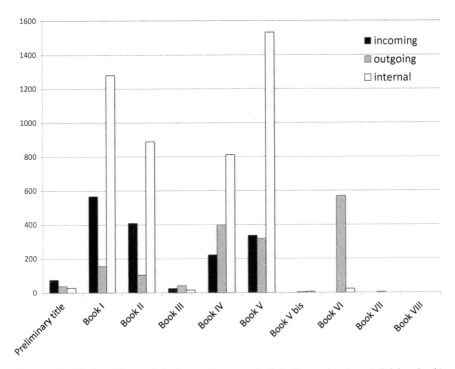

Fig. 2.6 Distribution of internal citations to the code of criminal procedure by subdivision (book)

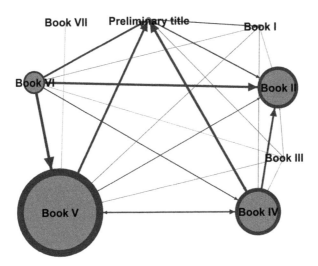

Fig. 2.7 Distribution of internal citations to the code of criminal procedure by subdivision (book)

2.6   Conclusion

Law complexity will not diminish or become out of date in the light of society progress and globalization of exchanges. The contemporary legislative inflation so criticises is probably only an aspect of the deep crisis regarding the sources of law. Indeed, the hieratic and state law is progressively supplanted by a multiple and disorganised law. In front of this explosion of sources of law, the development of computer science and of research using computerized or codified data could lead to the modification of the codification concept itself. Contemporary normative pluralism would undoubtedly be better understood by codes inspired by nodality dimension: it would thus increase the flexibility and security of the legal system. Indeed, as emphasised by the dean Cornu (1998): "who thinks writing on a stone, will have only written in the sand".

References

Agile Alliance (2016) Manifesto for agile software development. Agile Alliance, Corryton. https://www.agilealliance.org/agile101/the-agile-manifesto/. Accessed 30 Nov 2017

Boisvert M, Trudel S (2011) Choisir l'agilité: du développement logiciel à la gouvernance. Éditions Dunod, Paris

Bouille F (1977) HBDS (hypergraph based data structure) : un modèle universel de banque de données simultanément portable, répartie. Thèse d'État. Université Pierre et Marie Curie, Paris VI

Boulet R, Mazzega P, Bourcier D (2012) Réseaux normatifs relatif à l'environnement: structures et changements d'échelles. In: Bourcier D, Boulet R, Mazzega P (eds) Politiques Publiques Systèmes Complexes. Hermann, Paris, pp 9–17

Bourcier D, Thomasset C (1996) L'Écriture du droit face aux technologies de l'information. Diderot Éditeur, Paris

Catta E, Delliaux A (2010) Renvois et références inverses, outils de légistique. In: Vingt et unième rapport annuel de la Commission supérieure de codification. Ed. des Journaux Officiels, pp 70–75

Colin F (2012) Droit et complexité. Revue de la Recherche Juridique. Presses Universitaires Aix-Marseille 1:99–108

Commission Supérieure de Codification (2013) Vingt-quatrième Rapport Annuel. Ed. des Journaux Officiels, III.2, Paris, pp 9–10

Conseil d'État (1991) Rapport public: de la sécurité juridique. Collection Études et documents du Conseil d'État, n°43. Conseil d'Etat, Paris

Conseil d'État (2006) Rapport public: Sécurité juridique et complexité du droit. Collection Études et documents du Conseil d'État, n°57

Cornu G (1998) L'art du droit en quête de sagesse. Collection Doctrine Juridique. Presses Universitaires de France, Paris

Doat M, Le Goff J, Pedrot PH (eds) (2007) Droit et complexité: pour une nouvelle intelligence du droit vivant. Collection L'univers des normes. Presses Universitaires de Rennes, Rennes

Donnadieu G, Karsky M (2002) La systémique, penser et agir dans la complexité. Collection Entreprise & Carrières. Ed. Liaisons/Eyrolles, Paris

Millard E (2007) Éléments pour une approche analytique de la complexité. In: Doat M, Le Goff J, Pedrot PH (eds) Droit et complexité - Pour une nouvelle intelligence du droit vivant. Presses Universitaires de Rennes, Rennes, pp 141–153

Molfessis N (2006) Combattre l'insécurité juridique ou la lutte du système juridique contre lui-même. In: Rapport public: Sécurité juridique et complexité du droit. Collection Études et documents du Conseil d'État, n°57. Conseil d'Etat, Paris, pp 391–406

Morin E (1990) Introduction à la pensée complexe. Points/Seuil, Paris

Official Journal of the European Union (2012) Council conclusions inviting the introduction of the European Legislation Identifier (ELI) (2012/C 325/02). http://eur-lex.europa.eu/legal-content/EN/TXT/HTML/?uri=CELEX:52012XG1026(01)&from=HR. Accessed 30 Nov 2017

Ohno T (1989) L'esprit Toyota. Collection Productivité de l'entreprise. Masson, Paris

Schwab K, Sala-i-Martín X (2013) The global competitiveness report 2013–2014. World Economic Forum, Cologny. http://www3.weforum.org/docs/WEF_GlobalCompetitivenessReport_2013-14.pdf. Accessed 30 Nov 2017

Chapter 3
Organizational Consciousness *Versus* Artificial Consciousness

Claire Lajaunie and Pierre Mazzega

Abstract What is the capacity of an informal network of organizations to produce answers in response to complex tasks requiring the integration of masses of information designed as a high-level cognitive and collective activity? Are some network configurations more favourable than others to accomplish these tasks? We present a method to make these assessments, inspired by the Information Integration Theory issued from the modelling of consciousness. First we evaluate the informational network created by the sharing of information between organizations for the realization of a given task. Then we assess the natural network ability to integrate information, a capacity determined by the partition of its members whose information links are less efficient. We illustrate the method by the analysis of various functional integrations of Southeast Asian organizations, creating a spontaneous network participating in the study and management of interactions between health and environment. Several guidelines are then proposed to continue the development of this fruitful analogy between artificial and organizational consciousness (refraining ourselves from assuming that one or the other exists).

C. Lajaunie (✉)
INSERM, CERIC, UMR DICE 7318, CNRS, Aix Marseille University, University of Toulon, University of Pau and Pays Adour, Aix-en-Provence, France

Strathclyde Centre for Environmental Law and Governance (SCELG), University of Strathclyde, Glasgow, UK
e-mail: claire.lajaunie@inserm.fr

P. Mazzega
UMR5563 GET Geosciences Environment Toulouse, CNRS/University of Toulouse, Toulouse, France

Strathclyde Centre for Environmental Law and Governance (SCELG), University of Strathclyde, Glasgow, UK
e-mail: pierre.mazzegaciamp@get.omp.eu

3.1 "How Do Organizations Think?"

At first, it seems an awkward question. How can we assume that organizations think? Why would we push this incongruity to the point to ask ourselves how a network of organizations thinks? In a first place, let us justify the legitimacy, then the consistency of the question. If consensual uses of the notion of thought exist, there is in contrast no consensus about the concept itself. There are, of course, different neighbouring conceptions of what thought is, co-evolving with our practices, knowledge and more generally, according to the cultural (and thus historical) contexts among which they are called for.[1] A priori, it is not ruled out that thought itself can be considered in respect with a certain conception of organization's functioning.

The issue can be tamed if we assess it slightly differently, considering on an interrogative form the statement contained into the title of Mary Douglas's book, published in 1986 "*How institutions think*". Numerous are the institutions[2] which, through the cultural immersion we experience, are constituting the common environment of our subjective thoughts, the cognitive reference framework within which we are evolving, as individual or social groups, often without being aware of its impregnation. M. Douglas traces the genealogy of this corpus of ideas back to E. Durkheim: those ideas receiving a lukewarm or sometimes hostile[3] welcome, they almost fell into oblivion. Nevertheless, some authors followed up the development of the elements presented by Durkheim. But above all, the book of Olson (1965), reformulating the analysis of collective action for public goods production grounded on the rational (individual) behaviour theory, shed new light on the question of whether and to which extent thought depends on institutions. In response, this new formulation led to various critiques, especially those developed by M. Douglas: she essentially insists on the fact that Olson's theory, discounting small groups, cannot apply to all levels of social organization (without being able to explain it); she also observes that other factors of co-operation exist and cannot be captured by an utilitarian approach.

Of course, the scientific fame of those authors itself does not confirm the relevance of our initial question. But as works on the rational choice theory, works developed in Artificial Intelligence and even more those focusing on the conditions to be met in order to build an artifact endowed with consciousness (Cardon 2000) allow us to renew the context of these studies. More precisely, our approach intends

---

[1]We can quote here the conclusion to the Section entitled "conceptual stability and change" in the article (p. 1522) written by Hjørland (2009):"*Concepts are dynamically constructed and collectively negotiated meanings that classify the world according to interests and theories. Concepts and their development cannot be understood in isolation from the interests and theories that motivated their construction, and, in general, we should expect competing conceptions and concepts to be at play in all domains at all times.*"

[2]For example, the categories of time, space, causality, but also the grammatical forms of the language...

[3]Douglas (1986) op. cit., p. 11.

to explore an analogy with computational models of artificial consciousness (for a recent review, cf. Reggia 2013). Specific cerebral cortex regions are dedicated to specialized functions.[4] Several brain regions are simultaneously challenged and co-operate with each other in a network in order to generate sophisticated processes—particularly cognitive processes—of a higher level. Considered from in a general and abstract sense, those processes relate to an information integration process. Tononi (2008) developed a theory stating that the emergence of integrated information from the cerebral regions' network constituted a fact of consciousness; the diversity of processes operating is much like the observed diversity of consciousness experiences. The analogy between the functioning of organizations and of cerebral regions is extremely tempting and we chose to explore it further.

Indeed, the information integration is more than a simple juxtaposition or collection of information but it develops a synthesis at the level of the considered entities' network, the network thus functioning as a system. We interpret the various solutions generated by organizations networks responding to global as well as local changes (environment, health, economy...) as the result of the systemic process of the information integration. Section 3.2 presents a limited group of organizations dealing with health and environmental challenges in Southeast Asia in order to illustrate our approach. Transposing Tononi's (2004) consciousness model, in Sect. 3.3 we examine informational networks linking those organizations according to several functions they perform; then we evaluate their theoretical limits to function as an information integration system induced by the efficiency of the underlying informational networks. We also assess how the consideration of a corpus describing the entire network impacts the informational networks between organizations and their information integration capacity. Some options stemming from this analogy between artificial consciousness and artificial consciousness are presented in Sect. 3.4. Section 3.5 discusses the assumptions and limitations of the model we propose, before presenting our conclusions in Sect. 3.6.

3.2 Organizations Networks "Health-Environment" in Southeast Asia

Our research about organizational networks on health and environment in Southeast Asia, has been conducted within the framework of an international research project entitled BiodivHealthSEA. That project aimed at investigating the local impacts of global changes on zoonotic diseases (as those diseases constitute more than 60% of emerging diseases), focusing on rodent-borne diseases, in relation to biodiversity changes. The project analyses the local perception of biodiversity loss and their links to health through global governance, national public policies and the actions of

---

[4]Objects or people recognition, motor control systems, vision, audition, etc.

NGOs in the sectoral domains of health, environment, conservation and development.

In the context of the regional economic integration with the opening, by the end of 2015 of the ASEAN (Association of Southeast Asian Nations) Economic Community, the free movement of goods, services and persons will accelerate the pace of changes within the region. Indeed, Southeast Asia is a hotspot of biodiversity at threat subject to important environmental changes (land use changes, deforestation, and erosion of biodiversity) in relation to fast socio-economic changes (economic growth, migration, and wildlife and livestock trade). Those changes in turn cause the infectious diseases' emergence of potential global pandemics (Morand et al. 2014) that must be acknowledged at the regional level as well as the national level.

In that respect, our research led to review policies, agendas, or various kinds of initiatives on biodiversity or health at the regional level and to assess how health and biodiversity are connected in formal or informal settings. To take into account the diversity of actors and the way they try to coordinate their strength and goals (the goals themselves may be driven by international or regional policies), we identified different networks and initiatives. We have chosen those born from health and environmental considerations in general or those that were more specific (geographical area in Southeast Asia, topics, actors involved).

Since its creation, ASEAN has been characterized by its minimal institutional organization, a limited use of formal rules or the principle of non-interference in each other's domestic affairs. The so-called "ASEAN Way" favours national implementation and cooperative programmes and dialogues among members (Robinson and Koh 2002). The traditional "ASEAN Way" together with the realization that States actors have a limited ability to deal with global, regional and national challenges, led to the elaboration of regional programmes by States actors as well as other stakeholders. This "alternative regionalism" in the regional context is referred to "as a spontaneous, bottom-up process that recognizes the importance of a wide range of stakeholders in the making of regional systems and institutions" (Chandra 2009, p. 4). Thus we can affirm with Lallana that ASEAN as an institution is a network organization or we could consider it as a network of networks. Lallana adds an interesting comparison stating that "ASEAN operates much like the Internet" (Lallana 2012).

Our research interest here is to study how networks dedicated to health or environment in Southeast Asia interact, produce and share information but it is also to evaluate the ability to integrate information within a network of networks of organizations. As many networks related to the health or the environment exist in Southeast Asia (on environmental networks, cf. Elliott 2011), we decided to focus on some in order to illustrate our work.

We consider a regional organization which gathers all the ASEAN member states plus Timor Leste. The choice has been guided by the fact that this organization called SEAMEO (Southeast Asian Ministers of Education Organization) is an established organization celebrating its 50th anniversary in 2015. It is itself divided into 21 institutions specialized in different research and education areas, all producing knowledge and information. Within SEAMEO, we chose the institutions whose activities among the network are directly linked with issues regarding health and environment (agriculture, food and nutrition, history and tradition, cultural diversity, tropical medicine, tropical biology and public health).

The study of this network will allow us to determine the capacity of a network of organizations to produce answers in response to complex tasks that require the integration of masses of information designed as a high-level cognitive and collective activity. We examine if some network configurations are more favourable than others to accomplish these tasks. In this respect, we use the analogy between artificial consciousness and organizational consciousness presented Sect. 3.1, selecting some SEAMEO institutions to develop methodology and explore the potential of the analogy.

3.3 Multifunctional Organization Network

Mathematically, the number of networks created on the basis of a group of objects is indeterminate: it is the specific kind of link considered between these objects which generate a specific network. Thus, the network is not necessarily a priori or intentionally thought about or created, but it can be structured by the existence of the various entities forming the network. It is particularly true with social networks (family or neighbourhood ties, professional links. . .) and organization networks whether they are formal or not. We consider here three types of functions generating as many networks: (1) missions of the organizations previously described; (2) their governing board composition; (3) content of their training programmes.

How do we proceed[5]? For each organization, we gather information publicly available regarding one of those functions (information obtained through their websites). Each organization has an associated text corpus from which we can extract a list of keywords or key expressions[6] (and if necessary, to each keyword we associate a list of similar expressions). The keyword extraction step is optional. We use it here to reduce the information management load while giving the possibility to direct the informational network building to a specifically targeted research topic. A link is created between two organizations A and B if a least one pair of keywords[7]—respectively coming from A and B's corpus—appears in the corpus of the organization C (C being distinct or not from A and B). This link is weighted by the function of average mutual information $I_{AMI}[A, B]$[8] evaluated through corpus analysis, as described in the Annex (gathering all the equations). The auto information associated to an organization $I_{AMI}[A, A]$ is assessed in the same way (with $C \neq A$

---

[5]The method is described in detail and commented in Lajaunie and Mazzega (2016a).

[6]By keyword we mean a noun phrase, a word or even a word root: e.g. the root "agri" identifies all occurrences of themes related to agriculture in the corpus we use here.

[7]Note that in a pair of keywords (t_j, t_k) (tn, tm) we can have $t_j = t_k$.

[8]Note that $I_{AMI}[A, B] = I_{AMI}[B, A]$ and $I_{AMI}[A, B] \geq 0$.

otherwise no auto information will result from network affiliation). Taking account of all pairs of organizations, we create a network induced by the considered function, network represented by a graph which vertices are organizations and links are weighted by the values of average mutual information functions (or auto information). A null value indicates that there is no link.

The capacity Φ_{IIS} of the entities network (cerebral cortical regions in the case of Tononi (2004, 2008), organizations here) to behave as an information integration system is limited by the weakest informational link between entities groups within the network. As such, Φ_{IIS} is theoretically evaluated considering all possible partitions of the entities set,[9] when calculating for each of them average mutual information values and determining the minimal value. Without going into details, this approach is proposed by Tononi (2004) on a neuro-physio-pathological basis. For instance, it is observed that patients with cortex lesions may have cortex regions isolated one from the other and thus are deprived from some consciousness experiences.[10] In extreme cases, such injury can lead to the total absence of informational link between two groups of entities.

3.3.1   Network Induced by the Role and Missions of Organizations

Similarly, two organizations dedicated to completely disparate missions, without any link between one another, are not prone to work together and even less to conjointly conduct complex tasks. Figure 3.1a shows the informational network induced by the description of the role and missions of each of the five SEAMEO's organizations considered. Other texts that form an additional corpus can be added to the original corpus and considered in the analysis (e.g. a text describing the roles and missions of SEAMEO, see below).

We observe that RECFON presents strong informational links with the four other organizations. It also has the highest auto information rate: it means that RECFON's role within the network is understood only in regard with the roles and chores of other organizations in the network. Indeed, RECFON's missions are encompassing research, education and information in food and nutrition: thus, they can overlap BIOTROP's missions in biology, TROPMED's missions regarding public health or even those of SEARCA in agricultural research. In contrast, TROPMED's missions (null auto information) are defined only by self-reference, and the affiliation to the network does not change its extent.

---

[9]In theory only because the number of partitions of a set S of N elements very quickly increasing with N, we only consider the set of all bipartitions of S.

[10]O. Sacks' book (1998) describes such cases. Brain's plasticity allows reducing at least partially the incidences of those injuries.

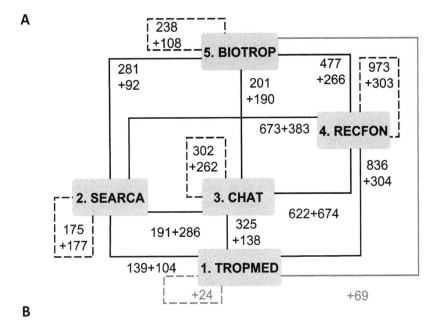

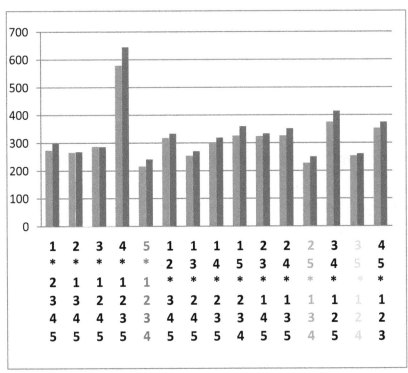

Fig. 3.1 (a) Informational network of roles and missions of the five organizations of SEAMEO considered (vertices in grey). Information function's values I_{AMI} are indicated on the links using the form "x+y" according to the following convention: x is I_{AMI} value without taking account of the

TROPMED and BIOTROP are not linked through their respective tasks. If we take account of the additional corpus describing SEAMEO's roles and charges as such, most of the informational links are strengthened, sometimes considerably (e.g. the link RECFON-SEARCA) and induce a link between TROPMED and BIOTROP.

Nevertheless, the adjunction of that corpus is very marginal regarding the change of the theoretical capacity of an organization network to integrate information and process complex collective tasks (Fig. 3.1b). It can be explained by the fact that if the network formalization may strengthen the informational flow between affiliated organizations, the organizations are not endowed with additional missions or competences. The partition limiting the network capacity to act as an information integration system split BIOTROP on one side and the four other organizations on the other side. A way to improve the network capacity to accomplish collective missions, while minimizing organizational changes, would probably go through a new definition of the role and missions of BIOTROP.

3.3.2 Network Induced by the Organization's Governance

To which extent the composition of the governing boards is improving (albeit to a various extent) the information flows between organizations? In order to answer, the corpus associated to each organization is now composed with the names of each member and their affiliations—department or agency (e.g. ministry) or faculty and university in the case of academic staff. The informational network induced by the composition of the governing boards is presented in Fig. 3.2a. Here the additional corpus is formed by the composition of the governing board of SEAMEO.

The network obtained is a complete graph. The fact that the Secretary General of SEAMEO is an *ex-officio* member of each board contributes to this result. Almost all link weightings have very close values one another, board compositions having a very similar shape. The adjunction of an additional corpus, here the composition of SEAMEO's Council changes very slightly the strength of informational links and the network's capacity to function as an information integration system through the functioning of its governing board (Fig. 3.2b). This last result reflects the fact that the Council of SEAMEO's network organizations is not the board of one network's organization. The bipartition limiting this capacity split SEARCA and BIOTROP on one side and the three other organizations on the other side.

Each board being composed of around 13 members, it is difficult to understand those results by a simple observation of the organization boards' composition.

Fig. 3.1 (continued) additional corpus C_+, +y the information input induced by the adjunction of this corpus. When $[x = 0; y \neq 0]$ the link is indicated in red; (**b**) $I_{AMI}[S_\kappa, S_\pi]$ values (y-axis) associated to each bipartition (S_κ, S_π) of the organization network (x-axis). The minimal value indicates the capacity Φ_{IIS} of information integration of the network

A

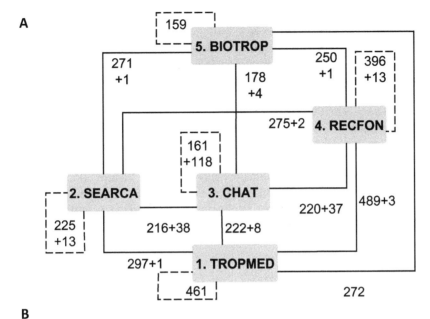

B

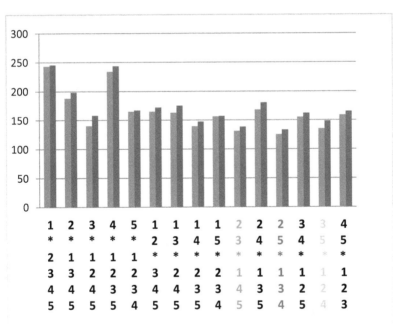

Fig. 3.2 (**a**) Informational network of the governing boards of the five organizations of SEAMEO (vertices in grey); (**b**) Values $I_{AMI}[S_\kappa, S_\pi]$ (y-axis) associated to each bipartition of the governing boards' network (x-axis). The minimal value indicates the capacity Φ_{IIS} of information integration of the network. For representation conventions, cf. Fig. 3.1

Actually, the informational network (Fig. 3.2a) incorporates much information. Figure 3.3 unfolds the entire network of institutions taking part to various governing boards (those taking part to SEAMEO's Council are not represented, this Council operating at another level). The strong visible symmetry of the graph is probably the reason of the homogeneity of information function's values of Fig. 3.2a (with one exception: the participation of eight organizations to the governing boards of TROPMED and RECFON induce a high mutual information value between those two organizations). We can notice the centrality (Freeman 1979) of SEAMEO's Secretariat as well as of the National University of Singapore (cf. Table 3.1). Nevertheless, it is a closeness centrality degree (in average SEAMEO's Secretariat is the closest from other organizations, it can be seen as the "centre" of the network). The strongest betweenness centrality degrees are associated to CHAT, BIOTROP and SEARCA: those organizations are linking together groups of institutions that would otherwise be relatively disconnected from one another.

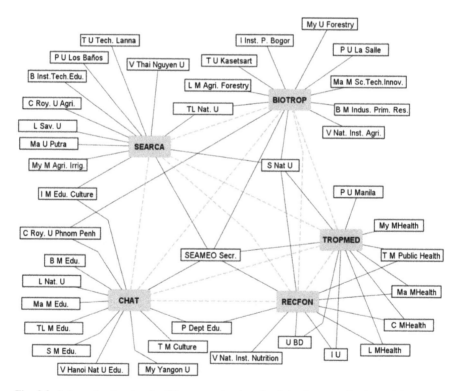

Fig. 3.3 Informational network of the governing boards of the five organizations of SEAMEO (vertices in grey; links in green dotted lines) and of organizations taking part to their respective boards. The Secretary General of SEAMEO is an ex-officio member of all the different boards. 1st Letter {*B* Brunei Darussalam, *C* Cambodia, *I* Indonesia, *L* Laos, *Ma* Malaysia, *My* Myanmar, *P* Philippines, *S* Singapore, *T* Thailand, *TL* Timor Leste, *V* Vietnam}; 2nd letter: {*M* Ministry, *U* University}

Table 3.1 List of ten organizations with the highest centrality degrees among the five SEAMEO's organizations or of organizations affiliated to their governing board (cf. graph, Fig. 3.3 without informational links in green: 44 vertices, 56 links)

N_e		B_{cent}		C_{cent}	
Org. name	Value	Org. name	Value	Org. name	Value
BIOTROP	1.00	CHAT	1.00	SEAMEO Secr.	1.00
CHAT	1.00	BIOTROP	0.99	BIOTROP	0.80
SEARCA	1.00	SEARCA	0.99	S Nat. U	0.80
RECFON	0.83	SEAMEO Secr.	0.96	CHAT	0.80
TROPMED	0.83	RECFON	0.53	SEARCA	0.80
SEAMEO Secr.	0.42	TROPMED	0.53	RECFON	0.77
S Nat. U	0.33	S Nat. U	0.44	TROPMED	0.77
10 ex-æquos	0.17	IM Edu. Culture	0.14	P Dept. Edu	0.67
		C Roy.U Phnom Peh	0.14	TL Nat. U	0.67
		TL Nat. U	0.09	C Roy.U Phnom Penh	0.67
		P Dept. Edu.	0.09	IM Edu. Culture	0.67

N_e number of links (or centrality degree, normalized by the higher centrality degree found in the graph), B_{cent} betweenness centrality degree, C_{cent} closeness centrality measure

3.3.3 Network Induced by the Organization's Training Courses They Provide

As all the organizations studied depend on SEAMEO (regional inter-governmental organization established among governments of Southeast Asian countries to promote regional co-operation in education, science and culture in the region), they all offer training courses detailed on their website. The corpus used here is the description of the course offers. The informational network induced by these offers is presented Fig. 3.4a. The SEAMEO network also promotes these courses on its website. The additional corpus is the description of the course offer as presented at the SEAMEO level. When this additional corpus is not taken into account, CHAT is apart from the other organizations (the network is not fully connected, CHAT is an isolated vertex). CHAT is indeed focusing on the promotion of co-operation regarding the study of history and traditions among SEAMEO's members, through research, human resource development, education and networking. The courses currently offered do not fit in the general line of courses proposed by the other organizations and regarding various aspects of their missions (agriculture, nutrition, health...).

Of course, SEAMEO's description of training courses (additional corpus) allows linking offers from the affiliated organizations (links in red, Fig. 3.4a) but does not change the incapacity ($\Phi_{IIS} = 0$) of organizations to propose courses that would integrate (not simply overlap) all the areas covered (bipartition of CHAT on one side versus the four other organizations on the other side, Fig. 3.4b). The additional corpus is not associated with a vertex of the graph (SEAMEO member organizations offer courses but not SEAMEO as such). Hence the bipartite summit that minimizes the information is the same: CHAT is an isolated organization on one side and the other organizations are on the other side.

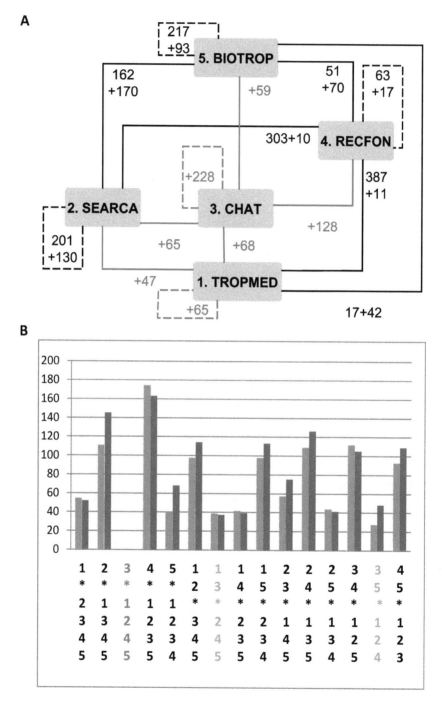

Fig. 3.4 (a) Informational network of the training courses proposed by the five organizations of SEAMEO (vertices in grey); (b) Values $I_{AMI}[S_\kappa, S_\pi]$ (y-axis) associated to each bipartition of the network of training courses (x-axis). The minimal value indicates the capacity Φ_{IIS} of information integration of the network. For representation conventions, cf. Fig. 3.1

Table 3.2 For each type of functioning of the organization network, the elements of the smallest part of the bipartition minimizing the average mutual information are in bold

Linking functions	Organization					Φ_{IIS}
Missions	TROPMED	SEARCA	CHAT	RECFON	**BIOTROP**	215 (+26)
Governance	TROPMED	**SEARCA**	CHAT	RECFON	**BIOTROP**	128 (+8)
Training	TROPMED	SEARCA	**CHAT**	RECFON	BIOTROP	0 (+0)

The value corresponding to the capacity of information integration Φ_{IIS} is indicated in the last column (and between brackets the gain of information obtained by the adjunction of the additional corpus)

3.3.4   Assessment of SEAMEO's Organizations

Although the five organizations we are considering here are members of a formalized network, SEAMEO, the informational links between them should be analysed under a specific perspective of characteristics (role and missions) or functions (administration and governance, courses) of affiliated members. The quality and structure of each network depends of the considered function. The formal network is efficient to process complex information integration tasks (that we relate to a form of organizational consciousness) in terms of governance (through governing boards) but are *a priori* unable to offer courses integrating in a synthetic way all the knowledge disseminated by its members (Table 3.2).

The information produced at the level of SEAMO's network allows a better link between organizations and modify their respective positions for the process of given functions. However, it cannot replace the role of organizations and thus cannot reinforce the network capacity to function like an information integration system that is to say to realize collectively high level cognitive tasks.

In a previous article (Lajaunie and Mazzega 2016a), we also studied the impact of the adjunction of a new organization C in the network. We notably observed that the entrance of C into the network can modify the intensity of informational link between organization A and B already in the network, or create an auto information on A, as C's functions lead to reconsider A's functions. On another hand, the information integration capacity being assessed *a priori*, it is possible to evaluate different scenarios. It can be done by adding organizations and depending on each considered function (mission, governance, courses), to choose the organization that will maximize the capacity of the extended network to process integrative collective tasks.

3.4   Organizational *Versus* Artificial Consciousness: Open Debate

So far, we have shown that the transposition of Tononi's model (2004, 2008) allows considering various organizations as components of several informational networks, corresponding to functions performed by those organizations, and evaluating *ex ante* their theoretical capacity to collectively conduct the integration of a large amount of information. The method gives the possibility to assess the impact of an additional organization or of an additional corpus describing the whole network on those informational networks and on their integration capacity. But those are only beginnings: the study must be completed aligning the idea of organizational consciousness to the theory of consciousness as an information integration system. The most interesting point is that diverse theoretical predictions on the emergence of consciousness—differentiated participation of some cerebral cortical regions to this emergence, the existence of connectivity patterns favouring more or less the integration of information, etc.—are significant regarding organization networks, and can be assessed. In the following sections, we present those predictions (many are relying on neuropsychiatric observations) as conjectures to explore in the case of organizations.

As for cerebral regions (CR), all the organizations of the network are not necessarily involved into the emergence of an organizational consciousness—or let us say to the information integration at the network's level. Moreover, the organizations involved in this process can participate only temporarily. According to the collective task to accomplish, some organizations will be activated while others will not,[11] following complex processes (not very predictable, nonlinear, or each time depending on different variables, or on unstable configurations of actors' relationships). At a lower systemic scale, the internal functioning processes of each organization (respectively AC) are likely to modify the quality of experience of consciousness by the network. Here, "quality of experience of consciousness" means type of actions that the organizations of the network are able to undertake collectively. At a superior systemic scale, networks of networks of organizations (or AC) exist and create other information integration structures and thus other experiences of consciousness.

It has also been demonstrated that the informational network connectivity of cerebral regions (and thus the capacity of Φ_{IIS}) evolves over time, for instance in response to a solicitation from the environment. There is a continuous rearranging in the case of organizations or at least in the case of SEAMEO (which we consider only partially here) and of its international or regional partners. Those solicitations come from the adaptation of regional strategic positioning vis-à-vis the emergence of economic or political challenges, shifting alliances, changes in the legal, political or economic context of international co-operation. This adaptation capacity is corresponding to the "ASEAN's way", flexible and adaptive way of decision-making. As underlined by Frost (2008), environmental, health, and human rights groups are forming information networks and uneven cross-border coalitions.

---

[11]It will be necessary to specify how to define and observe the network's state at a determined moment: the informational networks previously presented are creating the structure of informational exchanges (an equivalent to anatomic constraints of the brain); the network's state would correspond to the real functioning state of the network when realizing a specific collective task. To various activity patterns would correspond diverse consciousness experiences.

Various neuro- and physio-pathological works are also showing that learning processes induce a modification of physical substrate of cerebral areas (mainly through a rearranging and improvement of the inter-connectivity patterns) which in turn leads to an extension of the consciousness experience range. The input of information technology to the functioning of organizations' network offers a trivial analogy of this phenomenon (e.g. Scott 2000). Moreover, organizations are developing in collaboration a broad spectrum of activities resulting in co-learning processes (multilateral meetings, co-organizations of events, common synthesis or strategic reports, collaborative projects, creation of new governing boards, involvement into participatory management processes...). We should underline the fact that each of those activities can be seen as a specialized informational network involving the organization's members.

The field of possible analogies between dysfunction of the brain, on the one hand, and of organizations, on the other hand, is wide open. Works in this area are numerous whether it is in neuropsychiatry, administrative science or science of organizations. The flexibility and the genericity of our model should allow deepening and renewing the exploring of those useful analogies. Some cortex injuries are going with the loss of determined consciousness experiences.[12] The dissolution of an organization, its withdrawal from a collective project (or to a lesser extent its potential weaknesses) can be considered as an "organizational injury". According to our simulations, such a withdrawal induces a repositioning of each organization within the network relatively to the others, whatever the function considered. The organizations also show various forms of resilience overcoming some dys-functioning through a coordinated and negotiated redefinition of their own prerogatives or even through collective activities based on the integration of numerous information sources (e.g. by being proactive for the conception and implementation of inter-sectoral or inter-agencies projects to address the dynamic of emergence of new risks regarding health and environment). At the regional or international level, this resilience is generally translated by the integration of new partners or the creation of institutions favouring various actors' commitment at different levels of governance (for instance the creation of a virtuous circle between international coordination and national public policies[13]).

Practically we will pay attention to other theoretical inputs, relying particularly on two of them. Tononi's model (2004, 2008) is strongly grounded on the notion of a "complex", defined as a subset of elements (AC) that does not belong to a subset whose capacity Φ_{IIS} of information integration is higher. The accessible range of consciousness experiences is determined by static (anatomy, informational network a priori) and dynamic characteristics (functional states, patterns, processes, and

---

[12] After the brain's corpus callosum cut off, each hemisphere of the brain develops its proper experience of "private" consciousness, but only the left hemisphere can express its states of mind (Sperry 1984).

[13] Substituting an analysis based on the notion of influence for analyses regarding effectiveness and compliance, Bernstein and Cashore (2012) propose an approach of the link between global governance (e.g. international environmental regimes) and public policies closer to the bases of our model.

activating parameters of network's components) of complexes (one AC can be part of one or more complexes, thus partial overlap are possible). Considering the very limited number of organizations used to develop our examples, we did not try to identify those complexes among the combinatorics of possible merging of organizations. Nevertheless, this step, for each informational network, does not present any difficulty. Other works also offer interesting perspectives; particularly the analogy with the theory stating that consciousness depends on the existence of a top-down synergy of AC activities via a global neuronal workplace (Dehaene and Naccache 2000) remains to explore. Those authors start with the observation that the treatment of an enormous amount of information by the brain is possible without consciousness but that there is a prerequisite: the attention. Furthermore, consciousness itself is required for the realization of specific tasks like the sustainability of information, the realization of new operation combinations or the spontaneous generation of intentional behaviours. We will test the hypothesis that this role is assigned to international organizations.

3.5   Discussion

Modelling the structuring and functioning of organizations and groups of organizations is an active field of research. Many ongoing works propose to reproduce and integrate in a coherent way the most salient properties of organizations in generic representations, kinds of meta-models adaptable to many contexts via their instantiation. For example, Diaconescu and Pitt (2015) rely on the ideas developed by A. Koestler in the 1960s (Koestler 1969; see also Calabrese et al. 2010) on so-called "holonic" systems to account for the relative autonomy of organizations (internal structuring, roles, own resources, internal rules, choice of shared objectives) and for their successive interlocking in more integrative hierarchical structures of polycentric governance. They continue the study by Pitt et al. (2011), which explores via a logical formalization one of the principles exhumed by E. Ostrom and her colleagues (Ostrom 1991; Andersson and Ostrom 2008) concerning the conditions for the success of autonomous institutions of sustainable management of common goods. This "nested enterprises" principle is concerned with the efficiency of a system of systems ordering this management in layers and encapsulations of institutions starting from the local level. We note that at this level of abstraction, the modelling of organizations involved in the governance of common natural resources exploits an analogy with the conception of self-managing systems in the domain of autonomic computing (Lalanda et al. 2013). Noriega et al. (2014) propose a modelling of socio-cognitive systems that can combine human and artificial agents interacting via a web-mediated social space. This approach emphasizes the interactions between participants' behavioural norms, their implementation and the overall performance of the system. This very limited overview is quite representative of a rapidly expanding field, many other works underway on this topic developing innovative approaches (see e.g. Ghose et al. 2014; Aldewereld et al. 2016).

The approach presented here focuses on assessing effective (e.g. through the composition of governing boards, the institutionalized partnerships) or potential governance (partial recoveries of roles, missions, or training offers) of themes offered by a group of organizations. No prior condition constrains the type of organizations (organization in the common sense, network or network of networks of organizations, technical platforms, multi-agency initiatives, etc.), their legal status (public, private, mixed, governmental or not, etc.), the fact of being localized or geographically distributed, or their institutional arrangements (networks, encapsulations, hierarchies, etc.). The model is based on the empirical data produced by the organizations themselves. This is an advantage because it reduces the projection of an *a priori* view of the structure and functioning of organizations onto a reality where collaborations, management and assessment, influences and powers intertwine more than they obey a hierarchy.[14] But it also has its weakness since the analysis remains dependent on the information produced and updated by organizations, according to non-standardized templates. We overcome these limitations in part by analysing—when they exist—the joint productions of organizations, in particular with text mining and the analysis of the evolution of the terminology associated with a topic of interest.[15] Of course, the effective functioning of organizational networks depends on power relationship, strategic positioning or resources control, following changing configurations. Ideally, the assessment of concrete patterns of collaborations should be supplemented by sociological surveys in the field. However, in networks counting several tens or hundreds of organizations, this expectation seems out of reach. Nevertheless, the model presented here is also able to highlight the underlying informational networks and the collective capacities of actors on the basis of the analysis of surveys and interviews.

If the analogy between a possible organizational consciousness and artificial consciousness seems fruitful, it is not pursued without critical thinking. In fact our preliminary results can be used just as well as arguments going against the theory considering the complex process of information integration as artificial consciousness. The existence of that complex process is enough to develop our study without stating the hypothesis of a consciousness form, which is still lacking a consensual concept. At that stage, everything depends actually on a prerequisite acknowledging or not the possibility of an artificial consciousness.

Overall, our conviction is growing that the institutional sphere of governance is sufficiently complex and rapidly evolving to require the simultaneous use of several approaches,[16] each of which nourishes the analysis from a specific perspective and in mutually complementary ways.

---

[14] In addition, even though the neuronal network exists *a priori*, the consciousness experiences may modify its functioning and reciprocally: we observe the same for organizations.

[15] E.g. for the analysis of "health and environment" terminology in international biodiversity conventions see Lajaunie and Mazzega (2016b, 2017) and Lajaunie et al. (2018).

[16] See Mazzega and Lajaunie (2017) for an approach of governance modeling relying on Galois lattices, and Mazzega et al. (2018) for the introduction of the notions of dimensionality and conjugacy in governance modeling using simplicial complexes.

3.6   Conclusion

The need for inter-sectoral public policies, mainly in environment (considered in a broad sense) is already showing collective awareness regarding challenges and the necessity to consider simultaneously and conciliate different point of view. The difficulties resulting from their conception and implementation are acknowledged and lead to examine both the co-operation process between actors and the cognitive basis of the collective action (Funtowicz and Ravetz 1993; Head and Alford 2015). Indeed, their conception ideally requires processing a massive integration of information (data, knowledge, institutional constraints, arbitration between divergent interests...). Their implementation requires collaboration between many organizations with various and complementary competences in order to reach common objectives (e.g. creation of a public good). In this respect, recalling Tononi's perspective (2004, 2008) as well as the perspective adopted in this study, the developed activities are expressing a form of an organizational consciousness emerging at the organization network's level. This is an interesting point of view: it leads to view the need for inter-sectoral policies as the product of an "augmented" consciousness. It also encourages scrutinizing it as the stimulus favouring the development of such an organizational consciousness, and to consider public policies as the expression of that consciousness. To come back to a conception in line with the one developed by Douglas (1986), those organizational systems are also stimulating individual awareness. It can happen regarding the importance of specific issues (e.g. ecological awareness) and, to a higher level of organization, the production of *artifacts* such as public policies, judicial norms, some events (e.g. Conference of the Parties to various conventions) or associations.[17]

Inspired by Tononi's theory of consciousness (2004, 2008), we are building a model of functioning of a group of organizations, proceeding in two steps: using a description of a function ensured by each organization member, we set an informational network which vertices are organizations and links are weighted by mutual information functions. The weakest informational link between subsets of organizations expresses the capacity of the network to produce complex cognitive operations, the integration of information loads at the network level. We have thus analysed the three informational networks respectively induced by the mission, the governance

---

[17]We can broaden that perspective. A rich literature, at the confluence of various academic areas, proposes criteria in order to define or characterize the complexity of judicial, socio-environmental or political systems (e.g. Bourcier et al. 2012; Squazzoni 2014). Nevertheless, our experience leads us to consider a subjective aspect of complexity: can be qualified as complex any system that cannot be comprehended by an individual understanding: "comprehension" and not "analysis" because if analysis can be broken down into different elements, comprehension targets more precisely information and knowledge integration processes which is not the result of a simple juxtaposition of preset results. In other words, the understanding of complex systems requires the creation of the conditions of an organizational consciousness (and the development of tools and methodologies coming for computer science and artificial intelligence can contribute to developing organizational consciousness).

and the training offers of a group of five organizations belonging to SEAMEO's network in Southeast Asia. We estimated a priori their capacity to accomplish in an integrative and collective way their mission, to act according to an integrated governance (e.g. strategic decision-making) or to propose training synthesizing their own knowledge.

On the basis of those results, we pursue the analogy between artificial consciousness and the possibility of a form of organizational consciousness—perceptible and that can be modelled. Indeed, it opens a research field: on the analysis of public policies as consciousness experiences, on the involvement of some organizations in the realization of specific collective tasks (which leads to the notion of network state or the notion of contingent activation of its members), on the nature of dys-functioning of organizational networks and their resilience modes or even on the impact of the formalization of a network or entrance of new members on the organizations' capacity to function as information integration systems.

Acknowledgements This study is a contribution to two projects: (1) the GEMA project "Gouvernance Environnementale: Modélisation et Analyse" funded by CNRS (Défi interdisciplinaire: "InFIniti" InterFaces Interdisciplinaires Numérique et Théorique); (2) the Project (2017–2021) N° ANR-17-CE35-0003-02 FutureHealthSEA "Predictive scenarios of health in Southeast Asia: linking land use and climate changes to infectious diseases" (PIs: Serge Morand CNRS/CIRAD and Claire Lajaunie INSERM).

Annex

The corpus C_S associated with a network S composed of M organizations is built as the concatenation of the individual corpora C_m associated with each organization, symbolically:

$$C_S = \bigcup_{m=1}^{M} C_m \tag{3.1}$$

The *posterior*[18] probability of occurrence of the term t_n^j associated with organization X_j in the corpus C_m is given by

$$P\left[t_n^j(C_m)\right] = F_{oc}\left[t_n^j(C_m)\right] / F_{oc}\left[t_n^j(C_S)\right] \tag{3.2}$$

where $F_{oc}[x]$ is the number of occurrences of event x. The *posterior* probability of joint occurrence of two terms, t_n^j of X_j and $t_{n'}^l$ of X_l, in the corpus C_m is:

---

[18]We could *a priori* postulate a uniform distribution of occurrence of a given term between the various corpora. The posterior probability is here based on the analysis of the empirical texts.

$$P\left[t_n^j(C_m), t_{n'}^l(C_m)\right] = F_{oc}\left[t_n^j(C_m) \wedge t_{n'}^l(C_m)\right] / F_{oc}\left[t_n^j(C_S) \wedge t_{n'}^l(C_S)\right] \qquad (3.3)$$

The average mutual information between organizations X_j and X_l in the network S is estimated as:

$$I_{AMI}\left[X_j, X_l\right]_{C_S} = \left(N_j \times N_l\right)^{-1} \sum_{m=1}^{M+} \sum_{n=1}^{N_j} \sum_{n'=1}^{N_l} e_{nn'}^{jl}(m) \qquad (3.4)$$

N_j (resp. N_l) being the number of terms in X_j (resp. X_l). If we consider an additional corpus C^+ then $M+ = M + 1$ (otherwise $M+ = M$). The elementary information $e_{nn'}^{jl}(m)$ between terms t_n^j and $t_{n'}^l$ on corpus C_m is given by:

$$e_{nn'}^{jl}(m) = P\left[t_n^j(C_m), t_{n'}^l(C_m)\right] \ln \left\{ \frac{P\left[t_n^j(C_m), t_{n'}^l(C_m)\right]}{P\left[t_n^j(C_m)\right] P\left[t_{n'}^l(C_m)\right]} \right\} \qquad (3.5)$$

The elementary information $e_{nn'}^{jl}(m)$ is not zero (and therefore $I_{AMI}\left[X_j, X_l\right]_{C_S} \neq 0$) if term t_n^j of X_j and term $t_{n'}^l$ of X_l are both occurring in the same corpus C_m (whatever the value of m). The auto information $I_{AMI}\left[X_j, X_j\right]_{C_s}$ is not zero (self-loop on the graph) if at least one key term of X_j appears at least in one other corpus C_l, with $l \neq j$. The average mutual information between components S_κ and S_π of the S network bipartition is

$$I_{AMI}\left[S_\kappa, S_\pi\right]_{C_s} = N_{\kappa\pi}^{-1} \sum_{m=1}^{M+} \sum_{n=1}^{N_\kappa} \sum_{n'=1}^{N_\pi} e_{nn'}^{\kappa\pi}(m) \qquad (3.6)$$

the elementary information $e_{nn'}^{\kappa\pi}(m)$ being given by an equation similar to (3.5) except that term t_n^κ (resp. $t_{n'}^\pi$) is taken in the list (composed of $N_{\kappa\pi}$ term pairs $\left[t_n^\kappa, t_{n'}^\pi\right]$) of formed by all key terms of organizations belonging to the bipartition component S_κ (resp. S_π), no term appearing twice in the list. The capacity $\Phi_{IIS}[S]$ of network S to function as an Information Integrative System (IIS) is the amount of effective information that can be integrated across the informational weakest link of a subset of organizations. Limiting the search for this weakest link between bipartition components S_κ and S_π, we have:

$$\Phi_{IIS}[S] = min_{[S_\kappa, S_\pi] \in \Pi_2(S)} \left\{ I_{AMI}\left[S_\kappa, S_\pi\right]_{C_S} \right\} \qquad (3.7)$$

$\Pi_2(S)$ being the set of all bipartitions of S.

References

Aldewereld H, Boissier O, Dignum V, Noriega P, Padget J (eds) (2016) Social coordination frameworks for social technical systems. Law, governance and technology series. Springer, Basel. https://doi.org/10.1007/978-3-319-33570-4

Andersson K, Ostrom E (2008) Analyzing decentralized resource regimes from a polycentric perspective. Policy Sci 41:71–93. https://doi.org/10.1007/s11077-007-9055-6

Bernstein S, Cashore B (2012) Complex global governance and domestic policies: four pathways of influence. Int Aff 88(3):585–604

Bourcier D, Boulet R, Mazzega P (eds) (2012) Politiques Publiques Systèmes Complexes. Hermann, Paris

Calabrese M, Amato A, Di Lecce V, Piuri V (2010) Hierarchical-granularity holonic modelling. J Ambient Intell Humanized Comput 1(3):199–209. https://doi.org/10.1007/s12652-010-0013-3

Cardon A (2000) Conscience Artificielle – Systèmes Adaptatifs. Eyrolles, Paris

Chandra AC (2009) Civil society in search of an alternative regionalism in ASEAN. International Institute for Sustainable Development, Winnipeg. http://www.iisd.org/library/civil-society-search-alternative-regionalism-asean. Accessed 30 Nov 2017

Dehaene S, Naccache L (2000) Towards a cognitive neuroscience of consciousness: basic evidence and a workspace framework. Cognition 79(1–2):1–37

Diaconescu A, Pitt J (2015) Holonic institutions for multi-scale polycentric self-governance. In: Ghose A, Oren N, Telang P, Thangarajah J (eds) Coordination, organisations, institutions, and norms in agent systems X. LNAI 9372. Springer, Basel, pp 19–35

Douglas M (1986) How institutions think. Syracuse University Press, Syracuse

Elliott L (2011) ASEAN and environmental governance: rethinking networked regionalism in South East Asia. Procedia Soc Behav Sci 14:61–64. https://doi.org/10.1016/j.sbspro.2011.03.023

Freeman LC (1979) Centrality in social networks: conceptual clarification. Soc Netw 1(3):215–239

Frost EL (2008) Asia's new momentum. In: Frost EL (ed) Asia's new regionalism. Lynne Rienner, Boulder, pp 1–19. https://www.rienner.com/uploads/47e2d7961e70a.pdf. Accessed 30 Nov 2017

Funtowicz SO, Ravetz JR (1993) Science for the post-normal age. Futures 25(7):739–755. https://doi.org/10.1016/0016-3287(93)90022-L

Ghose XA, Oren N, Telang P, Thangarajah J (eds) (2014) Coordination, organizations, institutions, and norms in agent systems. LNAI 9372. Springer, Basel

Head BW, Alford J (2015) Wicked problems: implications for public policy and management. Adm Soc 47(6):711–739. https://doi.org/10.1177/0095399713481601

Hjørland B (2009) Concept theory. J Am Soc Inf Sci Technol 60(8):1519–1536. https://doi.org/10.1002/asi.21082

Koestler A (1969) Some general properties of self-regulating open hierarchic order (SOHO). In: Koestler A, Smythies JR (eds) Beyond reductionism. New perspectives in the life sciences. Hutchinson, London. http://www.panarchy.org/koestler/holon.1969.html. Accessed 30 Nov 2017

Lajaunie C, Mazzega P (2016a) Organization networks as information integration system - case study on environment and health in Southeast Asia. Adv Comput Sci Int J 5(2):28–39. http://www.acsij.org/acsij/article/view/461

Lajaunie C, Mazzega P (2016b) One health and biodiversity conventions. The emergence of health issues in biodiversity conventions. IUCN Acad Environ Law eJournal 7:105–121. http://www.iucnael.org/en/documents/1299-one-health-and-biodiversity-conventions

Lajaunie C, Mazzega P (2017) Transmission, circulation et persistance des enjeux de santé dans les conventions internationales liées à la Biodiversité et Conventions de Rio. In: Maljean-Dubois S (ed) Diffusion de normes et circulations d'acteurs dans la gouvernance internationale de l'environnement. Confluence des Droits, Aix en Provence, pp 61–80. http://dice.univ-amu.fr/sites/dice.univ-amu.fr/files/public/ouvrage_circulex_2017.pdf. Accessed 30 Nov 2017

Lajaunie C, Mazzega P, Boulet R (2018) Health in biodiversity-related conventions: analysis of a multiplex terminological network (1973–2016). In: Chen S-H (ed) Big data in computational social science and humanities. Springer, Taïwan, pp 165–182

Lalanda PH, McCann JA, Diaconescu A (2013) Autonomic computing. Principles, design and implementation. Springer, London. https://doi.org/10.1007/978-1-4471-5007-7

Lallana EC (2012) ASEAN 2.0: ICT, governance and community in Southeast Asia. Institute of Southeast Asian Studies, Singapore

Mazzega P, Lajaunie C (2017) Modelling organization networks collaborating on health and environment within ASEAN. In: Martinez RS (ed) Complex systems: theory and applications. NOVA Publications, Hauppauge, pp 117–148

Mazzega P, Lajaunie C, Fieux E (2018) Governance modeling: dimensionality and conjugacy. In: Sirmacek B (ed) Graph theory - advanced algorithms and applications. InTech Publisher, Reijika, pp 63–82. ISBN 978-953-51-3773-3. Open access at: https://www.intechopen.com/books/graph-theory-advanced-algorithms-and-applications/governance-modeling-dimensionality-and-conjugacy

Morand S, Jittapalapong S, Supputamongkol Y, Abdullah MT, Huan T (2014) Infectious diseases and their outbreaks in Asia-Pacific: biodiversity and its regulation loss matter. PLoS One 9(2): e90032

Noriega P, Padget J, Verhagen H, d'Inverno M (2014) The challenge of artificial socio-cognitive systems. In: 17th International workshop coordination, organizations, institutions and norms, Paris, May 2014. http://homepages.abdn.ac.uk/n.oren/pages/COIN14/papers/p12.pdf. Accessed 30 Nov 2017

Olson M (1965) The logic of collective action: public goods and the theory of groups. Harvard University Press, Cambridge

Ostrom E (1991) Governing the commons. The evolution of institutions for collective action. Cambridge University Press, Cambridge

Pitt J, Schaumeier J, Artikis A (2011) The axiomatisation of socio-economic principles for self-organizing systems. In: Fifth IEEE international conference on Self-Adaptive and Self-Organizing Systems (SASO), pp 138–147. https://doi.org/10.1109/SASO.2011.25

Reggia JA (2013) The rise of machine consciousness: studying consciousness with computational models. Neural Netw 44:112–131. https://doi.org/10.1016/j.neunet.2013.03.011

Robinson NA, Koh KL (2002) Strengthening sustainable development in regional inter-governmental governance: lessons from the "ASEAN way". Singapore J Int Comp Law 6:640–682

Sacks O (1998) The man who mistook his wife for a hat: and other clinical tales. Touchstone, New York

Scott JE (2000) Facilitating interorganizational learning with information technology. J Manag Inf Syst 17(2):81–113

Sperry R (1984) Consciousness, personal identity and the divided brain. Neuropsychologia 22 (6):661–673

Squazzoni F (2014) A social science-inspired complexity policy: beyond the mantra of incentivization. Complexity 19(6):5–13. https://doi.org/10.1002/cplx.21520

Tononi G (2004) An information integration theory of consciousness. BMC Neurosci 5:42. https://doi.org/10.1186/1471-2202-5-42

Tononi G (2008) Consciousness as integrated information: a provisional manifesto. Biol Bull 215 (3):216–242. https://doi.org/10.2307/25470707

Chapter 4
The Entity-Process Framework for Integrated Agent-Based Modeling of Social-Ecological Systems

Christophe Sibertin-Blanc, Olivier Therond, Claude Monteil, and Pierre Mazzega

Abstract The success of Integrated Assessment and Modeling of social-ecological systems (SESs) requires a framework allowing members of this process to share, organize and integrate their knowledge about the system under consideration. To meet this need and ease management of successful modeling processes, we present a conceptual framework for integrated agent-based modeling and simulation of SESs in the form of a formal *"entity-process meta-model"*, along with a distinction between three levels of models—conceptual, concrete and simulation—and characterization of the research question using indicators and scenarios. We then describe how to represent the structural and dynamic dimensions of SESs into conceptual and concrete models and to derive the simulation model from these two types of models. Finally, we discuss how our framework solves some of the challenges of integrated SES modeling: integration and sharing of heterogeneous knowledge, reliability of simulation results, expressiveness issues, and flexibility of the modeling process.

C. Sibertin-Blanc (✉)
Institute of Research in Computer Science of Toulouse, IRIT, Université de Toulouse, CNRS, UT1, Toulouse, France
e-mail: sibertin@ut-capitole.fr

O. Therond (✉)
Université de Lorraine, INRA, LAE, Colmar, France
e-mail: olivier.therond@inra.fr

C. Monteil
DYNAFOR, Université de Toulouse, INRA, Castanet-Tolosan, France
e-mail: monteil@ensat.fr

P. Mazzega
UMR5563 GET Geosciences Environment Toulouse, CNRS/University of Toulouse, Toulouse, France

Strathclyde Centre for Environmental Law and Governance (SCELG), University of Strathclyde, Glasgow, UK
e-mail: pierre.mazzegaciamp@get.omp.eu

© Springer Nature Switzerland AG 2019
R. Boulet et al. (eds.), *Law, Public Policies and Complex Systems: Networks in Action*, Law, Governance and Technology Series 42,
https://doi.org/10.1007/978-3-030-11506-7_4

57

4.1   Introduction

Environmental and natural resource (NR) management issues involve multiple interactions between ecological processes and many actors having diverse and contrasting interests and objectives (Reed 2008; Pahl-Wostl 2007). Many biophysical and anthropic processes act concurrently, directly or indirectly, at their respective scales of time, space and magnitude on NRs' states and dynamics. They occur in social-ecological systems (SESs) in which interactions within and between social and ecological subsystems give rise to emergent structures and non-linear processes at sub- and whole-system levels (Parrott 2011).

Integrated Assessment and Modeling (IAM) is an interdisciplinary approach to deal with environmental and NR management problems based on integrating models of all relevant system components into an integrated modeling platform (Jakeman et al. 2006). Such model-based methods collect data and knowledge from a wide range of scientific disciplines and integrate them to investigate a research question, most often in a "policy oriented context", to analyze system responses to changes and to design sustainable management strategies (Pahl-Wostl et al. 2000; Tol and Vellinga 1998; Ahrweiler and Gilbert 2015). The potential of integrated modeling to address NR management and policy problems is now well-established (Voinov and Bousquet 2010; Sterk et al. 2009; Bots and Daalen 2008; McIntosh et al. 2007; Jakeman et al. 2006; Oxley et al. 2004). Models are cognitive artifacts that are essential for making complex problems intelligible (Sterk et al. 2009; Conklin 2006). Modeling lies at the core of complexity science and, during the past few decades, it has played an increasing role in better understanding how complex systems function.

A model expresses an individual or collective representation that one or more observers build based on the knowledge that they share about a system of reference (SR) that they investigate for a given research question. Several computational paradigms are available for designing a model, such as system dynamics, equation-based, statistics, expert system, evolutionary (e.g., artificial neural networks), and cellular or agent-based models (ABMs) (Gilbert and Troitzch 2005; Parker et al. 2003). While all but the last example represent the SR by means of abstractions that characterize phenomena of interest, ABMs consider the component elements of the SR. An ABM is composed of related entities that correspond to well-defined elements of the SR, so that the model's organization mirrors the modeler's representation of the SR. An ABM also describes interdependent dynamics of these elements and thus allows functioning of the SR to be simulated. Notably, ABMs are particularly well suited for representing heterogeneous decision-making processes of social actors and spatial interactions between social actors and between them and their environment (Bousquet and Le Page 2004; Parker et al. 2003). Thus, ABMs are well suited to simulate SES behaviors and to assess potential effects of *what-if* scenarios for NR management issues (An 2012; Bousquet and Le Page 2004).

Concrete issues of NR management cross barriers between academic disciplines (Norgaard and Baer 2005), so that an integrated ABM includes disciplinary sub-models that each describes application of a specific scientific theory in the SR under consideration. These sub-models may be integrated in many ways, which fall more or less into two typical approaches (Voinov and Shugart 2013). According to the "*assemblage*" approach, each sub-model corresponds to a software component, and they are integrated by exchanging data, the output of one component being the input of others. This approach benefits from modules that are well-tested and theoretically well-founded. The risk, however, is to yield an "integronster" model (Voinov and Shugart 2013) that does not capture essential features of the SR, due to mismatches between modules in resolution, spatiotemporal scale, recursive data exchange, etc. According to the "*integral*" approach, the SR model is built as a whole in a transdisciplinary way, so that sub-models are interwoven into a common representation of the SR. This approach risks yielding to an *ad hoc* model that lacks theoretical bases; preventing this requires that each scientific theory be carefully tailored to the specific characteristics of the SR under consideration. This approach allows more accurate description but costs more.

In the integral approach, a conceptual framework is required to support integration of multiple heterogeneous sources of knowledge into a coherent description (model) of the SR. This framework will provide participants in a modeling project with a common language for expression, sharing and organization of their various knowledge and concerns (Binder et al. 2013).

In this article, we present such a conceptual framework for integrated agent-based modeling and simulation (IABM) of SESs in the form of a formal meta-model of SESs, called hereafter the "*entity-process* meta-model", along with a distinction between three levels of models—conceptual, concrete and simulation—and characterization of the research question using indicators and scenarios. A meta-model of a class of systems, here SESs, is a model of models of such systems, i.e., a formal definition of the nature of the elements that appear in SES models and how they may be related. Accordingly, a SES model is expressed using concepts provided by the meta-model. The entity-process framework is formal in that it also determines how simulation models are generated and executed on computers.

The main purpose of this framework is twofold:

- *Supporting integration and sharing of heterogeneous knowledge:* A typical integrated SES modeling project involves people with a variety of theoretical or empirical knowledge, viewpoints, concerns, duties and also stakes in project outcomes. They are scientists from ecological sciences, computer sciences or human and social sciences with a laboratory, field or intervention research perspective (Hatchuel 2001), along with, in case of participatory modeling (Voinov and Bousquet 2010), users of natural resources, managers, policy makers or third-party stakeholders. To address this heterogeneity, our meta-model purposes to allow modeling-project participants to build an integrated representation of the SR that is agreed upon, and thus well-understood, by everyone. In addition, the software implementation of the model must be reliable, so that team members may trust the simulation results.
- *Easing the modeling process:* Significant integrated modeling projects for SES have to face many difficulties, due to the (variable) number and diversity of

participants, the plurality of scientific disciplines, the complexity of the SR and the difficulty in formalizing the research question, gathering data, implementing the model, etc. (Kragt et al. 2013). They are risky projects often lasting several years and facing many hurdles; accordingly, methodological and organizational issues are of paramount importance for their success.[1] A meta-model shapes the form of a model and thus guides its design, development and management (Walden et al. 2015; ISO 2008). Thus, the second motivation for the entity-process framework is to ease management of modeling projects, especially distribution and coordination of its tasks.

Our entity-process framework has been used to guide the MAELIA integrated modeling project. The MAELIA project developed an agent-based simulation platform to study environmental, economic and social impacts of scenarios of water and land use and water management in combination with climate change. The platform is dedicated to support decision-making processes of organizations involved in managing water scarcity in the Adour-Garonne basin (southwestern France). Its modeling architecture and components, the calibration methods used, simulation performance, scenario construction and application examples were described in several articles (Gaudou et al. 2014; Mazzega et al. 2014; Murgue et al. 2014; Therond et al. 2014). Outcomes of the use of our entity-process framework during the MAELIA project are used in this chapter to illustrate its potential.

The next section (Sect. 4.2) presents the *entity-process framework*, which distinguishes two dimensions of SES models: structure and dynamics. Model *structure* describes SR components as a set of *entities* and *relationships* between them, while distinguishing *resources*, passive entities handled by processes, from *actors*, active entities having autonomous behavior. The *dynamic* dimension of a model is composed of *processes* that use and act upon entities, and so change the system. Interaction between a SR and its environment is addressed by distinguishing *internal processes*, under system control, from *external processes*, which only influence system behavior. Decomposing the model in structural and dynamic dimensions requires carefully assembling them together. The framework also distinguishes three levels of SR models: *conceptual, concrete* and *simulation*. Finally, it defines *indicators*, which determine how to observe phenomena of interest, and *scenarios*, which investigate hypotheses about the research question.

The entity-process meta-model is abstract in nature and thus does not specify how models should be depicted. The third section (Sect. 4.3) describes how to represent structural and dynamic dimensions of models at both conceptual and concrete levels. It also provides three kinds of *interaction diagrams* that show how processes interact through entities, how entities are handled by processes or how model subsystems interact. The fourth section (Sect. 4.4) is devoted to simulation models: it describes

---

[1]In this regard, SES modeling projects do not differ much from common software projects, of which only 39% succeed (delivered on time, on budget, with required features and functions), 43% were challenged (late, over budget or with less than the required features and functions), and 18% failed (cancelled prior to completion or delivered and never used) (Standish Group 2009, 2013).

how a simulation model is directly derived from conceptual and concrete models and how works the simulation engine that controls process executions. This *computational semantics* of the entity-process meta-model prevents participants in the modeling process from seeing models as black boxes. Section 4.5 discusses how the framework solves some of the challenges that integrated SES modeling projects face: integration and sharing of heterogeneous knowledge, reliability of simulation results, expressiveness issues, and flexibility of the modeling process. The conclusion summarizes the framework and mentions future work likely to increase its potential for the community of SES researchers.

4.2   The Entity-Process Framework for SES Modeling

The basic concepts of the entity-process meta-model are shown in Fig. 4.1. Accordingly, the *structure* of a SES model is composed of various kinds of *entities* and *relationships* between them, while its *dynamics* are composed of various kinds of

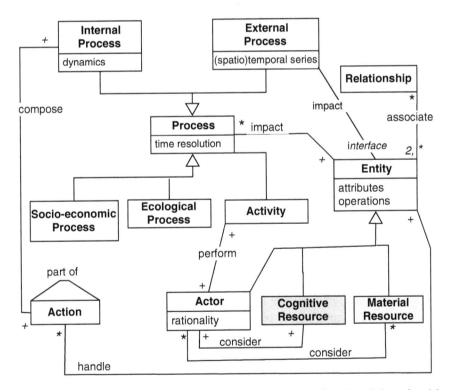

Fig. 4.1 UML class diagram of the entity-process meta-model for formal modeling of social-ecological systems. Symbols represent cardinalities of associations: "*": any number of elements (including none); "+": at least one element; "2, *": at least two elements

processes that handle and impact entities of the structure. The two dimensions of a model are closely related and determine each other, as discussed later. The entity-process framework also distinguishes three levels of models—conceptual, concrete and simulation—and considers indicators and scenarios.

4.2.1 Models' Structure: Entities and Relationships

Entities are SR components that have a distinctive existence and can be perceived, captured and acted out as such. Entities are referred to with nouns and can be distinguished from one another. They are *impacted* and *handled* by processes. An entity may be *permanent*, if it exists longer than the period during which the system is studied, or *transient*, if the system includes operations to make it to appear or disappear. An entity is described by a set of *attributes* that correspond to its features. A range of values is associated with each attribute of an entity. Some attributes are *constant*, having an immutable value on the time scale of the system, while others are *variable*. The *state* of an entity is defined as the values of its variable attributes. An entity is also endowed with *operations* that process its attribute values to change or get data about its state.

Cohesion among entities is ensured by *relationships*, associating two or more entities, that can be classified into two types. A *structural* relationship permanently associates entities related by their nature (e.g. a field always has a soil type). A non-structural, or *event* relationship, associates entities due to an action (e.g., a farmer owns a field until he/she sells it). At any moment, the *structure* of a system is defined as the set of its entities and structural links while its *state* is defined as the states of these entities and their event links.[2]

The meta-model distinguishes three kinds of entities: actors, material resources and cognitive resources. An entity is not fully categorized by the nature of the SR component to which it refers but by a modeling choice that assesses its role in the model for the question investigated. An *actor* is agent with some autonomy, such as an *individual*, a *population* of similar individuals or a *collective* (an organization, association, enterprise, etc.), who performs at least one activity. For example, a cattle herd can be considered as an actor if its behavior is not fully determined and controlled by some processes. On the contrary, a human entity who merely provides services without autonomous behavior could be classified as a (material) resource. An actor has *rationality*, which defines how it determines and conducts its activities, solves conflicts that could appear between them, and decides which action to execute (or not) at a given time. The *behavior* of an actor is the observable result that comes from exercising its rationality.

A *resource* is a passive object used by processes. *Material resources* are physical objects that stand somewhere at any time (e.g., water body, field, dam), while

---

[2]A link is an instance of a relationship between precise entities.

cognitive resources are immaterial entities that are involved in actors' exercise of rationality. They are information, beliefs, knowledge or expectations about facts, procedures or values that actors *consider* when conducting activities or designing strategies. A cognitive resource is *private* if it is usable by a single actor (e.g., a farmer's cropping system) or *common* if it is shared by several actors (e.g., weather forecasts). Some resources have both material and cognitive dimensions that are difficult to distinguish since they have a symbolic status; they are categorized according to the most relevant aspect. For example, money may be handled as banknotes (material resource) or as value (cognitive resource). Any information about a material resource used by an actor implies the existence of a related cognitive resource, which will be considered in the model only if required (e.g., an actor belief about the state of a water resource differs from its current state).

Accurate description of the SR's structure also requires expressing *integrity constraints*, which are restrictions on structure and state that ensure that the concrete model is a coherent description of a possible SR. Cardinalities of associations in UML class diagrams (Fig. 4.1) express such constraints e.g., "each process has to impact at least one entity". Other constraints deserve to be explicitly stated, such as "the gross margin of a farm is the sum of its fields' gross margins'" or "the up-down relationship between stream sections of a river basin is an order relationship (it includes no cycle)".

4.2.2 Models' Dynamics: Processes

Processes are SR elements likely to occur and whose occurrence produces changes in the state or structure of the system. They are preferably referred to with verbs. As in most ABM approaches, processes are conceptualized as acting in discrete time, and each has a *time-scale* attribute that determines at which time steps of a simulation it has to be activated by the simulation engine. Typical time steps are one hour, day, week, month or year; it is also possible to consider non-periodic processes whose next activation is calculated dynamically.

The framework distinguishes three kinds of processes: activities, ecological processes and socio-economic processes. An *activity* is a process to be *performed* by actors who aim to achieve goals based on their rationality (e.g., irrigate, decree a water-withdrawal restriction). An *ecological process* results from the action of biophysical laws (e.g., water runoff on soil, plant growth). It applies to material resources and influences a change in their states.[3] A *socio-economic process* is the overall result of human economic or social activities (e.g., changes in land use, diffusion of new technologies, changes in prices of agricultural inputs) which is not ascribed to

---

[3]In fact, ecological processes also apply to actors, who must have material support to work. For example, human actors are subject to aging. The fact that actors are also a material resource is not shown in Fig. 4.1 for clarity.

an actor. Only effects of a socio-economic process are described in the model, since it is not relevant to detail mechanisms that accomplish the changes.

SESs are open systems that interact with their *environment* (i.e., entities and processes of the world that lie outside the system although they influence its dynamics). While the boundary between a SR and its environment is often rather fuzzy, it must be clearly set in the model. To account for how a system is impacted by its environment, a secondary distinction between processes must be introduced: external vs. internal processes.

External processes are those not under control of the system; thus, their progress does not depend on the state of the system. External processes are described as (spatio-) temporal series that force, at each step of their time scales, new values of or variations in entities' states. These entities are conceptualized as *interface entities*, which may be impacted by both external and internal processes. They are similar in nature to other entities; thus, the change in status of a process (internal vs. external) entails no other modification in the model. For example, if the SR has a local or regional scale, weather data and technological innovations are supported by interface entities whose changes are determined by external processes.

Internal processes are processes which performance depends on the current state of the system. An internal process is composed of a set of *actions*, which can themselves be decomposed into *sub-actions*, and its *dynamics* describes the scheduling of actions and how they are performed at each time step of the process progress.

As integrity constraints place constraints on entities and relationships of the model's structure, the model's dynamics includes *behavioral constraints* on processes to deal with potential conflicts between processes that occur concurrently, typically when two processes intend to update a same attribute at a same time step of a simulation. The form and operation of behavioral constraints will be addressed in Sect. 4.4.

4.2.3 (De)composition of Models into Structure and Dynamics

According to this meta-model, the model of a SES consists of two types of primitive elements—entities and processes—unlike approaches such as object-oriented, agent-based or DEVS (Ziegler et al. 2000; Quesnel et al. 2007), which consider only a single type of primitive element (objects, agents, or processes, respectively). According to a dynamic view of the system, entities of the structure serve as a glue between the processes, while according to a structural view, processes of the dynamics cause entities to co-evolve.

Therefore, dynamics and structure of a model are strongly related. In a syntactical perspective, each process *impacts* at least one entity by changing its state or by creating or destroying entity instances or links. Conversely, each resource is *impacted* or *handled* by at least one process, and each actor *performs* at least one activity. In summary, an entity is included in the model only if it serves processes, and a process is included only if it impacts entities.

In an operational or functional perspective, dynamics and structure determine each other. Processes interact through entities: through changes it makes in the states of the entities it impacts, a process affects the course of processes, whose performance depends on the state of these entities. Moreover, at any moment during a simulation, the structure's state is the result of previous process executions and also determines how the next step of each process will be performed. To ensure that processes interact properly within the same world, there must be no ambiguity about the identities and attributes of the entities involved in the execution of each process.

4.2.4 Conceptual, Concrete and Simulation Models

During an integrated agent-based modeling project, one can distinguish three levels of models (see Fig. 4.2). The *simulation model* is the software run on computers, which includes program code, input files and all the software resources required to

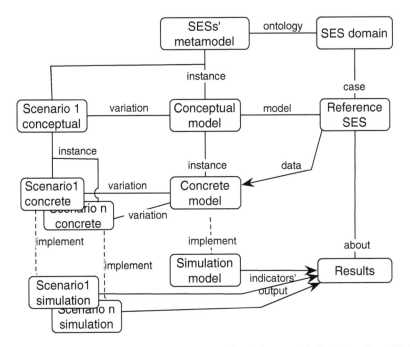

Fig. 4.2 Levels of models—conceptual, concrete and simulation—and their relationships with the reference social-ecological system (SES) to be modeled, the meta-model of SESs, scenarios and indicators. V1 to Vn correspond to the different incremental versions of the conceptual model

run the code properly. The *conceptual model* is an abstract description of a type of SR (e.g., water management systems in France) that defines types of SR elements (i.e., entities, relationships, processes) that have to be included in the model. Between the conceptual and simulation models, the *concrete model* represents a concrete SR (e.g., water management of a given watershed), describing its unique features and identifying all instances of the conceptual model's entity types that must appear in the simulation model (e.g., all fields, farms, farmers, dam managers of the SR). Thus, a conceptual model that is applied to different SRs will lead to a particular concrete model for each SR. In short, the concrete model is an instantiation of the conceptual model, and the simulation model is a software implementation of the concrete model.

Regarding structure, a conceptual model defines only the *type* of entities and relationships to be considered, where an *entity type* is defined by a name, a list of attributes and a list of operations, and a *relationship type* is defined by a name and the set of entity types it associates. A concrete model includes a set of instances of these entity types linked together by a set of instances of the relationship types that fulfill the integrity constraints.[4] For example, if the conceptual model includes a Water Agency actor, the concrete model will include a single instance of this type whose attribute values are based on characteristics of the water agency under study. Likewise, a material resource Field will be instantiated into the concrete model as the number of concrete fields in the geographic area of the SR. The same holds for relationships between entities: the relationship exploit between Farmer and Field in the conceptual model will give rise in the concrete model to concrete exploit links between each Farmer instance and the Field instances it works (Fig. 4.3).

Regarding dynamics, internal and external processes require different treatments. Internal processes, their dynamics and the actions they contain, are described in the conceptual model, while the concrete model provides specific values of generic parameters if needed. As for an external process, the conceptual model only provides the type of interface entities it impacts, while the concrete model includes input-data series specific to the SR. For example, the Weather Forecast external process will be described by a data series specific to the period and space considered.

4.2.5 Indicators and Scenarios

In IAM projects, indicators and scenarios determine the knowledge that can be delivered by model simulations in response to research questions. They express how the SR model is observed and tested depending on the aim of the project.

---

[4]Thus, models deal only with "entity types" and "entity instances", using the term "entity" when there is no ambiguity. The same holds for relationships, although relationship instances are preferably called "links".

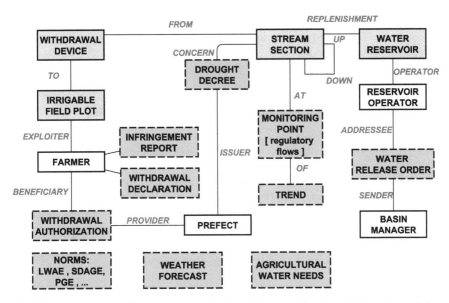

Fig. 4.3 Actor-resource diagram representing the subsystem of water withdrawals regulation (an extract of the conceptual model of the MAELIA project)

Indicators are a part of model definition since they determine which entities and processes to include in the model.

Indicators provide information about model internal behavior and outputs towards the SR's environment. Process executions cannot be observed directly; except for the computing resources they consume, only their effect on entities can be observed. Therefore, indicators are defined by aggregating states and distributions of entities and links. An indicator is defined by the list of entity attributes and relationships of the conceptual model involved in calculating it, how it is calculated and, optionally, how it should be displayed in the user interface of the simulation platform.

Scenarios intend to study effects of hypotheses on the SR. Typical scenarios are expressed as model variations, such as changes in (i) dynamics of internal processes (e.g., parameter values) (ii) data series of external processes that impact interface entities (e.g., climate-change scenarios), or (iii) instances and initial states of entities (e.g., state of water resources) and links of the concrete model. Scenarios may also change the conceptual model by adding or removing entities or processes or by changing the theory used to describe a process. In the MAELIA project, water-regulation scenarios include a new actor in charge of distributing water resources among farmers in a new type of management zone.

We claim that scenarios are merely models that have a specific role in the modeling project and correspond to hypothetical SESs or various views on, or possible futures of, the SR. They do not differ in nature from the model of the current functioning of the SR. Each scenario gives rise to an associated simulation model. Considering scenarios as models emphasizes that not all changes result in a new scenario. Designing a scenario requires paying attention to coherence among elements of this new model.

4.3 Expression of Conceptual and Concrete Models

The meta-model introduces a set of concepts and specifies logical relationships among them. Since it is abstract in nature, a concrete syntax must be defined to describe conceptual and concrete models, preferably with supporting diagrams. In line with breaking down SES models into structure and dynamics, conceptual models have *actor-resource* diagrams (to define entities and relationships of model structure), *process* diagrams (one for each process of model dynamics) and *interaction* diagrams (to illustrate interactions between entities and processes). Models' structure and dynamics are also described by concrete models.

4.3.1 Structural Models: Actor-Resource Diagrams

Concepts used to define model structure rely mainly on principles of the object-oriented approach (Meyer 1997). Accordingly, actor-resource diagrams use UML class diagram notations to represent actors, resources and relationships of the conceptual model structure (OMG 2005).[5] For example, an actor-resource diagram can describe entities and relationships involved in the Prefect's activity to decide whether or not to issue a drought decree, which restricts water uses (Fig. 4.3). UML stereotypes can be defined to distinguish actors, material resources, cognitive resources and interface entities using specific colors or borders in diagrams.

Actor-resource diagrams can focus on just a part of the conceptual model structure and have different levels of detail, showing only entity and relationship names (with or without cardinalities), or also showing attributes (only the public ones or also the private ones, with or without value ranges) and operations.

To describe conceptual model structure, an actor-resource diagram must be supplemented with elements that are not supported in UML class diagrams but necessary for specification of the simulation model, in particular:

- integrity constraints, expressed using either UML Object Constraint Language (OMG 2010) or any other way to express clear and unambiguous statements
- the main operations of each entity, specified in such a way that they can be accurately implemented in the simulation model

---

[5]UML notation is widely known and used, but other approaches, such as the Entity-Relationship formalism (Chen 1976) or knowledge representation with Descriptive Logic (Baader et al. 2003), could be used instead.

A concrete model structure defines the initial state of the simulation model, i.e. entity instances (including attribute values) and relationship links that must be initialized for any simulation. The concrete model lists external data files and bases that describe entities' instances and links, and how they must be processed to produce *initialization input files* of the simulation model. Attribute values of initial instances for some entity types can be set using probabilities. They can be used for single attributes (e.g., farmers' inclinations to respect administrative restrictions on water withdrawal) or on all instances of an entity type (e.g., the farmer population if they are not known individually).

4.3.2   Dynamic Models: Process Diagrams

In the conceptual model, each internal process gives rise to a *process diagram* that describes how it proceeds, its dynamics and its action(s).

Each process should be described using the formalism most appropriate for it, such as a system of equations (difference or differential), a state automaton , an algorithm, a decision-tree (Fig. 4.4) or a set of "event-condition-action" rules. Process diagrams are diverse due to the variety of processes in SESs and the levels of detail at which they are represented in a model. Nonetheless, each process diagram includes the following elements:

- precise specification of the process's *interface*, i.e., entity instances it accesses, input attributes whose states influence its performance, and output attributes whose states it changes
- the temporal (and possibly spatial) scale of the process
- description of how the process operates, especially whether it acts on many entities (e.g., runoff, which applies to every land unit of a hydrological sub-model), using a formalism appropriate for both examination by peers and correct implementation in the simulation model

An internal process does not generate a concrete process diagram unless specific parameter values need to be specified. In contrast, an external process mainly has concrete description that lists external data files and bases to be used and how they are pre-processed to produce the time series that will serve as a *forcing input file* during simulations.

4.3.3   Interaction Diagrams

Conceptual and concrete models convey sufficient information for producing the associated simulation model. Nevertheless, to ease overall understanding of the SR model, interaction diagrams are useful for showing at the conceptual level, the main interactions between the model's structure and dynamics. Interaction diagrams

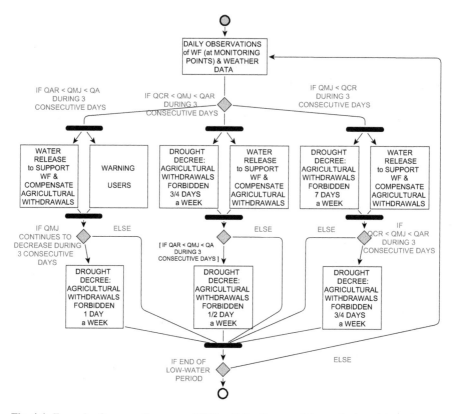

Fig. 4.4 Example of process diagram: an UML activity diagram of the prefect's activity to issue a drought decree (regulation of water withdrawals). QA (alarm flow), QAR (reinforced alarm flow), QCR (crisis flow) are compulsory levels of river water flow while QMJ is the daily average water flow (see Mazzega et al. 2014 for more details)

provide an overview of processes' semantics and entities' roles. Interaction diagrams can focus either on entities, processes or subsystems.

For example, an *entity-oriented interaction diagram* for water regulation and agricultural land-use in the MAELIA model (Fig. 4.5) summarizes activities performed by some actors and the main resources involved in their execution; thereby, it describes how actor behaviors depend on each other. A *process-oriented interaction diagram* (Fig. 4.6) highlights how activities interact through shared resources, showing communication flows and dependencies among processes. Ecological and socio-economic processes can also be shown in such diagrams.

In contrast, a *subsystem interaction diagram* shows how subsystems (composed of closely related entities and processes) interact through shared resources (Fig. 4.7). Indeed, likewise the system as a whole interacts with its environment by means of interface entities, it may be breakdown into subsystem. The MAELIA model can be broken down into four subsystems (Hydrology, Farming, Other uses, and

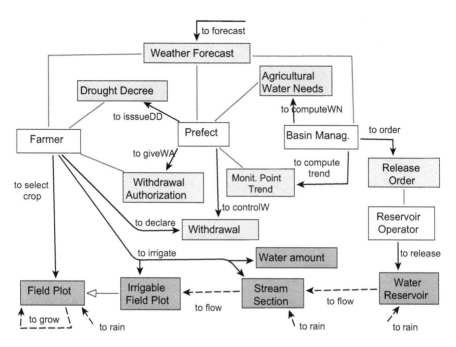

Fig. 4.5 Entity-oriented interaction diagram from the MAELIA model focusing on regulation of water withdrawal. Entities are represented as boxes and processes as arrows. White boxes represent actors, blue boxes material resources and green boxes cognitive resources. Dashed arrows represent ecological or socio-economic processes and link the most impacted entities. Solid arrows represent activities and link the performing actor to the most impacted entities. Gray lines link actors to the main cognitive resources they consider. External process arrows have no source

Regulation) that are defined according to the core subsystems of the SES General Framework (Ostrom 2009): *Resource system, Resource units, Users,* and *Governance system* (Fig. 4.8). In the MAELIA subsystem interaction diagram (Fig. 4.7), Hydrology subsystem gathers *Resource units* and *Resource system,* the former corresponding just to the structure of Hydrology; Regulation subsystem corresponds to the *Governance system* ; *User* is split into Farming and Other uses subsystems because the MAELIA model focuses on agricultural use of water resources. Interface entities between subsystems support *Interactions* and *Outcomes,* and external processes and indicators support interactions with *Related ecosystems* (Fig. 4.7).

Interaction diagrams have no formal semantics and simply arrange some elements of the model selected according to diagrams' objectives. They increase understanding of model organization by focusing on dependencies between its structure and dynamics. They may be useful during preliminary steps of model design to elucidate the entire SR's functioning.

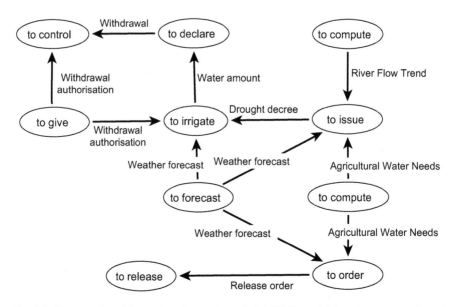

Fig. 4.6 Process-oriented interaction diagram from the MAELIA model focusing on regulation of water withdrawals. Processes are represented as ellipse (nodes) and entities as arrows. An arrow's source process impacts the resource while the target process's performance depends on the state of the resource

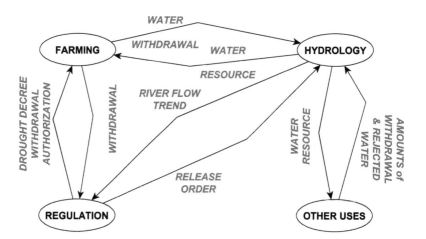

Fig. 4.7 Interaction diagram showing four subsystems of the MAELIA model connected by resources (arrows) that serve as interface entities

Fig. 4.8 Core subsystems
in a framework for
analyzing social-ecological
systems (adapted from
Ostrom 2009)

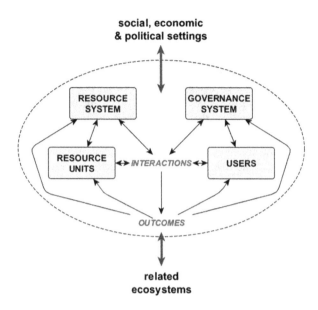

4.4   Computational Semantics of the Meta-model: Simulation Model

The entity-process meta-model does not only define conceptual and concrete models (i.e. *descriptive model*) of a SR; it also defines the structure and behavior of the simulation model that implements the descriptive model. The simulation model can be developed from scratch by translating the descriptive model into a programming language such as java, or C++, or preferably using a simulation platform such as Cormas (Bousquet et al. 1998), Gamma (Taillandier et al. 2012a), Repast Symphony (North et al. 2006), NetLogo (Wilenski 1999), OMS (Ahuja et al. 2005) or many others—see the SES simulation platforms reviewed in Laniak et al. (2013: Table 6). These platforms provide useful services, such as a graphical interface, simulation monitoring, or management of geographic information. We present principles of implementation according to the object-oriented approach (Meyer 1997), the standard paradigm for the development of ABM platforms.

Implementation of model structure is straightforward: each entity type is translated into a class, and each entity instance becomes an object of the class of its type. UML class diagrams have a well-defined semantics, and most UML tools automatically generate code corresponding to a class diagram, leaving only operations to be coded by hand.

Each internal process is also implemented as a class. The class of an ecological or socio-economic process has a single instance because it occurs only once at each time step (e.g., runoff operates in the same way at all times and places). The same holds for activities, and the rationality of an actor controls all activities it is allowed to perform. At each time step of a simulation, all processes whose temporal resolution corresponds to the step's time stamp are activated to perform an action according to the current state of the system.

The policy of the simulation-engine that activates processes at each time step of a simulation is crucial. It determines the temporal dimension of interactions among processes, which has been shown to influence results (Kubera et al. 2009; Caron-Lormier et al. 2008; Michel et al. 2003). The policy must reflect the modeling team's representation of the overall effect of performing processes, which leads to distinguishing *performance* of an action (pushing a door) from its actual *effect* (eventual opening of the door): processes perform actions independently of each other, and the overall effect of these actions is determined by each impacted entity once all actions have been performed (Ferber and Muller 1996). If an entity is subject to a single action, the effect of the action can occur immediately. If an entity experiences conflicting actions, however, the overall effect is decided according to *behavioral constraints* (cf. Sect. 4.2.2) that govern changes in the entity state. For example, if a farmer wants to withdraw more water than available from a reservoir, the effect will be to obtain only the quantity available. If several farmers want to do so, the reservoir's behavioral rules will determine whether some of them (e.g. selected at random) obtain the quantity desired while others get nothing or if each of them obtains only a fraction of the quantity desired. Behavioral constraints specify the overall effect of actions that cannot be completed simultaneously at the same time step of a simulation. Thus, at each time step, the simulation engine proceeds in two steps:

1. activate all ecological and socio-economic processes and the rationality of all actors to select the actions to be performed (in any order)
2. ask all entities to apply the effects of the actions that they undergo, according to behavioral constraints (in any order)

Thus, the overall effect of a time step is as if all processes operate concurrently (and not sequentially). In practice, the simulation engine does not need to call all entities at each time step, because conflicts likely to occur are not common and are known in advance. In addition, most conflicts can be prevented by an appropriate scheduling of processes, breaking down some processes, or introducing inoperative time lags. Thus, optimizations can allow to apply effects of most actions on the fly, while producing the same overall effect as the two-pass policy.

4.5 Discussion

As an epistemic tool, a framework's suitability relies on its ability to support production of good knowledge. This production involves many organizational, applicative, scientific and technological issues within a community of practice (Laniak et al. 2013). We address how the entity-process framework supports some of these issues, but methodological questions about how to address research questions (Schlüter et al. 2014; Jakeman et al. 2006) are out the scope of this article.

4.5.1 Integration and Sharing of Heterogeneous Knowledge

Despite the diversity of participants in a SES integrated modeling project, they must build a representation of the SR that includes the diversity of everyone's knowledge and is agreed upon, and thus well-understood, by everyone.

Every field of knowledge uses technical terms that condense domain-specific knowledge and ease communication between specialists. To be understood by people outside their domain, specialists must deconstruct these terms and rebuild them using simple and unambiguous concepts. To address this issue, our meta-model relies on basic concepts (Fig. 4.1), which are common knowledge.

It is understood, however, that no participant needs to acquire all the knowledge held by all others and thus becomes a specialist in each of the domains involved in the model. Separate definition of processes allows each specialist to express theories proper to his/her discipline using his/her favorite formalism and thus to include knowledge in the model that is not necessarily shared by others.

Thus, entity-process models feature two faces: overview and domain-specific. The *overview face* results from collaborative work of all team members, who are responsible for its quality and hold its (intellectual) ownership. This face includes the elements necessary to properly interpret simulation results: the structural model and the interfaces of processes. Understanding it requires only common knowledge about the SR, and it supports communication of the model to interested parties. In contrast, a *domain-specific face* includes technical elements about the representation of processes that fall within the scope of a specific domain and can be scrutinized by specialists.

Our framework may help address the great challenges of documenting a model for project needs and describing it for communication to others. To improve communication of model, common model-description's outlines are needed, such as ODD or TRACE protocols (Grimm et al. 2006, 2014). However, regarding the amount of work needed to write a model description, the best way is to follow the structure of the model; the description will be easier to understand if the model is well-structured according to a rigorous meta-model (see description of the MAELIA model in the Appendix). This meta-model could favor *open modeling*, i.e., easy access and wide availability of simulation models, in response to increasing demands for democratic rights, scientific scrutiny and public value extraction (Edmonds and Polhill 2015). Open modeling is largely a matter of good documentation. Improving understanding of descriptive models and reliability of simulation models is likely to favor the spreading of IABM, for which need increases as the extent and severity of environmental problems in the twenty-first century worsen (Parker et al. 2002).

4.5.2 Reliability of Simulation Results

In most IAM projects, the software-coding phase and the resulting simulation model looks like a black box to most participants in the modeling process (Resnick et al. 2000). Having no idea about the organization and functioning of the simulation model, they may feel to loose control over the modeling process and thus wonder whether the simulation model is a faithful implementation of the descriptive one. Lack of an overview of the simulation model often turns into a lack of confidence in simulation results that prevents their use to support decision-making about NR management. As a formal modeling language, the entity-process meta-model has two semantics: informal semantics toward the real world that interprets a model as a description of a given SR and a formal semantics toward the computer-technology world that generates a digital representation of the SR. Thus, if participants in the modeling process are confident about the descriptive model and the implementation of the computational semantics in the simulation model, they may trust the simulation results. Note that computational semantics eases model replication, which is essential to validate models (Axelrod 2005; Edmonds and Hales 2003; David 2013).

4.5.3 Expressiveness

Because a SES framework relies on ontological assumptions, it is necessary to examine the meta-model's *expressiveness* (i.e., nature of the knowledge that it may represent into entity-process models). In fact, this meta-model is *generic* in that it relies on abstract concepts that may be specialized for conceptual needs of a specific domain (e.g., material resource may be specialized as various types of natural resources). It is also *comprehensive* in that it deals with the main perspectives of SESs: openness (i.e., the interactions with the environment), structure, dynamics, endo- and exogenous evolution considered by scenarios and its functional dimension (ecosystem services it offers), which can be described as resources' attributes or operations. Thus, for a wide range of research questions about SESs, the concepts provided by the meta-model are sufficient for constructing necessary higher-level concepts.

The basic level of base concepts of the meta-model may be viewed as a drawback. However, the meta-model does not prevent considering higher-level compound entities or processes. In addition, the low level is necessary in order to obtain a modeling language that both allows members of a modeling team to communicate without ambiguity and has easy-to-understand and well-defined computational semantics.

The low level of the base concepts could even be beneficial for "community-of-practice" issues, which many authors consider to be of paramount importance. *"Without a common framework to organize findings, isolated knowledge does not cumulate"* (Ostrom 2009), because there is no way to compare models, adapt them to different research questions or reuse their parts.[6] Due to its generality, the entity-process meta-model could serve as a common framework for IABM, as the SES General Framework (Ostrom 2007, 2009) does for analytical approaches.

In SES models, the model of any process includes a causality pattern, i.e., a theory that is more or less implicit and well-founded scientifically. When modeling processes, the entity-process meta-model does not require using a given scientific theory. For example, in the MAELIA model, hydrology issues are handled by the SWAT model (Arnold et al. 1998), farmers select cropping systems according to Dempster-Fischer theory for decision-making (Taillandier et al. 2012b), daily crop management is described with "event-condition-action" rules, land-use and -cover changes rely on statistics and domestic water consumption is calculated with an econometric model (Reynaud and Leenhardt 2008). Thus, processes may be modeled in any way, be they empirical (i.e., reproducing process effects), mechanistic (i.e., detailing how mechanisms produce effects), based on statistics or in a system-dynamics form that abstracts the process as interdependent parameters.

From a wider viewpoint, there is recurrent debate in social sciences about the primacy of structure or action. From the structural standpoint, or *methodological holism*, action is nothing but the result of society's structure, while from the *methodological individualism* standpoint, society is nothing but the result of individuals' (inter)actions. Some social scientists pass the debate by giving the standpoints equal ontological status: social structures are means of social action, social action constructs social structures, and the core of social matter is the links between the two (e.g., Bourdieu 1990; Giddens 1984). The entity-process meta-model is agnostic in this regard; it accommodates all three positions by allowing teams to guide model design by structure, dynamics or their mutual dependencies.

4.5.4   Model Modularity and Organization of Modeling Processes

Modularity is a cornerstone principle in software engineering that requires that the syntax of software programs couples its units as loosely as possible (Dahl et al. 1972). Modularity greatly eases program design, development and maintenance by separating concerns as much as possible so that each unit focuses on a well-defined topic (Hürsch and Lopes 1995). Modularity is relevant for conceptual and concrete models, not just simulation models. It is closely related to the "nearly decomposability" of systems (Simon 1998, p. 197) that Ostrom (2007) recognizes as essential for SES analysis: *"Scientific progress has been achieved...when scholars have*

---

[6]In software engineering, research in the 1990s to improve software development by reusing code shifted towards model-driven development approaches and reuse of software models (Robinson et al. 2004; Schmidt 2006). Indeed, models favor an integrated view to tackle "wicked" problems, in which the problem itself is not well-understood until a solution is developed.

recognized that complex systems are partially decomposable in their structure". The importance of modularity increases with the complexity of the system, and a SES model inherits the complexity of its target SR. A model's modularity eases representation and processing of the knowledge it embeds and thus contributes to its sharing and integrating (cf. Sect. 4.1). It also supports differences in commitment of team members, some of whom are interested in only certain aspects of the model

The entity-process meta-model allows development of highly modular models, since they may be broken down into components that have well-defined delineations and connections in three independent directions:

- structural and dynamic dimensions
- subsystems that interact through resources (Fig. 4.7)
- conceptual, concrete and simulation models (Fig. 4.2)

Accordingly, model construction may be divided along these three directions (e.g., focusing on the structural dimension of a given subsystem in the concrete model). This decomposition extends to model structure and dynamics, since each entity is a well-delineated unit, and each process can be described independently once its interface is defined.

By defining the components necessary to build a model, a meta-model determines the tasks to be done and thus guides the modeling process. Modularity eases distribution and coordination of tasks among team members, since they can work in parallel on separate aspects, and so it improves *flexibility* of the modeling process. This flexibility is required for collaborative processes that inevitably face unknown factors.

Models are subject to many activities, not only construction (iterative) but also versioning, data collection (Altaweel et al. 2010), verification (Nuno 2013), validation (Evans et al. 2013), calibration (Tang et al. 2006), adaptation, application (Kleijnen 2005), communication and documentation (Grimm et al. 2006) and so on (Laniak et al. 2013). Model modularity is likely to ease performance of these activities, we consider two of them.

Modularity eases model *maintenance*, since a change in one component has limited consequences on others. Maintenance is a serious issue (Jacobson et al. 1999) because model development is a progressive and iterative process as new knowledge is considered, understanding of issues improves and initial results are obtained (Laniak et al. 2013). Sequential model versions are developed as team member proposals are discussed, amended, refined, simplified, discarded or considered again later. For example, SR boundaries are not defined at the outset, and identification of elements that must be included the model is likely to vary during the modeling process.

Calibration of a simulation model is essential for validating it. In this regard, integral models experience difficulties that are avoided by assemblage models, in which each module can be calibrated separately (Voinov and Shugart 2013). Calibrating an integral simulation model is a scientific challenge because processes are tightly interwoven, and many parameters that influence model results can interact with each other. To get an overview of model behavior and screen influential parameters, multiple sensitivity analyses must be performed. By clearly separating processes, entity-process modeling enables one to consider only certain subsets of processes while making others inactive, thus disentangling influences of and interactions between parameters step by step (e.g., Lardy et al. 2014).

4.6   Conclusion

This paper introduced an entity-process meta-model of SESs to provide scientists from various disciplines, possibly with NR management stakeholders, with a generic, comprehensive and formal framework to organize their knowledge about a SES into rigorous descriptive and simulation models. We also presented how to express conceptual and concrete models that conform to this meta-model, as well as computational semantics of the corresponding simulation model. Finally, we studied how the framework addresses some issues that IABM projects face. The main distinctive features of the framework are as follows:

1. It is individual-/agent-based, i.e., model elements correspond to SR elements, in contrast to analytical frameworks, which mainly describe the SR with abstractions; it thus allows development of models that simulate SR functioning.
2. It is highly modular, allowing a model to be broken down into well-delimited components whose connections and interactions are well-defined.
3. It relies on few concepts, which fall into common knowledge, and thus can be well-understood by all participants interested in the modeling process, and it offers mechanisms to aggregate elementary elements into higher-level constructs.
4. It is formal, in that it has well-defined computational semantics and thus ensures that simulation models comply with the descriptive model from which they are generated.

Some benefits of these features experienced in the MAELIA project have been highlighted. These seem good reasons to use this framework, even if they do not constitute a validation, which can be obtained only by successful uses.

The gap between analytical and agent-based approaches in the study of SESs hampers accumulation of knowledge found by these two ways, and development of a framework covering both would result in a rather artificial construct that fails to handle the essence of SESs. A more promising approach seems to be model-driven engineering tools (Bezivin 2005), which can transform a model (M1) conforming to one meta-model (MM1) into another model (M2) conforming to another meta-model (MM2) using translation rules from MM1 to MM2 (e.g., ATL model-transformation language; Jouault et al. 2008). For example, the SES General Framework (Ostrom 2007, 2009) could be represented as a meta-model, and correspondence rules could be defined between it and the entity-process meta-model.

Future work is also to develop an Integrated Development Environment to ease development of conceptual and concrete models, including tools to verify their coherence, and to automatically generate the skeleton of the corresponding simulation model.

Acknowledgements This work has been funded by the Thematic Network for Advanced Research "Sciences & Technologies for Aeronautics and Space" (RTRA STAE http://fondation-stae.net/) in Toulouse, France, under the MAELIA project.

Appendix

Outline of the MAELIA simulation platform that is organised according to the Entity-Process Framework. The full details and documentation are available on the MAELIA web-site http://maelia-platform.inra.fr/ (in French; Accessed 22 May 2018).

Entities

Reading the complete actors-resources diagram of the MAELIA platform is simplified by grouping entities into four parts or "modules". Each actor or resource (of which we give here only the labels) are endowed with attributes and operations (see below). The documentation also provides an overview description and the Actors-Resources diagram.

Agricultural Module

- Actors' labels: *farmers;*
- Cognitive resources' labels: *field bloc; irrigation bloc; cultivated species; cropping plan; cropping system; crop management strategy; weather area;*
- Material resources' labels: crop; farm; islet; irrigation device; field; water withdrawal device; agricultural soil;

Hydrology Module

- Labels of material resources: d*am; channel; homogeneous response unit; s*tream; *groundwater; local reservoir; hydrological soil; hydrological zone; average weathering zone;*

Regulation Module

- Actors' labels: *dam manager; agricultural water manager; water policy;*
- Cognitive resources' labels: *administrative sector; monitoring point; management unit; administrative zone;*

Other uses Module

- Actors' labels: *district; industries;*
- Material resources' labels: *domestic withdrawal device; industrial water withdrawal device; domestic reject device; industrial reject device;*

Processes

The labels of the main processes dynamically linking the entities (and programmed in the platform) are listed below. The documentation also provides an overview description of each modelled process and the corresponding interaction diagram.

Description of the scheduling of process activation ((by the simulator engine))
Description of the model initialisation

Agricultural Module

- *Cropping plan decision process;*
- Soil-Crop Dynamics (2 alternatives models): *"AqYield" (plant growth model, initially set for field crops); simple plant dynamics;*
- *Water withdrawal;*
- Crop Management Strategy: *plowing; sowing; hoeing; irrigation; harvest;*
- External processes: *field area change; farm economy; cropping plan (as data);*

Hydrology Module

- *Chanel hydrology;*
- Hydrology (2 alternative models): *hydrology simple model; SWAT model: [includes: land phase; water routing phase; local reservoir fulling];*
- External processes: *input flow; weather;*

Regulation Module

- *Withdrawal volume allocation; control and sanction; edict drought decree; dam water release*

Other uses module

- *Domestic water withdrawal; industrial water withdrawal; domestic water reject; industrial water reject;*
- External process: *population growth;*

Template for the Description of an Entity

Definition	System reference' element to which it refers, role, scale;
Activities	for actors only;
Attributes	Name, public/private; description; data type, unit, variable/constant; read/write process accesses;
Links	Name; description; target entity; read/write process accesses;
Operations	Name, public/private; functional description; input/output parameters; formal description;
Initialisation	Link to the Pre-processing section;
Discussion	Explanation of the modelling choices, ...
References	References to external documents (if required);
Implementation	Description of implementation details (only for the modellers);

Template for the Description of a Process

Definition	Purpose, internal/external;
Scale	Temporal, spatial scale(s) (if relevant);
Interface	Type, identity and attributes of accessed entities;
Scheduling	If applies to several entities;
Formal definition	Specification for implementation;
Validation	Results of sensitivity analysis, calibration, ...
Discussion	Explanation of the modelling choices, ...;
References	References to external documents (if required);
Implementation	Description of implementation details (only for the project's members);

Documentation provides further information on the following topics:

Pre-processing	Description of the data sources and processing to generate each of the input files for model initialisation and external processes;
Indicators	Available for everyone, information source entities and computation method;
Scenarios	For each scenario, one overview page and explanations about the differences with the standard (baseline) model;
Glossary	Definition of technical terms, parameters, acronyms, etc.

References

Ahrweiler P, Gilbert N (2015) The quality of social simulation: an example from research policy modeling. In: Janssen M, Wimmer M, Deljoo A (eds) Policy practice and digital science. Public administration and information technology, vol 10. Springer, Cham, pp 35–55. https://doi.org/10.1007/978-3-319-12784-2_3

Ahuja LR, Ascough JC II, David O (2005) Developing natural resource models using the object modeling system: feasibility and challenges. Adv Geosci 4:29–36. https://doi.org/10.5194/adgeo-4-29-2005

Altaweel MR, Alessa LN, Kliskey A, Bone C (2010) A framework to structure agent-based modeling data for social-ecological systems. Struct Dyn 4(1). https://escholarship.org/uc/item/7kw1h48n

An L (2012) Modeling human decisions in coupled human and natural systems: review of agent-based models. Ecol Model 229:25–36. https://doi.org/10.1016/j.ecolmodel.2011.07.010

Arnold JG, Srinivasan R, Muttiah RS, Williams JR (1998) Large area hydrologic modeling and assessment. I. Model development. J Am Water Resour Assoc 34(1):73–89. https://doi.org/10.1111/j.1752-1688.1998.tb05961.x

Axelrod R (2005) Advancing the art of simulation in the social sciences. In: Rennard J-P (ed) Handbook of research on nature inspired computing for economy and management. IGI Global, Hersey, pp 90–100

Baader F, Calvanese D, McGuinness DL, Nardi D, Patel-Schneider PF (2003) The description logic handbook: theory, implementation, applications. Cambridge University Press, Cambridge

Bezivin J (2005) On the unification power of models. Softw Syst Model 4(2):171–188. https://doi.org/10.1007/s10270-005-0079-0

Binder CR, Hinkel J, Bots PWG, Pahl-Wostl C (2013) Comparison of frameworks for analyzing social-ecological systems. Ecol Soc 18(4):26. https://doi.org/10.5751/ES-05551-180426

Bots PWG, Daalen CE (2008) Participatory model construction and model use in natural resource management: a framework for reflection. Syst Pract Action Res 21(6):389–407. https://doi.org/10.1007/s11213-008-9108-6

Bourdieu P (1990) The logic of practice. Polity Press, Cambridge

Bousquet F, Le Page C (2004) Multi-agent simulations and ecosystem management: a review. Ecol Model 176(3–4):313–332. https://doi.org/10.1016/j.ecolmodel.2004.01.011

Bousquet F, Bakam I, Proton H, Le Page C (1998) CORMAS: common-pool resources and multi-agent systems. In: Pasqual del Pobil A, Mira J, Ali M (eds) Tasks and methods in applied artificial intelligence. IEA/AIE 1998. Lecture Notes in Computer Science (Lecture Notes in Artificial Intelligence), vol 1416. Springer, Berlin, pp 826–837

Caron-Lormier G, Humphry RW, Bohan DA, Hawes C, Thorbek P (2008) Asynchronous and synchronous updating in individual-based models. Ecol Model 212(3–4):522–527. https://doi.org/10.1016/j.ecolmodel.2007.10.049

Chen P (1976) The entity-relationship model - toward a unified view of data. ACM Trans Database Syst 1(1):9–36

Conklin J (2006) Wicked problems and social complexity. In: Conklin J (ed) Dialogue mapping: building shared understanding of wicked problems. Wiley, Chichester, pp 3–40

Dahl OJ, Dijkstra EW, Hoare CAR (1972) Structured programming. Academic Press, London

David N (2013) Validating simulations. In: Edmonds B, Meyer R (eds) Simulating social complexity. Understanding complex systems. Springer, Berlin, pp 135–171

Edmonds B, Hales D (2003) Replication, replication and replication: some hard lessons from model alignment. J Artif Soc Soc Simulat 6(4). http://jasss.soc.surrey.ac.uk/6/4/11.html

Edmonds B, Polhill G (2015) Open modelling for simulators. In: Terán O, Aguilar J (eds) Societal benefits of freely accessible technologies and knowledge resources. IGI Global, Hersey, pp 237–254. https://doi.org/10.4018/978-1-4666-8336-5.ch010

Evans A, Heppenstall A, Birkin M (2013) Understanding simulation results. In: Edmonds B, Meyer R (eds) Simulating social complexity. Understanding complex systems. Springer, Berlin, pp 173–195. https://doi.org/10.1007/978-3-540-93813-2_9

Ferber J, Muller J-P (1996) Influences and reaction: a model of situated multi-agent systems. In: Proceedings of second international conference on multi-agent systems (ICMAS-96). AAAI, pp 72–79. https://aaai.org/Library/ICMAS/1996/icmas96-009.php. Accessed 30 Nov 2017

Gaudou B, Sibertin-Blanc C, Therond O, Amblard F, Auda Y, Arcangeli JP, Balestrat M, Charron-Moirez MH, Gondet E, Hong Y, Lardy R, Louail T, Mayor E, Panzoli D, Sauvage S, Sanchez-Perez JM, Taillandier P, Nguyen VB, Vavasseur M, Mazzega P (2014) The MAELIA multi-agent platform for integrated analysis of interactions between agricultural land-use and low-water management strategies. In: Alam SJ, van Dyke Parunak H (eds) Multi-agent-based simulation XIV, LNAI, vol 8235. Springer, Berlin, pp 85–100

Giddens A (1984) The constitution of society. Polity Press, Cambridge

Gilbert N, Troitzch KG (2005) Simulation for the social scientist. Open University Press

Grimm V, Berger U, Bastiansen F, Eliassen S, Ginot V, Giske J, Goss-Custard J, Grand T, Heinz SK, Huse G, Huth A, Jepsen JU, Jørgensen C, Mooij WM, Müller B, Pe'er G, Piou C, Railsback SF, Robbins AM, Robbins MM, Rossmanith E, Rüger N, Strand E, Souissi S, Stillman RA, Vabø R, Visser U, DeAngelis DL (2006) A standard protocol for describing individual-based and agent-based models. Ecol Model 198(1–2):115–126

Grimm V, Augusiak J, Fock A, Frank BM, Gabsi F, Johnston ASA, Liu C, Martin BT, Meli M, Radchuk V, Thorbek P, Railsback SF (2014) Towards better modelling and decision support: documenting model development, testing, and analysis using TRACE. Ecol Model 280:129–139. https://doi.org/10.1016/j.ecolmodel.2014.01.018

Hatchuel A (2001) The two pillars of new management research. Br J Manage 12(s1):S33–S39. https://doi.org/10.1111/1467-8551.12.s1.4

Hürsch W, Lopes CV(1995) Separation of concerns. Technical Report NU-CCS-95-03, Northeastern University, Boston

ISO (2008) ISO/IEC 15288:2008 systems and software engineering - system life cycle processes. International Organization for Standardization. http://www.iso.org/iso/catalogue_detail?csnumber=43564. Accessed 30 Nov 2017

Jacobson I, Booch G, Rumbaugh J (1999) The unified software development process. Addison-Wesley, Reading

Jakeman AJ, Letcher RA, Norton JP (2006) Ten iterative steps in development and evaluation of environmental models. Environ Model Softw 21(5):602–614. https://doi.org/10.1016/j.envsoft.2006.01.004

Jouault F, Allilaire F, Bezivin J, Kurtev Y (2008) ATL: a model transformation tool. Sci Comput Program 72(1–2):31–39. https://doi.org/10.1016/j.scico.2007.08.002

Kleijnen JPC (2005) An overview of the design and analysis of simulation experiments for sensitivity analysis. Eur J Oper Res 164(2):287–300

Kragt ME, Robson BJ, Macleod CJA (2013) Modellers' roles in structuring integrative research projects. Environ Model Softw 39:322–330. https://doi.org/10.1016/j.envsoft.2012.06.015

Kubera Y, Mathieu P, Picault S (2009) Interaction biases in multi-agent simulations: an experimental study. In: Artikis A, Picard G, Vercouter L (eds) Post-proceedings of the 9th international workshop engineering societies in the agents world (ESAW'08). LNCS, vol 5485. Springer, Berlin, pp 229–247

Laniak G, Olchin G, Goodall J, Voinov A, Hill M, Glynn P, Whelan G, Geller G, Quinn N, Blind M, Peckham S, Reaney S, Gaber N, Kennedy R, Hughes H (2013) Integrated environmental modeling: a vision and roadmap for the future. Environ Model Softw 39:3–23. https://doi.org/10.1016/j.envsoft.2012.09.006

Lardy R, Mazzega P, Sibertin-Blanc C, Auda Y, Sanchez-Perez JM, Sauvage S, Therond O (2014) Calibration of simulation platforms including highly interweaved processes: the MAELIA multi-agent platform. In: Ames DP, Quinn NWT, Rizzoli AE (eds) Proceedings of the 7th international congress on environmental modelling and software, San Diego, June 2014. http://www.iemss.org/sites/iemss2014/proceedings.php

Mazzega P, Therond O, Debril T, March T, Sibertin-Blanc C, Lardy R, Sant'ana DR (2014) Critical multi-level governance issues of integrated modelling: an example of low-water management in the Adour-Garonne basin (France). J Hydrol 519(Part C):2515–2526. https://doi.org/10.1016/j.jhydrol.2014.09.043

McIntosh BS, Seaton RAF, Jeffrey P (2007) Tools to think with? Towards understanding the use of computer-based support tools in policy relevant research. Environ Model Softw 22(5):640–648. https://doi.org/10.1016/j.envsoft.2005.12.015

Meyer B (1997) Object-oriented software construction, 2nd edn. Prentice Hall, Upper Saddle River

Michel F, Gouaïch A, Ferber J (2003) Weak interaction and strong interaction in agent based simulations. In: Hales D, Edmonds B, Norling E, Rouchier J (eds) Multi-agent-based simulation III. MABS 2003. Lecture Notes in Computer Science, vol 2927. Springer, Berlin, pp 43–56. https://doi.org/10.1007/978-3-540-24613-8_4

Murgue C, Lardy R, Vavasseur M, Leenhardt D, Therond O (2014) Spatiotemporal fine simulation of effects of cropping and farming systems on irrigation withdrawal dynamics within river basin. In: Ames DP, Quinn NWT, Rizzoli AE (eds) Proceedings of the 7th international congress on environmental modelling and software, San Diego, June 2014. http://www.iemss.org/sites/iemss2014/proceedings.php

Norgaard RB, Baer P (2005) Collectively seeing complex systems: the nature of the problem. BioScience 55(11):953–960. https://doi.org/10.1641/0006-3568(2005)055[0953:CSCSTN]2.0.CO;2

North MJ, Collier NT, Vos RJ (2006) Experiences Creating Three implementations of the re-past agent modeling toolkit. ACM Trans Model Comput Simul 16(1):1–25. ACM, New York, NY USA

Nuno D (2013) Chapter 8: Validating simulation. In: Edmonds B, Meyer R (eds) Simulating social complexity, Understanding Complex Systems. Springer, Berlin

OMG (2005) Documents associated with UML® Version 2.0, July 2005. Object Management Group. http://schema.omg.org/spec/UML/2.0/. Accessed 30 Nov 2017

OMG (2010) About the Object Constraint Language Specification Version 2.4, February 2014. Object Management Group. http://www.omg.org/spec/OCL/2.4/. Accessed 30 Nov 2017

Ostrom E (2007) A diagnostic approach for going beyond panaceas. PNAS 104(39):15181–15187

Ostrom E (2009) A general framework for analyzing sustainability of social-ecological systems. Science 325(5939):419–422. https://doi.org/10.1126/science.1172133

Oxley T, McIntosh BS, Winder N, Mulligan M, Engelen G (2004) Integrated modeling and decision-support tools: a Mediterranean example. Environ Model Softw 19(11):999–1010. https://doi.org/10.1016/j.envsoft.2003.11.003

Pahl-Wostl C, Schlumpf C, Büssenschütt M, Schönborn A, Burse J (2000) Models at the interface between science and society: impacts and options. Integr Assess 1(4):267–280

Pahl-Wostl C (2007) Transitions towards adaptive management of water facing climate and global change. Water Resour Manage 21(1):49–62

Parker P, Letcher R, Jakeman A et al (2002) Progress in integrated assessment and modelling. Environ Model Softw 17(3):209–217. https://doi.org/10.1016/S1364-8152(01)00059-7

Parker D, Manson S, Janssen M, Hoffmann M, Deadman P (2003) Multi-agent systems for the simulation of land-use and land-cover change: a review. Ann Assoc Am Geogr 93(2):314–337. https://doi.org/10.1111/1467-8306.9302004

Parrott L (2011) Hybrid modelling of complex ecological systems for decision support: recent successes and future perspectives. Eco Inform 6(1):44–49. https://doi.org/10.1016/j.ecoinf.2010.07.001

Quesnel G, Duboz R, Ramat E, Traoré MK (2007) VLE: a multi-modeling and simulation environment. In: Proceedings of the 2007 summer computer simulation conference, San Diego, July 2007, pp 367–374. https://pdfs.semanticscholar.org/0ba2/f0d9ccf88a52d128de5ee89f29923fb9af49.pdf. Accessed 30 Nov 2017

Reed MS (2008) Stakeholder participation for environmental management: a literature review. Biol Conserv 141(10):2417–2431. https://doi.org/10.1016/j.biocon.2008.07.014

Resnick M, Berg R, Eisenberg M (2000) Beyond black boxes: bringing transparency and aesthetics back to scientific investigation. J Learn Sci 9(1):7–30. https://doi.org/10.1207/s15327809jls0901_3

Reynaud A, Leenhardt D (2008) Mogire: a model for integrated water management. In: Sanchez-Marre M, Bejar J, Comas J, Rizzoli A, Guariso G (eds) International congress on environmental modelling and software - integrating sciences and information technology for environmental assessment and decision making. iEMS, Barcelona, July 2008. http://www.iemss.org/iemss2008/uploads/Main/S06-04-Reynaud_et_al-IEMSS2008.pdf

Robinson S, Nance RE, Paul RJ, Pidd M, Taylor SJE (2004) Simulation model reuse: definitions, benefits and obstacles. Simul Model Pract Theory 12(7–8):479–494. https://doi.org/10.1016/j.simpat.2003.11.006

Schlüter M, Hinkel J, Bots PWG, Arlinghaus R (2014) Application of the SES framework for model-based analysis of the dynamics of social-ecological systems. Ecol Soc 19(1):36. https://doi.org/10.5751/ES-05782-190136

Schmidt DC (2006) Model-driven engineering. IEEE Comput 39(2):25–31. http://ieeexplore.ieee.org/stamp/stamp.jsp?arnumber=1597083. Accessed 30 Nov 2017

Simon H (1998) The science of the artificial, 3rd edn. The MIT Press, Cambridge

Standish Group (2009) Chaos: a recipe for sucess. Standish Group International, Incorporated. http://www.projectsmart.co.uk/docs/chaos-report.pdf. Accessed 30 Nov 2017

Standish Group (2013) The Chaos Manifesto. Standish Group International, Incorporated. http://www.versionone.com/assets/img/files/CHAOSManifesto2013.pdf. Accessed 30 Nov 2017

Sterk B, Leeuwis C, van Ittersum MK (2009) Land use models in complex societal problem solving: plug and play or networking? Environ Model Softw 24(2):165–172. https://doi.org/10.1016/j.envsoft.2008.07.001

Taillandier P, Vo DA, Amouroux E, Drogoul A (2012a) GAMA: a simulation platform that integrates geographical information data, agent-based modeling and multi-scale control. In: Proceedings of PRIMA'10. LNCS, vol 7057. Springer, Berlin, pp 242–258

Taillandier P, Therond O, Gaudou B (2012b) A new BDI agent architecture based on the belief theory. Application to the modelling of cropping plan decision-making. In: Seppelt R, Voinov AA, Lange S, Bankamp D (eds) International Environmental Modelling and Software Society (iEMSs) 2012, Leipzig, pp 1–5. http://www.iemss.org/society/index.php/iemss-2012-proceedings

Tang Y, Reed P, Wagener T (2006) How effective and efficient are multiobjective evolutionary algorithms at hydrologic model calibration? Hydrol Earth Syst Sci Discuss 10:289–307

Therond O, Sibertin-Blanc C, Lardy R, Gaudou B, Balestrat M, Hong Y, Louail T, Mayor E, Nguyen VB, Panzoli D, Sanchez-Perez JM, Sauvage S, Taillandier P, Vavasseur M, Mazzega P (2014) Integrated modelling of social-ecological systems: the MAELIA high resolution multi-agent platform to deal with water scarcity problems. In: Ames DP, Quinn NWT, Rizzoli AE (eds) Proceedings of the 7th international congress on environmental modelling and software, San Diego, June 2014. http://www.iemss.org/sites/iemss2014/proceedings.php

Tol RSJ, Vellinga P (1998) The European forum on integrated environmental assessment. Environ Model Assess 3(3):181–191. https://doi.org/10.1023/A:1019023124912

Voinov A, Bousquet F (2010) Modelling with stakeholders. Environ Model Softw 25(11):1268–1281. https://doi.org/10.1016/j.envsoft.2010.03.007

Voinov A, Shugart H (2013) 'Integronsters', integral and integrated modeling. Environ Model Softw 39:149–158. https://doi.org/10.1016/j.envsoft.2012.05.014

Walden DD, Roedler GJ, Forsberg KJ, Hamelin RD, Shortell TM (eds) (2015) INCOSE systems engineering handbook: a guide for system life cycle processes and activities, 4th edn. Wiley, Hoboken

Wilenski U (1999) Netlogo. Center for connected learning and computer-based modeling. http://ccl.northwestern.edu/netlogo. Accessed 30 Nov 2017

Zeigler B, Gon Kim T, Praehofer H (2000) Theory of modeling and simulation, 2nd edn. Academic Press, New York

Part II
Complexity in Action and Policy Analysis

Chapter 5
An Interdisciplinary Study of Leptospirosis Surveillance Systems in Three Regencies of East Java, Indonesia

Bianca van Bavel, Fiona Larkan, Jarlath E. Nally, and Armand Purwati

Abstract In April–May of 2013, Sampang Regency (Madura Island), experienced extreme seasonal rains, and subsequent flooding, followed by dramatic peaks in reported leptospirosis. Local public health surveillance efforts responded to these events and an investigative regional report was launched by the Centre for Environmental Health Engineering and Disease Control, Sampang Regional Health Office. In light of this outbreak and targeted investigation, this study sought to combine existing surveillance data with descriptive household data to investigate leptospirosis incidence and its associated socio-environmental exposures in Sampang and two neighbouring regencies of Gresik and Surabaya in East Java, Indonesia. Leptospirosis has a complex and variable disease epidemiology. In order to identify environmental and social risk determinants of cases of leptospirosis, a total of 275 household questionnaires were administered across nine targeted sample sites in the regencies of Gresik, Sampang, and Surabaya, East Java, Indonesia. Univariate analysis and binomial logistic regression were used to analyze associations of independent predictor variables with suspected and probable case reporting.

Results revealed a history of leptospirosis in 30 respondents. Independent predictors that demonstrated significant association with reported leptospirosis were:

B. van Bavel (✉)
Centre for Global Health, Trinity College Dublin, Dublin, Ireland

Priestley International Centre for Climate, University of Leeds, Leeds, United Kingdom
e-mail: b.vanbavel1@leeds.ac.uk

F. Larkan
Centre for Global Health, Trinity College Dublin, Dublin, Ireland
e-mail: larkanf@tcd.ie

J. E. Nally
Bacterial Diseases of Livestock Research Unit, National Animal Disease Center, Agricultural Research Services, United States Department of Agriculture, Ames, IA, USA
e-mail: Jarlath.Nally@ars.usda.gov

A. Purwati
Dr. Soetomo Regional General Hospital, Institute of Tropical Diseases, Airlangga University, Surabaya, East Java, Indonesia

© Springer Nature Switzerland AG 2019
R. Boulet et al. (eds.), *Law, Public Policies and Complex Systems: Networks in Action*, Law, Governance and Technology Series 42,
https://doi.org/10.1007/978-3-030-11506-7_5

living in flood prone areas, recent history of in-house flooding, living in close proximity to refuse deposits, occupational farming, and using alternative sources of water for domestic use (artesian wells, rivers and collected rain water). Household access to piped or canalized running water had a negative association with reported leptospirosis outcomes. The results of the binary logistic regression analysis produced a model with overall fit. Across the nine targeted sample sites, significant discrepancies in surveillance reporting were found between each of the five corresponding health clinics, as well as the three regencies of Gresik, Sampang, and Surabaya, indicating distinct surveillance systems and health responses. While increases in rainfall and flooding events have been well established as determinants, this study highlights two additional key factors attributable to changes in the distribution of leptospirosis: socio-sanitary deprivation, as well as a lack of integrated public health surveillance systems. This research reinforces the success of certain local and adaptive surveillance initiatives, and recommends the wider integration of disciplinary efforts and resources across communities, institutions and sectors for effective public health action.

5.1   Background

Leptospirosis is one of the world's most widely distributed zoonoses, yet it is also one of the most neglected zoonotic infectious diseases. As a complex bacterial zoonosis caused by spirochetes of the genus *Leptospira*, the epidemiology of leptospirosis is variable for countries, communities and individuals of diverse social, ecological, and economic circumstances (Lau et al. 2010; Victoriano et al. 2009; Cook and Zumla 2009; Picardeau et al. 2014). Transmission occurs by means of exposure to pathogenic leptospires in contaminated urine; either directly through contact with infected urine or tissue of animal reservoirs, such as rodents and livestock, or indirectly through contaminated water or soil (Adler and de la Peña Moctezuma 2010; Bharti et al. 2003; Jena et al. 2004). Most infections occur through indirect transmission via environmental or social exposures to contaminated sources; such as sewage, water, refuse, and soil (Goeijenbier et al. 2013; Victoriano et al. 2009; Vinetz et al. 2005; Schneider et al. 2013; Lau et al. 2010; Reis et al. 2008; Adler and de la Peña Moctezuma 2010). Significant socio-economic and environmental factors associated with higher risk of infection include poor sanitation, inadequate waste management and water treatment, crowded living conditions, as well as agricultural and occupational practices (Lau et al. 2010; Felzemburgh et al. 2014; Schneider et al. 2013; Riley et al. 2007). Evidence has shown periods of increased rainfall, subsequent flooding, soil saturation, and stagnant water to be correlated with increased seroprevalence and outbreaks of leptospirosis (Amilasan et al. 2012; Goeijenbier et al. 2013; Sarkar et al. 2002; Smith et al. 2013; Felzemburgh et al. 2014). Furthermore, it is predicted that continued changes in climate (patterns of rainfall and temperature rise), human demography, and behaviour (population growth, urbanization, land use, travel, and trade) will also impact the incidence, distribution, and burden of leptospirosis (Githeko et al. 2000; Lau et al. 2010; Sarosa 2006; Alderman et al. 2012; Schneider et al. 2013; Jena et al. 2004; Hartskeerl et al. 2011). There is also a well-documented association with the acquisition of leptospirosis linked to related occupations; such as faming, breeding, butchering, veterinary practice, and garbage collection (Adler and de la Peña Moctezuma 2010; Schneider et al. 2013).

Despite a large geographical distribution across the global South and North, there is a disproportionate burden of leptospirosis concentrated in tropical wet climates; with low-and middle-income, resource poor settings being hotspots for disease. It is projected that numerous serovars of *Leptospira* may be present in any one of these locations (Adler and de la Peña Moctezuma 2010; Cosson et al. 2014). Since confirmation of leptospirosis is often limited to hospitalized patients, reported incidences—0.1–1 cases per 100,000 persons per year in temperate climate; >10 cases per 100,000 persons per year in humid (sub) tropical climate; >100 cases per 100,000 persons affected during outbreaks—are based on severe leptospirosis cases only; meaning the disease-to-infection ratio is largely underestimated, with the number of mild cases anticipated to be many times greater than the reported burden of severe cases (Hartskeerl et al. 2011). A recent publication by Torgerson et al. (2015) estimates the global burden of leptospirosis—approximately 2.90 million DALYs lost per annum; and equal to more 70% the global burden of cholera (GBD 2010)—bears most heavily on populations in the Western Pacific, sub-Saharan Africa, South-East Asia, as well as parts of Central and South America. Previous estimates for these areas are restricted due to limited resources and capacities; conflated diagnoses with acute endemic febrile illnesses such as Malaria and Dengue (Biggs et al. 2011; Crump et al. 2011; Manock et al. 2009; Sarkar et al. 2012); as well as lack of supportive legislation and unreciprocated policy at the level of surveillance (Hartskeerl et al. 2011).

The highest reported incidence of leptospirosis in the Asia-Pacific is found in South-East Asia and Oceania (Pappas et al. 2008). The WHO South-East Asia Regional Office (SEARO) produced a report on the state of leptospirosis in 11 member states (WHO 2009). The highest reported annual incidence rates (>10 per 100,000) were in Bangladesh, Nepal, Thailand, and Sri Lanka; followed by incidence rates in India and Indonesia of 1–10 per 100,000 (Victoriano et al. 2009). However, most national incidence data in this region is often limited to outbreak reports or specific case studies, with Bhutan, Timor-Leste, DPR of Korea, Maldives, and Myanmar having little or no published data on human leptospirosis epidemiology (WHO 2008). Now recognized as a disease of global importance, as access to surveillance resources and diagnostics measures improve, the distribution and burden of leptospirosis are anticipated to grow disproportionately (Bharti et al. 2003; Gamage et al. 2012).

5.2 Methods

In April–May of 2013, Sampang Regency (Madura Island), experienced extreme seasonal rains, and subsequent flooding, followed by dramatic peaks in reported leptospirosis. Local surveillance efforts responded to these events and an investigative regional report was launched by the Centre for Environmental Health Engineering and Disease Control, Sampang Regional Health Office (Penyakit 2014). In light of this outbreak and targeted investigation, this study sought to combine existing surveillance data with descriptive household data to investigate leptospirosis incidence and its associated socio-environmental exposures in Sampang and two neighbouring regencies of Gresik and Surabaya in East Java, Indonesia.

5.2.1 Study Setting

The province of East Java is located on the south-eastern tip of Java Island, it is home to over 39 million people and it consists of (29) regencies and municipalities (BPS 2010). Gresik Regency (7°15′39″S; 112°65′61″E) population 1.307 million people (McDonald 2014; BPS 2010), is a coastal port with large manufacturing and industrial sectors. Surabaya (7°15′55″S, 112°44′33″E) population 2.765 million (McDonald 2014; BPS 2010), is a main seaport and commercial city, located in the Delta Brantas Region. Sampang Regency (6°50″–7°13″S, 113°80″–113°39″E) population 876, 950 (BPS 2014), is located on Madura Island, one of the lowest income settings in East Java (2012), with heavy dependence on subsistence agricultural practices (BPS 2010). Figure 5.1 depicts the location of the three regencies within the context of East Java Province, Indonesia.

5.2.2 Study Population

Data collection occurred from April–May (2014). The study population was selected using provincial and regional hospital-based surveillance data for suspected, probable, and fatal cases of leptospirosis in 2013–2014; as reported by the East Javanese health authorities (DKPJT Dinas Kesehatan Provinsi Jawa Timur—Provincial Health Office, 2014). Based on these records, the three regencies with the highest reported figures were Gresik, Sampang, and Surabaya respectively (Tables 5.1 and 5.2). Multi-stage purposive sampling was performed to select for community health clinics within these regencies—Duduk Sampeyan and Cerme (Gresik); Banyuanyar and Kamoning (Sampang); Pecar Keling (Surabaya)—followed by systematically sampling household units from each preceding locality (Creswell 2013; Webb and Bain. 2010; Teddlie and Yu 2007; Tashakkori and Teddlie 2010).

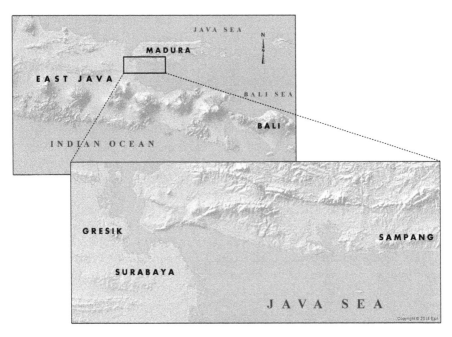

Fig. 5.1 IInset Map of Gresik, Surabaya, and Sampang Regencies within the context of East Java Province, Indonesia. This map was created using ArcGIS® software by Esri. ArcGIS® and ArcMap™ are the intellectual property of Esri and are used herein under license. Copyright © Esri. All rights reserved

Table 5.1 Total number of leptospirosis cases and incidence rates as reported by selected Provincial Health Authorities in 2013–2014

Provincial Health Authority	Individual cases[a]	IR/100,000
Surabaya	55	1.99
Gresik	94	7.19
Sampang	150	17.11

IR incident rate
[a]Includes the total number of fatal, probable, and suspected cases

Table 5.2 Total number of leptospirosis cases and incidence rates as reported by selected Sampang Community Health Clinic Authorities in 2013–2014

Community Health Clinic Authorities	Individual cases[a]	IR/10,000
Sampang	102	4.63
Banyuanyar	62	9.97
Kamoning	34	6.47

IR incident rate
[a]Includes the total number of fatal, probable, and suspected cases

In standard practice, a four-fold or greater rise in agglutination titre between two consecutive serum samples is confirmation of leptospirosis infection, and in the event that no other samples or testing are available, an IgM titre of 1:80 to 1:160 is the minimal cut off for suspected cases of infection (WHO 2003; Palmer et al. 2005). At the level of community health clinics, case probability was often defined solely using positive Rapid Diagnostic Test (RDT) results. Estimating the incidence of febrile illness, like leptospirosis, in resource-poor, infrastructural-deficient settings often requires the use of alternative methods based on multiple assumptions (Biggs et al. 2013; Crump et al. 2003; Paul et al. 2011; Thriemer et al. 2012). For instance, research has been used to validate the collection of self-reported information over a specified time period on adjusted crude rates of incidence, prevalence, and burden, including the assessment of health seeking behaviour and social networks, as a reliable substitute when surveillance records are insufficient or unavailable (Oksanen et al. 2010; Crump et al. 2003; Paul et al. 2011; Webb and Bain 2010). This study corroborated cases of leptospirosis actively reported in 2013–2014 by provincial and regional health authorities using self-reported epidemiological methods to characterize the population both in terms of positive and negative disease associations.

5.2.3 Questionnaires

Informed by existing tools and methods used in the literature, questionnaires were developed by the research team and administered to produce characterizations of household demographics, domestic environment, socio-economic and flooding exposure (Reis et al. 2008; Vanasco et al. 2008; Barcellos and Sabroza 2000; Bhardwaj et al. 2008; Marmot et al. 2008). 'Domestic Environment' variables referred to the local context of sanitation, crowding, water, and waste management for the immediate areas around the home and neighbourhood. 'Recent History of Flooding' variables quantified exposure to in-house flooding or contact with flood water occurring since the last month, coinciding with the end of rainy season (April, 2014).

The data gathered from the questionnaires was coded and manually entered into SPSS, a statistical analysis software. Descriptive statistics were used to define and compare the study population. Univariate analyses were used to calculate the odds ratios (OR) for association of predictor variables with the outcome of reported leptospirosis. A multi-level analytical approach was used to investigate the effects of interactions both within and between variables. A binary logistic regression model was applied. Variables with higher inter-correlation or those with high numbers of missing data were removed from the final regression model. Wald test and Pearson Chi-Square tests with Cramer's V measures were used to compare associations of predictor variables. All p values are 2 sided and evaluated for statistical significance at the ($p < 0.05$) level with (95%) confidence.

5.2.4   Ethical Considerations

Ethical approval was obtained by Irish and Indonesian research institutions, as well as Indonesian health authorities for both primary data collection and secondary data analysis. Individual consent was obtained from study participants, however, due to issues of patient confidentiality, no personal identifiers were used to link individual records for analysis.

5.3   Results

5.3.1   General Demographic and Descriptive Statistics

Of the 282 questionnaires distributed, 275 were completed and returned, resulting in a 97.5% response rate. Responses represented a total of 1268 household members. The study population had a uniform distribution of age (n = 271; median: 41; range: 18–81) and gender (n = 250; 111 male: 139 female), representing a total of 1268 household members. 50.9% (n = 140) of the surveyed population were rural residents, and 49.1% (n = 135) urban residents; these totals included 165 households from flood prone areas and 110 from non-flood prone areas (60%:40%). Of those living in flood zones, a third (n = 56) reported experiencing in house flooding within the past month (March–April, 2014), with just over half (n = 86) having been exposed to flood waters. The majority of all respondents reported some element of daily exposure, be it direct or indirect, to known leptospirosis reservoirs; with 240 reported living less than 20 m from an open sewage system and 242 reported daily rodent sighting in their home. Furthermore, 40.2% of those households surveyed did not have access to running water, with 75.4% of households relied on alternative sources of water for domestic use, including artesian wells, rivers, and collected rain water.

5.3.2   Reported Associations of Leptospirosis

Overall, 10.9% (n = 30) of the 275 households confirmed reports of suspected or probable leptospirosis infection. The median age of this cohort was 45 (range 20–70) years. Farming or animal related occupations (breeder, butcher, or veterinarian) were more likely in respondents reporting cases of leptospirosis than those without (50% compared to 24.9%; $P = 0.035$). Households with up to primary education reported higher frequencies of reported leptospirosis (53.5% versus 34.6%; $p = 0.046$). Neighbourhood housing density was negatively associated with reported cases (OR: 0.40; $p = 0.018$). Nearly all, 96.7% (n = 29), of those reporting cases of

Table 5.3 Selected independent predictor variables for reported suspected or probable cases of leptospirosis

| | Reported case history n = 30 | | |
Social-environmental associations	OR	95% CI	P
Living in Sampang regency	3.55	1.29–9.74	0.014
Living in Banyuanyar clinic catchment	4.80	1.00–23.05	0.050
Living in Kamoning clinic catchment	5.67	1.22–26.41	0.027
Living in a flood zone	4.06	1.50–10.98	0.006
In house flooding within the past month	4.43	1.90–10.33	0.001
Type of residence (rural)	1.61	0.74–3.49	0.230
Housing density ($\geq$50 HH/10,000 m^2)	0.40	0.18–0.85	0.018
Access to PDAM	0.44	0.20–0.95	0.037
Water source at HH (artesian well)	6.28	1.80–21.94	0.004
Water source at HH (river)	4.37	0.92–20.86	0.060
Last completed level of HH education ($\geq$SMP)	0.46	0.22–0.99	0.049
Level of HH income (<Rp. 1,000,000)	2.27	0.99–5.20	0.054
Living <20 m to open sewage	4.16	0.55–31.74	0.170
Living <20 m to refuse depot	2.57	1.15–5.74	0.021
Frequency of refuse pickup (daily)	3.80	1.28–11.29	0.016
Occupational farming	2.76	1.23–6.18	0.014
Gender (male)	1.61	0.71–3.65	0.250

OR Odds Ratio; CI Confidence Interval; HH Household; PDAM Per Perusahaan Daerah Air Minum Regional Drinking Water Company; SMP Primary Level Education; Rp. Indonesian Rupiah (Indonesian currency)

leptospirosis were living less than 20 m from open sewage and 93.3% (n = 28) reported daily rodent sighting in their home.

Analysis of determinants (Table 5.3) revealed that reported cases of leptospirosis were significantly associated with living in a flood-prone area (OR: 4.06; 95% CI: 1.50–10.98) and using alternative water sources for domestic consumption (artesian wells, river, and rain water collection) (OR: 3.33; 95% CI: 1.49–7.45). Additional associations for reported leptospirosis cases included: recent history of in house flooding (OR: 4.43; 95% CI: 1.90–10.33), living less than 20 m from open refuse deposit (OR: 2.57; 95% CI: 1.15–5.74), and farming (OR: 2.76; 95% CI: 1.23–6.18). Access to piped water in-house through the regional drinking water company (PDAM) was negatively associated with case reporting (OR: 0.44; 95% CI 0.20–0.95). The presence of domestic animals (chickens, livestock, cats, and dogs), gender, type of residence (rural or urban), and reported contact with flood water did not demonstrate significant associations ($P > 0.05$).

The results from the univariate analysis are presented in Tables 5.4 and 5.5 disaggregated by community health clinic catchment and regency. Results of the binary logistic regression analysis produced a model with overall fit (X^2 (15, $n = 228$) = 32.45; $p = 0.006$; −2 Log Likelihood = 121). Overall percentage classifications of the model were; sensitivity (8.3%), specificity (98.5%), PPV (Positive Predictive Value) (40%), NPV (Negative Predictive Value) (90.1%). A

Table 5.4 Percentage of participants disaggregated by regency, according to significant individual and household level variables

	Household variable %				Individual variable %	
	Access to PDAM	Artesian well source	History of flooding	<20 m to refuse	Occupational farming	Reported leptospirosis
Surabaya N = 50	94.0	28.0	2.0	22.0	0	4.0
Sampang N = 139	66.9	50.4	37.4	63.3	31.7	16.5
Gresik N = 86	29.1	33.7	3.5	36	25.6	5.8

PDAM Perusahaan Daerah Air Minum Regional Drinking Water Company
Definitions: History of flooding, refers to the occurrence of in-house flooding within the last month

reliable difference in leptospirosis reporting was found between the five community health clinic catchments (X^2 (4, $N = 262$) = 11.15, $p = 0.025$), as well as between the three regencies (X^2 (2, $N = 262$) = 10.57, $p = 0.005$).

5.4 Discussion

The study aimed to explore determinants of leptospirosis across social and environmental boundaries. The findings from this study are congruent with previous studies on acquired leptospirosis in humans, which have identified environmental mechanisms along with driving socio-economic factors as directly contributing to an increased burden of leptospirosis (Schneider et al. 2013; Lau et al. 2010; Felzemburgh et al. 2014; Maciel et al. 2008; Ko et al. 1999; Barcellos and Sabroza 2000).

While the initial investigation launched by the regional authorities in Sampang found increased incidence of leptospirosis in connection with extreme rainfall and flooding events (Amilasan et al. 2012; Goeijenbier et al. 2013; Sarkar et al. 2002; Smith et al. 2013), this study highlights two additional key factors attributable to changes in the distribution of leptospirosis: socio-economic and sanitary deprivation; as well as a lack of integrated public health surveillance and mandated notification system (Hartskeerl et al. 2011).

5.4.1 Socio-Sanitation Deprivation

Higher infection rates of leptospirosis have been associated with more densely populated, urban slum areas, lacking access to adequate waste management and improved sanitation (Schneider et al. 2013; Riley et al. 2007; Lau et al. 2010; Ko et al. 1999; Felzemburgh et al. 2014; Maciel et al. 2008; Barcellos and Sabroza

Table 5.5 Household characterisations by community health clinic catchment according to socio-economic and environmental variables

Type of residence (density)	Access to PDAM	Artesian well source	In-house flooding	<20 m from sewage	<20 m from refuse	Daily HH rodent sightings	HH income <Rp. 1,000,000	HH education ≤1°	Incidence of leptospirosis
Gresik regency									
Duduk Sampeyan N = 36 — Rural	0	16.7	0	88.6	63.9	83.3	52.8	52.8	8.3
Cerme N = 50 — Rural	50.0	46.0	6.0	98.0	16.0	100.0	24.0	18.4	4.0
Sampang regency									
Banyuanyar N = 64 — Urban	76.6	37.5	37.5	85.9	46.9	95.3	29.3	31.3	16.7
Kamoning N = 75 — Rural	58.7	61.3	37.3	81.1	77.3	74.7	62.3	54.1	19.1
Surabaya regency									
Pacar Keling N = 50 — Urban	94.0	28.0	2.0	91.8	22.0	90.0	17.8	24.0	4.0

All numbers indicate the percentage of total respondents

PDAM Perusahaan Daerah Air Minum Regional Drinking Water Company

Definitions: History of flooding, refers to the occurrence of in-house flooding within the last month

2000). Apart from a negative association between neighbourhood housing densities and reported leptospirosis cases, the study revealed similar results for disease determinants as found in the literature (Table 5.3). Determinants of sanitation coverage, waste management, water treatment, as well as the number of inhabitants per household were not restricted to urban areas of higher housing densities as much as they were more general socio-economic gradients found across the sample population (2008; Marmot et al. 2008; Reis et al. 2008; Riley et al. 2007) and, in particular, rural farming communities. This was evidenced by the fact that majority of respondents lived in close proximity to an open sewage system and lacked improved water sources for everyday domestic use. Further supported by the negative association of case reporting and access to canalized water through the regional drinking water company (PDAM), access to improved water sources could be considered preventative and a safe alternative to using unprotected and untreated sources. Such socio-sanitation deprivations drive repeated exposure to contaminated environments and increase the rate of infection among impoverished populations (Felzemburgh et al. 2014).

Despite efforts by the government, including additional support received through partnering with bilateral and multilateral donor agencies and the regional drinking water company (PDAM), Indonesia still faces immense challenges to improve the provision of safe water and basic sanitation services and infrastructure (Haryanto and Sutomo 2012; Martínez-Santos 2017; Patunru 2015). While recent figures indicate that 87% of the population now have access to 'improved water sources', there is incomplete information about the safety and reliability of that water supply and the number of households that have sustainable access to safe-quality drinking water (Martínez-Santos 2017; WHO UNICEF 2017). Notwithstanding, budget allocations set out in the current National Development Plan (2015–2019) appear only to cover 12% of what is actually needed in order to address these gaps in service provision (Patunru 2015). Without financial investment and government prioritization at the central, provincial, and district levels the regional drinking water company, PDAM, lacks the capacity to reliably provide (distribute, regulate, and carry) safe-quality water to households. Additional challenges include limited involvement and partnership with the private sector, poor quantity and quality of primary water sources, and low levels of community awareness and participation (Haryanto and Sutomo 2012). Even though the household sanitation characteristics of this study cohort were complementary to a disease specific health outcome, this research can still be used to communicate the impact of poor sanitation and water quality, as well as advocate for healthier domestic environments.

5.4.2 Distinct Surveillance Systems

Optimizing the standard of diagnostic capacities (specificity) with the level of placement within the healthcare system (sensitivity) is a massive challenge for surveillance (Crump et al. 2003). Even though established hospital-based surveillance is more likely to have reliable diagnostic measures, this level of healthcare is unlikely to capture many of the mild and less severe presentations, particularly for communities lacking access to healthcare resources all together (Crump et al. 2003; Felzemburgh et al. 2014). Other studies have highlighted the need to integrate surveillance at a community level in order to capture the extent of burden on more vulnerable, under-resourced populations (Paul et al. 2011; Halliday et al. 2012; Maciel et al. 2008; Riley et al. 2007). This study has taken a similar approach to investigate the integration of surveillance across multiple levels of a health system and inform our understanding of disease epidemiology. With the intention of corroborating provincial and regional health authority surveillance data, case incidences for 2013–2014 were applied as a control for our model (Tables 5.1 and 5.2). As anticipated, localised figures obtained from the household survey indicated a comparatively high infection-to-disease ratio; this is in part due to errors of misclassification. While we predicted similar structural and resource constraints for surveillance across the three regencies, the reporting discrepancies between the three regencies $(X^2 (2, N = 262) = 10.57, p = 0.005)$, as well as between the five community health clinic catchments $(X^2 (4, N = 262) = 11.15, p = 0.025)$, would suggest distinct surveillance mechanisms and subsequent public health responses. These discrepancies could be attributed to diversity in surveillance system capacities and regulations (Halliday et al. 2012; Hartskeerl et al. 2011). Poor communication between authorities, institutions, and sectors could also account for some of the discrepancies in surveillance reporting and responses. The extent of vigilance and local awareness of leptospirosis in Sampang, following the flooding in 2014, are exemplar of effective surveillance being used to stimulate public health action. Given this response, it is recommended that surveillance be standardized and mandatory with instilled networks of communication across local, regional, and provincial levels.

Surveillance initiatives can play an integral role towards strengthening the structural and functional capacities of local health systems (Zhou et al. 2013). Regrettably, within both the context of this study as well as other low-and middle-income settings, surveillance and subsequent public health responses are limited by both human resources and technological capacities (Bharti et al. 2003; Picardeau et al. 2014). Particularly where diagnostic restrictions prevent the delineation of suspected, probable, and confirmed incidences complementary and novel approaches can help increase the sensitivity of surveillance measures while bringing systems closer to the level of affected communities. In order to do so, adaptive surveillance tools need to start by assessing social networks of communities (Paul et al. 2011), patterns of health-seeking behaviours (Biggs et al. 2013; Crump et al. 2003), as well as epidemiological and historical factors of disease exposures (Sarkar et al. 2012). Resources need to be reallocated and integrated with existing surveillance efforts in order to optimize health responses (Coulibaly and Yameogo 2000; Halliday et al. 2012) and find a way to increase the sensitivity of surveillance without compromising the specificity of diagnostics. The coordination of these demands marks a challenge for systems, especially in endemic regions, and will require the political support of regional and national authorities.

5.4.3   Limitations

The biggest limitation to this study was the lack of standard diagnostic methods to estimate incidence of leptospirosis. As mentioned before, estimating the incidence of febrile illness in resource-poor, infrastructural-deficient settings often requires the use of alternative methods based on multiple assumptions (Biggs et al. 2013; Paul et al. 2011; Thriemer et al. 2012; Crump et al. 2003). While not conventional, given the availability of resources at the local level of community health clinic catchments, the use of self-reported epidemiological methods to characterize the population using both positive and negative associations of disease to complement active surveillance data from regional health authorities was considered a reliable alternative in this context. The researchers recognize the significant subjectivity and potential error of misclassification in these combined retrospective and social epidemiological and molecular methods, and exercise caution in their interpretation (Marmot and Steptoe 2007; Oksanen et al. 2010). We recommend these methods be replicated in several representative populations before inferring incidence at a broader regional, provincial, and/or national level.

5.5   Conclusion

In conclusion, the findings from this study corroborate those existing in the literature and recognize leptospirosis as having a complex and variable disease epidemiology with diverse patterns of incidence and burden across people, place, and time. While increases in rainfall and flooding events have been well established determinants, this study also exemplifies two additional key factors attributable to changes in the distribution of leptospirosis: socio-economic and sanitary deprivation, as well as a lack of integrated public health surveillance. Though through a disease specific lens, these conditions are seen as potential sources of exposure, most are truly general public health concerns that require action—i.e. improving access to safe and reliable domestic water sources through increased regional PDAM coverage, capacity, and funding; ensuring adequate sanitation; improving water treatment and waste management for both rural and urban communities; increasing disease awareness and surveillance strategies in flood zones, as well as farming communities. Given the reported situation of leptospirosis and its underlying socio-environmental determinants in these hotspots and vulnerable populations there needs to be an emphasis on reducing the potential of transmission in everyday exposures and contaminations. This research reinforces the success of local and adaptive surveillance initiatives and calls for wider integration of efforts and resources across communities, institutions, and sectors. As well, the results of this study can be used to communicate associated impacts of poor domestic environments and demand for healthier circumstances in such deprived communities. Interdisciplinary dialogue is recommended to inform leptospirosis research, strengthen surveillance, and affect public health action.

Acknowledgements The research was facilitated through extension of an existing academic collaboration between Professor Eric van Gorp (Erasmus Medical Centre, Rotterdam) and Professor Usman Hadi (Dr. Soetomo Teaching Hospital, University of Airlangga, Surabaya). The authors would like to extend special appreciation for the contributions from the community health clinics and regional DKK staff (Dinas Kesehatan Kabupaten, Regional Health Office), as well as the research team from the Institute for Tropical Diseases, Surabaya. Additional thanks to the reviewers for their helpful comments and contributions, which the authors feel have enhanced the manuscript. As well as thanks to our colleague, Angus Naylor (Priestley International Centre for Climate, University of Leeds), for his expertise with mapping. We would also like to acknowledge the passing of our dear co-author and colleague, Fiona Larkan, whose contributions and impact extend far beyond the scope of this work.

This research was conducted in accordance with the Declaration of Helsinki and was granted ethical approval by appropriate regional and local Indonesian authorities, DKPJT, DKK, University of Airlangga Surabaya, as well as the Health Policy and Management and Centre for Global Health Research Ethics Committee, Trinity College Dublin. Informed written consent was obtained from all participants by way of their completion and return of anonymized questionnaires. Participation in this study was completely voluntary and included consenting individuals of 18 years or older. Any further information and documentation that would support these processes and statements will be made available to the Editorial Board upon request.

The authors declare they have no competing interests.

BvB was the principal investigator on the study, designed the study, collected and analysed the data, and wrote the paper. FL assisted in the study design, in particular incorporating mix-methodology, and edited the paper. JEN assisted with background, in-depth analysis, and edited the paper. AP assisted with the design, implementation, and collection of data. All authors read and approved the final manuscript.

Questionnaire

Questionnaire Version 3
ENGLISH (Pilot)
April, 2014

DATE: └─┴─┘ └─┴─┘ └─┴─┴─┴─┘ (dd-mm-yyyy)
TIME: _____
LOCATION: _____
ADMINISTERED BY: _____
PARTICIPANT ID: _____

DEMOGRAPHIC
Date of birth: └─┴─┘ └─┴─┘ └─┴─┴─┴─┘ (dd-mm-yyyy)
Gender: [MALE/ FEMALE]
Address: _____
Level of Education: (Last Full Year Completed)
> [1]Primary
> [2]Secondary
> [3]Post-Secondary

DOMESTIC (HOUSEHOLD) *Description of Residence/Neighbourhood*
Type   [RURAL / URBAN / SUBURBAN]
Type   [INFORMAL / FORMAL]
Flood Prone Area
> [Y / N]
Number of Persons in Household _____
Approximate Housing Density _____ (HH/100 M²)
Frequency of Rodent Sightings/Signs
> [1] Daily
> [2] Several Times a Week
> [3] Several Times a Month
> [4] Seldom
> [5] N/A
Presence of Other Animals; Dogs, Cats, Chicken, Livestock
> [Y / N]

DOMESTIC (HOUSEHOLD) *Description of Water Supply and Sanitation*
Access to Piped Running Water
> [Y / N]
Frequency of Water Supply
> [1] Daily
> [2] Several Times a Week
> [3] Several Times a Month
> [4] Seldom
> [5] N/A
Length of Water Supply Interruption
> [1] Hours
> [2] Days
> [3] Weeks
> [4] N/A

Questionnaire Version 3
ENGLISH (Pilot)
April, 2014

Frequency of Waste Collection
[1] Daily
[2] 2-3 Times a Week
[3] 1 Time a Week
[4] 1 Time every 2 Weeks
[5] N/A
Access to Plumbing and Improved Sanitation
[Y / N]
Type of Toilet
[1] Private
[2] Shared
[3] Public
[4] Other
Proximity to Open Sewage System
[1] <20 M
[2] 20-100 M
[3] >100 M
Proximity to Open Refuse Deposit
[1] <20 M
[2] 20-100 M
[3] >100 M

OCCUPATIONAL

Rural or Animal Centred (Includes: Agricultural Work, Farming, Fishing, Abattoir Work, Forestry, and Veterinary Care Sanitation and Waste Management)
[Y / N]
Does Work Require You To Use Protective Equipment (Gloves, Footwear, Masks)
[Y / N]

SOCIO-ECONOMIC

Average Monthly Household Income
[1] < Rp.1000.000
[2] Rp.1000.000 – Rp.5.000.000
[3] > Rp.5.000.000
Head of Household Level of Education: (Last Full Year Completed)
[1] Primary
[2] Secondary
[3] Post-Secondary

HISTORICAL

Previous Known Cases of Leptospirosis
[Y / N]
Previous Cases of Flooding
[Y / N]
Frequency of Flooding
[1] Daily
[2] Weekly
[3] Monthly
[4] Yearly
[5] N/A
Previous Contact with Flood Water
[Y / N]

Questionnaire Version 3
BAHASA INDONESIA (Final)
April, 2014

KUISIONER

TANGGAL: ⌊_⌊_⌋   ⌊_⌊_⌋ ⌊_⌊_⌊_⌊_⌋ (dd-mm-yyyy)

LOKASI: _____

KODE :_____

DEMOGRAFI

Tanggal Lahir ⌊_⌊_⌋   ⌊_⌊_⌋ ⌊_⌊_⌊_⌊_⌋ (dd-mm-yyyy)

Jenis Kelamin [Laki/Perempuan]

Alamat: _____

Pendidikan Terakhir

    [1] SD

    [2] SMP

    [3] SMA

    [4] Perguruan Tinggi

    [5] Tidak Sekolah

Pekerjaan

    [1] PNS/ ABRI/ POLISI

    [2] Pegawai Swasta

    [3] Petani

    [4] Peternak

    [5] Nelayan

    [6] Jagal (ayam/sapi/kambing)

    [7] Mantri Hewan

    [8] Ibu Rumah

    [9]Wiraswasta

    [10] Tidak Pekerjaan

Questionnaire Version 3
BAHASA INDONESIA (Final)
April, 2014

LINGKUNGAN *Kondisi Rumah/Lingkungan*

Type [Desa/ Kota]

Daerah Banjir [Ya / Tidak]

Jumlah anggota keluarga _____

Kepadatan Rumah _____ (Jumlah rumah/10, 000 m²)

Frekuensi melihat tikus di sekitar rumah/ lingkungan

[1] Setiap hari

[2] Beberapa kali dalam seminggu

[3] Beberapa kali dalam sebulan

[4] Jarang

Ada/tidaknya hewan lain disekitar rumah ; Anjing, Kucing , Ayam, Ternak (lingkari salah satu)

LINGKUNGAN *Kondisi Air dan Sanitasi*

Akses PDAM

[Ya / Tidak]

Jenis Sumber Air

[1] Air dalam kemasan

[2] Air Sumur

[3] Air Sumber

[4] Air Sungai

[5] Air Hujan/ lainnya

[6] Tidak Berlaku

Frekuensi Penggunaan Air

[1] Setiap hari

[2] Beberapa kali dalam seminggu

[3] Beberapa kali dalam sebulan

[4] Jarang

Questionnaire Version 3
BAHASA INDONESIA (Final)
April, 2014

KUISIONER

LINGKUNGAN *Kondisi Air dan Sanitasi*

Tipe Toilet

[1] Milik sendiri

[2] Milik bersama

[3] Umum

[4] Lainnya

Frekuensi Pembuangan Sampah

[1] Setiap Hari

[2] 2-3 kali seminggu

[3] Satu kali seminggu

[4] Dua kali seminggu

Jarak saluran air (got) dengan rumah/lingkungan

[1] <20 Meter

[2] 20-100 Meter

[3] >100 Meter

Jarak dengan tempat pembuangan sampah

[1] <20 Meter

[2] 20-100 Meter

[3] >100 Meter

Questionnaire Version 3
BAHASA INDONESIA (Final)
April, 2014

SOSIAL-EKONOMI

Penghasilan per bulan

[1] < Rp.1000.000

[2] Rp.1000.000 – Rp.5.000.000

[3] > Rp.5.000.000

Pendidikan terakhir kepala rumah tangga

[1] SD

[2] SMP

[3] SMA

[4] Perguruan Tinggi

[5] Tidak Sekolah

SEJARAH KASUS PENYAKIT

Pernah sakit Leptospira

[Ya / Tidak]

Kejadian Banjir dalam bulan terakhir

[Ya / Tidak]

Frekuensi Banjir

[1] Setiap Hari

[2] Setiap Minggu

[3] Setiap Bulan

[4] Setiap Tahun

[5] Lainnya

Kontak terakhir dengan air banjir

[Ya / Tidak]

References

2008. Economic impacts of sanitation in Indonesia: a five country study conducted in Cambodia, Indonesia, Lao PDR, the Philippines, and Vietnam under the Economics of Sanitation Initiative (ESI). In: Pacific WASPEAAT (ed) Economics of sanitation initiative. World Bank, Jakarta

2012. Human Development Index (HDI) by Province and National: 1996–2012. Badan Pusat Statistik, Indonesia. http://sp2010.bps.go.id/. Accessed 30 Nov 2017

2014. Buletin Epidemiologi Jawa Timur. In: Timur DKPJ (ed) Indonesia

Adler B, de la Peña Moctezuma A (2010) Leptospira and leptospirosis. Vet Microbiol 140 (3–4):287–296. https://doi.org/10.1016/j.vetmic.2009.03.012

Alderman K, Turner LR, Tong S (2012) Floods and human health: a systematic review. Environ Int 47:37–47. https://doi.org/10.1016/j.envint.2012.06.003

Amilasan A-ST, Ujiie M, Suzuki M, Salva E, Belo MCP, Koizumi N, Yoshimatsu K, Schmidt W-P, Marte S, Dimaano EM, Villarama JB, Ariyoshi K (2012) Outbreak of leptospirosis after flood, the Philippines, 2009. Emerg Infect Dis 18(1):91–94. https://doi.org/10.3201/eid1801.101892

Barcellos C, Sabroza PC (2000) Socio-environmental determinants of the leptospirosis outbreak of 1996 in western Rio de Janeiro: a geographical approach. Int J Environ Health Res 10 (4):301–313. https://doi.org/10.1080/0960312002001500

Bhardwaj P, Kosambiya JK, Desai VK (2008) A case control study to explore the risk factors for acquisition of leptospirosis in Surat city, after flood. Indian J Med Sci 62(11):431–438

Bharti AR, Nally JE, Ricaldi JN, Matthias MA, Diaz MM, Lovett MA, Levett PN, Gilman RH, Willig MR, Gotuzzo E, Vinetz JM, Peru-United States Leptospirosis Consortium (2003) Leptospirosis: a zoonotic disease of global importance. Lancet Infect Dis 3(12):757–771

Biggs HM, Bui DM, Galloway RL, Stoddard RA, Shadomy SV, Morrissey AB, Bartlett JA, Onyango JJ, Maro VP, Kinabo GD, Saganda W, Crump JA (2011) Leptospirosis among hospitalized febrile patients in Northern Tanzania. Am J Trop Med Hyg 85(2):275–281. https://doi.org/10.4269/ajtmh.2011.11-0176

Biggs HM, Hertz JT, Munishi OM, Galloway RL, Marks F, Saganda W, Maro VP, Crump JA (2013) Estimating leptospirosis incidence using hospital-based surveillance and a population-based health care utilization survey in Tanzania. PLoS Negl Trop Dis 7:e2589. https://doi.org/10.1371/journal.pntd.0002589

BPS (2010) Sensus Penduduk 2010. Badan Pusat Statistik. http://sp2010.bps.go.id/. Accessed 30 Nov 2017

Cook GC, Zumla A (2009) Manson's tropical diseases, 22nd edn. Saunders Elsevier, Philadelphia

Cosson J-F, Picardeau M, Mielcarek M, Tatard C, Chaval Y, Suputtamongkol Y, Buchy P, Jittapalapong S, Herbreteau V, Morand S (2014) Epidemiology of *Leptospira* transmitted by rodents in Southeast Asia. PLoS Negl Trop Dis 8:e2902. https://doi.org/10.1371/journal.pntd.0002902

Coulibaly ND, Yameogo KR (2000) Prevalence and control of zoonotic diseases: collaboration between public health workers and veterinarians in Burkina Faso. Acta Trop 76(1):53–57

Creswell JW (2013) Research design: qualitative, quantitative, and mixed methods approaches. Sage Publications, Incorporated, Thousand Oaks

Crump JA, Youssef FG, Luby SP, Wasfy MO, Rangel JM, Taalat M, Oun SA, Mahoney FJ (2003) Estimating the incidence of typhoid fever and other febrile illnesses in developing countries. Emerg Infect Dis 9(5):539–544

Crump JA, Gove S, Parry CM (2011) Management of adolescents and adults with febrile illness in resource limited areas. BMJ 343:d4847. https://doi.org/10.1136/bmj.d4847

Felzemburgh RDM, Ribeiro GS, Costa F, Reis RB, Hagan JE, Melendez AXTO, Fraga D, Santana FS, Mohr S, Dos Santos BL, Silva AQ, Santos AC, Ravines RR, Tassinari WS, Carvalho MS, Reis MG, Ko AI (2014) Prospective study of leptospirosis transmission in an urban slum community: role of poor environment in repeated exposures to the *Leptospira* agent. PLoS Negl Trop Dis 8:e2927. https://doi.org/10.1371/journal.pntd.0002927

Gamage CD, Tamashiro H, Ohnishi M Koizumi N (2012) Epidemiology, surveillance and laboratory diagnosis of leptospirosis in the WHO South-East Asia Region. In: Lorenzo-Morales J
(ed) Zoonosis. InTech, Rijeka, pp 213–226. https://doi.org/10.5772/37694

Githeko AK, Lindsay SW, Confalonieri UE, Patz JA (2000) Climate change and vector-borne
diseases: a regional analysis. Bull World Health Organ 78(9):1136–1147

Goeijenbier M, Wagenaar J, Goris M, Martina B, Henttonen H, Vaheri A, Reusken C, Hartskeerl R,
Osterhaus A, van Gorp E (2013) Rodent-borne hemorrhagic fevers: under-recognized, widely
spread and preventable – epidemiology, diagnostics and treatment. Crit Rev Microbiol 39
(1):26–42. https://doi.org/10.3109/1040841X.2012.686481

Halliday J, Daborn C, Auty H, Mtema Z, Lembo T, Bronsvoort BMD, Handel I, Knobel D,
Hampson K, Cleaveland S (2012) Bringing together emerging and endemic zoonoses surveillance: shared challenges and a common solution. Philos Trans Roy Soc Lond B: Biol Sci 367
(1604):2872–2880. https://doi.org/10.1098/rstb.2011.0362

Hartskeerl RA, Collares-Pereira M, Ellis WA (2011) Emergence, control and re-emerging leptospirosis: dynamics of infection in the changing world. Clin Microbiol Infect 17(4):494–501.
https://doi.org/10.1111/j.1469-0691.2011.03474.x

Haryanto B, Sutomo S (2012) Improving access to adequate water and basic sanitation services in
Indonesia. Rev Environ Health 27(4):159–162

Jena AB, Mohanty KC, Devadasan N (2004) An outbreak of leptospirosis in Orissa, India: the
importance of surveillance. Trop Med Int Health 9(9):1016–1021

Ko AI, Reis MG, Dourado CMR, Johnson WD Jr, Riley LW (1999) Urban epidemic of severe
leptospirosis in Brazil. Lancet 354(9181):820–825. https://doi.org/10.1016/S0140-6736(99)
80012-9

Lau CL, Smythe LD, Craig SB, Weinstein P (2010) Climate change, flooding, urbanisation and
leptospirosis: fuelling the fire? Trans Roy Soc Trop Med Hyg 104(10):631–638. https://doi.org/
10.1016/j.trstmh.2010.07.002

Maciel EAP, De Carvalho ALF, Nascimento SF, De Matos RB, Gouveia EL, Reis MG, Ko AI
(2008) Household transmission of *Leptospira* infection in urban slum communities. PLoS Negl
Trop Dis 2:e154. https://doi.org/10.1371/journal.pntd.0000154

Manock SR, Jacobsen KH, De Bravo NB, Russell KL, Negrete M, Olson JG, Sanchez JL, Blair PJ,
Smalligan RD, Quist BK, Espín JF, Espinoza WR, MacCormick F, Fleming LC, Kochel T
(2009) Etiology of acute undifferentiated febrile illness in the Amazon Basin of Ecuador. Am J
Trop Med Hyg 81(1):146–151. https://doi.org/10.4269/ajtmh.2009.81.146

Marmot M, Steptoe A (2007) Whitehall II and ELSA: integrating epidemiological and psychobi-
ological approaches to the assessment of biological indicators. Biosocial Surveys. National
Research Council of the National Academies Washington DC, Chapter 2. https://www.ncbi.
nlm.nih.gov/books/NBK62431/. Accessed 30 Nov 2017

Marmot M, Friel S, Bell R, Houweling TAJ, Taylor S (2008) Closing the gap in a generation: health
equity through action on the social determinants of health. Lancet 372:1661–1669

Martínez-Santos P (2017) Does 91% of the world's population really have "sustainable access to
safe drinking water"? Int J Water Resour D 33(4):514–533. https://doi.org/10.1080/07900627.
2017.1298517

McDonald P (2014) The demography of Indonesia in comparative perspective. Bull Indones Econ
Stud 50(1):29–52. https://doi.org/10.1080/00074918.2014.896236

Oksanen T, Kivimäki M, Pentti J, Virtanen M, Klaukka T, Vahtera J (2010) Self-report as an
indicator of incident disease. Ann Epidemiol 20(7):547–554. https://doi.org/10.1016/j.
annepidem.2010.03.017

Palmer S, Brown D, Morgan D (2005) Early qualitative risk assessment of the emerging zoonotic
potential of animal diseases. BMJ 331(7527):1256–1260

Pappas G, Papadimitriou P, Siozopoulou V, Christou L, Akritidis N (2008) The globalization of
leptospirosis: worldwide incidence trends. Int J Infect Dis 12(4):351–357. https://doi.org/10.
1016/j.ijid.2007.09.011

Patunru AA (2015) Access to safe drinking water and sanitation in Indonesia. Asia Pac Policy Stud 2(2):234–244. https://doi.org/10.1002/app5.81

Paul RC, Rahman M, Gurley ES, Hossain MJ, Diorditsa S, Hasan AM, Banu SS, Alamgir A, Rahman MA, Sandhu H, Fischer M, Luby SP (2011) A novel low-cost approach to estimate the incidence of Japanese Encephalitis in the catchment area of three hospitals in Bangladesh. Am J Trop Med Hyg 85(2):379–385. https://doi.org/10.4269/ajtmh.2011.10-0706

Penyakit BBTKLDP (2014) Laporan Investigasi Potensi Risiko Kesehatan Akibat Bencana Banjir Di Kabupaten Sampang. In: Sampang DKK (ed) Sampang, Indonesia

Picardeau M, Bertherat E, Jancloes M, Skouloudis AN, Durski K, Hartskeerl RA (2014) Rapid tests for diagnosis of leptospirosis: current tools and emerging technologies. Diagn Microbiol Infect Dis 78(1):1–8. https://doi.org/10.1016/j.diagmicrobio.2013.09.012

Reis RB, Ribeiro GS, Felzemburgh RDM, Santana FS, Mohr S, Melendez AXTO, Queiroz A, Santos AC, Ravines RR, Tassinari WS, Carvalho MS, Reis MG, Ko AI (2008) Impact of environment and social gradient on *Leptospira* infection in urban slums. PLoS Negl Trop Dis 2: e228. https://doi.org/10.1371/journal.pntd.0000228

Riley L, Ko A, Unger A, Reis M (2007) Slum health: diseases of neglected populations. BMC Int Health Hum Rights 7:2. https://doi.org/10.1186/1472-698X-7-2

Sarkar U, Nascimento SF, Barbosa R, Martins R, Nuevo H, Kalofonos I, Kalafanos I, Grunstein I, Flannery B, Dias J, Riley LW, Reis MG, Ko AI (2002) Population-based case-control investigation of risk factors for leptospirosis during an urban epidemic. Am J Trop Med Hyg 66 (5):605–610

Sarkar J, Chopra A, Katageri B, Raj H, Goel A (2012) Leptospirosis: a re-emerging infection. Asian Pac J Trop Med 5(6):500–502. https://doi.org/10.1016/S1995-7645(12)60086-8

Sarosa W (2006) Indonesia. In: Roberts BH, Kanaley T (eds) Urbanization and sustainability in Asia: case studies of good practice. Asian Development Bank, Manila

Schneider M, Jancloes M, Buss D, Aldighieri S, Bertherat E, Najera P, Galan D, Durski K, Espinal MA (2013) Leptospirosis: a silent epidemic disease. Int J Environ Res Public Health 10 (12):7229–7234. https://doi.org/10.3390/ijerph10127229

Smith JKG, Young MM, Wilson KL, Craig SB (2013) Leptospirosis following a major flood in Central Queensland, Australia. Epidemiol Infect 141(3):585–590. https://doi.org/10.1017/S0950268812001021

Tashakkori A, Teddlie C (2010) Sage handbook of mixed methods in social & behavioral research. Sage, Thousand Oaks

Teddlie C, Yu F (2007) Mixed methods sampling: a typology with examples. J Mixed Methods Res 1:77–100. https://doi.org/10.1177/2345678906292430

Thriemer K, Ley B, Ame S, von Seidlein L, Pak GD, Chang NY, Hashim R, Schmied WH, Busch CJ-L, Nixon S, Morrissey A, Puri MK, Ali M, Ochiai RL, Wierzba T, Jiddawi MS, Clemens JD, Ali SM, Deen JL (2012) The burden of invasive bacterial infections in Pemba, Zanzibar. PLoS ONE 7:30350. https://doi.org/10.1371/journal.pone.0030350

Torgerson PR, Hagan JE, Costa F, Calcagno J, Kane M, Martinez-Silveira MS, Goris MGA, Stein C, Ko AI, Abela-Ridder B (2015) Global burden of leptospirosis: estimated in terms of disability adjusted life years. PLoS Negl Trop Dis 9:e0004122. https://doi.org/10.1371/journal.pntd.0004122

Vanasco NB, Schmeling MF, Lottersberger J, Costa F, Ko AI, Tarabla HD (2008) Clinical characteristics and risk factors of human leptospirosis in Argentina (1999–2005). Acta Trop 107(3):255–258. https://doi.org/10.1016/j.actatropica.2008.06.007

Victoriano A, Smythe L, Gloriani-Barzaga N, Cavinta L, Kasai T, Limpakarnjanarat K, Ong B, Gongal G, Hall J, Coulombe C, Yanagihara Y, Yoshida S-I, Adler B (2009) Leptospirosis in the Asia Pacific region. BMC Infect Dis 9:147. https://doi.org/10.1186/1471-2334-9-147

Vinetz JM, Wilcox BA, Aguirre A, Gollin LX, Katz AR, Fujioka RS, Maly K, Horwitz P, Chang H (2005) Beyond disciplinary boundaries: leptospirosis as a model of incorporating transdisciplinary approaches to understand infectious disease emergence. EcoHealth 2(4):291–306. https://doi.org/10.1007/s10393-005-8638-y

Webb P, Bain C (2010) Essential epidemiology. Cambridge University Press, Cambridge

WHO (2003) Human leptospirosis: guidance for diagnosis, surveillance and control

WHO (2008) Leptospirosis in South-East Asia: the tip of the iceberg? World Health Organization Regional Office for South-East Asia (SEARO), New Delhi

WHO (2009) Leptospirosis situation in the WHO South-East Asia region. World Health Organization Regional Office for South-East Asia (SEARO), New Delhi

WHO UNICEF (2017) Progress on Drinking Water, Sanitation and Hygiene: 2017 Update and SDG Baselines. World Health Organization (WHO) and the United Nations Children's Fund (UNICEF), Geneva. Licence: CC BY-NC-SA 3.0 IGO

Zhou X-N, Bergquist R, Tanner M (2013) Elimination of tropical disease through surveillance and response. Infect Dis Poverty 2:1. https://doi.org/10.1186/2049-9957-2-1

Chapter 6
Complexity of Scenarios of Future Health: Integrating Policies and Laws

Claire Lajaunie, Serge Morand, and Pierre Mazzega

Abstract In Southeast Asia, regional institutions insist on the crucial role of innovative research to address sustainable development challenges. Among those challenges, the increasing human dominance of the global landscape, particularly in regard to forest cover loss is of major concern. Such dramatic habitat changes are accelerating the biodiversity loss. This reduction in biodiversity through altered landscapes due to urbanization and agricultural intensification appears linked to major epidemiological changes in human diseases with higher disease risks and the emergence of novel pathogens resulting from increased contacts between wildlife, domesticated animals and humans.

It appears necessary to investigate the multiple impacts of the intensification of the circulation along the economic corridor Thailand-Laos (linking Myanmar to Vietnam) on the evolution of infectious diseases of public health interests. Integrating the various dimensions of complexity thanks to disciplines such as ecology and environmental sciences, health sciences, policies and law, we analyse retrospectively, and comparatively infectious diseases' dynamics associated to policies, land use and biodiversity changes. The need of prospective scenarios of health that are

C. Lajaunie (✉)
INSERM, CERIC, UMR DICE 7318, CNRS, Aix Marseille University, University of Toulon, University of Pau and Pays Adour, Aix-en-Provence, France

Strathclyde Centre for Environmental Law and Governance (SCELG), University of Strathclyde, Glasgow, UK
e-mail: claire.lajaunie@inserm.fr

S. Morand
CNRS ISEM/CIRAD ASTRE, Faculty of Veterinary Technology, Kasetsart University, Bangkok, Thailand
e-mail: serge.morand@cirad.fr

P. Mazzega
UMR5563 GET Geosciences Environment Toulouse, CNRS/University of Toulouse, Toulouse, France

Strathclyde Centre for Environmental Law and Governance (SCELG), University of Strathclyde, Glasgow, UK
e-mail: pierre.mazzegaciamp@get.omp.eu

© Springer Nature Switzerland AG 2019
R. Boulet et al. (eds.), *Law, Public Policies and Complex Systems: Networks in Action*, Law, Governance and Technology Series 42,
https://doi.org/10.1007/978-3-030-11506-7_6

113

embedded in the socio-ecosystems is crucial: we will thus produce scenarios of future health embodied in the One Health approach at the human-animal-environment interface and directed towards decisions-makers or communities concerned at the national or local scale.

6.1 Introduction

Even though since the United Nations Conference on the Human Environment (Stockholm, 1972), the awareness of inter-linkages between health and environment increased in the international arena, through various international conferences (United Nations Conference on Environment and Development, Rio 1992; World Summit on Sustainable Development, Johannesburg 2002) and a decisive involvement of the World Health Organization (WHO) in treaty-making processes, health issues were not taken into consideration as such, until recently, by the international environmental law. Few doctrinal works tempted to highlight the role that international environmental law could play in addressing health threats such as emerging diseases (Von Schirnding et al. 2002; Onzivu 2006) but disease issues are still poorly considered through the international environmental law perspective. As a consequence, to date there is a lack of evidence-based work into the field of environmental law.

In Southeast Asia, the development of evidence-based policies is called by different agencies such as United Nations Development Program and United Nations Environment Program in Southeast Asia (cf. the Poverty-Environment Initiative in Thailand, UNDP, UNEP, Government of Thailand 2010) or the United Nations Economic and Social Commission of Asia-Pacific (ESCAP 2014) and at the National level in Thailand or Laos.

While focusing on regional connectivity, regional institutions such as ESCAP insist on the crucial role of innovative research to address sustainable development challenges. Among those challenges, the increasing human dominance on the global landscape, particularly in regard to forest cover loss is of major concern in the tropics (Lewis et al. 2015; Cornu et al. 2017). Such dramatic habitat changes are highlighted as a major cause of accelerated biodiversity loss (Lynam et al. 2016; Civitello et al. 2015; Wilcove et al. 2013). This reduction in biodiversity through altered landscapes due to urbanisation and agricultural intensification appears linked to major epidemiological changes in human diseases with higher disease risks and the emergence of novel pathogens resulting from increased contacts between wildlife, domesticated animals and humans (Lloyd-Smith et al. 2009; Brearley et al. 2013; Morand 2018). Southeast Asia is a tropical region where both biodiversity is at high risk due to human activities and where infectious diseases are highly favoured (Coker et al. 2011; Horby et al. 2013; Gay et al. 2014; Morand et al. 2014a; Hotez et al. 2015).

It leads to different questions in the regional context of Southeast Asia: how international environmental law translated and implemented at the regional or national level can address health issues (such as diseases spread)? How regional organisations and initiatives on health or the environment or both could function together in an attempt to solve health issues? How environmental law at the regional or national level could take advantage of considering and integrating the questions related to disease ecology, biodiversity erosion, land use/land cover (LULC) change, and global changes in order to propose evidence-based policies and regulations fitting a specific local or regional context? This is the kind of issues we are addressing with the FutureHealthSEA project (2017–2021) by investigating the impacts of the intensification of the circulation along the economic corridor Thailand-Laos (linking Myanmar to Vietnam) on the evolution of infectious diseases of public health interests. Integrating ecology and environmental sciences with health sciences, policies and law, this project analyses retrospectively and comparatively infectious diseases' dynamics associated with policies, land use and biodiversity changes and combine predictive process-based scenarios and policy-driven storytelling scenarios of health incorporating disease ecology, biodiversity erosion, future land use and climate change regional impacts.

The need of prospective scenarios of health that are embedded in the social-ecological systems is a crucial issue. However, these scenarios cannot be limited to the results of phenomenological (statistical) models, although they show their interest for retrospective or comparative analyses, but they should be produced from process-based models (Sect. 6.2) integrating disease ecology modelling and be policy-driven (Myers et al. 2013; Mouquet et al. 2015). An excursion is proposed in Sect. 6.3 in the world of integrative impact assessment modelling to present some of the difficulties that arise when it comes to modelling public policies, but also the value of integrating them into the simulations as effective components of the evolution of a health-environment interaction system. This involves digitally simulating evidence-based scenarios that take into account existing or projected public policies and norms, and thus explore areas where public action can be expressed in the context of a science-policy dialogue (Sect. 6.4). Conclusions are drawn in Sect. 6.5.

6.2   The Need of Process-Based Prospective Scenarios

Previous projects[1] have shown that biodiversity and environmental changes, notably land use changes at regional to local scales are factors of health risks and of emergence of zoonotic diseases. They highlighted the fact that biodiversity is a source of pathogens diversity as well as a source of biological diversity as well and even cultural diversity (Morand et al. 2014b; Morand and Lajaunie 2018). They confirmed the importance of the spatio-temporal dynamics of the land use land cover

---

[1]ANR Project BiodivHealthSEA "Local impacts and perceptions of global changes: Biodiversity and Health in Southeast Asia" (2012–2016) and ANR Project Ceropath "Community Ecology of Rodents and their Pathogens in Southeast Asia" (2007–2011).

in determining the diversity of wildlife and their parasites, in particular through the use of network analyses (Bordes et al. 2016; Pilosof et al. 2015) with implications for human risk of zoonotic diseases. Regarding health, the insights gained from those projects underlined the necessity to understand the various dynamics at stake and to develop scenarios of future health embodied in the One Health approach at the human-animal-environment interface.

The One Health approach to manage the risks presented by animal diseases and zoonoses at the animal human-ecosystem interface started spreading into international environmental agreements related to biodiversity, acknowledging as such the role of biodiversity in addressing well-being and health issues (Lajaunie and Mazzega 2016). This acknowledgment leads to the creation of the Intergovernmental Platform on Biodiversity and Ecosystem Services (IPBES) modelled on the Intergovernmental Panel on Climate Change (IPCC) to be an efficient science-policy interface mechanism able to improve policy-relevant information about the state, trends and outlooks of human-environment interactions with a focus on the impacts of ecosystems change on human well-being. The Strategic Plan for Biodiversity 2011–2020[2] integrates this aspect by defining strategic goals and targets (Aichi biodiversity targets[3]) in order to halt the loss of biodiversity and thus contribute to human well-being. These Aichi targets, as well as the IPBES assessments and the One Health approach, implies a translation at the national level of those international strategies and Thailand is very committed into the implementation of these strategies and tends to have a leadership role at the regional level on these aspects.

In the context of climate change, the IPCC build scenarios and storylines describing different options of the evolution of the world through the twenty-first century by taking into account socio-economic factors. Thus, the scenarios proposed by the IPCC, called Special Reports on Emission Scenarios,[4] are based on factors such as the global population, economic development (expressed in annual Gross Domestic Product) or measure of equity (per capita income ratio). It is striking to see that the methodology of scenarios developed by the IPBES, which main goal is to strengthen the science-policy interface, is distinguishing between four different types of scenarios, supposed to play "important roles in relation to the major phases of the policy cycle".[5] Nevertheless, the IPBES does not seem to suggest the integration of policies and law as factors involved in the dynamic of change of biodiversity and of modification of the environment at large.

In addition, the Executive Secretary of the Convention on biodiversity in a note to provide its Subsidiary Body on Scientific Technical and Technological Advice (SBSTTA) relevant information on scenarios for the 2050 Vision for Biodiversity underlined the fact that "quantitative models that incorporate feedback regarding biodiversity change on ecosystem services and human well-being have not been

---

[2]https://www.cbd.int/sp/. Accessed 25 Feb 2018.

[3]https://www.cbd.int/sp/targets/. Accessed 25 Feb 2018.

[4]See e.g. https://www.ipcc.ch/pdf/special-reports/emissions_scenarios.pdf. Accessed 25 Feb 2018.

[5]See https://www.ipbes.net/scenarios. Accessed 25 Feb 2018.

incorporated into comprehensive scenarios" (SBSTTA 2017 §20). Among those feedbacks we must consider the spillover effects of policies and law (for instance on land use, agricultural policy, protected areas, forest logging).

However, few studies have allowed policy makers to anticipate the full health implications of their decisions, which implies that research effort should explore the multiple health outcomes of ecosystem alteration, taking into account the socio-ecological dynamic changes. Investigating multiple diseases of public health importance may then generate useful insights for policy (see Box 6.1). The emphasis should then be put on policy-driven research. Most of studies that put their scientific efforts in biodiversity conservation or ecosystem services tend to proceed from basic research to policy application, forgetting the advice of Myers et al. (2013) that a basic reversal of approach from policy-driven application to basic research with the objective of producing scenarios will participate to the increasing value of scientific results to society.

Box 6.1 Some Emerging Infectious Diseases Related to the Environment

Biological diversity and the complexity of interactions are also expressed by the large number of emerging or re-emerging infectious diseases (here in South-East Asia) linked to environmental dynamics through mechanisms and via specific paths. Four criteria guided our selection of diseases to be studied in the FutureHealthSEA project: (a) to address diseases with a significant impact on public health; (b) to select diseases allowing to explore the relative importance of environmental change, the role of domestic animals, wildlife and various vector types; (c) the availability of data on the entities and processes involved; (d) to allow a parsimonious use of scientific curiosities (the resources allocated to the project being limited). The diseases selected are the following:

Leptospirosis. The main types of leptospiroses considered (based on their genotyping and serotyping) differ in the importance of the factors of LULC change (e.g. through the intensification of agriculture and livestock farming) and environmental changes (water and soil), and dependence to survive outside the hosts, whether humans, livestock or wildlife, in their dynamics.

Scrub Typhus. Forest cover, which increases with altitude (very few forests in the plains) is one main determinant of the epidemiology of the scrub typhus (our terrain in Nan Province ranges between 100 m and 1700 m) through the changes of forest types, the diversity of the chigger mites' vectors and reservoirs, and the rodents hosts for chiggers development (Chaisiri et al. 2016, 2017). The spatial diffusion of scrub typhus is limited by the low dispersion of bacteria (trans-ovarian transmission from one mite generation to the next, no re-infection) but can be enhanced by dispersion of the mammalian hosts of the chiggers (Morand et al. 2019).

(continued)

Box 6.1 (continued)

Dengue. Dengue affects only humans preferentially in peri-urban areas and its epidemiology is well described in Vietnam (van Panhuis et al. 2015). Its vectors, *Aedes aegypti* and *Aedes albopictus*, show resistance to insecticides. The approach we develop could be transposable to other vector-borne diseases (babesiosis, bartonellosis, zika, chikungunya, Japanese encephalitis). We consider two types of transmission, simple vector-borne (mosquitoes/humans such as dengue, chick) and complex vector borne with reservoirs (ticks or fleas or mosquitoes/mammals/humans such as babesia, bartonella, Japanese encephalitis). We also investigate whether local development scenarios could provide the conditions for the re-emergence of malaria (via Anopheles mosquitoes) (Overgaard et al. 2015).

Melioidosis. Although it is a real threat, there are no systematic recording of melioidosis (*Burkholderia pseudomallei*) due to a telluric bacteria (Ribolzi et al. 2016), for which the modes of contamination are little known (Buisson et al. 2015).

In the scenarios, multi-level public policies will be considered via the impacts they are likely to have on land use-land cover, habitats or on health (e.g. prophylactic measures). We use various types of assessments (such as Strategic Environmental Assessment (World Bank 2009; Li et al. 2012) or Landscape Ecological Assessment (Mortberg et al. 2007; Lee and Oh 2012), different public policy appraisals (UNDP Thailand 2014) or case studies (UNDP Thailand 2014; OECD 2014) to help build scenarios. We aim at the production of indicators for decision makers from local to regional (ASEAN) level, along with their uncertainty and caveats about the limitations of their use, including ethical, and prospective proposals of strategic directions for evidence-based policies linked with the possible mitigation of outbreaks and spread of infectious diseases in the ASEAN economic corridor.

6.3 Integrating Policies and Regulations in Environment and Health Models

Technically, the future health scenarios we are developing are based on formal modelling and computer simulations. In recent years, impact assessment modelling has shown the interest (and possibilities) of integrating a variety of multi-scale environmental processes (Hamilton et al. 2015; Milat et al. 2015). Our purpose here is not to present this approach applied to the emergence of infectious diseases related to environmental changes, but to discuss the importance of integrating public policy representations and legal norms into simulation platforms, as integral components of social-ecological systems with direct impacts, though entangled through a myriad of processes, on the evolution of these systems.

6.3.1 On Policy Modelling

The term "policy modelling" covers a diversity of domains like social computing, policy analysis, visualisation (in policy modelling), citizen engagement, public opinion mining and sentiment analysis, visual analytics (including analytical reasoning) and linked data in open government information, trust in governance, public service aggregation, mash-ups and orchestration, just to mention a few items identified in the CROSSROAD (2010) project. In the present context, we focus on the development of formal representations of the entities and processes involved in a given public policy,[6] and the use of these representations in computers in order to simulate *in silico* the evolution of the state of these entities, eventually in interaction with other policy-driven, socially driven or environmental processes. A policy is by itself a complex system involving actors, material (natural resources, infrastructures, financial resources, etc.) and cognitive resources (data, knowledge, norms), which state changes under process' and actors' actions. A generic framework to represent a large set of such policies having potential impacts on social-ecological systems is described in Chap. 4 of this volume (Sibertin-Blanc et al. 2018). Its use makes it possible to clarify the concepts used in an interdisciplinary project, to share knowledge (especially between tenants from different disciplines) and to base the work on an abstract system of consensual knowledge representations. For example, the notion of "human well-being" may be considered as an indicator aggregating information on the state of variables related to the health of a population of (human) individuals but could equally well include information concerning the quality of the environment of this population (animal health, ecosystem health, . . .).

Several difficulties arise when it comes to modelling policies and their impacts, some of which are:

- A public policy simultaneously modifies the states of several actors and resources;
- The state of a resource is likely to modify the conditions of the implementation of a policy[7];
- The effect of a policy depends on its social acceptability and on the degree of compliance with which it is followed by various social groups;
- Each actor (individual or collective) interprets a policy (assuming he is aware of its existence and requirements) and integrates it in his own way into a behavioural strategy.

The identification of each process that a public policy solicits, of each activity and actor who carries it out, and the representation of how the state of the resources are

---

[6]For simplicity, we will consider here that the term "policy" also includes the class of norms and legal regulations. This shortcut is justified by the equally normative nature of public policies whose action aims to reach a different state of affairs than the current state.

[7]A change of state of a resource can also lead to the design and implementation of a targeted policy.

modified, are at the heart of impact modelling.[8] A parsimony principle guides the modelling: processes with little impact or impact on state variables of no interest for the issue considered are set aside.[9] The main areas of public policy that we take into account in the study of the emergence and epidemiology of the selected infectious diseases are presented in Fig. 6.1.

6.3.2   Entangled Process Dynamics

Regardless of their respective decision-making levels, all public policies and regulations and norms implemented in a given territory are supposed to act, simultaneously, on the behaviour of the actors, on the resources, and sometimes exert control over some processes (e. g. environmental services). The state of the various resources—biodiversity, soil, forests, water, air . . .—conditions in return the actions and possible behaviours of the actors, as well as the overall context of application of the policies and norms. The interactions take place in a continuous flow. Causality is diffuse, with changing intensities and orientations, and through evolving actors and resources networks.

Figure 6.2 is a highly stylised representation of interactions between resources and actors involved in the emergence and epidemiology of infectious diseases that we consider. At this level of abstraction, the labels of the entities or processes must be considered as classes whose main elements are, in a second phase of the modelling process, identified and represented in relation to the other entities and processes of the modelled system. For example, in this specific context the ecological concept of *habitat* brings together soils, bodies of water and vegetation (each of these entities being endowed with relevant state variables and functions capable of modifying the state variables of other entities). The *interactions* between the atmosphere and habitats or pathogens are also multiple (effects of precipitation, air humidity and temperature, for example). The complexity of this schema can be increased and its conceptual accuracy improved progressively for example by taking into account human settlements, which are important for synanthropic species such as some species of mosquitoes (*Aedes*), ticks (dogs, cattle), or rodents (*Rattus*). Larval mites are the reservoirs and vectors for Orientia tsutsugamushi while rodents are not, but they are the hosts for larval chiggers' development. Chiggers are linked with habitat as they need soil and vegetation to mature, reproduce (and to lay eggs for a new generation of infected/non infected larval mites). Some pathogens (Leptospira, Bulkholderia, some viruses) are directly in contact with the environment and are dependent upon its quality (pH, turbidity and others), some others are

---

[8]The processes themselves can be modified: the impact of deforestation on the water cycle—on runoff, recharge of groundwater, etc.—or soil depletion is a known example.

[9]From the point of view of modelling, such choices are guided by sensitivity analyses (see below).

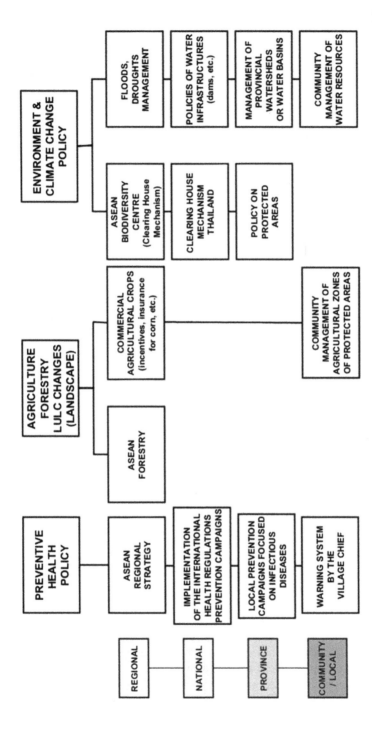

Fig. 6.1 Main public policies integrated into the modelling of the emergence of infectious diseases (see Box 6.1) in the province of Nan (Thailand). The left column shows the decision-making levels of their implementation

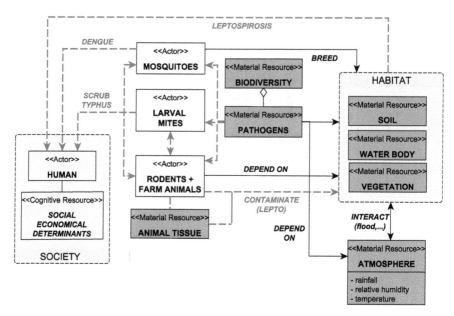

Fig. 6.2 Stylisation of the main interactions between resources and actors involved in the emergence and epidemiology of selected infectious diseases (disease-related links are in dashed lines)

in contact indirectly with the environment through their vectors (Bartonella, Orientia tsutsugamushi, Babesia).

An effective way to simulate the interactions between various public policies is to consider their impacts on resources whose changing state is "exposed" to the activity of the actors. If the empirical observation and formal representation of the direct interactions between actors often present insuperable difficulties (e.g. interactions between groups of rational strategic agents), the mediation of these interactions by the evolutionary state of the resources makes it possible to reproduce empirical dynamics.

Thus Figs. 6.1 and 6.2 are to be reconciled by connecting each public policy with each resource (characterised by its nature, if any geographical extension, etc.) it impacts in a potential or proven manner. For example, prophylaxis measures impact pathogens (considered in the meta-class of material resources for the purposes of this modelling of future health scenarios) and people's health. Incentives for the development of cash crops have observable effects (through LULC high resolution maps, landscape changes analysis, field surveys) on the forest, on the water cycle, therefore on habitats and biodiversity, but also on rodents, that in turn are candidate vectors of pathogens. Climate change has effects—direct or indirect—on just about every component and process of social-ecological systems.

It is important to emphasise what may seem like a paradox. A public policy is conceived *ex ante* according to a causal schema that wants its implementation to have well identified or even quantifiable effects. Of course, collateral, unexpected effects can also occur (especially because of the inventiveness of human actors). However, particularly in those policies and norms implementation whose pathways are interpenetrated by environmental dynamics (involving biological, bio-geochemical or physical processes) it is almost illusory to claim to attribute to each of the measures the share of changes that it has induced on the trajectory of evolution of the social-ecological systems empirically observed. A whole range of predictability of the evolution of the states of the actors and resources mixes (from quasi-certain predictions to the complete uncertainty for example concerning some collective decision-making) as well as effects delayed in time or in space, and effects cascading in a range of scales. Nevertheless, this observation, far from making the integrated impact assessment models obsolete, makes it indispensable (irreplaceable) through the simulation of process-based scenarios.

6.3.3   Integrated Impact Assessment Scenarios

The ability of the integrative model to represent with acceptable realism the dynamics of the social-ecological system is evaluated in comparison with a set of heterogeneous data related to the state variables of the model entities. *In silico* simulation of the interaction of processes and activities of virtual actors must reproduce as much as possible the past observations and data. The diversity of data types (on LULC changes, biodiversity, epidemiology, demography, economic data, stakeholder strategies, etc.) is essential to ensure relevant representativeness of the empirical information and thus verify the coherence of the integrative model.[10] The sensitivity analysis, which consists in testing the impact of different configurations of the integrative model on the observable variables, allows calibrating certain parameters, adjusting the model procedures and, if necessary, simplifying its representations. At the end of this phase, the model faithfully reproduces the trajectory of the social-ecological system as it has been observed and leads to an exhaustive description of the state of its variables considered as an initial system state from which the prospective scenarios will be simulated.

The business as usual scenario (BAU, see Fig. 6.3a) assumes that none of the conditions that governed the past evolution of the system will change in the future: the continuation of the simulation over the period of time of interest produces a description of the evolution of the system (and useful indicators) that will be used as a reference for comparison with other trajectories. Other scenarios can then be designed and simulated: modification of a compliance rate of the actors with the existing policies and regulations (condition set *C1* and trajectory *#T1* of Fig. 6.3a),

---

[10]Note, however, that this procedure cannot guarantee that another system of formal representations could pass this comparison test with the empirical data in just the same way. We will not develop this point, which raises questions about the ethics of modelling that we address elsewhere (see Mazzega 2018 *submitted*).

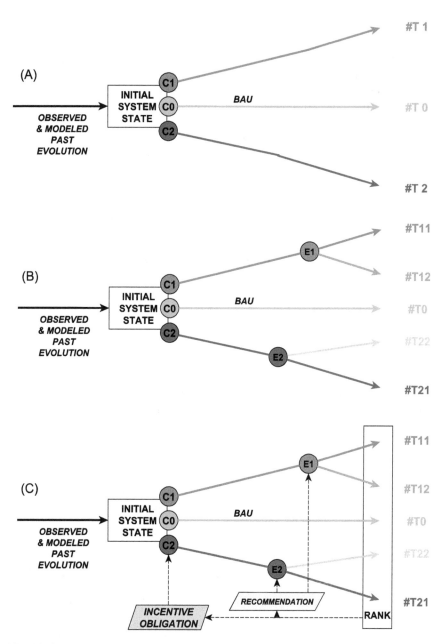

Fig. 6.3 Schemes of progressive constructions of scenarios (conditions Cj, event Ej, trajectory $\#Tjk$) and their possible use for the implementation of incentives or obligations (see text)

implementation of a new policy of health or biodiversity conservation (condition set $C2$ and trajectory $\#T2$ of Fig. 6.3a), etc., all other things being kept unchanged in the model simulation.

Many social and political interactions do not follow one another in a simply mechanistic way. Note however that ecosystem or biological dynamics present, from the point of view of modelling, behaviours just as little predictable, even poorly understood—like the biodiversity tipping points (Leadley et al. 2010). A relatively satisfactory approach to these phenomena is to consider as many potential events in time (these are *E1* and *E2* in Fig. 6.3b), and to make assumptions about the likely results of their occurrence. The way in which these assumptions are likely to modify the conditions of evolution of the subsequent trajectories are taken into account as so many branching sub-scenarios. The combinatorial of the scenarios' condition sets and events thus leads to diversifying the possible evolutions explored by simulation.

The scenarios are designed to provide analysis elements to specific communities—policy and decision makers, citizens or local communities, scientists—based on scientific knowledge and data that can be mobilized. By considering all intermediate and final states of modelled actors and resources, a likely trajectory of evolution can be perceived as the more desirable than another one, which leads to a hierarchical ranking of scenarios, from the more to the less desirable ones. Specifically, a desirable scenario may involve the implementation of incentives or obligations, or the consideration of specific policy recommendations if a given event occurs (Fig. 6.3c). However, this cycle can only be exploited if the conditions for a science-policy dialogue are well established, and this in the long term.

6.4   Science-Policy Dialogue for Informed Policies and Law

First, the results of the CERoPath project advocate focusing on diseases of public health importance for the area studied in order to facilitate a science-policy dialogue. This has been started with the BiodivHealthSEA project (2012–2016) for studies implemented at a local scale (village or district) by investigating zoonotic diseases or antimicrobial resistance at human—livestock—wildlife interface in Northern Thailand and Laos (Ribas et al. 2017; Olaitan et al. 2015, 2016). In 2006, the Nan Province was affected by a flood event and 1400 cases of leptospirosis were reported after the peak of the flooding, which led the government to set up a prevention campaign. The extensive survey of Leptospira infection in rodents gathered in 2008 and 2009 in the CERoPath project was compared to the human incidence of the disease from 2003 to 2012 gathered by the BiodivHealthSEA project in 168 villages with the collaboration of two district hospitals. Using an *ad hoc* developed land-use cover model, humans and rodents were observed as not infected in the same environment. Interestingly, there was a strong effect of public health campaigns conducted after the dramatic flood event of 2006. This study confirmed the role of the environment and particularly the land use in the transmission of bacteria, emphasised by the effects of the provincial public health campaigns on the epidemiological pattern of incidence, and questioned the role of wildlife as reservoirs (Della Rossa et al. 2016). Locally, health and environmental policies are highlighted as a key component of the epidemiological landscape. Similar ongoing studies concern the epidemiology of scrub typhus (Chaisiri et al. 2015).

A recent PhD study (Jaruwan Viroj, lecturer at Maha Sarakham University, enrolled in Montpellier University) constitutes another pilot study for future health scenarios. The epidemiology of leptospirosis and the public health policy are investigated by collecting the leptospirosis incidence data at the individual level (village) over 2004–2014 from the Department of Disease Control, the land use and socio-economic data (at the level of the village) from the Land Development Department, the Department of Public Health, and information on livestock and poultry than could carry Leptospira bacteria from the Department of Livestock Development.

Intensive survey with questionnaires and interviews of former infected and non-infected people (600 persons) has already been conducted, in order to obtain their perceptions and knowledge of the disease, its epidemiology, its control, and the potential roles of animal reservoirs. A second survey with questionnaires and interviews of health volunteers, public health officers, and community leaders (700 persons) has been given about for their perceptions on the strengths and weaknesses of leptospirosis control. All these data are already gathered and inte-grated in a linked geo-referenced database to be investigated statistically. The spatio-temporal epidemiology will be discussed in the light of a policy analysis of the leptospirosis surveillance and prevention scheme of Public Health (at both national and provincial levels).

This work contributes to the development of evidence-based policies and law. International environmental law (IEL) developed under the influence of ecology and both disciplines started to co-evolve since the 1970s (Turgut 2008). One distinctive feature of IEL is that it promotes cooperation among States to realise common gains (Bodansky 2010): there is an underlying notion of "general interest" as in public law, and this principle guides our research as it induces regional and transboundary cooperation, transposition of interesting solutions, common strategies. It also calls for a fluid interdisciplinarity due to the complex natures of social-ecological systems. Similarly, we think disease ecology, which studies host-pathogen interactions within the context of their environment and evolution, could play a decisive role for bridging public health and conservation policies. Furthermore, local participatory initiatives, community-based management of natural resources (Salam et al. 2006), specific customary law or regulations (on health, agriculture, forestry, biodiversity, water and soil) constitute case studies that can give insights for legal solutions and for evidence-based policies (Koon et al. 2012) that should be taken into account and up-scaled at the national level: we are studying some specific cases that could help to specify, confirm or modify national strategies and plans.

We consider that complex interplay of multiple contemporaneous environmental changes (e. g. LULC, climate change or exchanges intensification) on multiple dimensions of health need to be better assessed in order to gain utilities for public health policy, biodiversity conservation, and practices. The scenarios (Alcamo and Henrichs 2008; Biggs et al. 2007) we will produce are not "predictive" because of the multiplicity and the complexity of interactions associated to the contingency of political decisions but "prospective". As such they are directed towards decision makers (Alcamo and Henrichs 2008; Spierenburg 2012) or communities concerned at the national or local scale.

The main goal of the ongoing FutureHealthSEA project is thus to produce results that are reflecting local concerns, responding to the need of an evidence-based approach championed by national law such the new Thai rules and procedures for the Health Impact Assessment of Public Policies (National Health Commission Office; NHCO 2016). The United Nations Environment Programme is also calling for the development of evidence-based decision-making to reach the Sustainable Development Goals by 2030 (UNEP 2015). Indeed, we are aiming at developing a grounded research in line with the current considerations at the local, national or regional level and to build a dialogue between scientists and policy-makers to identify issues related to the interactions "biodiversity-infectious diseases" notably in order to facilitate the monitoring and assessment of public policies.

6.5 Conclusion

Assuming that changes in the environment and in the biodiversity whether they result from international or national policies or community actions have an impact on the evolution of health risks, the project proposes to prospective scenarios embodied in the One Health approach at the human-animal-environment interface to anticipate the influence of those changes. The originality of the project is to integrate law and policies regarding the environment and health as integral part of the various factors of changes. It requires to gather various types of data and to take different approaches into consideration. Addressing the different challenges, the project implies is rendered possible thanks to the implication of a variety of local and regional academic and institutional partners convinced by the interest of such an approach and willing to test it in concrete situations at the district, provincial or national level for instance.

Acknowledgements This work is a contribution to the ANR Project FutureHealthSEA (n° ANR-17-CE35-0003-02) "Predictive scenarios of health in Southeast Asia: linking land use and climate changes to infectious diseases" (PIs: S. Morand and C. Lajaunie). The Ecology and Environment Institute of the National Centre for Scientific Research (InEE CNRS, France) supports the International Multidisciplinary Thematic Network "Biodiversity, Health and Societies in Southeast Asia," Thailand (PI: S. Morand, CNRS/CIRAD) to which this study also contributes.

References

Alcamo J, Henrichs T (2008) Towards guidelines for environmental scenario analysis. In: Alcamo J (ed) Environmental futures: the practice of environmental scenarios. Elsevier, Amsterdam, pp 13–51

Biggs R, Raudsepp-Hearne C, Atkinson-Palombo C, Bohensky E, Boyd E, Cundill G, Fox H, Ingram S, Kok K, Spehar S, Tengö M, Timmer D, Zurek M (2007) Linking futures across scales: a dialog on multiscale scenarios. Ecol Soc 12:17. Available from http://www.ecologyandsociety.org/vol12/iss1/art17/. Accessed 25 Feb 2018

Bodansky D (2010) The art and craft of international environmental law. Harvard University Press, Cambridge

Bordes F, Caron A, Blasdell K, de Garine Wichatitsky M, Morand S (2016) Forecasting potential emergence of zoonotic diseases in South-East Asia: network analysis identifies key rodent hosts. J Appl Ecol 54(3):691–700. https://doi.org/10.1111/1365-2664.12804

Brearley G, Rhodes J, Bradley A, Baxter G, Seabrook L, Lunney D, Liu Y, McAlpine C (2013) Wildlife disease prevalence in human-modified landscapes. Biol Rev Camb Philos Soc 88:427–442. https://doi.org/10.1111/brv.12009

Buisson Y, Rattanavong S, Keoluangkhot V et al (2015) Melioidosis in Laos. In: Morand S, Dujardin J-P, Lefait-Rollin R, Apiwathnasorn C (eds) Socio-ecological dimensions of infectious diseases in Southeast Asia. Springer, Singapore, pp 89–104

Chaisiri K, McGarry JW, Morand S, Makepeace BL (2015) Symbiosis in an overlooked micro-cosm: a systematic review of the bacterial flora of mites. Parasitology 142(9):1152–1162. https://doi.org/10.1017/S0031182015000530

Chaisiri K, Stekolnikov AA, Makepeace BL, Morand S (2016) A revised checklist of chigger mites (Acari: Trombiculidae) from Thailand, with the description of three new species. J Med Entomol 53(2):321–342. https://doi.org/10.1093/jme/tjv244

Chaisiri K, Cosson J-F, Morand S (2017) Infection of rodents by Orientia tsutsugamushi, the agent of scrub typhus in relation to land use in Thailand. Trop Med Infect Dis 2(4):53. https://doi.org/10.3390/tropicalmed2040053

Civitello DJ, Cohen J, Fatima H, Halstead NT, McMahon TA, Ortega CN, Sauer EL, Young S, Rohr JR (2015) Biodiversity inhibits parasites: broad evidence for the dilution effect. Proc Natl Acad Sci 112(28):8667–8671. https://doi.org/10.1073/pnas.1506279112

Coker RJ, Hunter BM, Rudge JW, Liverani M, Hanvoravongchai P (2011) Emerging infectious diseases in Southeast Asia: regional challenges to control. Lancet 377(9765):599–609. https://doi.org/10.1016/S0140-6736(10)62004-1

Cornu J-F, Lajaunie C, Laborde H, Morand S (2017) Landscape changes and policies for biodiversity and environment conservation in Southeast Asia. In: Morand S, Satrawaha R, Lajaunie C (eds) Biodiversity conservation in Southeast Asia: challenges in a changing environment. Routledge EarthScan, London, pp 49–66

CROSSROAD (2010) A participative roadmap for ICT research in electronic governance and policy modeling – state of the art analysis. D1.2, FP7-ICT-2009-4 SA Project

Della Rossa P, Tantrakarnapa K, Sutdan D, Cosson JF, Chaisiri K, Tran A, Suputtamongkol S, Binot A, Lajaunie C, Morand S (2016) Environmental factors and public health policy associated with human and rodent infection by leptospirosis: a land-cover based study in Nan Province (Thailand). Epidemiol Infect 144(7):1550–1562. https://doi.org/10.1017/S0950268815002903

ESCAP (2014) ESCAP annual report 2014. United Nations economic and social commission for Asia and the Pacific, Thailand, 65 pp. Available at http://www.unescap.org/resources/escap-annual-report-2014. Accessed 25 Feb 2018

Gay N, Olival KJ, Bumrungsri S, Siriaroonrat B, Bourgarel M, Morand S (2014) Parasite and viral species richness of Southeast Asian bats: fragmentation of area distribution matters. Int J Parasitol Parasites Wildl 3(2):161–170. https://doi.org/10.1016/j.ijppaw.2014.06.003

Hamilton SH, ElSawah S, Guillaume JHA, Jakeman AJ, Pierce SA (2015) Integrated assessment and modelling: overview and synthesis of salient dimensions. Environ Model Software 64:215–229. https://doi.org/10.1016/j.envsoft.2014.12.005

Horby PW, Pfeiffer D, Oshitani H (2013) Prospects for emerging infections in East and Southeast Asia 10 years after severe acute respiratory syndrome. Emerg Infect Dis 19(6):853–860. https://doi.org/10.3201/eid1906.121783

Hotez PJ, Bottazzi ME, Strych U, Chang LY, Lim YAL, Goodenow MM, AbuBakar S (2015) Neglected tropical diseases among the Association of Southeast Asian Nations (ASEAN): overview and update. PLoS Negl Trop Dis 9:e0003575

Koon AD, Nambiar D, Rao KD (2012) Embedding of research into decision-making processes, background paper commissioned by the alliance for health policy and systems research to develop the WHO Health Systems Research Strategy, Public Health Foundation of India. Available on http://www.who.int/alliance-hpsr/alliancehpsr_backgroundpaperembeddingresearch.pdf. Accessed 25 Feb 2018

Lajaunie C, Mazzega P (2016) One health and biodiversity conventions. The emergence of health issues in biodiversity conventions. IUCN Acad Environ Law eJournal 7:105–121. Available on www.iucnael.org/en/documents/1324-iucn-ejournal-issue-7. Accessed 25 Feb 2018

Leadley P, Pereira HM, Alkemade R, Fernandez-Manjarres JF, Proenca V, Scharlemann JPW, Walpole MJ (2010) Biodiversity scenarios: projections of 21st century change in biodiversity and associated ecosystem services. Technical Series no. 50. Secretariat of the Convention on Biological Diversity, Montreal. 132 pp

Lee DW, Oh KS (2012) A landscape ecological management system for sustainable urban development. APCBEE Procedia 1:375–380. https://doi.org/10.1016/j.apcbee.2012.03.062

Lewis SL, Edwards D, Galbraith D (2015) Increasing human dominance of tropical forests. Science 349(6250):827–832. https://doi.org/10.1126/science.aaa9932

Li W, Liu Y, Yang Z (2012) Preliminary strategic environmental assessment of the great western development strategy: safeguarding ecological security for a new western China. Environ Manag 49(2):483–501. https://doi.org/10.1007/s00267-011-9794-1

Lloyd-Smith JO, George D, Pepin KM, Pitzer VE, Pulliam JR, Dobson AP, Hudson PJ, Grenfell BT (2009) Epidemic dynamics at the human-animal interface. Science 326(5958):1362–1367. https://doi.org/10.1126/science.1177345

Lynam AJ, Porter L, Campos Arceiz A (2016) The challenge of conservation in changing tropical Southeast Asia. Conserv Biol 30:931–932

Mazzega P (2018) On the ethics of biodiversity models, forecasts and scenarios. Asian Bioethics Review 10:295–312. https://doi.org/10.1007/s41649-018-0069-5

Milat AJ, Bauman AE, Redman S (2015) A narrative review of research impact assessment models and methods. Health Res Policy Syst 13:18. https://doi.org/10.1186/s12961-015-0003-1

Morand S (2018) Biodiversity and disease transmission. In: Hurst CJ (ed) The connections between ecology and infectious disease, advances in environmental microbiology. Springer, Berlin, pp 39–56

Morand S, Lajaunie C (2018) Biodiversity and health. ISTE Press/Elsevier, London/Oxford

Morand S, Jittapalapong S, Supputamongkol Y, Abdullah MT, Huan TB (2014a) Infectious diseases and their outbreaks in Asia-Pacific: biodiversity and its regulation loss matter. PLoS One 9(2):e90032

Morand S, Owers K, Bordes S (2014b) Biodiversity and emerging zoonoses. In: Yamada A, Kahn LH, Kaplan B, Monath TP, Woodall J, Conti L (eds) Confronting emerging zoonoses: the one health paradigm. Springer, Tokyo, pp 27–41

Morand S, Blasdell K, Bordes F, Buchy P, Carcy B, Chaisiri K, Chaval Y, Claude J, Cosson JF, Desquesnes M, Jittapalapong S, Jiyipong T, Karnchanabanthoen A, Pornpan P, Rolain JM, Tran A (2019) Changing landscapes of Southeast Asia and rodent-borne diseases: decreased diversity but increased transmission risks. Ecol Appl (in press)

Mortberg UM, Balfors B, Knol WC (2007) Landscape ecological assessment: a tool for integrating biodiversity issues in strategic environmental assessment and planning. J Environ Manage 82 (4):457–470. https://doi.org/10.1016/j.jenvman.2006.01.005

Mouquet N, Lagadeuc Y, Devictor V, Doyen L, Duputie A, Eveillard D, Faure D, Garnier E, Gimenez O, Huneman P, Jabot F, Jarne P, Joly D, Julliard R, Kefi S, Kergoat GJ, Lavorel S, Le Gall L, Meslin L, Morand S, Morin X, Morlon H, Pinay G, Pradel R, Schurr FM, Thuiller W, Loreau M (2015) Predictive ecology in a changing world. J Appl Ecol 52(5):1293–1310. https://doi.org/10.1111/1365-2664.12482

Myers SS, Gaffikin L, Golden CD, Ostfeld RS, Redford KH, Ricketts TH, Turner WR, Osofsky SA (2013) Human health impacts of ecosystem alteration. Proc Natl Acad Sci 110 (47):18753–18760. https://doi.org/10.1073/pnas.1218656110

NHCO (2016) Thailand's rules and procedures for the health impact assessment of public policies. National Health Commission Office, Bangkok, p 77. Available from https://en.nationalhealth.or.th/wp-content/uploads/2017/11/HIA2_ENG-final.pdf. Accessed 25 Feb 2018

OECD (2014) Towards green growth in Southeast Asia. Solutions for policy makers. Organisation for Economic Co-operation and Development, Paris, 28 pp. Available on https://www.oecd.org/dac/environment-development/Final%20SE%20Asia%20Brochure%20low%20res.pdf. Accessed 25 Feb 2018

Olaitan A, Thongmalayvong B, Akkhavong K, Somphavong S, Paboriboune P, Khounsy S, Morand S, Rolain J-M (2015) Clonal transmission of a colistin-resistant Escherichia coli from a domesticated pig to human in Laos. J Antimicrob Chemother 70(12):3402–3404. https://doi.org/10.1093/jac/dkv252

Olaitan AO, Chabou S, Okdah L, Morand S, Rolain JM (2016) Dissemination of the mcr-1 colistin resistance gene. Lancet Infect Dis 16(2):147. https://doi.org/10.1016/S1473-3099(15)00540-X

Onzivu W (2006) International environmental law, the public's health, and domestic environmental governance in developing countries. Am Univ Int Law Rev 21(4):597–684

Overgaard HJ, Suwonkerd W, Jeffrey Hii J (2015) The Malaria landscape: mosquitoes, transmission, landscape, insecticide resistance, and integrated control in Thailand. In: Morand S, Dujardin J-P, Lefait-Rollin R, Apiwathnasorn C (eds) Socio-ecological dimensions of infectious diseases in Southeast Asia. Springer, Singapore, pp 123–153

Pilosof S, Morand S, Krasnov BR, Nunn CL (2015) Potential parasite transmission in multihost networks based on parasite sharing. PLoS One 10:e0117909

Ribas A, Jollivet C, Morand S, Thongmalayvong B, Somphavong S, Siew CC, Ting PJ, Suputtamongkol S, Saensombath V, Sanguankiat S, Tan BH, Paboriboune P, Akkhavong K, Chaisiri K (2017) Intestinal parasitic infection and environmental water contamination in a rural village of Northern Lao PDR: identification of infection risk. Korean J Parasitol 55(5):523–532. https://doi.org/10.3347/kjp.2017.55.5.523

Ribolzi O, Rochelle-Newall E, Dittrich S, Auda Y, Newton PN, Rattanavong S, Knappik M, Soulileuth B, Sengtaheuanghoung O, Dance DB, Pierret A (2016) Land use and soil type determine the presence of the pathogen Burkholderia pseudomallei in tropical rivers. Environ Sci Pollut Res 23(8):7828–7839. https://doi.org/10.1007/s11356-015-5943-z

Salam A, Nogushi T, Pothitan R (2006) Community forest management in Thailand: current situation and dynamics in the context of sustainable development. New Forests 31 (2):273–291. https://doi.org/10.1007/s11056-005-7483-8

SBSTTA (2017) Scenarios for the 2050 vision for biodiversity, note by the executive secretary, subsidiary body on scientific, technical and technological advice CBD/SBSTTA/21/2, 15 September 2017

Sibertin-Blanc C, Therond O, Monteil C, Mazzega P (2018) The entity-process framework for integrated agent-based modeling of social-ecological systems. *This volume, chap.5*

Spierenburg M (2012) Getting the message across biodiversity science and policy interfaces – a review. GAIA 21(2):125–134. https://doi.org/10.14512/gaia.21.2.11

Turgut NY (2008) The influence of ecology on environmental law: challenges to the concepts of traditional law. Environ Law Rev 10(2):112–130. https://doi.org/10.1350/enlr.2008.10.2.012

United Nations Development Programme Thailand (2014) Country brief, strengthening the governance of climate change finance in Thailand. UNDP, Bangkok, 14 pp

United Nations Development Programme, United Nations Environment Programme, Government of Thailand (2010) Poverty/environment initiative framework in Thailand. Project document, strengthening inclusive and economic decision making for environmentally sustainable pro-poor development. UNDP, Bangkok, 29 pp

United Nations Environment Programme (UN Environment) (2015) The United Nations environ-
    ment programme and the 2030 agenda: global action for people and the planet. UNEP, Nairobi,
    8 pp
Van Panhuis WG, Choisy M, Xiong X et al (2015) Region-wide synchrony and traveling waves of
    dengue across eight countries in Southeast Asia. Proc Natl Acad Sci 112(42):13069–13074.
    https://doi.org/10.1073/pnas.1501375112
Von Schirnding Y, Onvizu W, Adede AO (2002) International environmental law and global public
    health. Bull World Health Organ 80:970–974
Wilcove DS, Giam X, Edwards DP, FIisher B, Koh LP (2013) Navjot's nightmare revisited:
    logging, agriculture, and biodiversity in Southeast Asia. Trends Ecol Evol 28(9):531–540.
    https://doi.org/10.1016/j.tree.2013.04.005
World Bank (2009) Strategic environmental assessment in East and Southeast Asia. A progress
    review and comparison of country systems and cases. In: Dusik J, Xie J (authors) World Bank's
    technical assistance program "Developing practice and capacity of strategic environmental
    assessments in East Asia and Pacific Region", 69 pp. Available from http://siteresources.
    worldbank.org/INTEAPREGTOPENVIRONMENT/Resources/
    SEAprogressreviewinEAPFINAL.pdf. Accessed 25 Feb 2018

Chapter 7
Architectural Pattern for Health Forecasting, Surveillance and Early Warning Systems

Ricardo De Gainza and Christine A. Romana

Abstract The French Institute for Public Health Surveillance (InVS, French Public Health Agency) described its complex activities of monitoring, surveillance and warning into official reports published in 2005, 2006 and 2011. Taking these documents as a starting point, we employed Object-Oriented Analysis (OOA) and Universal Modeling Language (UML) to design the architecture of a system able to suitably perform these activities. The conceptual framework of our modeling work implies studying (1) "risk exposure situation" to environmental health threats of human, animal or vegetal populations and (2) responsibilities of the system in charge of monitoring, reporting and warning in case of unacceptable risks. Three examples of environmental health threats illustrate the model: bluetongue (an insect-borne disease of animal populations presenting serious economic impact), human intoxication by chlordecone (a persistent organochlorine pesticide used until early 1990s in French West Indies for banana weevil borer control) and human intoxication by phycotoxins (natural metabolites produced by marine microalgae), due to ingestion of contaminated seafood.

7.1 Introduction

In 2005, the French Institute for Public Health Surveillance (InVS), a public organization created in 1998 under the authority of the French Public Health Ministry, published a white paper, *"L'alerte sanitaire en France - principes et organisation"*, defining "conditions and organization modes" for the French global warning system at national level (InVS 2005). In fact, the emergence of new health problems and environmental threats in France and other countries (contaminated

R. De Gainza (✉)
Pertina SARL, Paris, France
e-mail: rdegainza@pertina.com

C. A. Romana
UFR of Medicine, University of Paris Descartes, Paris, France
e-mail: cris.romana@invivo.edu

© Springer Nature Switzerland AG 2019
R. Boulet et al. (eds.), *Law, Public Policies and Complex Systems: Networks in Action*, Law, Governance and Technology Series 42,
https://doi.org/10.1007/978-3-030-11506-7_7

blood scandal, emerging of HIV, germs resistance to antibiotics, bioterrorism danger awareness after the 11 September 2001 attacks in the USA, 2003 high-mortality heat wave, etc.) asked for coordinated actions of all French public organizations at every administrative level.

This first report was followed one year after by another document, "Rapport de la mission d'évaluation et d'expertise de la veille sanitaire en France" (Girard et al. 2006), bringing improvements to health safety and health surveillance after having stated the fact that "the implemented system constituted a relatively confuse organization, with a considerably high number of interfaces, where it is often impossible to identify jobs and tasks, and without effective management". The missions then given to the InVS, "permanent observation of population health status", "public health monitoring and surveillance" and "early warning" were ratified by the French Public Health Policy law n°2004-806 (August 9, 2004). This law also adds an InVS mission of "contribution to public health crisis management", providing the Institute rights to access all public or private data needed to attain its goals.

A third report, "La veille et l'alerte sanitaires en France", specifies health surveillance and early warning concepts, surveillance systems structure and roles of each actor (InVS 2011). Health surveillance organization is depicted as constituted by "early warning systems based on periodic structured data collection and production of previously defined indicators" and a "monitoring system able to collect and analyze different kinds of signals". The authors propose that the early warning system must be based "[...] on a very proactive response to selected indicators for epidemiologic hazards, but also on a prospective monitoring on infectious or environmental phenomena of unknown nature that could present threats to public health".

It is interesting to note that, in all three reports, the surveillance and early warning system is described by means of a *functional decomposition,* "because it describes the activities it must accomplish" (Micheau et al. 2012; de Gainza et al. 2013). But, today, mastering of complex information systems is obtained rather by describing it as a set of classes and objects that collaborate with each other to realize system functionalities. System behavior, specified by functionality requirements, is obtained later by objects and classes communicating between them and with the outer world by means of messages (Coad and Yourdon 1993). In the case of surveillance and early warning systems, these messages can be assimilated to signals and/or events. We will propose in this paper an architectural pattern for such a system. This architecture has been conceived by using descriptions contained in the three InVS reports (2005, 2006 and 2011) as requirements for a Public Health Surveillance and Early Warning System. Other international organizations, as the European Center for Disease Prevention and Control (ECDC 2008) use equivalent descriptions.

The architectural pattern described in this publication is a *metamodel* that can be applied to any case of environmental health threat.

7.2   The Problem Scope: The Population Exposure

In our approach, system modeling is based on a simultaneous analysis of the problem domain and the system responsibilities within that domain (Coad and Yourdon 1993). The problem domain is the exposure of human, animal and vegetal populations to health environmental threats. The system responsibilities are to ensure monitoring, surveillance and early warning in case of non-acceptable risks (we will use in this case the term of nonconformity). If an alert is given, the system must ensure execution of actions needed to bring back risk at acceptable levels (we will use in this case the term of conformity).

The threat arises from an encounter between a population (human and/or animal and/or vegetal) and a hazard. The exposure situation (Fig. 7.1) represents such a contact and provides the information needed to assess its risk level (e.g. concentration of a chemical substance). Figure 7.1 shows the model of the exposure situation in Universal Modeling Language (UML) obtained by means of Object-Oriented Anlysis (OOA). UML is a graphic modeling language based on pictograms, usually employed in information systems architecture design. Even if used mostly in software development projects, OOA can be applied to any type of systems and is not limited to Information Technology. UML is based on a metamodel that defines the model elements (the concepts manipulated by the

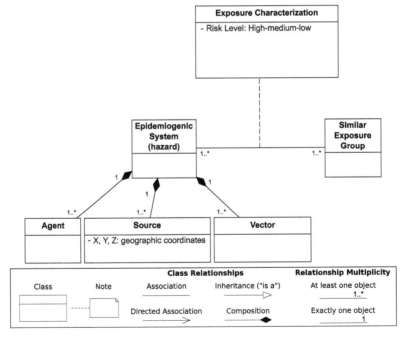

Fig. 7.1 Exposure situation modeled by Object-Oriented Analysis (OOA) in Universal Modeling Language (UML) (http://www.uml.org/)

language) and its semantics (their definition and the sense of its utilization). Each type of UML diagram has a structure (the modeling elements types are predefined) and carries a precise semantics. Together, the different UML diagram types offer a comprehensive view on both static and dynamic system aspects.

In our study's domain, we assimilate hazard to an epidemiogenic system (de Gainza et al. 2013, 2015). This epidemiogenic system is composed of three elements (Dor et al. 2009; de Gainza et al. 2013, 2015) (Fig. 7.1):

- source (e.g.: polluting industry or river, seaweed secreting toxic substances, etc.),
- agent (e.g.: bacteria, virus, parasite, chemical substance, contaminated food, etc.),
- agent vector (e.g.: the air that transports polluting particles, water transporting enterobacteria, an insect transporting and transmitting the malaria's parasite, the hands of a worker of the agri-food industry contaminated by salmonella, etc.).

The epidemiogenic system thus defines threats as arrangements or sets of sources, agents and vectors, related or connected as a whole, that could induce health problems (pathologies) within exposed populations (human and/or animal and/or vegetal).

Populations exposed to a particular epidemiogenic system under similar exposure conditions, constitute a Similar Exposure Group (SEG)[1] (Fig. 7.1). SEGs are always contained in an environment, the anthroposystem, which is composed by one or several sociosystem(s) and one or several natural or artificialized ecosystems (Lévêque et al. 2003). According to Lévêque et al., an anthroposystem belongs to a specific geographic space and evolves over time under the effect of external and/or internal factors. The anthroposystem concept supposes a systemic and dynamic vision of the interactions between human communities and environments, seen as a whole that could engender hazards (high-risk anthroposystem).

At last, the exposure situation characterization, or simply exposure, assembles the information about SEG and epidemiogenic system contact conditions. This information could, for instance, include substance concentration and state (pulverulence, volatility), ambient temperature and ventilation type when studying exposure to a chemical substance on a production chain. Risk level is computed as a two-factor product: plausibility (or probability) and gravity (or impact). Plausibility measures the probability of damage occurrence.[2] Gravity indicates the importance of damages in case of damage occurrence.[3] Exposure characterization properties will vary from one situation to another, but a risk level, estimated or assessed, will always be present.

---

[1] According to standard XP X 43-244 elements of occupational health vocabulary (December 1998), Similar Exposure Group is a group of persons, jobs or tasks presenting hazard exposure of same type and intensity.

[2] Norm NF ISO 31000: 2010.

[3] http://www.bivi.maitriserisques.afnor.org/layout/set/print/sitesautres/maitrisedesrisques/ofm/maitrisedesrisques/ii/ii40/ii4062/1.

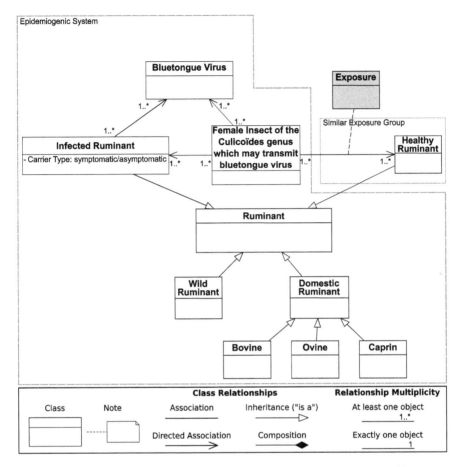

Fig. 7.2 Exposure situation of animal populations to bluetongue virus (BTV), or bluetongue, modeled by Object-Oriented Analysis and Universal Modeling Language, according to terms used in the European Council directive 2000/75/EC of 20 November 2000, article 2. Adapted from de Gainza et al. (2013, 2015). Source: Ministère de l'Agriculture et de l'Alimentation http:// agriculture.gouv.fr

An exposure situation model we carried out (de Gainza et al. 2013, 2015) is focused on a viral disease, the bluetongue, that affects many ruminant species, notably ovine (Fig. 7.2). Bluetongue, a non-zoonotic arboviral disease, affects certain wild and domestic species of cloven-hoofed ungulates. Non-contagious for man and originated in the Southern Hemisphere, Bluetongue strikes Corsica Island since the year 2000 and mainland France, as well as several other European countries, since 2006 (Charbonnier and Launois 2009). The causative agent, the bluetongue virus of the Reoviridae family, is spread through temperate and tropical regions of the world by biting Culicoïdes midges (Diptera: Ceratopogonidae). Ovine, and more rarely bovine, caprine and other domestic and wild ruminants are exposed. Bluetongue is a disease that causes "direct losses (mortality, abortion) and indirect losses (bad quality wool, growth lateness), often giving rise to export blocking" and "important losses for cattle breeders" (Perrin 2007).

In a similar way, it is possible to model exposure to Chlordecone (Fig. 7.3), a pesticide used to fight banana weevil in the French West Indies between 1972 and 1993. Chlordecone is listed as one of the Persistent Organic Pollutants (POP), chemical substances resistant to biotic and abiotic degradation. Strongly bioaccumulative, the pesticide can be transported over long distances and is ubiquitously found through the islands ecosystem (Bulletin Epidémiologique Hebdomadaire 2011; de Gainza et al. 2013). Because of its very high stability, low solubility and strong affinity with organic matter, the soils of the former banana plantations are today widely contaminated.

In terms of impact over human population health, Chlordecone was rated "possibly carcinogenic for man" (2B) by the International Agency for Research on Cancer (IARC) (Bulletin de veille sanitaire Antilles-Guyane 2012).

Chlordecone exposure model of Fig. 7.3 clearly identifies four types of exposure situation (in blue color). Exposure of consumers to foodstuff will include properties such as foodstuff contamination level, consuming frequency and exposed population age. Exposure of waterside residents to water will have, for instance, properties describing use of water made by exposed populations, e.g. washing, peeling or water filtering.

7.3 System Responsibilities According to the InVS in France

The InVS defined in 2011 the conceptual framework to be followed by French institutions in charge of Public Health surveillance,[4] early warning and response (Fig. 7.4). This conceptual framework must be applied at each deployment level (peripheral, intermediary, central) of early warning systems implementations (InVS 2011).

According to this conceptual framework, triggering of health surveillance early warnings is a four-step process:

(a) Signal collection (see Fig. 7.5).

Two signal types are considered:

(i) routinely collected indicators, reflecting individual or population health status or environmental exposure to hazardous agents: e.g. notifiable disease cases count, environmental pollutants concentration;

----

[4]According to the InVS, surveillance is a set of actions whose purpose is to identify unusual or abnormal events presenting a risk for human health.

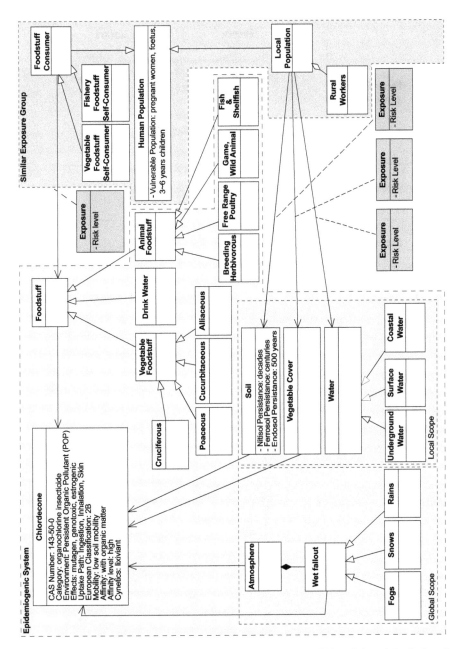

Fig. 7.3 Human populations exposure to chlordecone modeled by Object-Oriented Analysis and Universal Modeling Language. Ingestion of contaminated vegetables, meat and water is the first source of human risk. Three other risk exposure situations are due to human and animal populations contact with locally contaminated water, vegetable cover and soil. This model was obtained by interviewing domain experts. Adapted from de Gainza et al. (2013, 2015). Source: Ministère de l'Agriculture et de l'Alimentation http://agriculture.gouv.fr

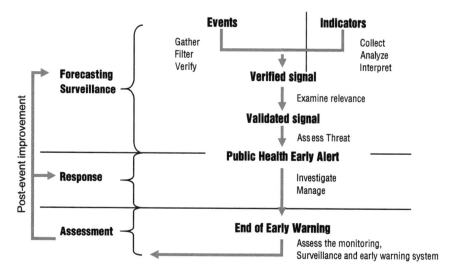

Fig. 7.4 Monitoring, surveillance and early warning systems conceptual framework (InVS 2011). Source: Santé Publique France https://www.santepubliquefrance.fr/

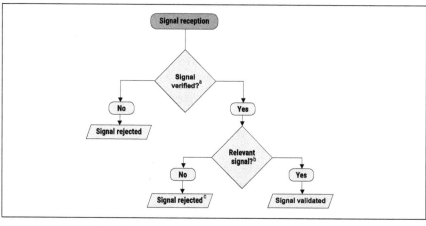

Fig. 7.5 Decision tree for events or indicator signal validation, according to French National Institute of Health Surveillance (InVS 2011). Source: Santé Publique France https://www. santepubliquefrance.fr/

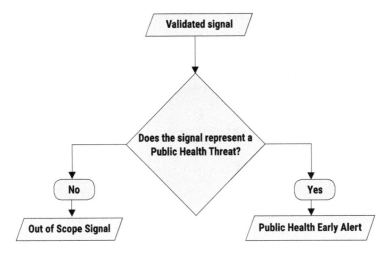

Fig. 7.6 Threat assessment and early warning characterization, according to the French National Institute of Health Surveillance (InVS 2011). Source: Santé Publique France https://www. santepubliquefrance.fr/

(ii) events related to public health threats: e.g. abnormal clinical presentation of hospital admitted patients, polluted site neighbors complaints, suspicious increase of unknown human pathology cases in a particular place or even short news from local newspapers.

(b) assessment of collected signals, following the InVS decision tree schematized in Fig. 7.5;

(c) threat impact assessment and alert triggering, as shown in InVS decision trees of Figs. 7.6 and 7.7;

(d) Response: early warnings trigger the response step, which includes two interactive approaches: alert management and complementary investigation (Fig. 7.8). Signal verification must confirm the existence of the event at the origin of the warning and cross-check data with other sources which may provide additional information on the event.

7.4   Which Architecture for Such a System?

We mean, as system architecture, "the conceptual model that defines the structure, behavior, and more views of a system" (Wikipedia). The responsibility of a surveillance, early warning and response system is to survey exposure situation. The exposure situation is then the source of the surveyed events and indicators.

Monitoring and surveying the anthroposystem to raise Public Health early warnings implicitly implies the existence of three essential elements (de Gainza et al. 2015):

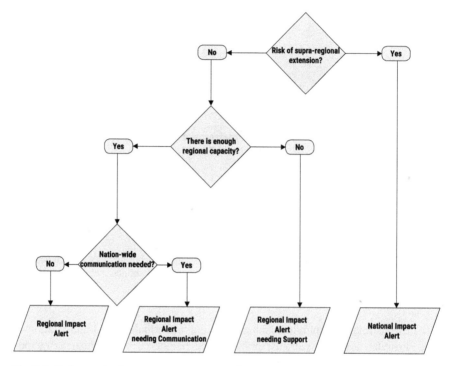

Fig. 7.7 Early warning impact assessment, according to the French National Institute of Health Surveillance (InVS 2011). Source: Santé Publique France https://www.santepubliquefrance.fr/

- *consensus* about the definition of the "wealthy" and "ill" states of the anthroposystem population, including, notably, a metric associated to "normality" and "pathology". The exposure situation model (see Fig. 7.9) shows that we can conceive exposure situation assessment as a comparison of the exposure situation being assessed with a standard exposure situation that we call *Referential Framework*. The referential framework takes account of existing consensus about "acceptable" or "unacceptable" exposure situations for a given threat in a given moment. Referential framework varies over time because it depends on social, economic, scientific and political consensus. Risk level thus expresses the gap measured during assessment.
- *knowledge on factors* (variables) that could allow to bring risk from unacceptable to acceptable level[5];
- *suitable tools* to bring back the "ill" anthroposystem to "normality", notably an institutional and political organization adapted to hazard and vulnerabilities of affected populations.

---

[5]Exposure situation risk level was defined in this study as join effect of two factors: probability of occurrence of damages on human or animal population health and potential severity of damages in case of occurrence (vulnerability) (de Gainza et al. 2015).

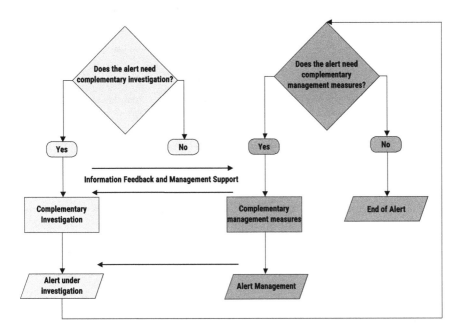

Fig. 7.8 Early Warning complementary investigation and management, after initial assessment and immediate management measures, according to the French National Institute of Health Surveillance (InVS 2011). Source: Santé Publique France https://www.santepubliquefrance.fr/

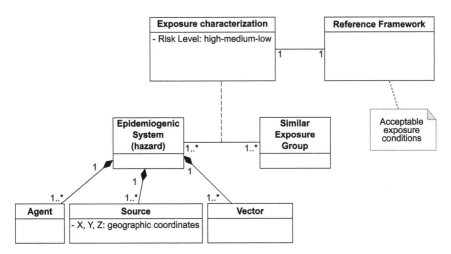

Fig. 7.9 Assessment: determining exposure situation risk levels by comparing its characterization with a baseline exposure, the threat's referential framework. The referential framework takes account of existing consensus about "acceptable" or "non-acceptable" exposure situations for a given threat in a given moment. Adapted from de Gainza et al. (2013, 2015). Source: Ministère de l'Agriculture et de l'Alimentation http://agriculture.gouv.fr

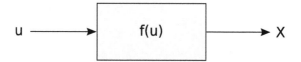

Fig. 7.10 Anthroposystem modeled as a block diagram. Adapted from de Gainza et al. (2013, 2015). Source: Ministère de l'Agriculture et de l'Alimentation http://agriculture.gouv.fr

The anthroposystem can then be modeled as a block diagram, a "dynamic system characterized by a set of output parameters X representing health and environmental conditions on which we can act by means of a command or control signal u" (Fig. 7.10).

Systems that survey and control the exposure situation (thought as encounter of a similar exposure group with the epidemiogenic system), monitor control variables X and manage actions in case of early warning. An early warning is triggered whenever a measurement raises an anomaly, that is, a nonconformity of the exposure situation with respect to the reference framework. The system must then generate the appropriate control signal u.

From this point of view, surveillance and control of a threat, in a given perimeter and territory, is a three steps iterative process:

- inventory of exposure situations, corresponding to contact points between epidemiogenic system and similar exposure groups,
- assessment of exposure situations, as systematic comparison between exposure situations and the referential framework, the "acceptable exposure situation", to assign a risk level,
- execution of corrective actions, namely acting on the anthroposystem, to bring it back to an "acceptable" state whenever risk level exceeds "acceptable" considered levels.

The implementation of these tasks and their iteration frequency will be specific to each threat.

To take account of this description, we added three new entities to the anthroposystem model: the *exposure measurement system*, the *exposure assessment system* and the *exposure control system*, respectively specialized in "surveillance", "assessment" and "management" tasks. The resulting configuration is that of a feedback system, represented in Fig. 7.11.

The "investigation and management of an early warning after initial assessment and immediate management actions" task, as proposed by the InVS (Fig. 7.8), has no dedicated entity in our feedback system of Fig. 7.11. This task is managed by the "exposure assessment system" block.

To summarize, the InVS gives the name of "surveillance systems" to systems operating on known environmental threats in order to detect signals that could trigger corrective action. We propose to represent such systems as *negative feedback*

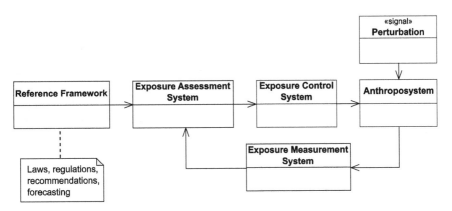

Fig. 7.11 Monitoring and early warning activities as a feedback system in UML. Adapted from de Gainza et al. (2013, 2015). Source: Ministère de l'Agriculture et de l'Alimentation http://agriculture.gouv.fr

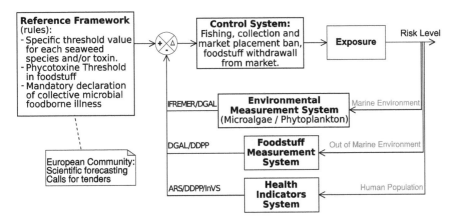

Fig. 7.12 Object-oriented model in UML of monitoring and early warning system for human intoxication with marine microalgae toxins. Adapted from de Gainza et al. (2013, 2015). Source: Ministère de l'Agriculture et de l'Alimentation http://agriculture.gouv.fr

systems (Åström and Murray 2008; Micheau et al. 2012). In practice, several measurements and/or control devices can coexist when surveying environmental threats to health. The topology of our feedback system can then include imbrications or chaining and Control Theory[6] provides the formal tools to represent and treat them. For instance, in the case of surveillance and early warning for microalgae phycotoxins, three measurement devices were found (Fig. 7.12) (de Gainza et al. 2015):

---

[6]Control Theory analyzes the properties of dynamic systems on which it is possible to act through commands.

- Phycotoxins surveillance on shellfish, performed by the French Institute for Research and Exploitation of the Sea (IFREMER), industrial and commercial public institute (EPIC status). IFREMER, in collaboration with the Directorate General for Food (DGAL, French ministry for agriculture and food), performs quality control of seafood products and marine environment (Decree of June 5, 1984 modified). Shellfish surveillance is carried out by the Phytoplankton and Phycotoxins Monitoring and Surveillance Network (REPHY), in their natural environment and in production and professional fishing areas.
- Outside shellfish natural marine environment (distribution logistics centers, markets and export control centers), follow-up is regulated by the Surveillance Plan managed by the DGAL[7] and implemented by the Departmental Population Protection Directorates (DDPP). Administration takes suitable measures whenever an early warning is confirmed.
- Collective Microbial Foodborne Intoxications (TIAC), are subject to mandatory notification to the InVS.[8] This obligation allows InVS, Regional Health Agencies (ARS) and DDPP to perform epidemiological and veterinary survey in order to identify TIAC responsible foodstuff and implement preventive measures.[9]

7.5   Discussion and Conclusion

Until 1984, the early warning organization in France was mainly based on notifiables diseases to sanitary authorities, mostly of infectious origin (Bouvet 1985). Starting from 1985, new measures were taken in order to develop the InVS surveillance system at national and international levels (InVS 2005):

- 1985, deployment of physicians and laboratories network and better treatment of information from the national reference laboratories;
- 1988, creation of the Nosocomial Disease Fight Committees in hospitals achieving early warning organization;
- 1992, creation of the National Public Health Network (RNSP) to strengthen surveillance activities, notably on infectious diseases and environmental health. Raise of diseases such as HIV, legionellosis or type C hepatitis, focused surveillance strategies on creation of laboratories and physician networks;

---

[7]A surveillance plan is an animal, vegetable or foodstuff random sampling campaign in order to assess a given contaminant prevalence within a given population and, consequently, consumer exposure to that hazard. http://agriculture.gouv.fr/plans-de-surveillance-et-de-controle. Accessed 5 Feb 2018.

[8]In application of article 3113-1 (D11-1) of Public Health Code and Circular concerning notification, investigation and response required in case of Microbial Foodborne Intoxication outbreak (JoRf #1487).

[9]Decree #2002-1089, August 07, 2002.

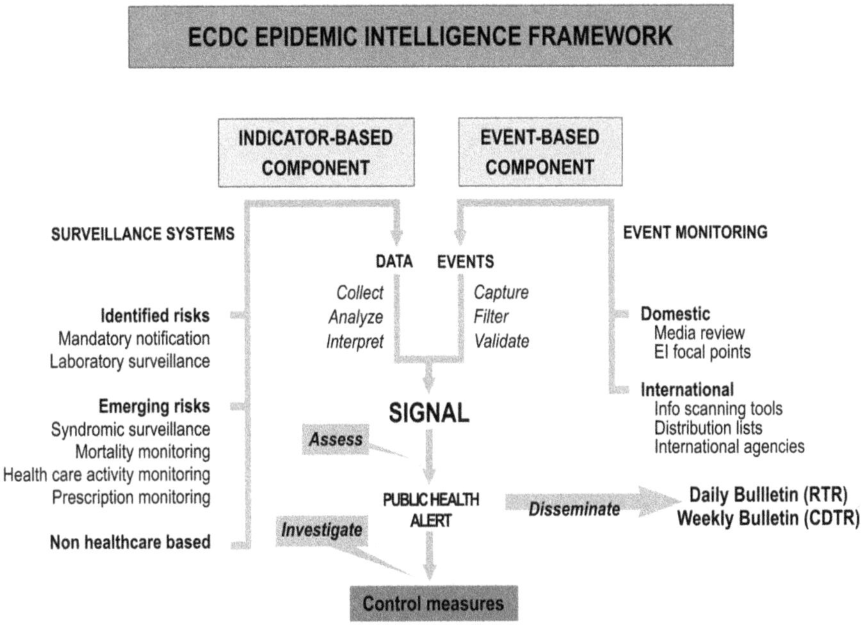

Fig. 7.13 Conceptual framework of monitoring, surveillance and early warning systems, according to the European Center for Prevention and Disease Control (adapted from ECDC 2008)

- 1998, lead poisoning becomes the first non-infectious disease subject to mandatory declaration in France;
- 1998, creation of the InVS, whose missions are public health sanitary monitoring, surveillance and early warning, completed by the Public Health Law of August 9 2004, which added a mission of crisis management contributions.
- 1990–2004, creation of international networks on transmissible diseases, charged of early detection of travel or alimentary health threats in Europe and, in 2004, of the European Centre for Disease Prevention and Control (ECDPC),[10] based in Sweden. ECDPC Epidemic Intelligence Framework covers activities of detection, identification, verification, analysis, assessment and investigation on events presenting potential threat to public health (Fig. 7.13) (ECDC 2008).

In France, early warning systems were built by successive contributions, particularly related with problems of infectious origin and, often, consecutively to sanitary

---

[10]The European Centre for Disease Prevention and Control (ECDPC) is an EU agency aimed at strengthening Europe's defences against infectious diseases. ECDC works in three key strategic areas: it provides evidence for effective and efficient decision-making, it strengthens public health systems, and it supports the response to public health threats. ECDC core functions cover a wide spectrum of activities: surveillance, epidemic intelligence, response, scientific advice, microbiology, preparedness, public health training, international relations, health communication, and the scientific journal Eurosurveillance.

crisis. This led, according to Jean-Yves Grall (2013), to "a health surveillance system [...] built essentially with successive layers, sometimes as reaction to crisis, in fact without global coherence" and induces "responsibility fragmentation in surveillance matters [...] split between several national agencies" (Fig. 7.14).

Five French national agencies are involved in health surveillance and early warning (Grall 2013): the French National Agency for the Safety of Medicines and Health Products (ANSM), the Nuclear Safety Authority (ASN), the Institute for Public Health Surveillance (InVS), the Agency of Biomedicine (ABM) and the Agency for Food, Environmental and Occupational Health & Safety (ANSES). Fragmentation is due, according to Grall (2013), mainly "to a succession of legislative measures taken in a disjointed way".

From the beginning of the twenty-first century, InVS strategy in surveillance matters increasingly incorporated environmental themes. But it is the high-mortality heat wave of spring 2003 that led to a different perception of sanitary early warning, showing that preventing populations from environmental health hazards needs use of statistical tools not specific to the environment, such as the number of emergency services admissions and mortality rates (InVS 2005).

Presently, early warnings are not only based, as stated, on factors measuring known threats but also on systems forecasting unknown phenomena (InVS): in 2009, for instance, the InVS conducted a study in order to inventory, class and prioritize environmental health threats with forecasting purposes (Dor et al. 2009). Objects-Oriented knowledge modeling provides an integrative point of view to approach surveillance systems. Figure 7.15 shows how Objects-Oriented description structures and contextualizes the functional description formulated by the InVS. Applied to surveillance and early warning in human, animal or vegetal health domain, this kind of analysis and modeling approach allows a better understanding of complex systems, such as health environmental threats, including multidisciplinary, multisectoral and territorial issues.

According to de Gainza et al. (2013, 2015), graphical modeling enables seamless information sharing between institutional actors in charge of surveillance and early warning. It also acts as an interface between expert's knowledge and operational tasks, particularly in IT projects. Application of this tool to forecasting, development and management of health surveillance and early warning systems could deliver better information and resource sharing, more precise characterization of surveillance and early warning target exposure situations and clearer management options when forecasting risks. Moreover, knowledge management in human, animal and vegetal health should become a European cooperation matter, as managers of different European countries translate directives in the field in different manners.

Systems built with this approach will last longer, as it is based on the identification of stable aspects of the domain, that is, on classes and objects strictly describing the problem domain and system responsibilities (Coad and Yourdon 1993).

This work constitutes a first approach and some important subjects would still need additional modeling: specific referential frameworks, for instance, in order to obtain operational definitions of risk level; assessment systems; objects properties; compliance of currently deployed information systems; role of non-governmental

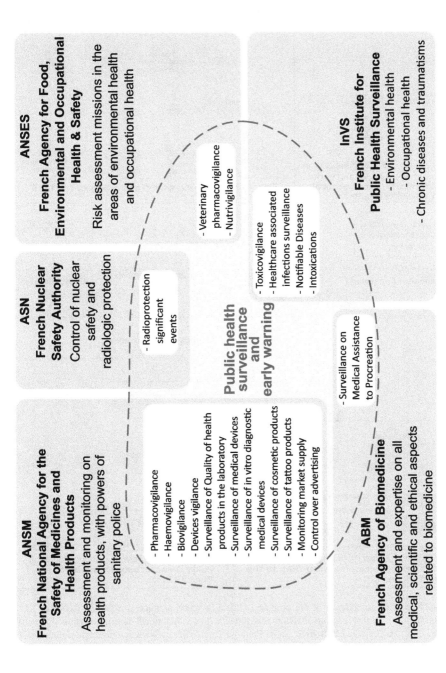

Fig. 7.14 Illustration of the fragmentation of the French health surveillance and early warning system. Missions of each agency are briefly described. Adapted from Grall (2013)

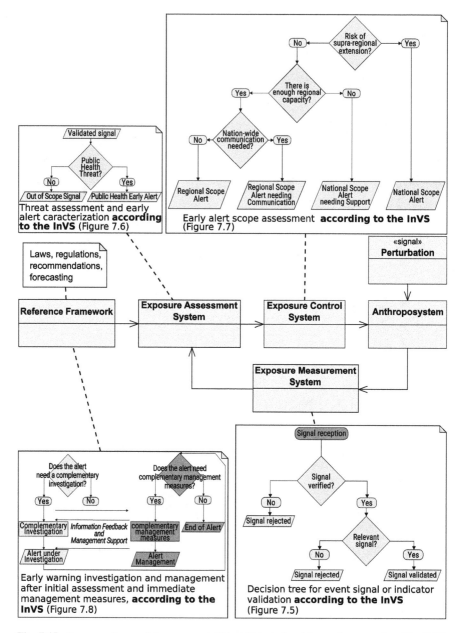

Fig. 7.15 Correspondence of the proposed Object-Oriented architectural pattern (see Fig. 7.11) with French National Institute of Health Surveillance (InVS) functional description (flow diagrams, Figs. 7.5, 7.6, 7.7 and 7.8, Source: Santé Publique France https://www.santepubliquefrance.fr/)

organizations and whistleblowers (journalists, physicians, farmers, breeders), appeared in the nineties and whose intervention can trigger, as Chateauraynaud stated in 2009, "multiple logics, going from surveillance to controversy, normalization or conflict".

References

Åström KJ, Murray RM (2008) Feedback systems: an introduction for scientists and engineers. Princeton University Press, Princeton. Available via http://www.cds.caltech.edu/~murray/books/AM05/pdf/am08-complete_22Feb09.pdf. Accessed 5 Feb 2018

Bouvet E (1985) Une nouvelle conception de la surveillance des maladies transmissibles. Bulletin Epidémiologique Hebdomadaire 20:81–82

Bulletin de Veille Sanitaire Antilles-Guyane (2012) Chlordécone aux Antilles: Actualités des études sur la santé n°4, April, 17 pp

Bulletin Epidémiologique Hebdomadaire (2011) Chlordécone aux Antilles: bilan actualisé des risques sanitaires n° 3-4-5, February, 48 pp

Charbonnier G, Launois M (2009) La fièvre catarrhale ovine. Collection Les savoirs partagés, CIRAD, Montpellier

Chateauraynaud F (2009) Les lanceurs d'alerte et la loi. Experts 83:44–47

Coad P, Yourdon E (1993) Analyse orientée objets. Masson, Paris

de Gainza R, Romana CA, Fosse J (2013) Modélisation des situations d'exposition et des dispositifs de surveillance et d'alerte pour la maîtrise des risques sanitaires (MaRiSa). Application à des exemples de dangers pour le consommateur et pour la santé animale (phycotoxines micro-algales d'origine marine, chlordécone, salmonelles et virus de la fièvre catarrhale ovine). Étude ministérielle DGAL-CCAP-2011-098, Ministère de l'Agriculture, de l'Agroalimentaire et de la Forêt, Paris, 89 pp

de Gainza R, Romana CA, Fosse J (2015) L'analyse orientée objets comme outil d'aide à la gestion des risques sanitaires. Notes et Etudes Socio-Economiques 39:107–130. Available via http://agriculture.gouv.fr/lanalyse-orientee-objets-comme-outil-daide-la-gestion-des-risques-sanitaires. Accessed 5 Feb 2018

Directive 2000/75/CE du conseil du 20 novembre 2000. FCO-Info. Available via http://www.fcoinfo.fr/spip.php?article69. Accessed 5 Feb 2018

Dor F, Karg F, Robin-Vigneron L (2009) Recensement et identification des menaces environnementales pour la santé publique. Environnement Risques & Santé 8:507–517. https://doi.org/10.1684/ers.2009.0302. Available via http://www.bdsp.ehesp.fr/Fulltext/410732. Accessed 5 Feb 2018

ECDC (2008) Surveillance of communicable diseases in the European Union – a long-term strategy: 2008–2013. European Centre for Disease Prevention and Control, Solna. Available via https://ecdc.europa.eu/en/publications-data. Accessed 5 Feb 2018

Girard J-F, Lalande F, Salmi L-R, Le Bouler S, Delannoy L (2006) Rapport de la mission d'évaluation et d'expertise de la veille sanitaire en France. Rapport technique, Ministère de la santé et des solidarités, Paris. Available via http://www.ladocumentationfrancaise.fr/rapports-publics/064000736/index.shtml. Accessed 5 Feb 2018

Grall J-Y (2013) Réorganisation des vigilances - Rapport de mission. Direction Générale de la Santé, Paris. Available via http://www.bdsp.ehesp.fr/Fulltext/473133. Accessed 5 Feb 2018

Institut de Veille Sanitaire (2005) L'alerte sanitaire en France - principes et organisation. Contribution de l'InVS à l'élaboration du Plan Régional de santé publique Plan d'action relatif à l'Alerte et à la Gestion des situations d'Urgence Sanitaire. Rapport d'un groupe de travail de l'Institut de veille sanitaire, Paris. Available via http://www.ladocumentationfrancaise.fr/rapports-publics/054000589/index.shtml. Accessed 5 Feb 2018

Institut de Veille Sanitaire (2011) La veille et l'alerte sanitaires en France. Ministère de Travail, de l'Emploi et de la Santé, Institut de Veille Sanitaire, Paris. Available via http://opac.invs.sante.fr/ doc_num.php?explnum_id=7055. Accessed 5 Feb 2018

Lévêque C, Muxart T, Abbadie L, Weil A, van der Leeuw S (2003) L'anthroposystème: entité structurelle et fonctionnelle des interactions sociétés-milieux. In: Lévêque C, van der Leeuw S (eds) Quelles natures voulons-nous? Elsevier, Paris, pp 110–129

Micheau J, Dor F, de Gainza R, Romana CA (2012) Menaces environnementales et systèmes d'alerte: conceptualisation et enjeux. Environnement Risques & Santé 11(6):493–501. Available via http://www.jle.com/fr/revues/ers/e-docs/menaces_environnementales_et_systemes_ dalerte_conceptualisation_et_enjeux_293245/article.phtml?tab=texte. Accessed 5 Feb 2018

Perrin A (2007) Contribution au développement de vaccins capripox viraux recombinants contre la Fièvre Catarrhale Ovine. Thèse de doctorat, Université Montpellier II - Sciences techniques du Languedoc, Montpellier. Available via http://bluetongue.cirad.fr/FichiersComplementaires/ 2007_Perrin_These_VaccinsCapripoxFCO.pdf. Accessed 5 Feb 2018

Chapter 8
Water Management and Development: The Limits of Coordination

Pierre Mazzega, Dominique Le Queau, Christophe Sibertin-Blanc, and Daniel Sant'Ana

Abstract Actors involved in water resource management and development policies from the large water cycle (at the river basin level) to the small water cycle (drinking water, sanitation and distribution) are numerous and diversified, in their institutional and economic positioning, as well as in the logic of the approaches they develop. In view of the expectations of a comprehensive policy in this field and of the obviously limited results obtained so far, the phasing of these approaches and the coordination of these actors is a major axis of the actions to be carried out in order to better manage the water resources. We argue the need for an explicit and assumed strengthening of the coordination of water stakeholders at all levels of governance. We question the reasons for these partial successes and failures and the way to overcome these difficulties, questions renewed on the basis of recent experiences. In particular, interdisciplinary and intersectoral collaboration using new hybrid modeling approaches (coupling multi-agent system, geographic information system, equation models, cellular automata, etc.), allows to precisely simulate the scenarios of evolution of water resource management and development, to assess *ex ante* their social, economic and environmental impacts and to anticipate the contribution of an

P. Mazzega (✉)
UMR5563 GET Geosciences Environment Toulouse, CNRS/University of Toulouse, Toulouse, France

Strathclyde Centre for Environmental Law and Governance (SCELG), University of Strathclyde, Glasgow, UK
e-mail: pierre.mazzegaciamp@get.omp.eu

D. Le Queau
Aeronautics and Space Science and Technology Foundation, Toulouse, France
e-mail: dominique.lequeau@fondation-stae.net

C. Sibertin-Blanc
Institute of Research in Computer Science of Toulouse, University of Toulouse 1, Toulouse, France
e-mail: sibertin@ut-capitole.fr

D. Sant'Ana
University of Brasilia, LACAM, Faculty of Architecture and Urbanism, Brasilia DF, Brazil
e-mail: dsantana@unb.br

© Springer Nature Switzerland AG 2019   153
R. Boulet et al. (eds.), *Law, Public Policies and Complex Systems: Networks in Action*, Law, Governance and Technology Series 42,
https://doi.org/10.1007/978-3-030-11506-7_8

increased coordination of water stakeholders in a logic of development-friendly actions.

8.1 Introduction

Our purpose is to share some thoughts on the management and development of water and associated resources. The positions expressed here result mainly from informal exchanges between the authors and some researchers and water actors. In order to discuss on the basis of concrete questions, we start from two observations: (1) target 7.C of the Millennium Development Goals (MDG 2012) "to halve, by 2015, the percentage of the population with no access to safe drinking water or basic sanitation services" under Objective 7 "ensuring a sustainable environment" has not been achieved in many countries (as already reported by MDG Rep. 2010); (2) the objectives of good status of waters covered by the Water Framework Directive (WFD 2000) are not achieved in many European hydrological basins (CPEC 2015), such as in France.[1] Many obstacles to achieving the Millennium Development Goals, or the objectives of the Water Framework Directive and other similar programs result from poor coordination of water and development actors. This regardless of the territorial base or of the social-ecological context (Oström 2009) of their implementation. Consequently, the absence of political or strategic objectives aiming at a better coordination of the actors is a gap that should be filled.

We propose here a systemic analysis of these deficiencies, based on a reflection on the existing system in France. In Sect. 8.2 we will quickly clarify the context of water management and the development of associated services. In Sect. 8.3 we present the bases of a method of analysis of public action[2] and public policies apprehended as complex systems (Bourcier et al. 2012; Mazzega et al. 2012). In Sect. 8.4, we develop a critique of mono-disciplinary approaches to water management and development (hereinafter WMD). Because of their too narrow field of analysis, these "panacea" approaches (see Oström 2007 in a broader context) claim to solve the problems of WMD outside the sociological and political frameworks of its concrete integration within a larger system of relationships, whose mere description—not to mention the dynamics—requires a wide interdisciplinary spectrum. We argue that the same factors limiting the success of these disciplinary approaches are also at work in the deficit of data production and sharing that would be required for the implementation of WMD (Sect. 8.5) or for the development of dedicated public services. In Sect. 8.6, we argue the interest of an interdisciplinary, integrative

---

[1]"France is committed, in the context of the Grenelle for Environment, not to ask for postponement in achieving the good ecological status of surface water bodies for more than a third of them", in MEDDE (2012), p. 34.

[2]Political sociology tends to favor the analysis of public action from now on (Hassenteufel 2008) to the detriment of life cycle analysis of public policies (Howlett and Ramesh 2003).

(including the large and the small water cycles) and multi-agents modeling approach of the WMD. The conclusions of this study are presented in Sect. 8.7.

8.2 Water Management and Development

8.2.1 Water Policy in France

The organization of water management in a European watershed—for example the Adour-Garonne basin in South-West France (~116,000 km^2)—derives from several normative levels (Gazzaniga et al. 2011): it is, first of all, the Water Framework Directive (WFD 2000) which mainly aimed at restoring the good ecological status of water and aquatic environments by 2015. At the national level, the laws of 1964, 1984 and 1992 lay the foundation for modern water resources management with: the principle of water management by watershed divided into water bodies, each being supposed to have a unified approach; the creation of basin committees that bring together representatives of key stakeholders; the objectives of preserving aquatic environments; water raised to the status of common heritage of the nation. The law on water and aquatic environments of 2006 (LEMA 2006) reinforces this system in order to reach the new objectives set by the WFD (2000). It also establishes the right of access to drinking water on conditions economically acceptable for each natural person.

At the level of each basin, with the support of the Basin Water Agency, the Basin Committee adopts a master plan for water planning and management (SDAGE in French) designed in a participatory manner, soliciting numerous associations (user associations, environmentalists, etc.) and other public or private water actors. Thus, the SDAGE 2010–2015 (SDAGE 2010) adopted for the Adour-Garonne basin in 2009, was revised in 2016.[3] It is accompanied by a program of measures and schemes of development and management by sub-basins. In France, the municipalities are responsible for investments and for the management of drinking water and sanitation services. This entire system and its continual adaptation to the environmental and ecological, but also economic and legal evolution, aims mainly to "stop the degradation of the environmental resources and ecosystems, resulting from the demographic growth, the economic development and the urbanization at the global scale" and to "provide universal access to drinking water and sanitation" as recalled by the Ministry of Environment and Sustainable Development in 2007 (MEDD 2007).

---

[3]The SDAGE 2016–2021 of the Adour-Garonne basin is available on http://www.eau-adour-garonne.fr/fr/quelle-politique-de-l-eau-en-adour-garonne/un-cadre-le-sdage/sdage-pdm-2016-2021.html Accessed 8 Feb 2018.

8.2.2 A Partial Success

However, the initial objectives set by the Directive could not be achieved every-where in 2015 (the objective having been lowered in France to reach the good ecological status of only 2/3 of the water bodies). Some reasons for this are:

- the initial state of some sub-basins was too degraded to allow the good status of the water to be reached by this deadline whatever the measures adopted (AEAG 2006);
- the existence of conflicts between the logic of "good" management of water with the logic—for example—of urban development, conflicts that are not solved by the legal opposability of the provisions envisaged by the SDAGE;
- the opposition of certain social groups to adapt those of their practices deemed incompatible with the objectives of the water policy;
- the reluctance, or even the refusal, of certain public authorities to implement unpopular provisions (e.g. restrictions on the use of the resource) particularly when they are likely to exclude part of their electorate.

Apart from the first point, these "reasons" all relate to a lack of coordination between the different actors in the water cycles. This syndrome ends up no longer being perceived: the great water cycle (at the scale of the hydrological basins) is totally dissociated from the small water cycle (drinking water, sanitation, water from the urban and rural zones) while both are primarily human affairs—those of resource users and operators, managers and policy-makers. Indeed, these policies are expressed in a complex context whose structure and evolution result from an interweaving of biogeochemical and physical processes, legal constraints and socio-logical, political and economic contingencies.

8.2.3 The Ontological Substrate of Water Policy

This occultation of the socio-ecological context which conditions the management and development of water resources mask a problematic disjunction: almost all the actors involved in water management at the basin scale seem to inhabit a sealed world, separated from the world of the actors of the small water cycle. Obviously, this is a fictional frontier. Indeed, in France at least, the modalities of financing water resources make drinking water users pay some of the externalities (pollution, degradation of aquatic environments) resulting from the activities of other social agents, farmers (surplus of nitrates and pesticides) and manufacturers (solid waste leachates, industrial wastelands, etc.) in particular (Bommelaer et al. 2011). The small water cycle finances the preservation of the large cycle, the Water Agencies redistributing a portion of the royalties collected from consumers towards the achievement of the priority objectives of the SDAGEs (Cour des Comptes 2015, p. 82 sq.). Moreover, behind water cycles there are water actors for which we use here a typology based on the different roles associated with the use of water: users, operators, managers, politicians. Thus, the management of public drinking water and sanitation services is dispersed in more than 30,000 municipalities or groups of municipalities.

Water policies structure a set of measures and mechanisms, more or less coherent, legalized by the public authorities, and aimed at managing and developing water resources from a given territory. They rely on legal and economic instruments (e.g. Shaw 2005), use an administration and deploy services, solicit different actors according to an *ad hoc* typology. From one country to another, the options chosen to implement national water policies are contrasted and differ in their mode of governance, financing mechanisms, nature of the water market, distribution of responsibilities and the accountability of programs, possible regulation of water services, links between land ownership and ownership of water resources (Sekhar et al. 2011), risk management systems (Pozzer and Mazzega 2013), etc.

In this sense any water management and development system is the expression of a specific political philosophy. The major political controversies are reflected in (and feed on) the debate over the right to water (Drobenko 2010), the water right, the economy and the governance of water. To take up a central idea of the book by Wight (2006), which deals more specifically with International Relations—and with a distortion of "politics" to "policy"—any (water) policy is an ontology (domain).

8.3 Resources, Actors, Norms

8.3.1 A Normative Ontology

It is indeed only a "domain" ontology because it is circumscribed by the semantics of the political sector concerned, and thus placed in a hierarchical gradation between core ontology (which theorizes time, space, relationship and other substantive concepts) and ontologies of more specialized applications. But any ontology is basically[4] "a formal, explicit specification of a shared conceptualization" (Grüber 1995) that "defines (specifies) the concepts, relationships, and other distinctions that are relevant to modeling a domain." (Grüber 2009). Strictly speaking, a policy *is* not a domain ontology but it *is based* on it. Even if it is a necessary fiction, the sharing of the conceptualization that it conveys is guaranteed by the authority that monopolizes the public domain and in the same movement legalizes the categorizations, the concepts and their interrelations, such as imposed through sectoral policy.

This authority is the State, through its administrations and services. This legalization is not necessarily legitimate for the actors concerned, as it often appears from

---

[4]As recalled by Guarinao et al. (2009), here is one of the first informal definitions of "ontologies" in the sense of computer science: "explicit specifications of conceptualizations". For the philosophical approach of ontology, see Varzi's book (2010).

the low effectiveness of measures decided but not applied. The State, however, is not an individual (singular agent) with cognitive abilities. It is made up of many actors, services, offices, organizations, etc. who may develop divergent opinions or oppose each other (Henry 2004). The ontology on which a water policy is based is nowhere explicit. In spite of this, the categorizations[5] that policies uses and publishes, the typologies that it validates or creates, the relations that it endorses or establishes, are imposed in the social field. The legalized ontology becomes a normative ontology established on the basis of the State's authority.[6]

8.3.2 *Manage and Develop Resources*

A simple terminological analysis of water policies (as well as of the description of the devices they deploy) shows that the terms with the most frequent and most diverse occurrences refer to material resources and to a lesser extent to cognitive resources. These terminological statistics are linked to the ontology revealed through the text describing the public policy concerned (Mazzega et al. 2011). We conjecture that this preferential attachment to resources structures many other public policies in which even the terms designating agents or actors are used under the category of (human) "resources".

In short, the State manages or develops water resources and resources mobilized for water management (infrastructures, finance, data and knowledge, etc.). It develops and diffuses a certain representation of these resources by means of a water policy. It targets the behaviors of water actors (mainly perceived through groups or social categorizations): pay for access, reduce pollution, share a finite resource, ensure a balanced allocation, participate and decide, etc. From this point of view, the representation of resources—concerning their state and evolution, the processes having an impact on these states—are all elements of an implicit public ontology (see Fig. 8.1). These representations of resources and their management form a sort of cognitive meta-resource that is taken up and used by various social groups and actors.

Usually, a public policy does not describe the ecological or environmental processes that induce the dynamics of interactions between natural resources because these processes are conceived as given, outside the field of public action. It is the case of the well-known environmental services that nature would lavish. On the other hand, the policies make explicit the role of the actors and their perceived behaviors as impacting the resources, directly or indirectly. The resources and their interactions are thus, in part but inextricably, socialized via the actors. Reciprocally, from the point of view of political ontology, interactions between actors are mainly

---

[5]For example, the State institutes certain resources as such, for example the "basin" in the 1964 law, the division into "hydrographic zones", the "water bodies", etc.

[6]This paragraph finds support in P. Bourdieu's course on the State (Bourdieu 2012).

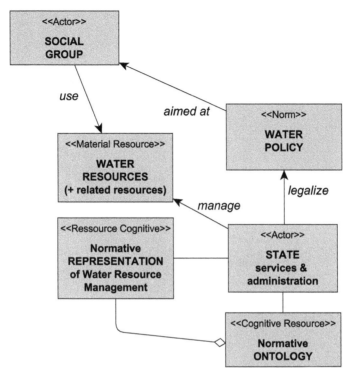

Fig. 8.1 The State institutes, manages and develops water or water-related resources, through a water policy that aims to circumvent the behavior of social groups, this policy being designed on the basis of an implicit ontology (see text)

mediated by the state of resources and its evolution. This "dual" viewpoint is fundamental because policies focus on the management of resources—central and well-designed entities of their ontology—and little or no on the coordination of actors.

8.3.3   Water Actors and Their Coordination

Although simple, the diagram of Fig. 8.1 summarizes the core of the political philosophy that the state diffracts both in society and through the prism of its internal divisions, by the institution of public policies. Two essential elements are omitted— omission without any doubt necessary for the action of the State:

- social groups are composed of individuals (who can belong simultaneously to several identified groups);

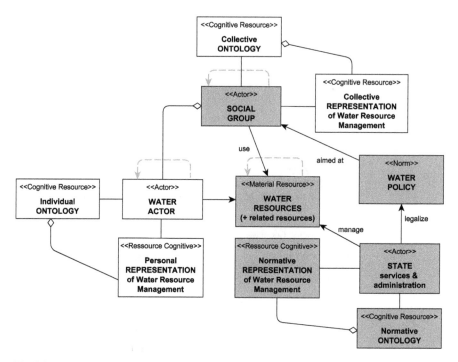

Fig. 8.2 Social groups and the individual actors that compose them also produce representations of resources within their own empirical ontologies. The dashed gray arrows suggest the existence of many other interactions between actors, between social groups, or between resources (e.g. biogeochemical, physical and ecological processes). Note: this figure incorporates the graph of Fig. 8.1

- each social group, each individual, is likely to produce a representation of resources, inserted in an idiosyncratic ontology (admittedly not explicit and not having the logical rigor of which the artificial intelligence is a requirement).

This broadening of our point of view is shown schematically in Fig. 8.2. The normative ontology of the state does not equally pervade all the representations of social groups, individuals, or all agents of the State. Generally, it ignored the empirical ontologies developed by social groups (collective or cultural ontology) and individuals.

Yet everything is organized, starting with governance, as if the normative ontology underlying public policy was shared in a homogeneous and uniform way among all actors. As a result, no explicit and assumed form of coordination is seen as necessary or supported at any level of governance. Thus, the coordination of the actors does not belong to the political ontology. This could explain why the coordination of the actors does not appear, to date, with the programs of the development goals, nor with the horizon of the sectoral policies. Assuming that there is a water policy whose objectives are accepted by all the actors involved, it does not follow that these actors have the same understanding of the objectives pursued, the same idea of the means to achieve them.

8.4 Value of Partial Approaches

Therefore, what do we mean by "coordination" of actors? To answer this question, we will show how some approaches that give preponderance to one dimension of the management and development of water resources are in fact embedded in systems of coordination of actors. Or at least that actors' coordination is supposed and necessary for the achievement of the objectives that the organization of public action in terms of governance, economy or resource engineering in particular. Thus, each angle of analysis and organization of the resource management becomes very valuable and induces its potential of expected effects by traversing the apparent detour from the creation of favorable conditions for the development of collective action.

8.4.1 Embedding of Governance

"Coordination" is different from "governance", understood as a multi-level organization mode of "the conditions that should be met for collective action regulation systems to maximize the normative expectations of its members". This definition borrowed from Lenoble and Maesschalck (2003) (and that they criticize) requires to found any theory of governance on a theory of the norm. On the other hand, the major condition for cooperation between the actors[7] is their adherence to a common project, and a coherent and compatible understanding between each group or actor. The coordination of actors, diverse in their social and cultural identities, in their public and private roles, in their paths, requires a dialogue, a minimum awareness of the ontology that each group has, and is out of reach of the normativity of its political ontology.

It then involves obtaining a minimum agreement on what the water policy actually covers, on its *a priori*, expectations and objectives and on the nature of the means it intends to implement. Lastly, agreement on the differentiated participation that it assumes on the part of each type or group of actors, regardless of their insertion in a governance scheme. The participatory conception of policies (or of measures that they promote) is not necessarily enough to ensure the support of all the actors in the project, and their projection into a future vision, which public policy tries to organize, after many negotiations and distortions. The normative nature of a

---

[7]Coordination is seen as a "dependency management": even hostile actors coordinate to confront one another. By cooperation we mean a positive coordination that aims to produce a synergy between actors.

legalized policy does not guarantee that the actors conform to it nor only share the most central conceptions of the political ontology on the basis of which it was conceived.[8]

The organizational schema of the political governance of resource management and development is essential here because it identifies the actors that must be worked on to foster cooperation at each concrete level of the implementation of the public policy, and for which partial objectives, on the basis of a shared understanding of the stakes.[9]

8.4.2 Embedding in Economy

In France, the Law of 21 April 2004 introduces a principle of recovering the cost of services related to the use of water (costs for the environment and resources included) from users of the resource. In 2007, the price of the drinking water and sanitation service in the big cities was lower than the European average price, while 90% of the major urban water purification costs investments were already made (Bommelaer et al. 2011). However, these prices show a great disparity from one region to another and between municipalities. These prices (including the operating costs of drinking water and sanitation services) are statistically higher in those that have opted for delegated services (Tavernier 2001). In 2008, 72% of the service was distributed among 8500 delegation contracts, the remaining 28% (direct management) being provided by public operators (FP2E 2008). In 2010, the improvement of sanitation efficiency remains one of the priority actions of the water agencies which devote 51% of the total amount of the 2010–2015 measurement programs associated with the SDAGE (see Sect. 8.2).

As we have said, the mechanism of water pricing leads to the transfer of the burden of externalities impacting aquatic resources (especially agricultural and industrial pollution) to consumers who are not responsible for it. Thus, at the level of watersheds, the sustainability of the resource is linked to the organization of this local service, which implies, beyond elected officials and local operators, the responsibility of many stakeholders (Barucq et al. 2010)—local authorities (French "collectivités territoriales"), departments and regions (through their support for investments), National Water Committee (advice on the price of water and quality

---

[8]It is a concrete problem of "alignment" of ontologies, of their coherence. Those of the various groups of actors do not align themselves because of the divergence of interests (for example, in the case of Sivens—see the chapter by C. Sibertin-Blanc in this volume - X. Beulin speaks of "water reservoir (retenue d'eau) "and not of "dam (barrage)"). An issue of conflicts of interest is to make one's own ontology prevail.

[9]In this sense, our interest is in the approach of Lenoble and Maesschalck (2003), which questions the question of the legitimacy of the norm less than "that of the conditions to be met to ensure its practical acceptance".

of services), State services (by water policy), European Union (terms and conditions of directives)—and requires their coordination.

The economic analysis also takes up the question of the optimal allocation of water resources at the level of the hydrological management unit, or even of a large basin. This type of approach takes into account the volumes of water that hydrology provides, the main quantitative uses (drinking water, industry, agriculture, etc.) through the demands associated with consumer profiles, and the associated pricing for each type of use (e.g. Reynaud and Leenhardt 2008). The available raw water comes from the hydrological cycle of the basin considered. This cycle is natural or partly artificial thanks to reserves whose use is left to the discretion of the individuals or the legal persons (when they are private). Part of this water volume can make the purpose of contracts, for example for supporting for the preservation of wetlands during low-water periods. It is interesting to note that, in the present state of our analytical capacities, the allocation of the large-scale resource is considered independently of the system of actors, resources and standards that operate in the management of drinking water and sanitation. The large-scale allocation would somehow determine, *a priori* and from the outside, the amount of water (large cycle) with which the complex game of water consumption (small cycle) can be organized. Identifying an optimum allocation is useful for a planner. But whether it expresses a Nash or Pareto equilibrium, the conditions for identifying such an optimum and its status of scientific result do not make it a tool for consultation and coordination of the actors concerned. The optimality of an allocation does not guarantee the social acceptance of the solution it justifies.

We will only mention the economic treatment of externalities—negative or positive—of the management of water resources, related to other activities (agriculture, industries) or to environmental services. We first note that a variety of solutions proposed to take into account these cross-sectoral aspects of water management, also accords with the same principles that guide water policies (especially the polluter-payer principle). Everything is a matter of interpretation, and therefore of negotiation and power relations between actors occupying specific positions in the economic system and on the social and political stage. The economic evaluation of the benefits (monetarisable or not; public health; preservation of biodiversity; amenities, etc.) resulting from environmental services (Birol et al. 2008) and the evaluation of the interest of the various key players to maintain these services or to choose other options, pose serious methodological difficulties.

Contingent valuation (Alberini and Kahn 2009) is currently one of the preferred tools and implemented in a spatial planning context, which can impact water resources (Birol et al. 2009; Ferreira and Marques 2015). This approach is criticized by economists (Venkatachalam 2004) but remains one of the few available based on a scientific approach. The production of these assessments proceeds by aggregating the individual statements of a willingness to pay, at the level of key social groups identified (key stakeholder groups). These statements are collected without taking into account the social environment, power relations, organizational or administrative constraints, legal norms, etc. This truly ontological omission is ambivalent. Although it is probably essential for designing and conducting stakeholder surveys, it is also likely to cause a lack of robustness of the results. The information that the contingent valuation provides is irreplaceable and would benefit from being immersed in a context of analysis based on the various forms of socialization of the actors.

8.4.3 Embedding in Engineering

Most major works or infrastructure projects are designed between engineers and present the mathematical evidence of a perfect fit to the problems they propose to solve. These pharaonic projects of transfer of water between basins (for example from the Rhone to Catalonia—ERN 2012, various projects of inter-basin transfers in India—NWDA 2012), of diversion of watercourses or of large dams in particular for the production hydro-electric production,[10] confirm the choice to favor certain economic activities in certain territories to the detriment of others. Most of these projects are supported by major international financial institutions. However, they are still faced with the expectations of a part of civil society (e.g. in India: Gupta and Deshpande 2004; Amarasinghe and Sharma 2008; in Brazil: Zhouri 2011), some of whose NGOs are spokespersons (e.g. BIC 2012). For local and even regional actors, there is a strong tension between benefiting from the economic windfalls (real or supposed) that a local development boosted by such projects can drain and preserve a sustainable environment—in the social-ecological sense of the term—certainly subject to evolution but to the more balanced rhythm of endogenous dynamics.

The technical aspect of the development of networks of water supply, sanitation, recovery and wastewater treatment is played out on more local scenes—the city, the neighborhood, the village—and therefore is less publicized. The economies of scale associated with these large networks are hampered by transportation and maintenance costs (e.g. road works). At present, the recovery of investments in the development and maintenance of these networks is achieved at the scale of several decades, horizon too distant and risky for many private companies. This is a real economic and regulatory engineering that is developing to ensure the conditions for sustainable financing of these services at costs acceptable for the consumer, and sustainable for the service providers (OECD 2009; da Cruz and Marques 2013). At the same time, rapid urban development, more or less governed by territorial and urban policies according to the level of national economic development, is leading to increasing demands for drinking water and wastewater treatment (Dziegielewski et al. 1993; Nauges and Wittington 2010).

---

[10]E. g. in the Amazon—Belo Monte dam on the Xingu, Santo Antônio and Jirau dams on Madeira, between countries: Guajará-Mirim project between Bolivia and Brazil, Garabi project between Argentina and Brazil, Corpus Christi hydropower project between Argentina and Paraguay, etc., IIRSA (2012).

Alternative approaches described as decentralized, supposedly adaptable, resilient and flexible (OECD HWP 2009) are envisaged or implemented, particularly in rural areas and emerging cities,[11] for which engineering solutions are indispensable technological inputs: water reuse (treated or untreated) for various uses, rain harvesting tanks, groundwater pumping, domestic filtration, etc. Many private companies are engaging in these rapidly expanding markets, particularly in emerging or developing countries,[12] which may also be of interest to developed economies.

This is also an issue of political philosophy: the organization of decentralized systems of water supply and treatment operates in fact a disengagement (or non-commitment) of the State in services for the public, by postponing on households the financial burden of access to drinking water and wastewater treatment for which a deficient service has negative impacts on public health. Two major questions arise: (a) at what scale should these alternative approaches be organized? (b) at which territorial scale should the transition from state ownership to private sector ownership take place in the case of centralized or decentralized approaches? These issues can only be usefully addressed by taking into account the technical opportunities, the socio-economic and institutional constraints, the environmental and urban conditions of each concrete situation.

8.5   Water Services and Data

Two aspects deserve special attention because they can contribute to the improvement of these assessments: the development of services *for* the environment and the production of data.

---

[11] In Brazil, since 2016, the Federal District and Brasilia have experienced the first water rationings linked to an unprecedented shortage of the resource. After conducting a study on the final domestic uses in various administrative sectors of the District (Sant'Ana 2011) and their modeling (Sant'Ana and Mazzega 2017), a project is underway (2017–2018) on the analysis of the potential of use rainwater and wastewater in public buildings (schools, hospitals, subways, shopping centers, airports, etc.), financed by the Water, Energy and Sanitation Regulatory Agency DF (PI: Dr. D. Sant'Ana).

[12] For example, in India, private ownership of land is transferred to groundwater, so that by investing in a well, a pump, and a truck, an individual can develop a private water supply service. This water supplies the customer who has installed a tank at home. The delivered water being likely to be polluted by deteriorated sewage pipelines, the filtering is carried out with the tap, in the kitchen by means of an ad hoc device.

8.5.1 Services et Innovations

The decentralized approach of water supply and sanitation and the creation of services are also a driving force of development. The viability of these services is based on scientific and technological innovation. Apart from services directly related to water, there is a high potential for innovation that can contribute to the transformation of practices, in several sectors of activity that have an impact on water resources.

Satellite remote sensing makes possible the emergence of new services that monitor, in near-real time, the levels of nitrates or moisture in agricultural soils, determine the growth stages of field crops or predict their productivity with some reliability and quantified accuracy. Remote sensing also allows to carry out a very precise cadastral survey of the agricultural parcels, used for declarations and requests for aid of the Common Agricultural Policy. Spatial observation of the color of the water also gives precise information on the eutrophication of the surface waters. This information leads to optimizing irrigation and controlling the use of agricultural inputs, which reduces operating costs without reducing productivity and limits the pollution of water tables and rivers. *In situ* sensors are being developed, their data entering into the composition of various indicators of the chemical and biochemical quality of water bodies,[13] and leading to significant progress in eco-toxicology and public and environmental health.

Actors' coordination intervenes here in the process of valorization of the innovation, by favoring the creation of companies and the organization of the market of the services and expertise. It is a real value chain that can be organized, driven by the interrelations between social actors, institutions and industry. Thanks to these interactions, the virtuous process of value creation is then facilitated by the emergence of places of debate where the distribution of responsibilities between public institutions and private operators as well as between ministries and local authorities can be discussed, and where training courses are organized for new environmental professions.

8.5.2 Water Data

All data collected about the water resource and its management are not useful. On the contrary relevant data is not collected. The collection of various data does not guarantee their compatibility. Access to data—even for non-commercial uses—is more a result of negotiation and exchange than compliance with normative

---

[13]For example, the Adour-Garonne basin is concerned by 33 priority substances identified by the WFD (2000), including 13 "priority hazardous" substances, 8 additional substances identified by Council Directive 76/464 / EEC (1976), and 86 others. Substances covered by the national program against water pollution by certain dangerous substances.

obligations to ensure their accessibility. The development of products adapted to targeted applications is a strong added value to the raw data which, most of the time, are not directly usable. These few remarks again draw the issues of actors' coordination. Controlling the production, holding and distribution of data (as well as the publication of statistics) is a form of control that is used knowingly by any organization providing services in this field. The publication of objective statistics can also filter information or make a tactical use of this information (Pettigrew 1972), opportunities that are used by both public authorities and some companies.

Thus, certain data are produced because it is possible and it justifies the activity of agents, without any other actual or even foreseeable use (for example in a context of heritage approach of the recorded information for possible future uses). Other water data remains inaccessible to non-commercial public use, either because it has a strategic dimension for the organization that holds it, or because it is likely to acquire commercial value. However, the use and dissemination of data is often accompanied by a duty to publish or by standards that satisfy the privacy of the information that may be disclosed (for example by imposing the anonymity of their geographic, fiscal, social referencing, or aggregated referencing).

8.5.3 Data Needs for Management Tools

In contrast, many data do not exist, are unreliable or are only available on media that require a transfer on a digital support. Some of this data would be needed to conduct a more rational management of water resources, linking the large and small water cycles. They would be useful for evaluating public water policies, or for documenting sustainable tools for management and resource development. The creation of databases and information systems precisely meets the needs of a program that would bring together and coordinate the skills and efforts of many agents, from users to institutional managers and scientists. In the MAELIA platform[14] (Gaudou et al. 2014; Mazzega et al. 2014; Therond et al. 2014) for example, which allows the simulation of the impacts of the public policies of water in the Adour-Garonne basin, in the South-West of France, we gather a large spectrum of data:

- Environmental data (topography, pedology, hydrology and geochemistry);
- Land cover and land use data and their changes;
- Data specific to agricultural techniques and productions (crop productivity, plot register, yields, agricultural prices, amount of aid, etc.),
- Socio-economic data (requests for drinking water, for irrigation and industry, tariffs, etc.), or
- Demographic data and scenarios;
- Data from simulations of regional impacts of climate change.

---

[14]http://maelia-platform.inra.fr/ (accessed January, 2018).

Other information relates to the behavior of key stakeholders—farmers' choice of crop rotation procedures, irrigation strategy, mobilized technologies, dam management method, but also volumes of water withdrawn, volumes discarded, etc. These data are used to calibrate the functioning of the modeling platform before using it for the construction of prospective scenarios for the evolution of the resource (March et al. 2012), related economic activities and territories on the horizon 2030. In addition to collecting data from the institutions that manage them, their formatting and integration into a GIS that provides the spatial layers of the multi-agent system, their harmonization are required to verify integrity constraints which guarantee the consistency of the model.[15] Some other pieces of information are incomplete and requires making modeling choices.[16]

The removal of such ambiguities improves the performance of the platform and leads to more and more realistic integration of the small water cycle into the large hydrological cycle and the multi-scale dynamics of territorial development. However—the leitmotif of this contribution—its construction also requires the coordination of many actors.

8.6 Support of Modeling

How to favor the cooperation of the actors within complex systems where dynamically intersect multi-level decision-making processes, economy of the commons, regulation, actors' games and environmental constraints? How to take into account—and in charge by the various territorial communities or the industrial sectors—, the environmental externalities? How to prioritize them in new services to rationalize and improve water management? The interests of the actors, the issues they envision, imagine or promote, are unlikely to change on their own. Should not we then work on their representations (or ontologies) and on how they evolve under the effect of external pressures or constraints specific to the actors' games? The modeling approach is a way forward to help achieve these ends.

---

[15]Using modeling terminology: "Integrity constraints are restrictions on the instantiation of entities and relationships that provide the ability to interpret the concrete model as a description of a coherent and achievable world." (Sibertin-Blanc et al. 2018, *this volume*).

[16]For example, we have the volumes of raw water distributed by municipality without knowing exactly where the water was taken, in what body of water—river, lake, hollows, canal, underground water—essential information to assess the impact of the water uses on the water cycle.

8.6.1 Integrative Modeling

Companion modeling (Barreteau et al. 2013)—designed through participatory processes—is very useful in identifying, illustrating and sometimes resolving conflicts arising from resource management. It facilitates the harmonization of behaviors through an awareness of actors who can, at least virtually, get out of the system in which they are positioned, and analyze the impact that their actions may have on its highly interactive dynamic, and the risks they thus incur to their environment. The vices of the models—stylization of the facts, omission of dynamics estimated of second rank, analytical reduction of the complexities, etc.—are the somewhat virtues of the modeling process—explanation of assumptions, sharing of knowledge, testability (falsifiability) of hypotheses and modes of representation, possibility of improving representations, confrontations with data, etc.

Thanks to pioneering work, and to the increase of numerical computation performances, the hybrid modeling of social-ecological systems (or eco-anthropo-geosystems)—combining multi-agent system, geographical information system and equation models—is increasingly allowing to couple the dynamics of the biosphere, the geophysical and geochemical environment, and an anthroposphere (combining economy, rational actors' games, social structures, legal and social norms, governance multilevel). This type of modeling brings together the latest disciplinary scientific innovations, harmonizes them, integrates them into a simulation platform. These new approaches will allow, at least to a certain extent, to go beyond the distinction between individualism and methodological holism by integrating them into a single virtual device. The synergy of companion modeling and hybrid modeling leads to the production of tools for simulating social, economic and environmental impacts, and the effects of the management and development policies for water resources.

8.6.2 Modeling Collective Action and Coordination

Much work has been done to understand the dynamics of collective action (beginning with Mr. Olson's seminal work—1971) and coordinating actors (e.g. Mailliard et al. 2007). The formalization goes far beyond the decontextualized representations of game theory (e.g. Axelrod's classic book 1984), and is rich in experiences and surveys of actors—users, politicians, managers, operators, companies, administrators, judges, etc.—operating in real situation. Recent modeling work based on the sociology of organized action (Crozier and Friedberg 1977) leads to the evaluation of the social acceptance of the implementation of agricultural public policies (Sibertin-Blanc et al. 2006; Sibertin-Blanc 2018; Adreit et al. 2011) or water policies, based on surveys and interviews. Various scenarios can be constructed that—all things being equal—simulate the effects of structures and cooperation between agents, at the most significant levels of governance and at relevant territorial scales.

Modeling of urban water management and sanitation services can be integrated into the modeling of water resources management at the watershed scale at a high level of abstraction that builds on invariants, the existing similarities between different contexts (e.g. Brazil versus France). Such a modeling platform is then instantiated on the contextual data of the watershed or water basin in question and the cities and rural areas it includes: demographic, economic, sociological, environmental data (geology, rainfall, hydrology, impacts of climate change, etc.). and geographical data (land cover and land uses, uses of soils, transport networks and infrastructure, etc.) (see Sect. 8.5.2).

8.6.3   Concrete Perspectives

Beyond the mobilizable elements of the theory (in the various disciplines concerned), the global understanding of the concrete conditions of the coordination of the actors will be made possible and will enable to overcome specific difficulties of water management and development through a work associating these same actors. The sharing of experiences and points of view engendered by the multiplicity of ontologies carried by the various actors is favored. This will allow to identify rules, to make guiding hypotheses or to formalize regularities revealed by these virtual interactions. In short, the understanding of collective action requires new modes of collaboration in original partnership frameworks where knowledge is shared from all points of view and co-builds the new knowledge required to overcome certain management, development and governance problems of water resources.

8.7   Conclusion

Obstacles to achieving "good" water management and development practices—the criterion of achieving such objectives could be the achievement of the development goals considered from the nationally to the municipal level—are largely underestimated. We argue here that the weakness, if not the absence, of consensus on water management and development objectives, the relativity of the views of the different actors combined with the lack of dialogue and coordination, are part of these obstacles too poorly taken into account. Other obstacles stem from this central limitation: lack of intersectoral policy; solutions advocated from a too small or unilateral vision of actual problems; lack of acquisition, consistency and access to water data; delay in the development of environmental services related to water. A detailed understanding of these barriers sets the conditions for overcoming them through inter-stakeholder, intersectoral, interdisciplinary, inter-agency approaches.

We do not question the relevance of disciplinary approaches to water management and development (see Sect 8.4), nor the usefulness of the solutions they advocate. Each of them is objectively grounded and develops a specific rationality. However, their partial and reductive nature jeopardizes the expected benefits. These approaches are to be articulated methodically (a methodological option being modeling) and to be immersed in a broader cognitive and informative environment, allowing for example to evaluate the impacts that they are likely to induce outside their intended field of application and of effectiveness (intersectoral issues: water agriculture, water energy, water development of territories, etc.), to take into account the constraints induced by these other fields, and to share the points of view of the other actors (users, managers, politicians, scientists).

However, a last critical point must be mentioned. The ontology underlying the opinion developed in this article is the result of numerous discussions within projects with scientific actors. Do these positions—and therefore the ontology that founds them—have more interest or use than those of other water actors, users of the resource, managers, politicians? Here too, the answer is political: it depends on the place one intends to give to scientific knowledge (which is not all knowledge) in the political process of management and development of water resources. Nevertheless, we advocate a rapprochement of scientific-theoretical-applicative approaches towards the concrete problems of organization of water management and development, on the one hand, and correlatively closer and intentional collaboration between scientific circles and water actors and decision makers.

The achievement of the Millennium Development Goals in 2015 has met with many difficulties, in line with the ambitions of the United Nations project, challenges that persist and oppose the achievement of the new Sustainable Development Goals.[17] One of the difficulties that seems to us to cross each of these objectives, and that we find in the implementation of water policies at regional, national and local scales, is the lack of consideration for the coordination of the actors and for the conditions for carrying out collective action at all levels of governance of development projects. In this contribution, we have argued this point of view from the analysis of the management and development of water resources, notably by relocating the drinking water supply and sanitation services in a broader context of territorial development and water resources management at the watershed or basin scale.

The development of a participatory hybrid modeling program (see Sect. 8.6) focused on the development of basic sanitation services in a large city, would address key issues of local water resources development and demonstrate the feasibility of the method and its potential contributions for ensuring environmental sustainability.

---

[17]http://www.undp.org/content/undp/en/home/sustainable-development-goals.html.   Accessed 5 Feb 2018.

Acknowledgements Colleagues from the MAELIA project in Toulouse are warmly thanked for the rich intellectual environment they create. Other forums proved to be fertile, such as Working Group 4 "Institutional and societal approaches, in terms of actors and decisions" of the Water Competitiveness Cluster (Montpellier, France), and the Working Group on "Space Services for the Environment" of the STAE Foundation (www.fondation-stae.net/). ADASA Regulatory Agency for Water, Energy and Sanitation of the Federal District; Brazil; http://www.adasa.df.gov.br/), through the *Projecto de Pesquisa sober viabilidade de sistemas prediais de aproveitamento de águas pluviais and reúso de águas cinza em edificações do Distrito Federal* (PI: D. Sant'Ana), allows the continuation of a fruitful dialogue, involving researchers, teachers, students and water professionals, between Brazil and France.

References

Adreit F, Roggero P, Sibertin-Blanc C, Vautier C (2011) Using Soclab for a rigorous assessment of the social feasibility of agricultural policies. Int J Agric Environ Inf Syst 2(2):1–20. https://doi.org/10.4018/jaeis.2011070101

AEAG (2006) État des ressources. Agence de l'Eau Adour-Garonne. Information available via http://www.eau-adour-garonne.fr/fr/etat-des-ressources-gestion-quantitative.html. Accessed 5 Feb 2018

Alberini A, Kahn JR (eds) (2009) Handbook on contingent valuation. Edward Elgar, Cheltenham

Amarasinghe UA, Sharma BR (2008) National river linking project: analyses of hydrological, social and ecological issues: overview of the workshop proceedings. In: Amarasinghe UA, Sharma BR (eds) Strategic analyses of the National River Linking Project (NRLP) of India, Series 2. Proceedings of the Workshop on Analyses of Hydrological, Social and Ecological Issues of the NRLP, New Delhi, 9–10 October 2007. International Water Management Institute, Colombo, pp ix–xxiii

Axelrod R (1984) The evolution of cooperation. Basic Books, New York

Barreteau O, Bots PWG, Daniell KA, Etienne M, Perez P, Barnaud C, Bazile D, Becu N, Castella J-C, Daré W, Trebuil G (2013) Participatory approaches. In: Edmonds B, Meyer R (eds) Simulating social complexity: a handbook. Springer, Berlin, pp 197–234

Barucq C, Ait-Kaci A, Enrich J-J (2010) Les services publics d'eau et d'assainissement en France. Données économiques, sociales et environnementales. FP2E – BIPE, Paris. Available via http://www.fp2e.org/userfiles/files/publication/etudes/12684096832_Rapport_BIPE_FP2E_2010.pdf. Accessed 5 Feb 2018

BIC (2012) Latin America: problem project. Bank Information Center, Washington, DC

Birol E, Koundouri P, Kountouris Y (2008) Using economic valuation techniques to inform water resources management in the southern European, Mediterranean and developing countries: a survey and critical appraisal of available techniques. In: Koundouri P (ed) Coping with water deficiency. Springer, Berlin, pp 135–155

Birol E, Koundouri P, Kountouris Y (2009) Assessing the economic viability of alternative water resources in water-scarce regions: combining economic valuation, cost-benefit analysis and discounting. Ecol Econ 69(4):839–847. https://doi.org/10.1016/j.ecolecon.2009.10.008

Bommelaer O, Devaux J, Tremblay M, Noel C (2011) Le financement de la gestion des ressources en eau en France. Etudes & Documents n°33, Commissariat Général au Développement, Paris. Available via http://www.side.developpement-durable.gouv.fr/EXPLOITATION/DEFAULT/doc/IFD/IFD_REFDOC_0510976/le-financement-de-la-gestion-des-ressources-en-eau-en-france Accessed 5 Feb 2018

Bourcier D, Boulet R, Mazzega P (eds) (2012) Politiques publiques systèmes complexes. Hermann, Paris

Bourdieu P (2012) Sur l'Etat. Cours au Collège de France 1989–1992. Raisons d'Agir/Seuil, Paris

Council Directive (1976) Council directive 76/464/EEC of 4 May 1976 on pollution caused by certain dangerous substances discharged into the aquatic environment of the Community. Available via http://eur-lex.europa.eu/ Accessed 5 Feb 2018

Cour des Comptes (2015) Les agences de l'eau et la politique de l'eau: une cohérence à retrouver. Cour des Comptes, Paris. Available via https://www.lemoniteur.fr/articles/les-agences-de-l-eau-et-la-politique-de-l-eau-une-coherence-a-retrouver-29077953 Accessed 5 Feb 2018

CPEC (2015) Directive-cadre sur l'eau et directive sur les inondations - mesures à prendre pour atteindre le «bon état» des eaux de l'Union européenne et réduire les risques d'inondation. COM (2015) 120 final, Commission au Parlement Européen et au Conseil, Bruxelles. Available via http://ec.europa.eu/environment/water/water-framework/pdf/4th_report/COM_2015_120_fr. pdf. Accessed 5 Feb 2018

Crozier M, Friedberg E (1977) L'Acteur et le Système. Point Seuil, Paris

Da Cruz N, Marques R (2013) A multi-criteria model to determine the sustainability level of water services. IWA. Water Asset Manage Int 9(3):16–20. Available via http://eprints.lse.ac.uk/59754/ Accessed 5 Feb 2018

Drobenko B (2010) Le Droit à l'Eau: une Urgence Humanitaire. Ed. Johanet, Paris

Dziegielewski B, Opitz EM, Kiefer JC, Baumann DD (1993) Evaluating urban water conservation programs: a procedures manual. American Water Works Association, Denver

ERN (2012) European Rivers Network; Information available via http://www.rivernet.org/rhonebarcelone/welcome_f.htm Accessed 5 Feb 2018

Ferreira S, Marques R (2015) Contingent valuation method applied to waste management. Resour Conserv Recycl 99:111–117. https://doi.org/10.1016/j.resconrec.2015.02.013

FP2E (2008) Les services publics d'eau et d'assainissement en France - Données économiques, sociales et environnementales, 3° ed., FP2E - BIPE, Paris

Gaudou B, Sibertin-Blanc C, Therond O, Amblard F, Auda Y, Arcangeli JP, Balestrat M, Charron-Moirez MH, Gondet E, Hong Y, Lardy R, Louail T, Mayor E, Panzoli D, Sauvage S, Sanchez-Perez JM, Taillandier P, Van Bai N, Vavasseur M, Mazzega P (2014) The MAELIA multi-agent platform for integrated analysis of interactions between agricultural land-use and low-water management strategies. In: Alam SJ, van Dyke Parunak H (eds) MABS 2013, LNAI 8235. Springer, Berlin, pp 85–100. https://doi.org/10.1007/978-3-642-54783-6_6

Gazzainga J-L, Larrouy-Castéra X, Marc P, Ourliac J-P (2011) Le Droit de l'Eau. Litec, Paris

Grüber TR (1995) Toward principles for the design of ontologies used for knowledge sharing. Int J Human-Comp Stud 43(5–6):907–928. https://doi.org/10.1006/ijhc.1995.1081

Grüber TR (2009) Ontology. In: Ling L, Tamer OM (eds) The Encyclopedia of database systems. Springer, Berlin

Guarinao N, Oberle D, Staab S (2009) What is an ontology. In: Staab S, Studer R (eds) Handbook on ontologies, international handbooks on information systems. Springer, Berlin, pp 1–17. https://doi.org/10.1007/978-3-540-92673-3

Gupta SK, Deshpande RD (2004) Water for India in 2050: first-order assessment of available options. Curr Sci 86(9):1216–1224. Available via http://www.iisc.ernet.in/~currsci/may102004/1216.pdf Accessed 5 Feb 2018

Hassenteufel P (2008) Sociologie Politique: l'Action Publique. Coll. U Sociologie, Armand Colin, Paris

Henry N (2004) Public administration and public affairs, 9th edn. Prentice-Hall Inc, Upper Saddle River

Howlett M, Ramesh M (2003) Studying public policy – policy cycles and policy sub-systems. Oxford University Press, Oxford

IIRSA (2012) Iniciativa para la Integración de la Infraestructura Regional Suramericana. Information available via http://www.iirsa.org/Page/Detail?menuItemId=28 Accessed 8 Feb 2018

LEMA (2006) Loi n°2006-1772 du 30 décembre 2006 sur l'eau et les milieux aquatiques. JORF n°303 (31/12/2006), texte n°3, p. 20285 sq. Available via http://www.legifrance.gouv.fr/ Accessed 5 Feb 2018

Lenoble J, Maesschalck M (2003) Toward a theory of governance. The action of norms. Kluwer Law International, Alphen aan den Rijn

Mailliard M, Amblard F, Sibertin-Blanc C, Roggero P (2007) Cooperation is not always so simple to learn. In: Terano T, Kita H, Deguchi H, Kijima K (eds) Agent-based approaches in economic and social complex systems IV. Springer, Berlin, pp 147–154

March H, Therond O, Leenhardt D (2012) Water futures: reviewing water-scenario analyses through an original interpretative framework. Ecol Econ 82:126–137. https://doi.org/10.1016/j.ecolecon.2012.07.006

Mazzega P, Bourcier D, Bourgine P, Nadah N, Boulet R (2011) A complex-system approach: legal knowledge, ontology, information and networks. In: Sartor G, Casanovas P, Biasiotti MA, Fernández Barrera M (eds) Approaches to legal ontologies: theories, domains, methodologies. Springer, Berlin, pp 117–132

Mazzega P, Boulet R, Libourel T (2012) Graphs for ontology, law and policy. In: Zhang Y (ed) New frontiers in graph theory. InTech Publ., Reijika, pp 493–514. https://doi.org/10.5772/35046

Mazzega P, Therond O, Debril T, March H, Sibertin-Blanc C, Lardy R, Sant'Ana D (2014) Critical multi-scale governance issues of the integrated modeling: example of the low-water management in the Adour-Garonne basin (France). J Hydrol 519:2515–2526. https://doi.org/10.1016/j.jhydrol.2014.09.043

MDG (2012) Millennium development goals. United Nation, New York. Information available via http://www.un.org/millenniumgoals/ Accessed 5 Feb 2018

MDG Rep. (2010) Millennium development goals report. United Nation, Department of Economic and Social Affairs, New York

MEDD (2007) La politique de l'eau en France. L'expérience française au service de l'action internationale. Ministère de l'Ecologie et du Développement Durable, Paris. Available via http://www.side.developpement-durable.gouv.fr/EXPLOITATION/DEFAULT/doc/IFD/IFD_REFDOC_0504186/La-politique-publique-de-l%2D%2Deau-en-France-l-experience-fran%C3%A7aise-au-service-de-l%2D%2Daction-internatio Accessed 5 Feb 2018

MEDDE (2012) Mise en œuvre de la directive-cadre sur l'eau pour un bon état des eaux en 2015. SG/DICOM/BRO/DGALN_12014. Ministère de l'Écologie, du Développement durable, des Transports et du Logement, Paris

Nauges C, Wittington D (2010) Estimation of water demand in developing countries: an overview. World Bank Res Obs 25(2):263–294

NWDA (2012) Inter-basin water transfer. National Water Development Agency, New Delhi. Information available via http://www.india-wris.nrsc.gov.in/wrpinfo/index.php?title=Inter_Basin_Water_Transfer_Links Accessed 5 Feb 2018

OECD (2009) Managing water for all: an OECD perspective on pricing and financing – key messages for policy makers. OECD Environment Directorate Climate, Biodiversity and Water Division, Paris. Available via http://www.oecd.org/env/resources/managingwaterforallanoecdperspectiveonpricingandfinancing.htm Accessed 8 Feb 2018

OECD HWP (2009) Alternative ways of providing water. Emerging options and their policy implications. Report of the OECD Horizontal Water Programme, OECD Environment Directorate Climate, Biodiversity and Water Division, Paris. Available via http://www.oecd.org/env/resources/42349741.pdf Accessed 8 Feb 2018

Olson M (1971) The logic of collective action. Harvard University Press, Harvard

Oström E (2007) A diagnostic approach for going beyond panaceas. PNAS 104(39):15181–15187. https://doi.org/10.1073/pnas.0702288104

Oström E (2009) A general framework for analyzing sustainability of social-ecological systems. Science 325:419–422. https://doi.org/10.1126/science.1172133

Pettigrew AM (1972) Information control as a power resource. Sociology 6(2):187–204. https://doi.org/10.1177/003803857200600202

Pozzer C, Mazzega P (2013) A redução de risco de inundação no Brasil: uma prioridade no quadro legislativo do país. Paranoá 10:25–36. https://doi.org/10.18830/issn.1679-0944.n10.2013. 12121

Reynaud A, Leenhardt D (2008) MoGIRE: a model for integrated water Management. In: Mimeo LERNA. Intern. Congress on Env. Modelling and Software, IEMSS 2008, Barcelona

Sant'Ana D (2011) A socio-technical study of water consumption and water conservation in Brazilian dwellings. PhD Thesis, Oxford Institute for Sustainable Development School of the Built Environment. Oxford Brookes University, Oxford

Sant'Ana D, Mazzega P (2017) Socioeconomic analysis of domestic water end-use consumption in the Federal District, Brazil. Sustain Water Resour Manag. https://doi.org/10.1007/s40899-017-0186-4

SDAGE BAG (2010) Schéma directeur d'aménagement et de gestion des eaux du bassin Adour-Garonne 2010–2015. Comité de Bassin Adour-Garonne. Version présentée au Comité de Bassin le 16 Nov 2009. 143 pp. Available via http://www.eau-adour-garonne.fr/fr/quelle-politique-de-l-eau-en-adour-garonne/un-cadre-le-sdage/sdage-pdm-2010-2015.html. Accessed 8 Feb 2018

Sekhar M, Javeed Y, Bandyopadhyay S, Mangiarotti S, Mazzega P (2011) Groundwater management practices and emerging challenges: lessons from a case study in the Karnataka State of South India. In: Findikakis AN, Sato K (eds) Groundwater management practices. IAHR monographs. CRC Press, Boca Raton

Shaw WD (2005) Water resource economics and policy: an introduction. Edward Elgar, Cheltenham

Sibertin-Blanc C (2018) Analysis of actors' conflicts around the realization of a public equipment. This volume, Chap. 10

Sibertin-Blanc C, Amblard F, Mailliard M (2006) A coordination framework based on the sociology of organized action. In: Boissier O, Padget J, Dignum V, Lindemann G, Matson E (eds) Coordination, organizations, institutions and norms in multi-agent systems. Lecture notes in computer sciences, vol 3913. Springer, Berlin, pp 3–17

Sibertin-Blanc C, Therond O, Monteil C, Mazzega P (2018) The Entities-Processes framework for integrated agent-based modeling of social-ecological systems. This volume, Chap. 5

Tavernier Y (2001) Rapport d'information sur le financement de la gestion de l'eau, n°3081. Assemblée Nationale. Commission des Finances, de l'Economie Générale et du Plan, Paris

Therond O, Sibertin-Blanc C, Lardy R, Gaudou B, Balestrat M, Hong Y, Louail T, Mayor E., Nguyen VB, Panzoli D, Sanchez-Perez JM, Sauvage S, Taillandier P, Vavasseur M, Mazzega P (2014) Integrated modelling of social-ecological systems: the MAELIA high-resolution multi-agent platform to deal with water scarcity problems. In: Ames DP, Quinn NWT, Rizzoli AE (eds) International Environmental Modelling and Software Society 7th International Congress on Environmental Modelling and Software. San Diego, pp 1833–1840. Available via http://www.iemss.org/society/index.php/iemss-2014-proceedings. Accessed 8 Feb 2018

Varzi AC (2010) Ontologie. Coll. Science et Métaphysique, Les Editions d'Ithaque, Paris

Venkatachalam L (2004) The contingent valuation method: a review. Environ Impact Assess Rev 24(1):89–124. https://doi.org/10.1016/S0195-9255(03)00138-0

WFD (2000) Directive 2000/60/EC of the European Parliament and of the Council of 23 October 2000 establishing a framework for Community action in the field of water policy. Available via http://eur-lex.europa.eu/en/. Accessed 8 Feb 2018

Wight C (2006) Agents, structures and international relations – politics as ontology. Cambridge studies in international relations. Cambridge University Press, Cambridge

Zhouri A (2011) A Tensões do Lugar. Hidrelétrica, Sujeitos e Licenciamento Ambiental. Editora UFMG, Belo Horizonte

Chapter 9
Formal Analysis of the Conflictive Play of Actors Regarding the Building of a Dam

Christophe Sibertin-Blanc

Abstract French people were astonished to learn of the death of an opponent to the construction of a dam in the Sivens forest, in the Tarn department (France), during clashes with the police on the night of 25 to 26 October 2014. However, the violence of the means deployed to realize this work and the determination of opponents, together woven in the play of all the actors of this project, foreshadowed the possibility of such a drama. Using a formal analysis framework based on the sociology of organized action, we present a model of this interaction system whose simulation results highlight the overdetermined nature of the emergence of a conflict of extreme intensity. Variations in this model allow the identification of the main determinants of this conflict and to consider other possible futures.

9.1 Introduction

The dam project in the forest of Sivens, initiated by the General Council of Tarn in 2007, consisted in making a water reservoir of 1.5 million m^3 on the course of Tescou, a tributary of the Tarn in the Garonne basin, mainly for irrigation of agricultural land (up to 70%) and support for low water (30%), for a cost of € 8.4 million. This project provoked a strong protest, motivated by the disappearance of 18 hectares of a wetland recognized as "major importance of the department from the point of view of biodiversity" (GéoDiag and Ecogéa 2007; SCOP Sagne 2010), while, oversized, it was not a "suitable solution" (Forray and Rathouis 2014; Forray and Roche 2015).

This opposition manifested itself in two different ways. In June 2012 a Collective with a strong expertise on all the aspects of the project tried, without success, to alert the decision makers and the courts about the insufficiencies of the project. In 2013,

C. Sibertin-Blanc (✉)
Institute of Research in Computer Science of Toulouse, IRIT, Université Toulouse-Capitole, CNRS, Toulouse, France
e-mail: sibertin@ut-capitole.fr

© Springer Nature Switzerland AG 2019
R. Boulet et al. (eds.), *Law, Public Policies and Complex Systems: Networks in Action*, Law, Governance and Technology Series 42,
https://doi.org/10.1007/978-3-030-11506-7_9

the site has been occupied by "Zadistes[1]", to prevent the carrying out of the preparatory works (tracking, collection of protected species, ...) and in 2014 to prevent deforestation works. The logging took place from 1 to 20 September 2014. During this period, the occupiers tried to prevent deforestation (settling in the trees, burrowing on the path of the machines . . .) but the support of law enforcement forces allowed the loggers to complete their work. Just before starting the concreting of the embankment on Monday, October 27, a coordination of opponents organized the 25 a meeting gathering several thousand people.

On the night of 25 to 26 October 2014, a project opponent, Rémi Fraisse, was killed by an offensive grenade during clashes between anti-riot forces and a group of opponents. This event raised a lot of emotion in the whole country (the two previous deads go back to 1986 and 1977) and led to the abandonment of the project without the passions subsiding on the ground.

The violence continued until the expulsion of the site on March 6, 2015, when the General Council of Tarn acknowledged "the impossibility of continuing any activity related to the progress of the work" while deciding a new project of "water reservoir for agriculture, resized according to the location of the site". The following summer was an opportunity for some to show the existence of water resources and for others the deplorable state of the cultures. Access to the site still banned at the end of 2015 remained monitored until the end of 2016. The "transaction protocol" between the State and the General Council of Tarn, prior to the development of a new project, has been concluded on December 11, 2015.[2] The cancellation by the Administrative Court of all the decrees regarding to the construction of the dam gave right to the opponents on June 30, 2016. The initial project being definitively sold out, the wetland site has been rehabilitated (October 2017) and the Prefect has initiated on 14 November 2016 the elaboration of a new territorial project (still in progress at the end of 2018).

How could we get here? In the press and elsewhere, many people have testified (Camille 2014), sought to understand what may have happened (Foissac 2015) or analyzed the dysfunctions in the management of this project (Souchay and Laimé 2015; Lefetey and Bové 2015), the Parliament and the League of Human Rights have undertaken inquiry commissions... On the Google search engine, the word "Sivens" gives 517,000 results (June 1, 2015). As a matter of fact, in September 2014, several voices launched alerts: the disproportion of resources deployed on the site by the police and the violence of the confrontation are likely to cause a serious accident (Foissac 2015; Bès et al. 2015). These warnings lead us to believe that Rémi Fraisse's death is not a fortuitous event but the unfortunately predictable result of the logic of the stakeholders involved in this project (Grossetti 2004): in this process

---

[1]Name given to people who occupy a *Zone A Défendre* (Area to Be Defended).

[2]Announced by the Ministry for environment and sustainable development on February 27, 2015, this protocol stipulates that (1) the General Council renounces this project, (2) does not attack the State for the cancellation of the decree authorizing the works, and (3) the State compensates the General Council for € 3.3 million.

initiated in 2007, the behavior of each one led, in September 2014, the conflict to a level of intensity that should have warm of the possibility of a tragedy.

This chapter proposes an analysis of the conditions of the occurrence, in fact the production, of such a level of conflict by modeling the actors' representations and strategies which determined the behaviors they adopted one vis-à-vis others and that led to the drama. By model, we mean a quantified description of the system consisting of the actors, their means of action and their mutual dependencies. Such a model is obviously reductive, this is the price to pay to make intelligible the complexity of the interactions between the actors, but the simplification entailed by this reduction does not prevent from accounting faithfully the essential features of the game among the actors. Such a model escapes the subjectivity of natural language and can serve as a support for the confrontation between divergent analyses of events: if we agree on the semantics of the model, that is on the interpretation of value scales of numerical variables, the points of disagreement will be clearly established as disputes over certain elements of the model. Finally, by calculating analytical properties and performing simulations, such a model produces results likely to highlight certain characteristics of the system's structure and the main determinants of its configuration (Axelrod 1997; Gilbert 2004).

In the second section of this chapter, we present the analysis framework and the tools we use to develop and study our model. In the next two sections, we present the model itself: the identification of the actors and their means of action then the quantification of their mutual dependencies. We then highlight some structural properties of the model, and the simulation results show the inevitability of a maximum level of confrontation. Finally, we consider changes in the strategy of the actors that lead to a model in which the level of conflict remains circumscribed, and thus highlight *a contrario* its main determinants. In conclusion, we note the paradigmatic nature of the Sivens dam project and synthesize the modeling approach.

9.2   The SocLab Model of a System of Organized Action

Organized action system (OAS) is understood as a set of actors who interact in a more or less well-defined organizational context (a company, an association, a political system, etc.) or in a more diffuse way around a concern of which they are stakeholders. The SocLab approach for the modeling and study of OAS is based on the sociology of organized action developed by M. Crozier and E. Friedberg (Crozier 1963; Crozier and Friedberg 1977); a detailed presentation can be found in Sibertin-Blanc et al. (2013). The SocLab software allows studying an OAS by defining its constituent elements (its structure) and calculating indicators on structural features of the action system and on potential behaviors of actors, by exploring its state space (what everyone could do *in abstracto*) and by carrying out simulations that indicate how the actors are likely to behave in practice.

The structure of an OAS consists of (see Fig. 9.1):

- a set of *actors*, individuals or collectives, each of them having means of action relating to the concern of the system;
- a set of relationships (or *relations*) that support interactions between actors.

Each relation is *controlled* by an actor and each actor *depends* on a number of relations for the achievement of its goals.

A relation is based on a (or a set of) resource(s) that is regulated by the actor who controls it; this control gives it a means of action and therefore a certain flexibility in the management of this resource, and the behavior adopted by this actor with regard to this resource is modeled by the *state* of the relation. This state will be more or less beneficial to each of the dependent actors and it is evaluated on a scale of value from −10 (overall very penalizing) to 10 (overall very favorable) which characterizes its level of cooperation vis-à-vis all other actors in the system.

The *stake* an actor places on a relation depends on the importance of the underlying resource for achieving its objectives: the more a resource is needed to achieve an important objective, the more the actor will have a high stake on the associated relation. The stakes are quantified on a scale from 0 (zero) to 10 (crucial) and the sum of the stakes of each stakeholder is normalized to 10.

The *effect* of a relation on an actor is a function that determines to what extent, depending on the state of the relation, the relation impairs or facilitates the achievement of the actor's goals, whether it is the possibility of access to this resource according to his needs, a hindrance or contribution to the achievement of his

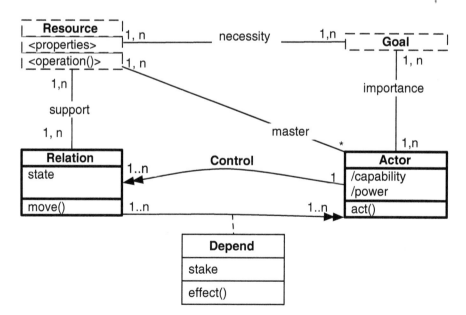

Fig. 9.1 The structure of a system of organized action in the form of a UML class diagram

objectives. The effect on an actor of a relation according to its state models, on a scale ranging from −10 (worst) to 10 (optimal), the contribution of this relation to the realization of the actor's objectives.

Finally, an actor can maintain certain *solidarity*, personal or organizational, with other actors. This is reflected in the consideration of the situation of other actors in the assessment of its own situation. Solidarity is expressed on a scale ranging from −1 (complete hostility) to 1 (complete adhesion).

We call *configuration* of an OAS the vector of the behavior of each of the actors, that is of the state of each of the relations. A configuration provides each actor with a certain *satisfaction* that assesses the extent to which its objectives are achieved, or at least made accessible, due to the behavior of all the actors. When an actor has solidarity only with himself, his satisfaction in a configuration $s = (s_r)_{r \in R}$ of the OAS is expressed in the form:

$$satisfaction(a, s) = \Sigma_{r \in R} \; stake(a, r) \, ^* \; effect_r \, (a, s_r) \qquad (9.1)$$

where R is the set of relations, *stake(a, r)* the stake of actors a on the relation r, and *effect_r (a, s_r)* is the effect on a of the relation r being in the state s_r. The value of the satisfaction of an actor is thus in the interval [−100, +100].

In the general case, the satisfaction of an actor has the form:

$$satisfaction(a, s) = \Sigma_{b \in A} \; solidarity(a, b) \, ^* \; \Sigma_{r \in R} \; stake(b, r) \, ^* \; effect_r \, (b, s_r) \quad (9.2)$$

where A is the set of actors and *solidarity(a, b)* the solidarity of a for the actor b.

In a dual way, we can quantify the power exercised by an actor in a given configuration as the sum of his contributions, through the relations he controls, to the satisfaction of other actors, in the form:

$$power(a, s) = \Sigma_{r \in R; a \; controls \; r} \; \Sigma_{c \in A} \; \Sigma_{b \in A} \; solidarity(c, b) \, ^* \; stake(b, r) \, ^* effect_r \, (b, s_r)$$
$$(9.3)$$

The scales of quantification used for the stakes, the state of relations and their effects are obviously arbitrary, but that does not have any consequence. Indeed, as far as the satisfactions and powers of the actors are concerned, the values themselves are not significant: only the comparisons and the percentages (*i.e.* the values in proportion) are likely to be interpreted in the terms of the modeled system. This interpretation requires that each value of the state of a relation (in the interval [−10, 10]) be characterized by a concrete behavior of the actor who controls this relation.

The structure of the model of an OAS makes it possible to carry out calculations which highlight some of its properties, we will give some examples. In addition, this structure defines the rules of a game among the actors in which they exchange their behaviors through the effect of the relations they control: when an actor modifies the state of relations he controls, it increases or decreases (depending on the shape of the effect functions) their contribution to the satisfaction of the actors who depend on it. According to a hypothesis of rationality of the actors, each one tries to achieve its objectives as best as possible, which amounts to obtaining the highest possible satisfaction. Everyone will therefore test different behaviors, in order to find one that encourages others to give it a good level of satisfaction, until an equilibrium configuration is reached in which no one sees how he could increase its satisfaction. This game therefore gives rise to a collective learning to find how everyone must behave in order to better achieve his objectives, that is to say, a joint search for a configuration of the game that provides everyone with a level of satisfaction that suits its expectations.

This social game differs from games considered in economics in that the objective of the game is not the maximization of actors' satisfactions, but to reach a quasi-stationary state. In such a configuration of the game, each one has obtained a satisfaction which he judges acceptable and so does not seek any more to modify the state of the relations which he controls. The behavior of the actors equilibrates each other and the system of action can function durably in this way, it is in a regulated configuration. The SocLab software includes an algorithm for the simulation of this collective learning. Assuming the bounded rationality of actors (Simon 1982), he calculates sustainable, socially plausible configurations. Its main properties are described in Sibertin-Blanc and El Gemayel (2013).

The model of the Sivens dam OAS that we present here is based on feedback from participants in this system that we interviewed during spring and fall 2015, quantitative data being recorded with the interview form given in the appendix. We will argue this model with the elements that we think are most significant, as the entire Sivens dam project is very well documented.

9.3 The Actors of the Model

Let us start by identifying the actors involved in the construction of the Sivens dam, we will then study the quantification of their mutual dependencies. Over the period 2007–2015, the system of action around the dam project has evolved, because of the succession of the holders of the Ministry of Ecology but also, endogenously, because of the evolution of the representation of actors. The model that we present here corresponds to the situation that, from the re-investment of the site by the Zadists on August 15, 2014, prevailed at the time of the tragedy.

Some elements of the national and regional context in which this dam project took place shed light on the actors' motivations. Faced with the virulence of opposition to the construction of a new airport[3] and although all authorizations were granted, in May 2014 the State resigned to suspend all operations in progress until the exhaustion of the lawsuits filed by the opponents. It is on this occasion that appeared the

---

[3]Designed to replace the Nantes city airport, The Notre-Dame-des-Landes airport project, which dates back to the 1970s, was finally abandoned in January 2018.

notion of ZAD ("Zone of Deferred Development" instituted in "Zone To be Defended") against "Large Imposed and Useless Projects", emergent movement of the contestation of big development projects in which the occupants of Sivens took place. In the course of 2014, other projects challenging the legitimacy of policies experienced the same vicissitudes (Subra 2014).

In application of the European Community Water Framework Directive (WFD 2000), the French Water and Aquatic Environments Act (LEMA 2006) introduced new rules for the calculation of abstraction volumes available for irrigation with a new organization of their distribution between farms. The Adour-Garonne basin annually has a structural deficit of about 250 million m^3 (Mercailloux 2014), while agriculture represents 11% of jobs in the Tarn department and 7.1% in the Tarn-and-Garonne. In the Adour-Garonne basin, the introduction of these new regulation gave rise to a very hard conflict between the agricultural profession and public authorities, which led to arrangements between the State and the regional Chambers of Agriculture, totally contradictory with the new regulation (Souchay and Laimé 2015; Chamber of Agriculture Tarn-et-Garonne 2011).

The report of the Court of Auditors (2015) concerning the Water Agencies recommends more transparency and selectivity in the awarding of grants and to "put in place a mechanism for preventing conflicts of interest for members of the authorities of Water Agencies and their staff ". For example, the same people sit on the General Councils of Tarn, the Adour-Garonne Water Agency which finances the dam at 52% and the CACG. Even if, in this case, no individual fault has been identified, this logic of cross-legitimization hampers the listening of divergent points of view (Lefetey and Bové 2015).

The system of action around the project to build a dam in the forest of Sivens involves a large number of actors, both because of the institutional complexity of a highly administered country like France and of the diversity of modes of expression of "civil society". The analysis of the interests, stakes, impact of their actions on the others and strategies of these actors makes it possible to note convergences which allow the grouping of several actors of the field into a single actor of the model. This results in a simplification of the game that does not necessarily distort it and improves its understanding.

None of the actors we have identified is a homogeneous entity; each constitutes in itself a system of action, with its internal conflicts and contradictions, which could be analyzed. What justifies the groupings that we have made are the dependencies of each actor and the effects of his behavior on others. More precisely, let's consider the network whose nodes are the entities involved in the game and having an arc, either positive or negative, from an entity A towards a entity B according to the nature of the impact of the behavior of A on B. The quantification of the model will show that the five actors in our model correspond to clusters that maximize the positive arcs within each group and the negative arcs between groups.

The model we present focuses on the occurrence of the fatal accident resulting from the clash between some opponents of the dam and the police. Organized around these two actors in the field, this model comprises five actors: the State (the regulator), the General Council of the Tarn department (CG, the project owner), the Company of Development of Coteaux de Gascogne (CACG, the project supervisor), the Testet Collective (legalist opponent) and the Zadists (activist opponent). Each actor controls a single relationship that is based on the means of action or resources it controls.

9.3.1 The State

By State, we mean the ministers who have directly intervened in the game: the Minister of Ecology and Sustainable Development—in this case D. Batho (until June 2013) and then P. Martin, S. Royal appointed in May 2014 only concerned herself late in the matter—and the Minister of the Interior, supported by the Minister of Agriculture and the Prime Minister. We also mean the Departmental Director of Public Security and the police forces over which he has authority. The Prefect of Tarn (Josiane Chevalier until August 30, 2014 then Thierry Gentilhomme) is the local representative of the State.

What are the means of action of the State? On the one hand, the granting of authorizations necessary for the realization of the dam and on the other hand the commitment of the police to protect the realization of the works. If these means of action are of very different natures, they have been put into play by the State in convergent ways with similar effects on the other actors, so that their dissociation would unnecessarily complicate the model. The State actor therefore controls a single relation, *support*, whose negative values correspond to a strict control of the legality and relevance of the project undertaken by the CG and a certain tolerance with regard to the occupation of the zone of works by the Zadists, and positive values to the reverse behaviors.

9.3.2 CG: The Council of Tarn Department, Local Authorities and Pro-Dam Farmers

The *Council of Tarn department* is the leader of the pro-dam coalition: owner of the project initiated in 2007 and definitively adopted by the department's permanent commission in May 2013, it finances it by 10%, just like the council of Tarn-et-Garonne department. This project dating back to 1978 was reactivated by a new CACG's report (2001) indicating a need for 1.5 mm^3 of water and made possible by the acquisition of the Sivens Forest (1976) and two adjacent farms (in 1997 and then in 2002). The *Council of Tarn-et-Garonne*, where are located the main beneficiaries of the project for the profitable cultivation of corn seed, is also very attached to the realization of the dam, in accordance with its support to the productive agriculture. It is the same for most local politicians such as the *Mayor of Lisle sur Tarn* (newly elected in 2014), town on which the dam is to be built, the *deputy* or the *Association of mayors and elected in Tarn*. The National Federation of Farmers' Unions

(*FNSEA*) and its authority in Tarn department (*FDSEA*), as well as *Young Farmers* and *Rural Coordination*, are agricultural professional unions that enlist and mobilize farmers (Callon 1986) to demand the construction of dams (Mercailloux 2014), just like the *Tarn Chamber of Agriculture* where they represent the majority. The policy implemented by the GC is (consistent with) the one they wish to be adopted. Finally, this coalition is supported by the *Avet* (Water Life Tescou Association) which has aroused, on the occasion of the construction of the dam, the constitution of a real militia of people who do not support the presence and way of life of the Zadists.

The means of action of the CG are the communication in the press and with the population to justify the project, and the establishment of the administrative acts necessary for the realization of the works, in particular the work orders for the project supervisor, the CACG. The means of action of agricultural unions are the support (protests, press, leaflets . . .), at national and local levels, for the construction of the dam, occasionally accompanied by the Avet. Avet's means are commando operations and intimidation in situ. These various means of action have been activated jointly in the same direction, which allows us to gather them in a single relation, *commitment*. Its positive values correspond to the implementation of these means for the construction of the dam and against the opponents, its negative values to the refusal of the dam.

9.3.3 The Coteaux de Gascogne Development Company (CACG)

The CACG has been the delegated developer of the project since 2009 and is the very likely manager of the future dam, but here, we consider it as the project supervisor of its construction. The CACG is a mixed economy company with 200 employees dedicated to "the land design, equipment and economic development of the Midi-Pyrénées and Aquitaine regions" whose mission is, among others, the control of water. It is the only major operator of this type in Midi-Pyrénées. The CACG has been interested in making this water reservoir since 1983 (Lefetey and Bové 2015). It was the CACG which, after a preliminary draft in 1989, drew up the 2001 report that led to the adoption of the dam project and did not examine other alternatives. Costs and oversizing were identified by experts appointed by S. Royal (Forray and Rathouis 2014; Forray and Roche 2015). This report served as a basis for further administrative documents, notably the master plan of water development and management (SDAGE), which allowed financing the dam project by the Adour-Garonne Water Agency. This report has not been accessible during the public utility investigation which ended in November 2012.

The action of the CACG is carried out by the *construction* of the dam, whose positive values correspond to its determination to build it.

9.3.4   The Testet Collective

This actor brings together the "*Collective for the safeguarding of the Testet wetland*" (http://www.collectif-testet.org/) and the numerous local and national associations it mobilized to challenge the legality as well as the relevance and the cost of this dam, or to criticize the way its construction was conducted. The *Confédération Paysanne* agricultural Union went in the same direction, as well as the online newspaper *Reporterre* (http://www.reporterre.net) which closely followed the entire project. The Collective has a very strong expertise on all aspects of the project. The competent agencies, namely the *CNPN* (National Council for the Protection of Nature), the *CDPNE* (Departmental Committee for Nature and Environment Protection) and the *ONEMA* (National Office for Water and Aquatic Environments), concluded in the same way as the Collective. It turns out that the State can override their opinions, so that these instances do intervene in the game only by the echo that the Collective gives to their opinions. The Collective's means of action is to make its proficiency recognized by the authorities concerned, the courts and the public. The positive values of the *expertise* relation it controls correspond to an important activity for that.

9.3.5   The Zadists

While the Collective embodies the legalistic—even co-managerial—modality of the militant protest, the Zadists embody the activist modality by the concrete occupation of the field. We group under this term all the people who have participated in one way or another in the occupation of site of the construction of the dam, accompanying those who instituted it in Zone A Defendre (Area To be Defended)[4] from autumn 2013: participants at meetings organized on site, hosted occasionally or living in the area, coming from afar or nearby residents bringing material and food necessary for daily life on this isolated site.

Their motivations are diverse, polarized towards ecology or towards the challenge of "big useless imposed projects", they are defenders of biodiversity, anti-capitalists, anarchists, antispecists, vegans … (Truong 2014). As a result, they have involvement (search for a way of life free of constraints, egalitarian and autonomous, pacifists, rejection of the barrage, hostility to the police force) and behaviors (physical commitment by binding to the top of trees or by burying themselves on the passage of the machines, clowning around, exactions, confrontations with the security forces) extremely differentiated. But any decomposition of the community of occupants into autonomous actors would be more or less arbitrary and we will only consider here the emergent effect of these behaviors. This actor controls the *occupation* relation, whose positive values correspond to the deployment of strong obstacles to the progress of the work.

---

[4]https://tantquilyauradesbouilles.wordpress.com Accessed 25 Feb 2018.

9.3.6 Other Actors

There are other stakeholders involved in the dam project which, for a variety of reasons, do not appear among the actors in the model.

The Adour-Garonne Water Agency: it is an essential partner of the project, since it finances 52% of it. AEAG's policy is to finance the works recommended by the SDAGE, which it decided to do on November 4, 2013 concerning the Sivens dam, after the Minister of Ecology P. Martin removed the restrictions on the financing of this type of work put by his predecessor D. Batho. In 2014, the Water Agency no longer had to intervene in the progress of the project and there is no reason to consider it as an actor of our model. Following the tragedy, AEAG's policy was to stand aside from the conflicts to preserve its legitimacy in the development of the forthcoming "Territory Project".

The European Union: The dam was to be financed by 24% by the EU, via the European Agricultural Fund for Regional Development. As early as November 2013, the EU asked Paris for an explanation of this project, then warned in July 2014 of the possibility of an infringement procedure to the Water Framework Directive. As the State has ignored these warnings, the EU will intervene as an actor only after the triggering of this procedure on November 26, which notifies the impossibility for the EU to finance this dam.

The Testet Collective won its case in 2016 for all the annulment actions it filed in 2013 and 2014. On the other hand, it lost all the suspension summonses before the *Administrative Court* and the *High Court*, with even a condemnation with the expenses of justice. Technically, it appears that during the period we are considering, the court has aligned itself with the prefecture and has therefore not behaved as an autonomous actor.

The neighbors: the pro-dams are grouped with the CG, the anti-divided between the Testet Collective and the Zadists.

The media: Essentially, the national newspapers did not consider the subject until the death of R. Fraisse and thus did not intervene in the system of action that we consider here. At the local level, major media have not engaged to the point of having an impact on the evolution of the project. The main newspaper in the region is *La Dépêche du Midi* whose boss is Chairman of the Tarn-et-Garonne Council (since 1985) and the Radical Left Party (since 1996). Implicitly favorable to the dam, it factually reported events since the beginning of the project, but without analyzing the project on its merits. The same is true of the main local TV channel, *FR3*, which, however, gave more voice to the various parties. The *free Tarn* newspaper reported the project closely, with more analysis on the merits.

9.4 Quantification of the Model

Our model therefore consists of five actors, each of them controling one relation (Table 9.1). Quantification of dependencies (stakes and effect functions) of each actor on relations is established from the data collected during interviews with participants, using the form given in the appendix. We argue the values of stakes and effect functions presented in Table 9.2, without justifying them in detail for lack of space.

9.4.1 The State

The State puts only two points of stakes on the relation it controls, *support*, because it is sufficiently established to depend only little of its own behavior. The form of its own effect function shows that what suits it best is to exercise its power but without excess (the maximum is reached for a cooperativeness of 4 on a scale $[-10, 10]$). Not taking into account the unfavorable opinions of the environmental agencies, the State gives little importance to the expertise (1 point), and takes more account of the occupation of the site (2 points) of which it must control the possible excesses. The sum of the stakes of the State is only 5 because it has, in addition, a solidarity of 0.5 with the CG according to the free administration of territorial entities principle. This very strong support for the CG is due to the proximity of the Minister P. Martin (notably President of the Council of Gers, headquarters of the CACG) with the supervisor of the project and the commitment of the prefect in favor of the dam. The State depends on relations *commitment* and *construction* only through his solidarity with the GC.

9.4.2 The CG

The retrospective analysis conducted by Foissac (2015) provides worthy insights into the behavior of T. Carcenac, Chairman of the Tarn Council. The CG relies on

Table 9.1 The actors of the model, groups of actors in the field

Actors of the model	Actors in the field	Controled relations
State	Concerned ministers, police forces, prefect	Support
CG	Tarn and Tarn-et-Garonne councils, local politicians, agricultural community, Avet association	Commitment
CACG	The Coteaux de Gascogne development company	Construction
T_Collective	Testet collective, the environmentalist movement (associations, union, green political party), environmental agencies	Expertise
Zadists	Visitors and occupants of the site	Occupation

Table 9.2 Matrix of dependencies, effect function and stake, of actors (in columns) on relations (in rows)

	State	CG	CACG	T_collect.	Zadists	Relevance
support	2.0	2.0	0.5	1.5	2.5	9,5
commitment	0.0	**3.0**	2.5	0.5	1.0	8,5
construction	0.0	3.0	**4.0**	2.5	1.5	12,5
expertise	1.0	0.5	0.0	**3.0**	1.0	5,75
occupation	2.0	1.5	3.0	2.5	**4.0**	13,75

On the diagonal, the dependence of the actor on the relation it controls (the stake in boldface). For effect functions, the horizontal axis corresponds to the behavior of the actor controlling the relation (from non-cooperative to left to cooperative to the right), the vertical axis to the resulting satisfaction of his objectives for the dependent actor. The last column "Relevance" indicates the sum of the stakes placed on each relation. Each actor has a solidarity of 1 towards itself, the State has also a solidarity of 0.5 for CG. (Table produced with the SocLab software)

the State (2) whose authorizations are essential for the realization of the project. With his democratic legitimacy, the CG is very determined that the dam project, voted by 43 out of 46 councilors, be completed (3), even at the expense of its wetland preservation policy and its charter of citizenship (Foissac 2015). It is equally important that the CACG makes every effort to build the dam (3). It gives little importance to the expertise (0.5: he does not acknowledge the meeting requests from the Collective) and values it negatively since it calls into question the project. As for the occupation of the site, it obviously contravenes its objectives and arouses sometimes violent hostility on the part of the Avet.

9.4.3 The CACG

The CACG relies on the State to protect access to the site (0.5), but above all on the commitment of the GC (2.5). Privately owned company whose turnover fell by 10% between 2012 and 2013, the realization of this dam is essential from its point of view (4). It takes no account of the expertise and is very bothered by the occupation of the site (3).

9.4.4 The Testet Collective

Although the Declarations of Public Utility and General Interest and other authorizations were signed (October 2013), the Collective still relies on the State for suspension summonses (1.5). It no longer hopes to be heard by GC (0.5) and is very worried by deforestation, which is gradually destroying the wetland (2.5). Its own expertise is essential for the Collective (3) because it bases its existence and legitimates its opposition to the project. Even if the Collectif wishes to stand out from the Zadists, especially its excesses, the occupation of the site remains his only recourse (2.5) against the "state of necessity" established by the start of work.

9.4.5 The Zadists

The intervention of the police reinforces the action of the Zadists by advertising (2.5), to a certain extent beyond which they can no longer prevent the progress of work. Beyond a certain level, the actions of the militias actually degrade their living conditions (1). They attach less importance to the construction of the dam (1.5) than to their emblematic fight against the State (Bès et al. 2015). Even if the Zadists give limited credit to the legalistic strategy of the Testet Collective, its expertise justifies their action and is indispensable to them (1), as long as he does not occupy the first place. For them, occupying the ZAD is essential (4): this is what bases their identity. Some people are aware that an excessive influx of occupants prevents the establishment of a common culture, and therefore compromises the effectiveness of the action, especially as the site's resources are limited. Others, less politicized or less experienced, value the confrontation in itself and, for example, do not resist the provocations of the police. The effect of occupation on Zadists is the result of these two trends.

9.5 Model Analysis

The death of an opponent of the project during clashes with anti-riot police is an event whose possibility increases with the importance of State's support (support → 10) and the vigorous occupation of the area (occupation → 10). These are the two relations that we will consider with the greatest attention.

9.5.1 Structural Analysis

The structural analysis of a model makes it possible to highlight some structural properties and the range of possibilities. Table 9.3 shows the most satisfactory configurations for each of the actors, and the most global satisfactory and unsatisfactory (i.e. summing the satisfaction of the actors). It appears that everyone would have the opportunity to achieve its goals (satisfaction between 90.4 and 100) ... as long as others agree.

Regarding conflicts, the comparison of the columns of this Table shows that (1) the main conflict is between the State, the CG and the CACG on the one hand and the Collective and the Zadists on the other hand (the maximum satisfactions of the ones corresponds to negative satisfactions of the others, the maximum and minimum global satisfaction clearly distinguish the two groups); (2) the interests of the State are the most convergent with the general interest (its maximum is the closest to the global one)—not surprising to this fact, the opposite would call into question the validity of the model—and (3) the Collective is particularly in conflict with the GC and the Zadists with the CACG. This last result is not trivial, it cannot be easily deduced from the data in Table 9.2 and draws attention to a significant fact: the direct opposition on the ground lies between the Zadists and the CACG, and that on the legality and relevance of the project between the Testet collective and the GC.

What is the range of influence that each actor can exercise, that is to say, his ability to contribute to the achievement of the objectives of others and thus influence their behavior?

The relevance of the relations (see Table 9.2) could lead us to believe that the Zadists and the CACG are the most powerful actors since the relations they control receive the most stakes. It is not so. The configurations of the maximum and minimum global satisfaction (first and last columns of Table 9.3) are also those in which each actor adopts the behavior that maximizes or minimizes the influence he exerts. Table 9.4 shows these extrema and the amplitude of influence that each actor is able to exercise. The GC benefits from a great range of influence because of the combination of the stakes and the orientation of the effects of his behavior: there are 7 points of stakes on the increasing effect functions of the relation commitment and only 1.5 points on the decreasing effect functions; for the Zadists, the ratio is 6.5/7.25 so that the overall effect of their behavior is always divided, what is positive for some being offset by what is negative for the others.

Table 9.3 Configurations providing actors (in column) their greatest satisfaction (e.g., the second column describes the configuration that gives the maximum satisfaction to State, 90.4)

		Satisfactions						Minimum
		Maximum						
		GLOBAL	State	CG	CACG	T_collect.	Zadists	GLOBAL
State of Relations	Support	5.0	8.0	10.0	−10.0	−10.0	5.0	−10.0
	Commitment	10.0	10.0	10.0	10.0	−10.0	−10.0	−10.0
	Construction	10.0	10.0	10.0	10.0	−10.0	−10.0	−10.0
	Expertise	10.0	10.0	−10.0	−10.0	10.0	6.0	−10.0
	Occupation	−3.0	−10.0	−10.0	−10.0	5.0	10.0	10.0
Satisfaction of actors	State	77.3	**90.4**	74.6	19.6	−72.8	−27.0	−93.4
	CG	73.1	85.5	**99.5**	59.5	−96.4	−67.5	−89.5
	CACG	79.0	100.0	100.0	**100.0**	−85.0	−100.0	−100.0
	T_collective	3.5	−36.2	−99.2	−69.2	**100.0**	60.0	34.5
	Zadists	15.9	−39.9	−64.1	−95.4	43.3	**97.9**	30.0
	GLOBAL	**248.7**	199.8	110.7	14.5	−110.9	−36.5	**−218.3**

In rows, the state of each relation (the higher this value, the more the actor who controls this relation acts energetically) and below, the satisfaction of each actor; in boldface, the satisfaction of the actor whom maximum satisfaction is reached in this configuration (table produced with the SocLab software)

Table 9.4 The range of influence that each actor is able to exercise (table produced with the SocLab software)

	State		CG		CACG		T_collective		Zadists	
	Behavior	Influence	Behavior	Influence	Behavior	Influence	Behavior	Influence	Behavior	Influence
Minimum	−10	−59	−10	−61	−10	−45	−10	−40	10	−13
Maximum	5	53	10	61	10	45	10	41	−3	49
Range		112		122		90		82		61

The "best" (the configuration of the global maximum) would be that the State supports moderately (5) and the Zadists do not occupy (−3), thus avoiding the possibility of an accident. But are the losers likely to accept this?

9.5.2 Simulation Results

The SocLab simulation algorithm provides an answer to this question by computing configurations in which it is plausible that the play of actors is regulated. Simulations are repeated because the algorithm has a part of randomness (when an actor does not know what behavior to adopt, he chooses it randomly). The simulation results, the details of which can be found at (Sibertin-Blanc 2016), are therefore amenable to statistical analysis (Villa-Vialaneix et al. 2014). We are interested here only in the average and the dispersion of the variables. The deviation of the state of a relation is an indicator of the room of maneuver, or indecision, of the actor who controls this relation. Table 9.5 shows these results.

With regard to the state of relations, the State supports (10) and the Zadists occupy (10) the maximum of their possibilities, the conditions of the occurrence of an accident are therefore met. In addition, the deviation is zero, all simulations lead exactly to the same blocking configuration: the game is overdetermined, no actor sees how it could behave otherwise.

As regards the satisfaction of actors, the CG appears as the winner and the Testet collective as the loser, the other actors being in an intermediate situation. These results correspond to what should have happened if the game had not been dramatically interrupted by the death of an opponent: the concreting of the dike was to begin on October 27th. Apart from the State, the behaviors adopted by the actors correspond to a Nash equilibrium: each one adopts the behavior which suits it the best, not counting on the others to achieve his objectives. This regulation is all the more stable as it is in line with the interest of the majority—CG, the CACG and the Collective (100% of their influence)—but opposed to that of the Zadists. These results are robust: the simulations of the models obtained by randomly varying each stake of ±1.5 around its value (while keeping to 10 the total stakes of each actor), produce the same configuration.

Table 9.5 Results of 100 simulations that all give the blocking configuration (table produced with the SocLab software)

	State of relations			Satisfaction of actors		Influence of actors	
	Average	Deviation		Value	Proportion	Value	Proportion
Support	10.0	0.0	State	37	71%	37	86%
Commitment	10.0	0.0	CG	61	80%	61	100%
Construction	10.0	0.0	CACG	40	70%	45	100%
Expertise	10.0	0.0	T_collective	5	52%	41	100%
Occupation	10.0	0.0	Zadists	30	65%	−13	0%
			GLOBAL	172	84%	172	84%

9.6 Models for Moderation of the State-Zadist Conflict

What other representations and strategies of actors would change the structure of the game to the point of moderating the conflict between the State and the Zadists?

On the side of the State, one could expect that the police mobilization remains proportionate and that its solidarity with CG under the free administration of territorial entities principle does not exceed its attention to the expertise of agencies. The productivist orientation of Minister Martin and the prefect's personal commitment to the dam led the State to manifest its preference for the construction of the dam.

On the side of the principal concerned, the CG owner, one would expect that he accompanies less the agricultural community and that it values positively the expertise of the Testet collective.

On the side of CACG and Testet collective, their representation is the expression of their raison d'être and they have no reason to change it.

For the Zadists finally, better organized they could have coordinated to better control the excesses of some of them. This can be taken into account in the model by limiting the state of the relation occupation to 7.

The distribution of the stakes of this second model is given in Table 9.6, the solidarity of the State with CG being reduced to 0.3 and the effect functions remaining the same (see Table 9.2), with the exception of the function of the relation expertise on the CG whose slope becomes increasing.

Simulation results of this second model are shown in Table 9.7. The importance of the deviation (second column) of the support relation leads to look at the dispersion of the results. It turns out that the State balances between two very different behaviors: a third of the simulations give exactly the same blocking configuration as before (in Table 9.5), except the limitation of the occupation to 7. So, we have a chance in three that the conditions of the occurrence of an accident are met. The other simulations, whose average and deviation are indicated in the third and fourth columns, give configurations that we will describe as moderate. In these configurations, if the CG, the CACG and the Testet collective adopt almost the same behaviors as in the previous model, the expected change, a moderation of the support by the State and occupation by the Zadists, is well

Table 9.6 Matrix of stakes of actors regarding relations in model 2 (in bold, stake of the actor on the relation it controls) (table produced with the SocLab software)

	State	CG	CACG	T_collective	Zadists	Relevance
Support	**2.0**	2.0	0.5	1.5	2.5	9.1
Commitment	0.0	**2.0**	2.5	0.5	1.0	6.6
Construction	0.0	2.5	**4.0**	2.5	1.5	11.25
Expertise	3.0	2	0.0	**3.0**	1.0	9.6
Occupation	2.0	1.5	3.0	2.5	**4.0**	13.45

Table 9.7 Results of 100 simulations of model 2

	State of relations					Satisfaction of actors		Influence of actors	
	Average	Deviation	Average	Deviation		Average	Proportion	Average	Proportion
Support	6.6	3.3	3.4	0.6	State	50	77%	46	99%
Commitment	9.7	0.6	9.5	0.8	CG	58	79%	36	99%
Construction	9.8	0.5	9.7	0.7	CACG	48	74%	32	99%
Expertise	10	0.1	9.9	0.2	T_collective	20	60%	94	100%
Occupation	6.2	1.2	5.4	1.2	Zadists	45	73%	13	40%
					GLOBAL	221	94%	221	94%

The third and fourth columns show the results for simulations that do not produce the Table 9.5 configuration. On the right, results concerning the actors in these moderate configurations (table produced with the SocLab software)

Table 9.8 Simulation results of a model that dismisses the possibility of a dramatic accident; State controls the authorization and policing relations (table produced with the SocLab software)

	State of relations			Satisfaction of actors		Influence of actors	
	Average	Deviation		Value	Proportion	Valeur	Proportion
Authorization	−4.06	2.06	State	43.4	68.5%	61.4	99.6%
Commitment	9.12	1.12	CG	37.8	68.5%	24.5	98.5%
Construction	9.78	0.36	CACG	43.3	71.8%	24.4	99.0%
Expertise	9.91	0.13	T_collective	22.8	61.9%	78.3	99.6%
Occupation	6.32	2.1	Zadists	41.0	73.2%	0.1	27.2%
Policing	5.1	1.2	GLOBAL	188.4	87.3%	188	87%

achieved. This results in a 10% improvement in global satisfaction, for the benefit of the State, the Testet collective and the Zadists (gain of about 15 satisfaction points each). The outcome of the game is much more balanced: the Collective is no longer ridiculed, the State exercises its full power and it is not sure that the dam is built.

What are the determinants of the possibilities offered by this model? It is not the change of CG's representation however the most concerned and powerful actor (cf. Table 9.4): one obtains the blocking configuration even if he grants more stakes to the expertise that to the construction of the dam. Nor is it the ceiling on occupation of the Zadists at 7, which, in all the variants of this model, has just the direct effect of limiting the state of this relation.

It is thus the change of the State's representation which opens an alternative way. This fact is well established insofar as it is not sensitive to a variation of ± 1 of actors' stakes. In this model 2, the State dissociates, more than in the previous model, the exercise of its two functions, the issue of authorizations and the maintenance of order.

For the blocking configuration to be frankly discarded, the State, as a simple regulator, must abandon its solidarity with the GC and attach equal importance to the expertise-authorization and occupation-policing aspects. We then obtain the results of Table 9.8, (Sibertin-Blanc 2016) gives details on this model and model 2.

Some properties are common to the simulation results of each of these models; they are images of characteristics (of our apprehension) of this system of action that deserve to be noted:

- The state of the relations commitment, construction and expertise is close to their maximum value with a small deviation, while the deviation of relations controlled by the State and Zadists is significant. This is due to the focus of our models on the conflict between the State and the Zadists; their representation of the game is more complex and gives them more room for maneuver, while the other three actors are essentially auxiliary to this conflict.
- The Testet collective is the actor who always gets the least satisfaction, although his contribution to the whole (94 in the model 2) can be very high; the legalistic opposition is a thankless role.
- On the other hand, the Zadists still exercise a very weak influence; they have their own way of playing the game, which does not fit with that of the other actors.

9.7 Conclusion

In their report submitted on October 27, 2014, and therefore drafted before the occurrence of the drama, N. Forray and P. Rathouis wanted "Sivens to be considered as a turning point in the management of water in Adour-Garonne, the last project of an era, the first stage of a major evolution". This seems to be the case with, *e.g.,* the circular of 4 June 2015 concerning the financing by the water agencies of the substitution reservoirs, the law of 8 August 2016 for the reconquest of biodiversity, nature and landscapes following the Richard report (2015), or the modification of the nature and use of munitions used in law enforcement operations following the report (Baudet and Miramon 2014).

Contrary to what some have said,[5] the death of R. Fraisse will not have been useless, since it allowed to stop the implementation and to make visible the failures of the Sivens dam project, considering both its management and its purpose (water management). Compared to complex projects with innumerable tangled issues such as the airport of Notre Dame des Landes, the stakes of this project were relatively modest: 8 M €, 12 to 17 ha of wetland and corn seed growing in about 20 farms. The contrast between the relative simplicity of this project and the gravity of the accident to which it gave rise makes the Sivens dam project a paradigm for these "Imposed Large Unnecessary Projects" which arose to serious conflicts between the French administrative and political systems and new citizen movements bearing a conception of the common good that is sustainable, meaningful and effective from the environmental, social and economic points of view (Foissac 2015).

Beyond the legislative and regulatory evolution mentioned above, the awareness of the disastrous consequences of such hiatus encourages the use of the National Public Debate Commission to guarantee the democratic legitimacy of these projects. It also highlights the need for participatory deliberation approaches for the elaboration of a project that is shared and agreed by the actors of a territory. Such processes greatly benefit, in support, from methods and tools based on integrative modeling and simulation such as Wat-A-Game (Abrami et al. 2012) or Maelia (Therond et al. 2014). Used as a negotiation support tool for the management of socio-ecological systems (Barreteau 2003; Bommel et al. 2014; Adreit et al. 2011), modeling makes it possible to objectify the positions and behaviors of the stakeholders and to highlight the consequences of their choices by simulation.

The SocLab model presented here has another concern, since it does not focus on the matter of the project but on the social dimension of the process of its design and implementation. This model is diagnostic assistance in that it is problematized around the question it aims to illuminate (in this case the State-Zadist conflict). Given the issue studied, the models presented here stand at a meso level, intermediate between the micro level that would examine the interactions between the physical actors in the field and the macro level for which the Sivens dam project would only constitute one episode among others.

The SocLab meta-model of Organized Action Systems provides firstly a process for the acquisition (see Appendix) and the representation (see Tables 9.1 and 9.2) of knowledge about the system that we consider. The quantitative nature of this representation makes it possible to highlight properties which, although the direct consequence of what one has put in the model, are not for all that trivial and whose robustness can be evaluated by analyzes of sensitivity.

---

[5]"To die for ideas is one thing, but it's still relatively stupid and silly", T. Carcenac (La Dépêche du Midi, 27/10/2014).

SocLab offers the possibility of testing hypotheses by observing the consequences of modifications made to the model. Each of these tests is a thought experiment capable of extending the knowledge and deepening the understanding of the model. In this way, we have been able to uncover constituent elements of the structure of the studied system of action that could be its essential determinants.

Appendix

This form is used to collect data from actors in the field to quantify the model. We start by presenting to the interviewee the architecture of the model using Fig. 9.1 and the interpretation of the effects functions, so that he knows how his statements will be used to fill a column of Table 9.2.

	Interviewee:	Resources		
	As model's actor:	R1	R2	- - -
1.	**What are the resources do you need** to perform your tasks, to achieve your objectives? **What does matter** for you?			
2.	**On who do you depend** to access the resource, to use it according to your own need? Who controls the resource?	<actor name>	<actor name>	<actor name>
3.	**How much important** is that resource for your own work (on a scale 0 . . . 10)?			
	What is the behavior of the person who controls the resource that would be (answers to the following questions will serve to draw the shape of effect functions):			
4.	**a- the worst case for you?** describe this behavior			
5.	Assess the effect of this behavior on your capability to achieve your objectives (on a scale −10 . . . 0)			
6.	**b- the best case for you?** describe this behavior			
7.	Assess the effect (on a scale 0 . . . 10)			
8.	**c- the neutral case, neither favourable or unfavourable?** describe this behavior			
9.	Assess the effect (on a scale −10 . . . +10)			
10.	**d- the behavior that you experience usually?** describe this behavior			
11.	Assess the effect (on a scale −10 . . . +10)			
12.	**Who does matter for you?**			
	Favorably (on a scale 0 . . . 10)	Actor XX:		
	Adversely (on a scale −10 . . . 0)	Actor YY:		

References

Abrami G, Ferrand N, Morardet S, Murgue C, Popova A, De Fooij H, Farolfi S, Du Toit D, Aquae-Gaudi W (2012) Wat-A-Game, a toolkit for building role-playing games about integrated water management. In: Seppelt R, Voinov AA, Lange S, Bankamp D (eds) Proceedings of Sixth International Congress on Environmental Modelling and Software. 2012 iEMSs Meeting, Leipzig, pp 1912–1919. Available on http://www.iemss.org/sites/iemss2012//proceedings/E2_0811_Abrami_et_al.pdf Accessed 25 Feb 2018

Adreit F, Roggero P, Sibertin-Blanc C, Vautier C (2011) Using SocLab for a rigorous assessment of the social feasability of agricultural policies. Int J Agric Environ Inf Syst 2(2):1–20. https://doi.org/10.4018/jaeis.2011070101

Axelrod R (1997) Advancing the art of simulation in the social sciences. In: Conte R, Hegselmann R, Terna P (eds) Simulating social phenomena. Lecture notes in economics and mathematical system, vol 456. Springer, Berlin, pp 21–40

Barreteau O (2003) The joint use of role-playing games and models regarding negotiation processes: characterization of associations. J Artif Societies Soc Simul 6(2). Available on http://jasss.soc.surrey.ac.uk/6/2/3.html. Accessed 25 Feb 2018

Baudet M, Miramon G (2014) Rapport relatif à l'emploi des munitions en opérations de maintien de l'ordre. IGPN/E/N°14-1899-I. Inspection Générale de la Police Nationale, Ministère de l'Intérieur, Paris, 41 p (13 Nov 2014)

Bès M-P, Blot F, Ducournau P (7/2015) Sivens: when dialogue breaks down. The making of a tragedy. Justice Spatiale - Spatial Justice n°8/2015. Available on https://www.jssj.org/article/sivens-quand-le-dialogue-devient-impossible-chronique-dun-drame-annonce/. Accessed 25 Feb 2018

Bommel P, Diegue F, Bartabur D, Duart E, Montes E, Pereira M, Corral J, Lucena CJ, Morales Grosskopf H (2014) A Further step towards participatory modelling. Fostering stakeholder involvement in designing models by using executable UML. J Artif Soc Soc Simul 17(1):6. https://doi.org/10.18564/jasss.2381

CACG (2001) Confortement de la ressource en eau sur le bassin du Tescou. Conseil Général du Tarn-et-Garonne, Montauban, 140 + 41 p. Available on http://www.collectif-testet.org/79+telecharger-le-rapport-cacg-2001.html. Accessed 25 Feb 2018

Callon M (1986) The sociology of an actor-network. In: Callon M, Law J, Rip A (eds) Mapping the dynamics of science and technology. Macmillan, London, pp 19–34

Camille (12/2014) Sivens sans retenue: feuilles d'automne. Edition la Lenteur, 158 p

Chambre d'agriculture Tarn-et-Garonne (2011) Visite de Nicolas Sarkozy dans le Tarn-et-Garonne: des avancées sur l'irrigation (Mars 2011)

Court of Auditors (2015) Les agences de l'eau et la politique de l'eau : une cohérence à retrouver. Cour des Comptes, Paris, https://www.ccomptes.fr/fr/documents/30121

Crozier M (1963) The Bureaucratic phenomenon. University of Chicago Press, Chicago

Crozier M, Friedberg E (1977) Actors and systems: the politics of collective action. The University of Chicago Press, Chicago

Foissac R (9/2015) Sivens, pour comprendre. Un Autre Reg'Art, Albi (Sept 2015)

Forray N, Rathouis P (10/2014) Expertise du projet de barrage de Sivens (Tarn). Rapport n° 009953-01, Conseil Général de l'Environnement et du Développement Durable. Ministère de l'Ecologie, du Développement Durable et de l'Energie, Paris, 62 p. Available on https://www.ladocumentationfrancaise.fr/var/storage/rapports-publics/144000641.pdf

Forray N, Roche P-A (1/2015) Mission pour un projet de territoire du bassin du Tescou (Midi-Pyrénées). Rapport n° 009953-02, Conseil Général de l'Environnement et du Développement Durable. Ministère de l'Ecologie, du Développement Durable et de l'Energie, Paris, 57 p. Available on http://www.ladocumentationfrancaise.fr/var/storage/rapports-publics/154000052.pdf. Accessed 25 Feb 2018

GéoDiag and Ecogéa (2007) Recensement des cours d'eau et des milieux aquatiques à « caractère patrimonial » sur le bassin Adour-Garonne – Cours d'eau remarquables. Agence de l'Eau

Adour-Garonne, Toulouse, 28 p. Available on http://oai.eau-adour-garonne.fr/oai-documents/56542/GED_00000000.pdf. Accessed 25 Feb 2018

Gilbert N (2004) Quality, quantity and the third way. In: Holland J, Campbell JR (eds) Methods in development research: combining qualitative and quantitative approaches. ITDG Publications, London, pp 141–148

Grossetti M (2004) Sociologie de l'imprévisible - Dynamiques de l'activité et des formes sociales. Presses Universitaires de France, Paris

Lefetey B, Bové J (2/2015) Sivens, un barrage contre la démocratie. Les Petits Matins, Paris

LEMA (2006) Loi n°2006-1772 du 30 décembre 2006 sur l'eau et les milieux aquatiques. JORF n°303 (31/12/2006), texte n°3, p. 20285 sq. Available via http://www.legifrance.gouv.fr/. Accessed 5 Feb 2018

Mercailloux L (2014) Le bassin Adour-Garonne manque d'eau. Les Echos, Prais (27/10/14)

Richard A (6/2015) Démocratie environnementale: débattre et décider - Rapport de la Commission spécialisée du Conseil national de la transition écologique sur la démocratisation du dialogue environnemental. Ministère de l'Ecologie, du Développement Durable et de l'Energie, Paris, 74 p. Available on http://www.ladocumentationfrancaise.fr/rapports-publics/154000364/index.shtml. Accessed 25 Feb 2018

SCOP Sagne (2010) Retenue de Sivens - Caractérisation des zones humides. Conseil Général du Tarn, Albi, 15 p. Available on http://www.collectif-testet.org/uploaded/Etude-impact-EP-2012/Annexes-EI/annexe-4-rapportzh-na-1.pdf. Accessed 25 Feb 2018

Sibertin-Blanc C (2016) Interplay of actors about the construction of a dam. CoMSES Computational Model Library. Available on https://www.openabm.org/model/5307/version/1. Accessed 25 Feb 2018

Sibertin-Blanc C, El Gemayel J (2013) Boundedly rational agents playing the social actors game - how to reach coopération. In: O'Conner L (ed) Proceedings of 2013 IEEE/WIC/ACM International Joint Conferences on Web Intelligence (WI) and Intelligent Agent Technologies (IAT), Atlanta, November 2013. https://doi.org/10.1109/WI-IAT.2013.135

Sibertin-Blanc C, Roggero P, Adreit F, Baldet B, Chapron P, El Gemayel J, Mailliard M, Sandri S (2013) SocLab: a framework for the modeling, simulation and analysis of power in social organizations. J Artif Societies Soc Simul 16(4):8. Available on http://jasss.soc.surrey.ac.uk/16/4/8.html. Accessed 25 Feb 2018

Simon HA (1982) Models of bounded rationality: behavioral economics and business organization, vol 1 and 2. The MIT Press, Cambridge

Souchay G, Laimé M (2/2015) Sivens, le barrage de trop. Seuil-Reporterre, Paris

Subra P (2014) Géopolitique de l'aménagement du territoire, 2de édition. A. Colin, coll. Perspectives Géopolitiques, Paris

Therond O, Sibertin-Blanc C, Lardy R, Gaudou B, Balestrat M, Hong Y, Louail T, Mayor E, Nguyen VB, Panzoli D, Sanchez-Perez JM, Sauvage S, Taillandier P, Vavasseur M, Mazzega P (2014) Integrated modelling of social-ecological systems: the MAELIA high-resolution multi-agent platform to deal with water scarcity problems. In: Ames DP, Quinn NWT, Rizzoli AE (eds) International Environmental Modelling and Software Society 7th International Congress on Environmental Modelling and Software. San Diego, pp 1833–1840. Available via http://www.iemss.org/society/index.php/iemss-2014-proceedings. Accessed 8 Feb 2018

Truong N (2014) La résistance des renoncules. Le Monde, Paris (4/11/2014)

Villa-Vialaneix N, Sibertin-Blanc C, Roggero P (2014) Statistical exploratory analysis of agent-based simulations in a social context: using self-organizing maps to define a typology of behaviors. Case Stud Bus Ind Gov Stat CS-BIGS 5(2). Available on https://hal.archives-ouvertes.fr/hal-00940788/document. Accessed 25 Feb 2018

WFD (2000) Directive 2000/60/EC of the European Parliament and of the Council of 23 October 2000 establishing a framework for Community action in the field of water policy. Available via http://eur-lex.europa.eu/en/. Accessed 8 Feb 2018

Part III
Complexity and Networks

Chapter 10
Exploiting the Web of Law

Radboud Winkels

Abstract Within the OpenLaws.eu project, we attempt to suggest relevant new sources of law to users of legal portals based on the documents they are focusing on at a certain moment in time, or those they have selected. In the future we attempt to do this both based on 'objective' features of the documents themselves and on 'subjective' information gathered from other users ('crowdsourcing'). At this moment we concentrate on the first method. In Sect. 10.2 I describe how we *create* the web of law if it is not available in machine readable form, or extend it when that is necessary. Next, I present results of experiments using analysis of the network of references or citations to suggest these new documents. In Sect. 10.3 I describe two experiments where we mix the use of network analysis with similarity based on the comparison of the actual text of documents. One experiment is based on simple bag-of-words and normalisation, the other uses Latent Dirichlet Allocation (LDA) with added n-grams. A small formative evaluation in both experiments suggests that text similarity alone works better than network analysis alone or a combination, at least for Dutch court decisions.

10.1 Introduction

More and more sources of law are (freely) available online in Europe and the rest of the world. It concerns both legislation and case law and possibly others like legal commentaries. Professionals may already get lost in the multitude of information, let alone ordinary citizens and (small and medium sized) enterprises. Traditionally commercial publishers provide this information, plus support for access. Legal experts write commentaries for them, editors provide links between different (types of) sources and warn subscribers for interesting new developments and case law. Now that large amount of sources of law become electronically available online,

R. Winkels (✉)
Leibniz Center for Law, University of Amsterdam, Amsterdam, Netherlands
e-mail: winkels@uva.nl

© Springer Nature Switzerland AG 2019
R. Boulet et al. (eds.), *Law, Public Policies and Complex Systems: Networks in Action*, Law, Governance and Technology Series 42,
https://doi.org/10.1007/978-3-030-11506-7_10

the question is whether new ways for supporting access can be developed. One stream of research may be directed towards *crowdsourcing*, have users of legal information share their collections of material, the links they see between different sources, their commentaries, etc. Another stream of research is directed at (semi-) automated linking and clustering of sources of law, analysis of the network of law to find authoritative sources or predict the change of opinion of higher courts, etc.[1] In the OpenLaws.eu project we explore both approaches (Wass et al. 2013).[2]

We are developing a platform that enables users to find legal information more easily, organize it the way they want and share it with others. The primary focus is on legal professionals, but ultimately the platform should be useful for everybody. The OpenLaws Internet platform is based on open data, open innovation and open source software. This means that OpenLaws integrates legal communities and IT communities in the design and in the operation of the system.

In this paper I will first describe how we *create* the web of law if it is not available in machine readable form, or extend it when that is necessary (Sect. 10.2). Next, I will explain how we *recommend* sources of law to users given a current document they are investigating based on network analysis. The focus will be on legislation and case law. In Sect. 10.3 we will add other document features, particularly 'text similarity', to suggest interesting new documents. I will also present small formative *evaluations* of all approaches and in Sect. 10.4 end with conclusions and further research.

10.2 Creating a Web of Law

Sources of law form a network of (parts of) documents, they cite and reference each other. We distinguish three types of documents:

- *Legislation*: legal rules of a generally binding character, typically has explicit processes for declaring rules in force and for modifying existing rules. Typically has a complex reference structure. The bibliographic distinction (Saur 1998) between 'works' and 'expressions' is of critical importance, because the text changes over time. 'Expressions' are the different versions of a 'work', e.g. 'article x of law y in force at date t' and the same article at date '$t+1$' where the text differs. Figure 10.1 presents an example of a legislative network.
- *Case Law*: legal decisions on individual cases that have a formative influence on future decisions on similar cases. This is most obviously the case for the judiciary, but other arbitration bodies may in practice be relevant in everyday live (for instance arbitration courts for consumer complaints). These documents are typically never changed over their lifetime, and do not have to be declared in force or

---

[1]These topics occur in a series of international workshops on "Network Analysis in Law (NAiL)" I have been organizing since 2013.

[2]See: https://info.openlaws.com/openlaws-eu/.

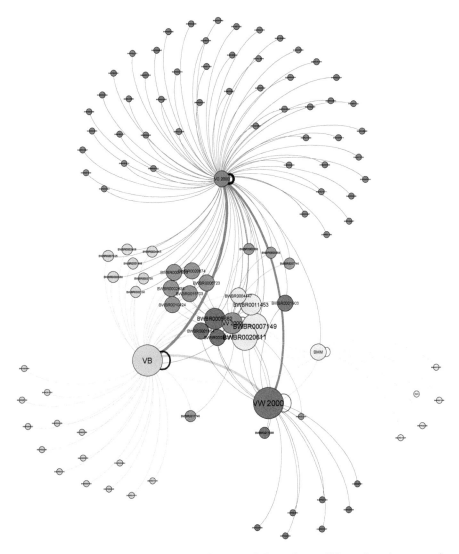

Fig. 10.1 The network of Dutch Immigration Law. Colours denote different laws (e.g. green is "Vreemdelingenbesluit" (VB)); size of nodes the relative importance of the law based on number of ingoing and outgoing references. The references are depicted as lines between nodes (node labels are of no importance for this illustration)

retracted. Legal decisions may be selectively published, however, depending on their formative influence on future decisions. Cases cite other cases and—depending on the legal system—legislation.

- *Commentaries*: documents that function as expert commentary on legal rules and decisions. These documents typically make references to rules or decisions, but otherwise share little in terms of structure or metadata with sources of law. Legal publishers and their products fall under this category.

Several researchers have applied network analysis to legal documents, but never for recommending new documents and only to one type of data at a time: for establishing the authority of case law as in Fowler and Jeon (2008) and Winkels et al. (2011), or analyzing the structure of legislation as in Liiv et al. (2007) and Mazzega et al. (2009). Van Opijnen (2014) uses links to legislation in Dutch case law when deciding upon the relevance of a particular case, but not to suggest other relevant sources of law and not as an applied context for legislation. In our work, we use network analysis of both legislation and case law to recommend potentially interesting new sources of law.

10.2.1 Legal Portals

Most of the sources of law available online are stand-alone web services or data-bases, containing one type of documents, not linked to other sources. For instance, the Dutch portal for case law[3] contains a (small) part of all judicial decisions in the Netherlands. Case citations in these decisions are sometimes explicitly linked, references to legislation are not.[4] From earlier research we know that professional users of legal documents would like to see and have easy access to related ones from other collections. E.g. when we evaluated a prototype system that recommends other relevant articles and laws to users of the official Dutch legislative portal, they told us they would like to see relevant case law and parliamentary information as well (Winkels et al. 2013).

Another problem of existing portals and data bases is that not even all internal links are explicitly represented. This is especially true for so called relative links like "the previous article", or "the second sentence of article x" and incomplete ones ("that law" or "article y" without the law that it is part of).

If these links are not given, we can try to find them automatically. For inter- and intra-legislation links we have shown this can be done very effectively for the Dutch case (de Maat et al. 2006) and others for other jurisdictions (e.g. Palmirani et al. 2003 for Italy; Tran et al. 2013 for Japan). For inter-case law links it is a bit more difficult, but we have shown it works for the Dutch case (Winkels et al. 2011 and so did Van Opijnen 2014). That leaves finding citations in case law to legislation and possibly finding links in other sources of law like commentaries to both case law and legislation. In this paper we will focus on finding references to legislation in Dutch case law and how we can use these to improve access to Dutch sources of law.

The data available in the Dutch official portals is not ideal for further analysis like natural language parsing or network analysis.[5] For legislation we started transferring the data to an RDF linked data format in 2011 and storing it at the Metalex Document

---

[3] rechtspraak.nl.

[4] Recently one has started to add some links to cited legislation in metadata, but not all and it does not give information on *where* in the text the citation occurs, nor how often.

[5] In 2016 a new version of the Dutch legislative portal was launched that overcomes many of the problems.

Server (Hoekstra 2011). The server currently contains 45,165 document versions (March 2016), and this number is growing every day since every change to the wetten.nl site is added to the triplestore. In Winkels et al. (2013) we describe how we generate networks for legislation using SPARQL queries on the RDF data. Here we will describe how we build a network of relations between case law and legislation.

10.2.2 The Dutch Case Law Portal

The Dutch portal for case law contains a small, but growing part of all judicial decisions in the Netherlands. Case citations in these decisions are sometimes explicitly marked in metadata (e.g. the first instance case); references to legislation only the main one(s) in recent cases. The texts are available in an XML format, basically divided in paragraphs using <para> tags, with a few metadata elements. The most relevant metadata for our purpose are:

- The date of the decision (*'Datum uitspraak'*)
- The field(s) of law (*'Rechtsgebieden'*)
- The court (*'Instantie'*).

The court decisions do not contain inline, explicit, machine readable links to cited legislation or other cases. So even when the metadata contain such references, we do not know in which paragraph the case or article was cited. We resort to parsing techniques to make these citations explicit and count them. We chose to work with a subset of all case law to start with; those cases that were tagged as belonging to 'immigration law' and that contained the actual text of the verdict. That gave us 13,311 documents to work with.

For locating references to legislation in case law we use regular expressions as we have done in the past together with a list of names and abbreviations of Dutch laws (de Maat et al. 2006). This list also contains the official identifier of the law (the BWB-number), which can be used for resolving the reference later on. We consider high precision to be more important than high recall.[6] Users will forgive us if we miss a reference, but be annoyed by false ones. We evaluated this procedure by checking 25 randomly selected documents by hand. These documents contained 163 references to legislation of which 141 were correctly identified (recall of 87%). There was one false positive (precision of 99%). The references we missed were mostly those to the *'Vreemdelingencirculaire'* ('Aliens act', a lower law that has a different structure than regular ones) and treaties with very long names like *'Europees Verdrag tot bescherming van de rechten van de mens en de fundamentele vrijheden'* ('Convention for the Protection of Human Rights and Fundamental Freedoms'). When we tried to

---

[6]Precision gives the percentage of all references we find that is relevant or correct. Precision of 100% means *all* references we find are relevant or correct. Recall gives the percentage of all relevant or correct references there are, that we actually find. A recall of 100% would mean we find *all* relevant or correct references.

capture this with regular expressions, they would match too easily, often matching entire sentences where they should have matched only the law. We declared these conventions outside the scope of this first experiment.

Resolving the references was a bit trickier, since sometimes they used anaphora, e.g. referring to 'that law'. In such cases, the citation was resolved by using the previous law identifier if it existed, i.e. we assume that the complete law was introduced just before in the text and resolved correctly. We used the same process for resolving ambiguous title abbreviations; e.g. 'WAV' is an abbreviation of '*Wet Arbeid Vreemdelingen*' (law on labour for immigrants), '*Wet Ammoniak en Veehouderij*' (law on ammonia and livestock) and '*Wet Ambulancevervoer*' (law on ambulance transport). Most of the time the full title is used before the abbreviation is used.

Another issue is determining the exact version of the law the case refers to. Typically, a judge will refer to the version that is in force at the moment of the decision, but it may also be the version that was in force at the time of the relevant facts, or even sometimes an earlier version of the relevant law, etc. We cannot decide which version is the correct one without interpreting the content of the case. Therefore we decided to resolve the reference to the 'work' level of the source of law, i.e. no particular version.[7] The resulting references are added to the XML of the case law document. The final network of the 13,311 case documents has 85,639 links to legislation (on average 6.5 references per case); the links connect the ECLI identifier[8] of the case with the BWB identifier of the (part of) law it refers to.

We evaluated the resolving process by checking 250 random ones by hand. Of these, 234 should have been resolved since the other 16 were outside of the scope of this experiment. 198 were resolved correctly (a recall of 85%). We had 10 'false' positives, i.e. references that were declared out of scope, so a precision of 95%. The results were good enough to continue.

Since case decisions may refer to the same source of law, e.g. an article, more than once, we count the number of references and compute the weight of the link between the case and the article as: $W = {}^1/n$ where n is the amount of occurrences of a certain reference and W is the weight of the edge. The lower the weight, the stronger the impact on the network is.

10.2.3 Recommending Sources of Law

When a user clicks an article in our prototype legislative recommender portal, related case law and legislation is retrieved:

---

[7]Bibliographic conventions distinguish four levels of documents: work, expression, manifestation and item (Saur 1998).

[8]'European Case Law Identifier'; see Council of the European Union conclusions on ECLI at: http://eur-lex.europa.eu/legal-content/EN/ALL/?uri=CELEX:52011XG0429(01).

1. The system checks whether the article appears in the case law network. If so, it creates a so-called ego graph, a local network containing all the nodes and edges within a certain weighted distance from the current node (Newman 2010). We start searching with a weighted distance of 0.4 and gradually increase it up to 2.0 until we have a sufficiently large, but still manageable network.
2. To find relevant legislation, the system also checks whether the current node is in the legislative network of the MetaLex document server. If so, it again creates an ego graph, this time for an unweighted network. To control the size of the graph, we use only references coming from the selected version (expression) of the current node.
3. If we have two local networks, we want to combine them in order to (better) predict the importance of legislative nodes. To do this, we need to assign weights to the legislative graph. We chose the value 0.1 as it allows the legislative network to influence the result but not overrule the case law references.
4. Finally, we use betweenness centrality on the combined network to determine the most relevant articles for the current focus. *Betweenness centrality* is a measure of centrality in a graph based on shortest paths. For every pair of nodes in a graph, there exists at least a shortest path between the nodes such that either the number of edges that the path passes through (for unweighted graphs) or—as in this case—the sum of the weights of the edges (for weighted graphs) is minimized.
5. The results are shown to the user in the top of frame A of Fig. 10.2.

10.2.4 A Formative Evaluation

We asked several professional users of the Dutch Immigration Service to use the prototype system and fill in an evaluation form afterwards. It was a small study; three users replied. The purpose of a formative evaluation (as opposed to a summative one) is to evaluate work in progress and adapt the design. It is to see whether one is on the right track. The three users were positive; they appreciated the clean and uncluttered interface and indicated that it was easy to understand without help. They also liked the indication of the number of times a case was referring to an article when you click on a case. They noted that the inclusion of case law added suggestions of relevant articles that were not available in a previous system (Winkels et al. 2013). They complained about the slowness of the system and the fact that references to the '*Vreemdelingencirculaire*' were missing (as we explained above).

10.3 Adding Other Document Features

In the previous experiment we only exploited the web of references between documents. Now we will explore whether we can improve suggestions for relevant documents by including other features, notably similarity measures based on the

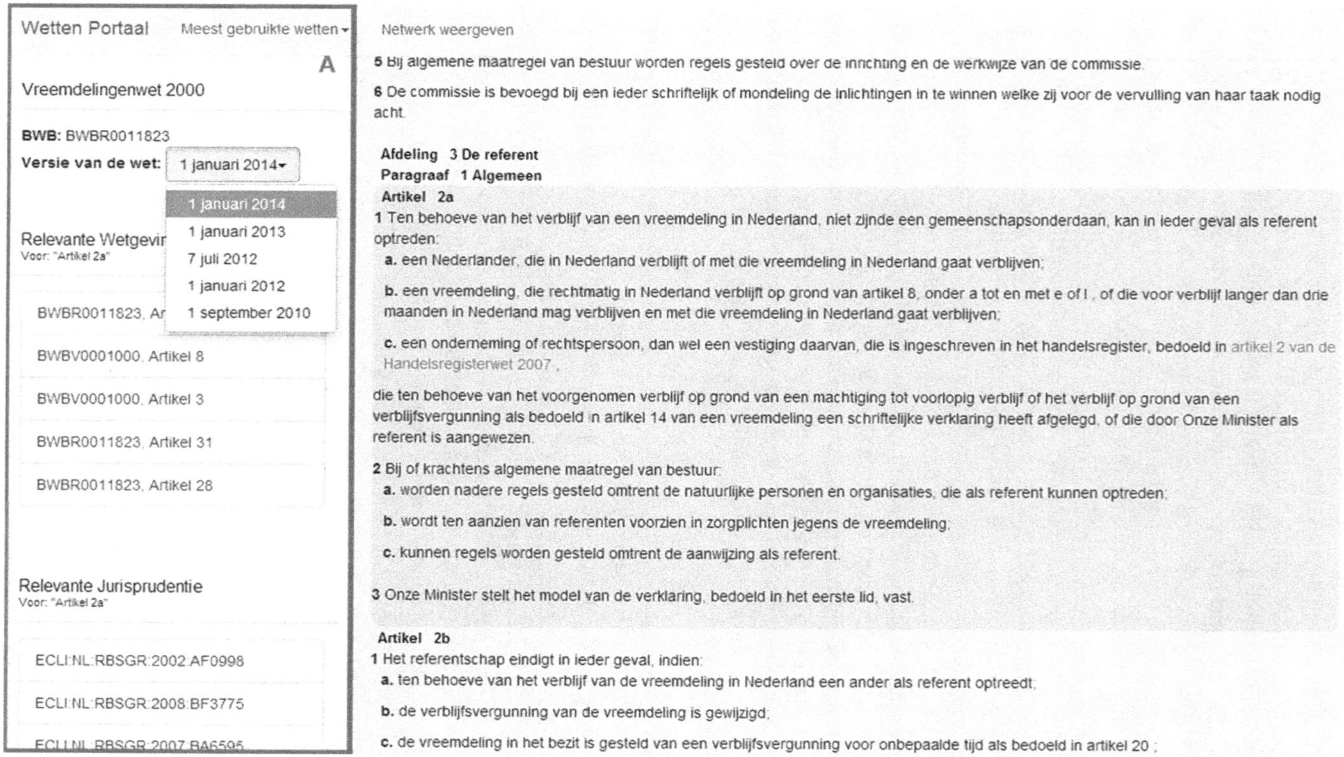

Wetten Portaal   Meest gebruikte wetten ▾   A

Vreemdelingenwet 2000

BWB: BWBR0011823
Versie van de wet: 1 januari 2014 ▾

1 januari 2014
1 januari 2013
7 juli 2012
1 januari 2012
1 september 2010

Relevante Wetgevir...
Voor: "Artikel 2a"

BWBR0011823. Ar...

BWBV0001000 Artikel 8

BWBV0001000 Artikel 3

BWBR0011823. Artikel 31

BWBR0011823. Artikel 28

Relevante Jurisprudentie
Voor: "Artikel 2a"

ECLI:NL:RBSGR:2002:AF0998

ECLI:NL:RBSGR:2008:BF3775

ECLI:NL:RBSGR:2007:BA5595

Netwerk weergeven

5 Bij algemene maatregel van bestuur worden regels gesteld over de inrichting en de werkwijze van de commissie.

6 De commissie is bevoegd bij een ieder schriftelijk of mondeling de inlichtingen in te winnen welke zij voor de vervulling van haar taak nodig acht.

Afdeling 3 De referent
Paragraaf 1 Algemeen
Artikel 2a

1 Ten behoeve van het verblijf van een vreemdeling in Nederland, niet zijnde een gemeenschapsonderdaan, kan in ieder geval als referent optreden:

a. een Nederlander, die in Nederland verblijft of met die vreemdeling in Nederland gaat verblijven;

b. een vreemdeling, die rechtmatig in Nederland verblijft op grond van artikel 8, onder a tot en met e of l, of die voor verblijf langer dan drie maanden in Nederland mag verblijven en met die vreemdeling in Nederland gaat verblijven;

c. een onderneming of rechtspersoon, dan wel een vestiging daarvan, die is ingeschreven in het handelsregister, bedoeld in artikel 2 van de Handelsregisterwet 2007.

die ten behoeve van het voorgenomen verblijf op grond van een machtiging tot voorlopig verblijf of het verblijf op grond van een verblijfsvergunning als bedoeld in artikel 14 van een vreemdeling een schriftelijke verklaring heeft afgelegd, of die door Onze Minister als referent is aangewezen.

2 Bij of krachtens algemene maatregel van bestuur:

a. worden nadere regels gesteld omtrent de natuurlijke personen en organisaties, die als referent kunnen optreden.

b. wordt ten aanzien van referenten voorzien in zorgplichten jegens de vreemdeling.

c. kunnen regels worden gesteld omtrent de aanwijzing als referent.

3 Onze Minister stelt het model van de verklaring, bedoeld in het eerste lid, vast.

Artikel 2b

1 Het referentschap eindigt in ieder geval, indien:

a. ten behoeve van het verblijf van de vreemdeling in Nederland een ander als referent optreedt.

b. de verblijfsvergunning van de vreemdeling is gewijzigd.

c. de vreemdeling in het bezit is gesteld van een verblijfsvergunning voor onbepaalde tijd als bedoeld in artikel 20 ;

Fig. 10.2 The user has article 2a of the Immigration law in focus. Current version is January 2014 (see pull-down menu at left). Relevant other articles are presented in window A (red or dark border) on the left and below that relevant case law

comparison of the actual text of documents. As stated in the introduction, we focus on case law in this study.

Relevancy for case law is hard to define; it is subjective, depends on the task or problem of the user searching for case law and also on the type of user. For a student or novice, well known landmark cases might be very relevant, while for a legal expert these are probably not. He or she will be more interested in less known or very recent new cases. In previous research we have concentrated on legal expert users and we still are, but we will also have a look at the preferences of novices.

10.3.1 Reference Similarity Combined with Text Similarity

The first experiment concerns case law within the Dutch tax domain, about 6000 documents. They were taken from the official Dutch portal based on the metadata 'Field(s) of law' (see above). After some pre-processing in which XML tags and strange characters were removed, we used the same parser as described earlier to detect references to legislation. A small test revealed that this time overall recall of the parser was only 55%. Main reason is missing names and abbreviations of tax laws and the use of different terms in the tax domain (like 'protocol') compared to other domains of law.

The effect of these omissions is multiplied if a case refers to the same item more than once.

Our hypothesis is that 'similar' cases can be identified by similarity in the legislation they cite and by similarity of the words used in the judgements. As a baseline we use the similarity in words used (text similarity): Bag-of-words combined with normalised TF/IDF weighting and cosine similarity.[9]

TF/IDF corrects for frequency of terms and normalisation for the length of documents; otherwise documents with highly frequent words and long documents would be overrated by the cosine similarity measure. For any document in our set (the focus document) we can now select the n-most similar other documents from that set. The left part of Table 10.1 gives an example for the ten most similar documents found this way for a verdict of the court of Amsterdam of 2010 (BO1378[10]) on the value of a house. The most similar case is one of the court of Alkmaar of 2008 (BC6103[11]), also on the value of a house.

The same algorithms are used to calculate the reference structure similarity between two documents. The right part of Table 10.1 gives the ten most similar

---

[9]TfidfVectorizer of SciKit-learn (Pedregosa et al. 2011) was used with minimal document frequency set to 1 and maximum to.7.

[10]http://deeplink.rechtspraak.nl/uitspraak?id=ECLI:NL:RBAMS:2010:BO1378.

[11]http://deeplink.rechtspraak.nl/uitspraak?id=ECLI:NL:RBALK:2008:BC6103.

Table 10.1 Ten most similar documents to RBAMS-2010-BO1378 according to bag-of-words (left) or bag-of-references (right)

	ECLI-NL-RBAMS-2010-BO1378			
	Bag of words		Bag of references	
1	RBALK-2008-BC6103	0.72	RBSGR-2008-BD1495	0.89
2	RBDOR-2010-BM0117	0.69	RBUTR-2010-BU4490	0.73
3	RBALK-2011-BQ0469	0.64	RBOVE-2014-951	0.69
4	RBARN-2006-AY9465	0.64	RBALK-2008-BD7537	0.69
5	RBDOR-2010-BO5257	0.62	RBALK-2007-BB9105	0.69
6	RBAMS-2011-BV6758	0.61	RBAMS-2011-BQ424	0.65
7	RBDOR-2010-BM2339	0.61	RBALK-2008-BC4175	0.64
8	GHAMS-2013-CA2684	0.61	RBALK-2012-BX0044	0.59
9	RBAMS-2011-BR6478	0.60	RBALK-2008-BD5937	0.58
10	RBHAA-2006-AZ2187	0.59	GHAMS-2001-AD8208	0.57

documents based on that method. Here number 1 is a verdict of the court of The Hague of 2008 (BD1495[12]) on pollution tax for commercial property.

The final step combines the bag-of-words similarity score and the bag-of-references similarity score by taking the average of the two scores. Now we can determine the n most similar documents for any *focus* document. We chose to only take into account the focus documents that have at least four outgoing references for now, this because of the relatively low recall of the parser. If a focus document has only one outgoing reference, the bag-of-references similarity scores will be either 0.0 or 1.0; this may be acceptable in a later stage with a superior reference parser, but at this stage these extreme scores are too uncertain.

Formative Evaluation

A small group of experts was asked to evaluate the system. They were asked to first read a focus document, randomly selected from a prepared database[13] and shown on an evaluation website that was created for this purpose. Subsequently they were asked to read six recommended documents and rank them on relevancy to the focus document. The most relevant one is ranked first (1), the least relevant last (6). The six documents were three with the highest similarity scores for the baseline implementation (bag-of-words only) and three documents with the highest similarity scores for the bag-of-words combined with the bag-of-references. They were also asked to give an overall score for the relevance of a suggestion on a scale from 1 to 10 with

---

[12]http://deeplink.rechtspraak.nl/uitspraak?id=ECLI:NL:RBSGR:2008:BD1495.

[13]Because we are interested in whether adding the bag-of-references to the similarity scores improves performance, documents that had recommendations that occurred in both sets were removed.

ECLI (Uitspraak)	(Meest relevant)	1	2	3	4	5	6	(Minst relevant)	Score relevantie
ECLI:NL:HR:2005:AR7771		•							3
ECLI:NL:HR:2008:BG4247						•			4
ECLI:NL:GHARN:2001:AD6171			•						7
ECLI:NL: GHARN:2001:AB2912					•				1 (Niet relevant)
ECLI:NL:RBALK:2010:BQ0425			•						10 (Zeer relevant)
ECLI:NL:GHARN:2000:AA7210							•		7

Fig. 10.3 Adapted from a screenshot of the evaluation site (in Dutch)

Table 10.2 Results expert evaluation

	Average rank	Average score
Bag-of-words only (baseline)	3.06	5.58
Bag-of-words with bag-of-references	3.94	4.46

1 representing 'not relevant' and 10 'very relevant'. This was done to assess the overall quality of suggestions. Even very bad suggestions may be ranked after all. Figure 10.3 gives an example screen from the evaluation site. Our intuition was that it is easier to rank suggestions for relevance than to assess the overall relevance of a suggestion.

This method of evaluation is rather subjective if a small amount of test subjects is used, but if can serve to determine if the research is heading in the right direction and find possible bugs and errors (Shani and Gunawardana 2011).

Four experts evaluated 18 cases; 15 unique ones and 3 the same for all experts. Results are presented in Table 10.2. It is clear that adding the bag-of-references worsens performance. This may partly be due to the fact that only 55% of references were found.

It may also be that similarity in references reflects something else than similarity in text. To further investigate this aspect, we examined to what extend the bag-of-words approach suggests the same documents as the bag-of-references approach. We analysed the top ten recommendations for 1000 focus documents for both approaches. We ignored recommendations with a similarity score of zero. Of the remaining 9528 recommendations, 1135 were recommended by both algorithms (about 12%).

Again, the amount of overlap may turn out to be higher with a better performing parser. Another explanation is that similarity in references reflects a more abstract commonality than our evaluators could spot or found useful.

10.3.2   Network Analysis Combined with Topic Modelling

A more advanced approach of comparing similarity of texts than the bag-of-words approach discussed above is that of *topic modelling*. A topic model represents a document, a court judgement in this case, as a mixture of topics. A topic is a set of words or phrases. Perhaps the most common topic model currently in use is Latent

Table 10.3 Example output of 3 suggestions for case ECLI:NL:RBSGR:2009: BH7787

Case	Similarity measure
ECLI:NL:RBSGR:2009:BH7787	100.00
ECLI:NL:RBSGR:2004:AQ5970	99.28
ECLI:NL:RBDHA:2015:4915	99.01
ECLI:NL:RVS:2004:AQ5615	98.67

Dirichlet Allocation (LDA) from Blei et al. (2003). One downside of this approach is that it treats documents as bags of words, i.e. ignores word order and therefore word phrases like 'European Union' or 'our Minister'. Several extensions of LDA have been proposed, one of which is Turbo Topics (Blei and Lafferty 2009) which starts like LDA, but subsequently significant words that are preceding or succeeding topic-words are searched in the texts and added to the topic model. In this experiment we use the open source implementation of Turbo Topics in MALLET.[14]

To be able to compare the results with suggestions purely based on network analysis, we decided to use the same domain as in the earlier work described above, namely immigration law (Winkels et al. 2014). After some pre-processing and selection of those cases with actual content, we worked with a set of nearly 13,500 cases.

Formative Evaluation

After all cases were represented as mixtures of topics, we selected the n best suggestions for each case by calculating the similarity between the topic mixtures. We calculate the sum of squared errors between a specified case and all other cases and convert this to a similarity value ranging from 0% to 100% overlap. Table 10.3 gives an example for three suggestions for case ECLI:NL:RBSGR:2009:BH7787 (a case of 2009 of the court of The Hague about a refugee from Turkey who was a courier for PKK) with similarity measures. It obviously has a similarity measure of 100% with itself. Next comes a case from the same court of 2004 with a similarity in topics of more than 99% (also about a member of the PKK), etc.

For this project, the evaluators consisted of three novices, two legal experts with experience in the immigration law, and two legal experts without experience in this field. For the results the four legal experts were pooled together, since there was no difference in their evaluations.

The evaluators were given five randomly selected cases for which they ranked three suggestions from best to worst, and for which they stated whether any of the three suggestions is good enough for a recommender system. One of the three suggestions was most similar according to the method using a topic model, another was the most relevant based on the references to legislation according to Winkels et al. (2014) and one of the suggestions was based on a combination of the two methods. For the combination of the two methods, a list of the top 200 suggestions according to the topic model was obtained (for each randomly selected case), and

---

[14]MAchine Learning for LanguagE Toolkit, McCallum (2002).

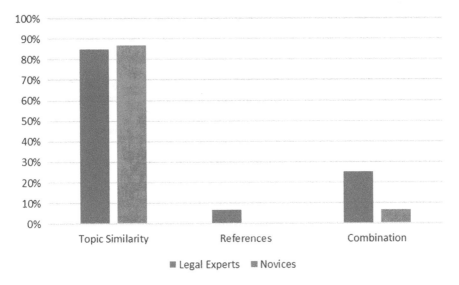

Fig. 10.4 Percentage of evaluators that thought a suggestion was good enough for recommendation

also a list of the top ten suggestions according to the references to legislation. The first suggestion from the top ten list that appeared in the other list of the top 200 suggestions, was chosen as the suggestion based on both methods. The evaluators were unaware of which suggestion was obtained by which method.

Both legal experts and novices showed significant preference for the suggestions based on topic similarity. The legal experts wanted to see 85% of the suggestions based on topic similarity in a recommender system, for the novices this was 87% (see Fig. 10.4). The legal experts ranked the suggestions based on topic similarity as best suggestion 80% of the time, while the novices always ranked the suggestion based on topic similarity as best suggestion. This indicates that suggestions based on topic similarity can give useful suggestions within Dutch case law.

10.4   Conclusions

We described results of research that is part of the OpenLaws.eu project. Ultimate aim is to deliver a platform for using, sharing and enriching big open legal data. Besides offering users the opportunity to collect, organize and annotate legal data, we also want to offer automatic suggestions based on analysis of existing data. In the future that may also be based on user-generated data. Users of OpenLaws can already annotate sources of law, highlight sections or phrases, group sources together in folders and link a source to other sources. In the future, this data can be analysed as well to improve suggestions for other users.

For now the recommendations are based on the analysis of official sources of law. We have presented first results for available data in the Netherlands. Based on analysis of the network of both legislation and case law, we offer users suggestions for interesting material based on their current focus document.

We have shown that it works quite well to automatically find and resolve references to legislation in Dutch case law. The parser was perhaps a bit over-fitted for the immigration domain, since it performed less well in the tax domain. It can easily be improved, but we will have to check whether this has repercussions for the immigration domain and how it performs in other legal fields. The prototype system will perform much better when running on a proper server. We also did not exploit the network of case law itself this time. In Winkels et al. (2011) we showed that this can be used to estimate the authority of cases, so if we include this the suggestions of relevant case law should be improved.

The network of references can be used to provide users of the legislative portal with relevant judicial decisions given their current focus and moreover, suggest additional relevant legislative sources. Another next step is adding legal commentaries and doctrine to the network and possibly parliamentary data.

When compared with suggestions of case law based on similarity of the actual text of the judgements, whether seen as just 'bags of words' or as a mixture of 'topics', users seem to prefer those over the suggestions based on network analysis or similarity in reference structures. We still have the intuition that similarity in reference structure indicates some common feature of cases, but perhaps it is too abstract for users. In our first experiment we treated the references as an unordered set; perhaps we should retain the order and try again.

In the future we will use some additional features as:

- The relative frequency of the reference in a court decision (what van Opijnen (2014) called 'multiplicity').
- The hierarchical position of the law cited, e.g. whether the referred law is a European directive or treaty, or a governmental decree.
- Document structure level of the reference. A lower document structure level (e.g. article or clause instead of a chapter) suggests a more specific reference, which could indicate a different role.
- The date of a case, preferring more recent cases for expert users. We can assume experts are well aware of older (landmark) cases, and will be more interested in (very) recent ones.

Acknowledgements Part of this research is co-funded by the Civil Justice Programme of the European Union in the OpenLaws.eu project under grant JUST/2013/JCIV/AG/4562. I would like to thank my students: Erwin van den Berg, Bart Vredebregt and Wolf Vos who performed the experiments.

References

Blei DM, Lafferty JD (2009) Visualizing topics with multi-word expressions. https://arxiv.org/pdf/0907.1013.pdf. Accessed 30 Nov 2017

Blei DM, Ng AY, Jordan MI (2003) Latent Dirichlet allocation. J Mach Learn Res 3:993–1022. http://www.jmlr.org/papers/volume3/blei03a/blei03a.pdf. Accessed 30 Nov 2017

de Maat E, Winkels R, Engers T (2006) Automated detection of reference structures in law. In: van Engers T (ed) JURIX 2006. IOS Press, Amsterdam, pp 41–50

Fowler JH, Jeon S (2008) The authority of Supreme Court precedent. Soc Netw 30(1):16–30. https://doi.org/10.1016/j.socnet.2007.05.001

Hoekstra R (2011) The MetaLex document server - legal documents as versioned linked data. In: Aroyo L et al (eds) The Semantic Web – ISWC 2011. Lecture notes in computer science, vol 7032. Springer, Berlin, pp 128–143. https://doi.org/10.1007/978-3-642-25093-4_9

Liiv I, Vedeshin A, Täks E (2007) Visualization and structure analysis of legislative acts: a case study on the law of obligations. In: ICAIL 2007 Proceedings of the 11th international conference on artificial intelligence and law. ACM Digital Library, New York, pp 189–190. https://dl.acm.org/citation.cfm?id=1276353. Accessed 30 Nov 2017

Mazzega P, Bourcier D, Boulet R (2009) The network of French legal codes. In: ICAIL 2009 Proceedings of the 12th international conference on artificial intelligence and law. ACM Digital Library, New York, pp 236–237. https://dl.acm.org/citation.cfm?id=1568271. Accessed 30 Nov 2017

McCallum AK (2002) Mallet: A machine learning for language toolkit. http://mallet.cs.umass.edu

Newman M (2010) Networks: an introduction. Oxford University Press, Oxford

Palmirani M, Brighi R, Massini M (2003) Automated extraction of normative references in legal texts. In: 9th international conference on artificial intelligence and law. ACM Digital Library, New York, pp 105–106. https://dl.acm.org/citation.cfm?id=1047815. Accessed 30 Nov 2017

Pedregosa F, Varoquaux G, Gramfort A, Michel V, Thirion B, Grisel O, Blondel M, Prettenhofer P, Weiss R, Dubourg V, Vanderplas J, Passos A, Cournapeau D, Brucher M, Perrot M, Duchesnay E (2011) Scikit-learn: machine learning in Python. J Mach Learn Res 12:2825–2830. http://www.jmlr.org/papers/volume12/pedregosa11a/pedregosa11a.pdf. Accessed 30 Nov 2017

Saur KG (1998) Functional requirements for bibliographic records: final report/IFLA Study Group on the Functional Requirements for Bibliographic Records. UBCIM publications New series vol 19, München. https://www.ifla.org/files/assets/cataloguing/frbr/frbr.pdf. Accessed 30 Nov 2017

Shani G, Gunawardana A (2011) Evaluating recommendation systems. In: Ricci F, Rokach L, Shapira B, Kantor P (eds) Recommender systems handbook. Springer, Boston, pp 257–297. https://doi.org/10.1007/978-0-387-85820-3_8

Tran OT, Le Nguyen M, Shimazu A (2013) Reference resolution in legal texts. In: Proceedings of the fourteenth international conference on artificial intelligence and law. ACM Digital Library, New York, pp 101–110. https://dl.acm.org/citation.cfm?id=2514601.2514613. Accessed 30 Nov 2017

van Opijnen M (2014) Op en in het web. Hoe de toegankelijkheid van rechterlijke uitspraken kan worden verbeterd. PhD Thesis in Dutch, University of Amsterdam

Wass C, Dini P, Eiser T, Heistracher Th, Lampoltshammer Th, Marcon G, Sageder C, Tsiavos P, Winkels RGF (2013) OpenLaws.eu. In: Proceedings of the 16th international legal informatics symposium IRIS 2013, Salzburg, February 2013, pp 209–212. https://pure.uva.nl/ws/files/2517952/167594_OPENLAWS.eu_IRIS13.pdf. Accessed 30 Nov 2017

Winkels RGF, de Ruyter J, Kroese H (2011) Determining authority of Dutch case law. In: Atkinson K (ed) JURIX 2011. IOS Press, Amsterdam, pp 103–112

Winkels RGF, Boer A, Plantevin I (2013) Creating context networks in Dutch legislation. In: Ashley K (ed) JURIX 2013. IOS Press, Amsterdam, pp 155–164

Winkels RGF, Boer A, Vredebregt B, van Someren A (2014) Towards a legal recommender system. In: Hoekstra R (ed) Legal knowledge and information systems. JURIX 2014: the twenty-seventh international conference. Volume 271 of frontiers in artificial intelligence and applications. IOS Press, Amsterdam, pp 169–178

Chapter 11
Environmental and Trade Regimes: Comparison of Hypergraphs Modeling the Ratifications of UN Multilateral Treaties

Romain Boulet, Ana Flávia Barros-Platiau, and Pierre Mazzega

Abstract In analyzing the ratifications of Multilateral Environmental Agreements (MEAs) and United Nations-based trade agreements, this study pursues two goals: first, to provide evidence of the limitations of the role played by the United Nations in promoting sustainable development as a bridge between both regimes, although member states are roughly the same; second, on a methodological side, to contribute to the exploration of the use of hypergraphs to model a dynamic in International Relations, as illustrated by analyzing empirical data easily accessible and available on the web. We use 3550 ratification dates of MEAs (1979–2015) and 834 ratifications of trade agreements (1963–2014) available on the website of the United Nations Treaty Collection. The hypergraph-based analysis of the temporal successions of ratifications highlights informal communities of countries whose contours emerge through this uncoordinated process of ratification. The European countries and more specifically members of the European Union, and their Atlantic allies stand out as having the leadership of the construction of a global environmental order. However, no formally established community of countries emerges from the chronology of ratification of the United Nations trade agreements. In this particular UN context, none of the contemporary trade powers is even central to this dynamic. Indeed, most trade negotiations take place outside the United Nations arena, particularly in the framework of the World Trade Organization, or in regional, bilateral, or even minilateral partnerships.

R. Boulet (✉)
Univ Lyon, Jean Moulin, iaelyon, Magellan, Lyon, France
e-mail: romain.boulet@univ-lyon3.fr

A. F. Barros-Platiau
IREL, Institute of International Relations, University of Brasilia, Brasilia DF, Brazil
e-mail: anabarros@unb.br

P. Mazzega
UMR5563 GET Geosciences Environment Toulouse, CNRS/University of Toulouse, Toulouse, France

Strathclyde Centre for Environmental Law and Governance (SCELG), University of Strathclyde, Glasgow, UK
e-mail: pierre.mazzegaciamp@get.omp.eu

© Springer Nature Switzerland AG 2019
R. Boulet et al. (eds.), *Law, Public Policies and Complex Systems: Networks in Action*, Law, Governance and Technology Series 42,
https://doi.org/10.1007/978-3-030-11506-7_11

11.1   Introduction

Under the aegis of the United Nations (UN), most multilateral[1] treaties are negotiated by about 200 sovereign States for years, and then are eventually signed and
ratified by some or most of these States. Although negotiation processes are at the
center of the research agenda in International Relations, these processes leading to
ratifications, on the contrary, are still very little studied. However, the ratification
processes vary according to the country considered, in particular according to the
interactions among public and private, domestic and multinational actors, this
alongside many other determinants (Lantis 2009). In addition to this, ratification
does not mean the full implementation of the international obligations contracted
through the agreements, which ultimately depends on the true willingness of the
State to meet these commitments, and to devote the means necessary to their
achievement.

Although trade negotiations take place mostly outside the UN, they are directly
connected to the UN legal and diplomatic framework. Multilateral, bilateral or
minilateral arenas such as the European Union (EU), the World Trade Organization
(WTO) (Falkner 2015), the Triad NAFTA, the G7, the BRICs, the Trans-Pacific
Partnership (TTP) or the Trans-Pacific Trade and Investment Partnership (TTIP)
have proliferated.[2] Similarly, minilateral or regional arrangements also exist in the
various environmental regimes (on climate change, protection and conservation of
biological diversity, ocean resource management and governance, etc.) as illustrated
by the examples of the regional agreements, specific conventions, such as the Arctic
Council and the Antarctic System, to name only a few of them. Trade and the
environment were usually treated in the UN negotiations as separate international
regimes[3] during the reconstruction of the Western liberal order or even after the
collapse of the bipolar order in the 1990s. But the links between them are increasingly recognized in both regimes as a requisite to get closer to the conditions for
sustainable development, according to the strengthening of the international obligations established by the multilateral agreements. The WTO agreement of 1995 is the

---

[1]Regional treaties concern restricted communities of States.

[2]The European Union is the most successful political arrangement and the only one that covers the
commercial and environmental agendas. The Triad composed by Washington, Brussels and Tokyo
was only an informal arrangement to reinforce the emergence of Japan in the 1980s. NAFTA is the
result of Washington's leadership on Toronto and Mexico. The TTP and the TTIP are both mega
accords that suffered heavily with Donald Trump's trade policy since 2016. The G7 is the group of
the most industrialized countries united to drive the global economy outside the UN framework.
BRICS is the informal group of emerging countries—Brazil, Federation of Russia, India, China,
South Africa—under Chinese leadership. The two latter are more economic than trade-oriented, but
they do foster intra-group trade.

[3]According to Krasner (1983), p. 141, it is "sets of implicit or explicit principles, norms, rules, and
decision-making procedures around which actor expectations converge, in a variety of areas of
international relations."

most emblematic example[4] of this trend. Thus, processes of juxtaposition, privatization and fragmentation of these two regimes (and complex of regimes)[5] represent a challenge for the UN over the coming years (Karns et al. 2015). Both regimes are linked because the trade and environment agendas have never been so intertwined (UNEP 2017a,b).

To better understand this dual evolution, this article analyzes the agendas of multilateral negotiations and the place/role of States on the basis of the ratifications of treaties that follow these negotiations. The interest of an analysis using mathematical modeling and the theory of international relations related to trade and environment is twofold. First, it is to test whether the UN manages to function as a reasonably homogeneous system, that is to say, to play the role of "constructor of the social world" to use the words of Barnett and Finnemore (2004). If the ratification of multilateral treaties shows a convergence of States parties to the two regimes, the contribution of the United Nations can be considered as significant. Then, the analysis of the results obtained will establish valid correlations concerning this trade-environment relation. If both of these assumptions are true, sustainable development—relying on the three pillars of economic viability, environmental preservation and social justice—can be seen as a structuring concept of international relations, just like the affirmation by Shelton and Kiss (2007) concerning International Environmental Law. If the results are too contrasted, it would be wise to consider the UN as an epiphenomenon (Mearsheimer 2001; Barnett and Finnemore 2007; Viola and Franchini 2018) playing only a marginal role. As a consequence, it may be argued that the sustainable development principle fails to structure both the international public law and the international relations.

In Sect. 11.2 we rapidly expose the logic that governs the elaboration and possible ratification of international treaties in trade and environment respectively. Then (Sect. 11.3) we present the data we use and the proposed analysis based on hypergraphs, defining this mathematical object and detailing the tools used in this study. In Sect. 11.4 we expose and compare the results of our analyzes carried out on the domains of environment and trade respectively. Section 11.5 discusses the contribution and limitations of the approach we have developed in the context of IR analysis, these limitations being mainly related to the specificity of the ratification dynamics according to the international regime approach.

---

[4]The WTO is not part of the United Nations, but relations between the two organizations have been governed since 1995 by the "Arrangements for Effective Cooperation with Other Intergovernmental Organizations".

[5]The debate on international regimes took shape around the 1970s. Using functional, strategic, and organizational arguments, Keohane and Victor (2010) described a regime complex as "a loosely coupled set of specific regimes".

11.2 Ratification of Trade and Environmental Treaties

11.2.1 The UN Convergence on Trade and Environment

One objective of the UN is to ensure more cohesion to a global trade and environmental governance by setting the basic rights and duties for all the States members. Within the United Nations, seen as a normative and material structure,[6] a myriad of public and private actors meet (IISD/UNEP 2005; Karns et al. 2015). From an institutional viewpoint, both areas—trade and environment—also shared a difficult start in the multilateral governance architecture. The International Trade Organization (ITO) could not be created following the refusal of the US Congress to ratify the charter in the late 1940s. More than three decades later, the United Nations Environment Program (UNEP) was established as the first step in building a real organization. Immediately after the 1992 Rio Summit, the World Trade Organization was created under the leadership of Washington, thus, confirming the predominance of the logic concerned with the regulation of trade over the one ensuring a sustainable management of the environment and natural resources. In response, in the year 2000, the UN orchestrated the global agenda through the Millennium Development Goals (MDGs) followed in 2015 by the Sustainable Development Goals (the SDGs or Global Goals),[7] so as to build a more harmonious and favorable context to sustainable development up to 2030. Recently the UNEP was renamed UN Environment but without structural changes.[8]

11.2.2 Three Factors of the Interlocking of the Two Regimes

Despite the limitations posed by the separation of the trade and environmental regimes over the past seven decades, there are several simultaneous interlinking factors, especially embedded in political, economic and legal approaches. A first factor is the economic approach that has been adopted to improve the collective management of natural resources. The concern regarding neo-Malthusian approaches of raw materials shortages in function of the population explosion in some Third World countries, leading to significant market imbalances (Meadows et al. 1972), is at the origin of the 1972 United Nations Conference on the Human Environment (UNCHE). Over time, market instruments such as quotas, labels and certifications have been used more extensively in environmental regimes. The Convention on International Trade in Endangered Species of Wild Fauna and

---

[6]According to the neoliberal and institutional research in International Relations, neo-realists, like Susan Strange (1998), prefer to describe the power structure as material.

[7]Including Goal 9 which deals with sustainable and inclusive industrialization.

[8]https://www.unenvironment.org/ Accessed 9 Feb 2018.

Flora (CITES[9]) is an example of the use of market instruments to protect endangered species. Another example is the global climate regime, having created the flexibility mechanisms with the 1997 Kyoto Protocol and encouraged carbon markets, allowing entrepreneurs to participate directly in solutions for the mitigation of greenhouse gas impacts. In the forest quasi-regime (de Carvalho 2012), REDD and REDD+ mechanisms have been designed to counter deforestation. Thus, under the 2015 Paris Agreement similar mechanisms have been proposed. At the Rio summit in 2012, the green economy was promoted as the new bridge between the commercial and environmental regimes.[10]

A second factor is based on the development of scientific knowledge. Among the key concepts linking both regimes, "sustainable development" was established in the Brundtland Report (1987) as a major concept triggering conciliatory efforts to promote international cooperation and effective multilateralism, linking trade, social justice and the environment. In the same vein, the concept of "global commons" established by the scientific community (Ostrom et al. 2002), provides a framework for a more sustainable management of shared resources. It also agreed on the concept of an "Anthropocene" (Crutzen and Steffen 2003; Biermann et al. 2012), reinforcing human responsibility to treat the environment as a set of goods and to consider the importance of ecosystem services (Nakicenovic et al. 2016).

A third factor in the overlap of the two regimes has been the recognition of legal principles, starting with the sustainable development. Trade and environment share the logic of State differentiation used in the framework of the GATT and the WTO with regard to the least developed countries: the States are sovereign but they possess asymmetrical capacities and different historical development trajectories, hence the principle of common but differentiated responsibilities consolidated in environmental law, especially in the climate regime. The Cartagena Protocol[11] on Biosafety to the Convention on Biological Diversity corroborated the precautionary principle, against the principle of non-discrimination of the WTO. As a result, countries had the right to refuse the purchase of living genetic modified organisms, in order to avoid risks that are still poorly known to consumers' health and the risks of biological contamination. The WTO Dispute Settlement Body further developed the precautionary principle and contributed to its inclusion in commercial litigation. The polluter-pays principles and the right to development, advocated by the countries of the South, are also present in the UN talks on trade and environment.

---

[9]CITES: https://cites.org/eng/disc/text.php Accessed 9 Feb 2018.

[10]https://sustainabledevelopment.un.org/index.php?menu=1225 Accessed 9 Feb 2018.

[11]Cartagena Protocol, adopted on 29 January 2000 and entered into force on 11 September 2003: http://bch.cbd.int/protocol/ Accessed 9 Feb 2018.

Table 11.1 Compared main ingredients of norms creation

	Environment	Trade
Main actors	UN, EU	USA, EU, China
Main International Organizations	UNGA, UNEP, UNDP, IPCC	GATT, UNIDO, UNCTAD, WTO
Highlights	1972, 1992, 2002, 2012	1970s, 1994
International Law	Rather declaratory (soft law)	Rather mandatory (hard law)
Paradigms	Sustainable development, global commons, differentiated responsibilities, MDGs and Global Goals	Free-trade, non-discrimination, regional integration, green economy, blue economy

11.2.3 However Two Orthogonal Directions

The environmental logic was previously concerned with issues that were treated as exclusive problems of sovereign States, such as pollution or the appropriation and consumption of raw resources. It then turned to more cross-border collective action issues (such as the fight against acid rain and oil spills), and then to global issues (such as the loss of biodiversity, climate change and its impacts, marine resource management, or nuclear contamination). Thus, the construction of international regimes since the last century attests to the internationalization of environmental issues, whose central concept was the ecological interdependence (OCDE 1982). States are asked to accept negative international obligations such as not to cause harm beyond their national jurisdiction, and positive obligations such as to prevent, cooperate, inform, repair the damages caused. Environmental agreements are therefore negotiated for the sake of preservation (fragile or threatened ecosystems), conservation (the most rational use of resources possible) or collective management, on behalf of present and future generations. Since 1972 (UNCHE, Stockholm), the UN has been organizing summits to promote the sustainable development agenda, the main ones being held in 1992 (Rio de Janeiro Earth Summit), 2002 (World Summit on Sustainable Development, Johannesburg) and 2012 (United Nations Conference on Sustainable Development – or Rio + 20).

The commercial logic is quite distinct (see Table 11.1). First, it is based on the *lex mercatoria*, European medieval customary law, with its own codes of conduct. Then, its main purpose is not to protect the Planet or its natural resources, but to build a material and normative structure for free trade and, to a lesser extent, the integration of markets at the global level. Its stage of internationalization began five centuries earlier, with the great European navigators. Private and public actors interact intensely in complex and asymmetrical interdependencies. Agreements in the UN framework are less numerous and effective than those established outside it. A strong assumption is that the trading powers prefer to negotiate with each other, like the United States and China, because the South forms a majority in the UN organizations (Devin and Smouts 2012) and the WTO. As a consequence, the Doha

Round[12] has been stalled for too long following several deep disagreements, aggravated by the 2008 crisis on the Euro-Atlantic axis. This partly explains why these States will not appear very much in the graphs below.

Taking into account countries individually since 1972, the two largest economies in the world, industrial and technological powers, polluters and emitters of greenhouse gases are the United States of America and China. Today they are also the biggest investors in technologies related to the "green economy", in particular to ensure their energy security. The USA is also the largest promoter of free trade since the establishment of the United Nations, but in environmental regimes it does not ratify most important agreements, despite its decisive participation. In addition, President Donald Trump denounced the Paris Agreement on Climate Change[13] in June 2017. On the contrary, China participates in the environmental debates and ratifies the major agreements, which does not constitute a guarantee that the Asian giant will implement them. It also participates in trade talks, bringing the G77/China, the BRICs and the G20 as central players, with increasing weight since its official WTO entry and the implementation of Ji Xiping's active diplomacy with the 2017 Rejuvenation Plan.

The European Union, for its part, is the only stable community in the environment regime, playing a central role in its region and within the United Nations (see below). It is irrefutably a central player in environmental and commercial law and can therefore be considered as a normative power in these two areas (Laïdi 2006), even after the conclusion of the BREXIT.[14] However, the EU is entangled in and weakened by current crises and contemporary Euro-skeptic rhetoric.

11.3 Data Analysis with Hypergraphs

Does the analysis of the history of the ratification of multilateral environmental and trade agreements corroborate the landscape of international relations just described? Can some information on ratifications be used to produce empirical evidence based on accessible and open data, about this divide between the logic of preserving the environment and the logic of growth through international trade? In order to answer these questions which concern as much a theme of globalization as a methodological reflection, we will, first of all, recall and present some results obtained on the ratification of the MAEs (Sect. 11.3.1) and then introduce (Sect. 11.3.2) hypergraphs and the associated analysis procedure (Sect. 11.3.3).

---

[12]Last WTO round of negotiations began in 2001, the Doha Development Program aimed to reduce trade barriers and facilitate the expansion of world trade.

[13]https://ec.europa.eu/clima/policies/international/negotiations/paris_fr Accessed 9 Feb 2018.

[14]The exit of the United Kingdom from the European Union voted in 2016.

11.3.1 Previous Results

In a previous work (Boulet et al. 2016), we analyzed 3550 ratifications related to 48 multilateral environmental agreements (MEAs) listed in chapter XXVII "Environment" of the United Nations Treaty Collection.[15] The analysis covering a period of 35 years (1979–2014) involves more than 195 countries (or entities like the EU with a mandate to sign and ratify these agreements). A first simple graph built on the basis of a rule[16] of succession of ratifications has made it possible to identify communities of MEAs emerging from this ratification dynamics and to interpret these communities of treaties according to the fundamental interests of the signatory countries (Boulet et al. 2016). A second rule,[17] somehow dual to the first, leads to build another graph where the vertices are the countries. Using various algorithms, we identify informal communities of countries[18] emerging from this ratification history (see Table 11.2) and represent them on a geographical map (Fig. 11.1).

The most salient result is the presence of the community gathering mainly Euro-Atlantic countries. Through the inclusion of all its States members the European Union is the only formal institution included in such an informal community[19] emerging from 35 years of ratification of MEAs. The calculation of the centralities of the vertices of the graph underlines even more the predominant place of European countries, in particular countries from Northern Europe and Norway (see Table 11.3).

From now our goal is twofold: (a) to enrich and improve this graph-based approach by introducing hypergraphs as a way to overcome problems related to the representation and modeling of simultaneous ratifications that are occurring recurrently in the database (see Sect. 11.4.1); (b) to explore what the hypergraph-based approach could bring to two highly differentiated areas of international policy and how it would be useful to conduct critical comparative analyzes (this is done on a small scale since we consider only the UN trade treaties).

---

[15]https://treaties.un.org/pages/Treaties.aspx?id=27&subid=A&lang=en Accessed 9 Feb 2018.

[16]There is a directed link from agreement A1 to agreement A2 if A2 is the first agreement ratified after agreement A1 by a same country.

[17]There is a directed link from country C2 to country C1 if C2 is the first country after C1 to have ratified the same MEA.

[18]We describe as "stable" the informal communities presented here in the sense that the list of countries that each one of them contains is found whatever the algorithm used.

[19]Indeed, none of the other formal communities (economic, political, strategic, security, …)— ASEAN, BRICs, African Union, MERCOSUR, …—appear in any of the countries communities induced by the history of ratifications.

Table 11.2 Main country communities underlying the MEAs ratifications graph (see Fig. 11.1)

Community (colour on Fig. 11.1)	Members
C1 38 members (red)	Austria, Belarus, Belgium, Bulgaria, Canada, Croatia, Cyprus, Czech Rep., Denmark, Estonia, EU, Finland, France, Germany, Greece, Hungary, Ireland, Italy, Japan, Jordan, Latvia, Liechtenstein, Lithuania, Luxembourg, Netherlands, Norway, Poland, Portugal, Romania, Russian Fed., Slovakia, Slovenia, Spain, Sweden, Switzerland, Ukraine, UK, USA
C2 32 members (blue)	Angola, Bahrain, Bangladesh, Bolivia, Burundi, Chad, Colombia, Comoros, Congo, Gambia, Ghana, Guinea, Haiti, Iran (Islamic Rep.), Israel, Kazakhstan, Kyrgyzstan, Madagascar, Mauritania, Micronesia (Fed.), Mozambique, Myanmar, Namibia, Pakistan, Palau, St. Vincent & Grenadines, Suriname, Swaziland, Turkmenistan, Vanuatu, Yemen, Zimbabwe
C3 22 members (green)	Antigua & Barbuda, Brazil, Chile, China, Ecuador, El Salvador, Ethiopia, Fiji, Guatemala, India, Kenya, Lesotho, Malaysia, Mali, Mauritius, Mexico, Morocco, Paraguay, Tanzania (Un. Rep.), Tunisia, Venezuela (Rep.), Zambia
C4 16 members (yellow)	Algeria, Barbados, Cambodia, Cameroon, Cuba, Congo (Dem. Rep.), Dominican Rep., Equatorial Guinea, Eritrea, Honduras, Kuwait, Lao (Dem. Rep.), Niger, Papua New Guinea, St. Kitts & Nevis, Sudan
C5 16 members (grey)	Arab Emirates (Un.), Bahamas, Bhutan, Dominica, Kiribati, Marshall Islands, Oman, Saudi Arabia, Senegal, Seychelles, Singapore, Sri Lanka, St. Lucia, Syria (Arab Rep.), Uganda, Uzbekistan

11.3.2 Directed Graphs and Hypergraphs: Definitions

Let us start by recalling definitions of graphs and hypergraphs. A *graph* is a set $V = \{v_1, v_2, . . ., v_n\}$ of vertices and a set E of edges, an edge being a subset of V with two elements. This simple (one often speaks of a *simple graph*) and binary (there exists or not a relation between two vertices) structure can be enriched by the addition of weight on the edges (*weighted graph*) or by the addition of an orientation on the edges (*directed graph*). So, a *directed graph* is defined by a set $V = \{v_1, v_2, . . ., v_n\}$ of vertices and a set E of directed edges, a directed edge being defined by a source vertex and a target vertex. Figure 11.2 illustrates these definitions.

A *hypergraph* is defined by a set $V = \{v_1, v_2, . . ., v_n\}$ of vertices and a set E of hyperedges, a hyperedge being a subset of V with several (two or more) elements. A directed hypergraph is a set $V = \{v_1, v_2, . . ., v_n\}$ of vertices and a set E of directed hyperedges, a directed hyperedge being defined by a set of source vertices and set of target vertices; these source set and target set being disjoint. Figure 11.3 illustrates these definitions.

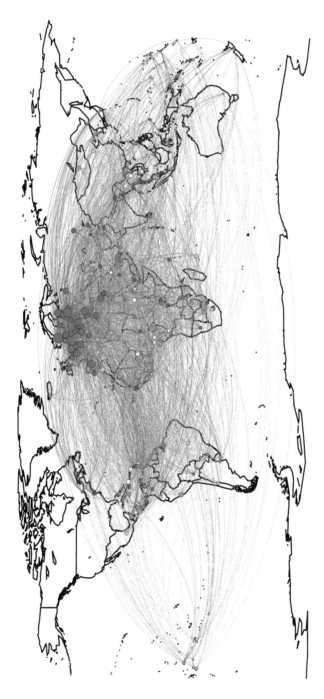

Fig. 11.1 The oriented graph associated with the ratifications of the MEAs by the 197 countries of the world. The vertices (countries) are colored according to their membership to a stable community revealed by the analysis (Table 11.2). The size of the vertices is proportional to their betweenness centrality measure. A link takes the color of its source vertex. [Figure prepared with *Gephi* for the graph and *Inkscape* for the map]

Table 11.3 Most central countries in the graph of environmental ratifications

Closeness centrality (rank)	Betweenness centrality (rank)
1. Norway	1. Hungary
2. France	2. Norway
3. Hungary	3. Lithuania
4. Luxembourg	4. Belgium
5. Spain	5. Austria
6. Netherlands	6. Spain
7. Finland	7. Estonia
8. Lithuania	8. Romania
9. Bulgaria	9. Netherlands
10. Denmark	10. Finland

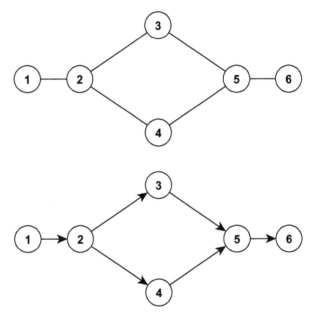

Fig. 11.2 Top: a graph whose set of vertices is {1, 2, 3, 4, 5, 6} and whose set of edges is {{1,2}, {2,3}, {2,4},{3,5},{4,5},{5,6}}. Bottom: A directed graph on the same set of vertices having 6 directed edges represented by arrows going from the source to the target

11.3.3 Analysis of a Directed Hypergraph

Our analysis of a directed hypergraph is based on its incidence matrix. The incidence matrix B of a directed hypergraph on n vertices and m directed hyperedges is the $n \times m$ matrix whose rows are labeled by vertices from 1 to n and whose columns are labeled by the directed hyperedges from 1 to m. The (i,j) entry of B is 1 if vertex i is a target of hyperedge j, -1 if vertex i is a source of hyperedge j and 0 otherwise (Gallo et al. 1993). Note that the sign is conventional and our analysis is not influenced by these conventions. The matrix B can be seen as an individual/variables matrix where individuals are the vertices and variables are the directed hyperedges taking values 0, 1 or -1. The mean of a variable is 0 if and only if the directed hyperedge has as many sources as targets. In multidimensional descriptive statistics, it is often

Fig. 11.3 Top: a
hypergraph whose set of
vertices is {1, 2, 3, 4, 5, 6}
and whose set of hyperedges
is {{1,2},{2,3,4},{3,4,5},
{5,6}}. Bottom: a directed
hypergraph on the same set
of vertices and having
4 hyperedges represented
par arrow hyperedges going
from sources toward targets

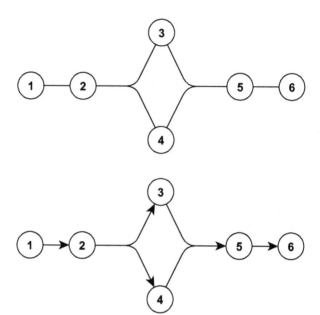

customary to center-reduce variables in order to erase the effects of scales between
variables expressed in different units or with different orders of magnitude. Here it is
not useful because it is interesting to highlight hyperedges with multiple sources and
goals.

A principal component analysis based on the diagonalization of the matrix B^TB
allows defining new orthogonal factors which are linear combinations of original
variables given by the k eigenvectors associated to the k largest eigenvalues of B^TB.
So, we can embed the rows of B in a Euclidean space of dimension k. The vertices of
the directed hypergraph are then points of $\mathbb{R}^k$ whose coordinates are given by Bu,
u being an eigenvector of B^TB. Once the vertices of the directed hypergraph are
embedded in $\mathbb{R}^k$ we apply usual methods of unsupervised clustering such as k-means
ascending hierarchical clustering in order to detect some communities of vertices of
our directed hypergraph.[20] Another point of view is spectral embedding: the vertices
of the directed hypergraph are embedded in $\mathbb{R}^k$ and the coordinates are given by the
eigenvectors of BB^T. When the hypergraph is a graph, BB^T is the Laplacian matrix
and we recognize the usual spectral clustering (von Luxburg 2007).

Thanks to this embedding in $\mathbb{R}^k$, the central vertices can be defined as the vertices
closest to the center of gravity (barycenter) of the scatter-plot of $\mathbb{R}^k$. The definition of
this notion of centrality differs from the usual notions of centrality of betweenness of
closeness. In order to avoid any confusion, we will call it *embedding centrality*.

---

[20]The choice in the convention of the sign in the definition of B has no effect in this approach,
indeed if $\tilde{B}$ the matrix built with the converse convention we have $\tilde{B} = -B$ and $\tilde{B}^T\tilde{B} = B^TB$.

11.4 Hypergraph-Based Comparison of Environment and Trade Ratifications

11.4.1 Modeling by Hypergraphs

A weak point of modeling by simple graphs is that it artificially increases the degree of the vertices representing the countries that have proceeded to simultaneous ratifications, thus being able to bias some indicators, in particular the indicators of centrality. To overcome this problem, we proceed to a modeling based on directed hypergraphs where there is a directed hyperedge from a *source set* A of vertices (countries) and a *target set* B of vertices if and only if all the countries in A have ratified simultaneously a treaty just before countries in B ratify simultaneously that treaty. Sets A and B may contain a single country. Thus, simultaneous ratifications do not increase the degree of the vertices in A or B as can be seen on Fig. 11.4 which is an example of hypergraph construction for a single treaty.

The hypergraph resulting from a set of treaties is then the union of hypergraphs built for each treaty: the vertices (resp. hyperedges) are the union of the set of vertices (resp. hyperedges) of hypergraphs for each treaty. Let us note that this union is not the disjoint union of hypergraphs because the set of vertices are not disjoint.

11.4.2 Results in the Field of the Environment

We produced the hypergraph induced by the same data used in the work presented previously, say the 3550 ratifications of 48 MEAs. The method exposed in Sect. 11.3.3 provides a clustering of the vertices (thanks to an embedding followed by an ascendant hierarchical clustering). A large community clearly emerges (cf. Table 11.4) containing countries from continental Europe, among which 27 are countries of the EU (only Malta is not classified in this group and UK is a member of the EU and belongs to this group over the considered time period).

This community stands out clearly in the sense that the best partitioning is a bipartition with on the one hand these 36 countries of continental Europe and, on the other hand, the rest of the world. Other partitions resulting from division at different levels of resolution (thus varying the number of communities) do not reveal other communities corresponding to politico-economic groups or formal communities.

According to the embedding centrality, most central countries are European countries (Fig. 11.5). These results correspond to the strengthening of multilateral institutions through the development of public international law in general and environmental law in particular promoted by these countries. From the beginning of the twentieth century, not only these Western countries are the main sources and architects of an articulation of doctrines, institutions and principles relating to the environment, but they also served as models to other countries keen to improve the legal and political framework of their public action.

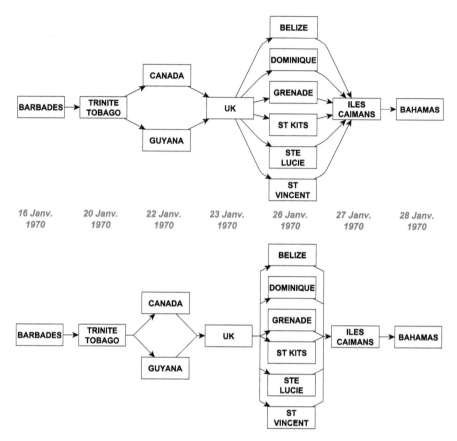

Fig. 11.4 Top: example of modeling by a directed graph of a few successive ratifications of the agreement establishing the Caribbean Development Bank. Bottom: modeling by an oriented hypergraph of the same data

Table 11.4 Countries constituting a community in the hypergraph of environmental ratifications

Albania	Austria	Belarus	Belgium	Bulgaria	Croatia
Cyprus	Czech Rep.	Denmark	Estonia	EU	Finland
France	Germany	Greece	Hungary	Ireland	Italy
Latvia	Liechtenstein	Lithuania	Luxembourg	Moldava	Netherlands
Norway	Poland	Portugal	Romania	Serbia	Slovakia
Slovenia	Spain	Sweeden	Switzerland	UK	Ukraine

The precautionary principle, for example, is inspired by German regulations, while the polluter-pays principle has been consolidated by the OECD. Both have been adopted in multilateral and national texts on other continents. In addition, the first ministries of the environment were created in developed countries, while other states followed after the UNCHE. Europeans, having undertaken to develop their

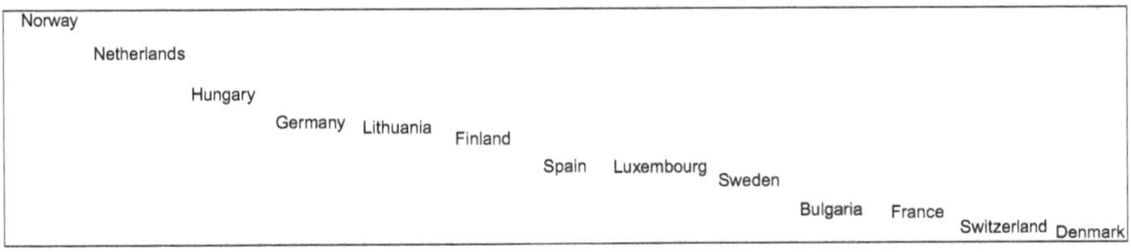

Norway
Netherlands
Hungary
Germany Lithuania
Finland
Spain Luxembourg
Sweden
Bulgaria France
Switzerland Denmark

Fig. 11.5 List of the most central countries (ranked from left to right by decreasing embedding centrality) in the hypergraph of ratifications of UN environmental agreements (1979–2014)

environmental law earlier than the rest of the world in general, and collectively in the context of the development of EU law, tend to ratify environmental agreements at the same pace. Our results obtained from the hypergraph-based analysis corroborate the thesis that the EU is both a material and normative structure (Laïdi 2006) in environmental matters.

As far as the rest of the world is concerned, most of the time regional organizations have failed to generate deep and effective cooperation to address environmental challenges, thus regional governance is less obvious. The case of the governance of the Amazon is a typical example: the Amazon Cooperation Treaty[21] signed in 1978 may suggest that regional cooperation on environmental issues is effective, while its impact on the foreign policies of the Member States has always been and remains very limited. It is therefore not surprising that they do not form regional communities appearing in the graphs constructed from ratifications.

11.4.3   Results in the Field of Trade

We apply the same method of modeling and clustering for UN trade-related treaties. We have 834 ratifications from 1963 to 2014, covering 23 commercial treaties listed in Chapter X of the United Nations Treaty Collection. There is a large, heterogeneous community (Table 11.5) that contains none of the world's top 10 economic powers. We have another, smaller, emerging community that contains three of the world's major economic powers (China, Japan and USA in community C2 in Table 11.5).

Concerning the embedding centralities (shown in Fig. 11.6), we have a central position of some African countries (there are five treaties related to Africa), the USA and China being at the sixth and ninth ranks respectively.

---

[21]See the website of the Amazon Cooperation Treaty Organization http://otca.info/portal/ Accessed 9 Feb 2018.

Table 11.5 Three communities—C1 to C3—detected in the hypergraph of ratifications of UN trade agreements

C1	Antigua and Barbuda, Azerbaïdjan, Bahreïn, Bolivia, Bosnia and Herzegovina, Brunei, Bulgaria, Costa-Rica, Croatia, United Arab Emirates, Eritrea, Estonia, Greece, Guatemala, Hong-Kong, Cayman Islands, Marshall Islands, Solomon Islands, Turks and Caicos Islands, British Virgin Islands, Iceland, Kiribati, Latvia, Lithuania, Malta, Micronesia, Monaco, Montserrat, Nauru, Nicaragua, Niue, Oman, Palau, Portugal, Czech Republic, San Marino, Serbia, Slovakia, South Sudan, East Timor, Turkmenistan, Tuvalu, Vanuatu
C2	Belgium, China, Denmark, Egypt, Gabon, Guinea, Japan, Liberia, Libya, Malaysia, Republic of Korea, Thailand, USA, Zambia
C3	Comoros, Gambia, Honduras, Iraq, Lesotho, Malawi, Niger, Qatar, Samoa, Senegal, Vietnam, Yemen

Fig. 11.6 List of most central countries (ranked from left to right by decreasing embedding centrality) in the hypergraph of ratifications of UN trade agreements

Table 11.6 Main information concerning the ratification data

	Environment	Trade
Period studied	1979–2014	1963–2014
Number of agreements (identified by the UN)	48	23
Number of "countries" (vertices)	197	198
Number of ratifications	3550	834
Number of non-simultaneous ratifications	3334	717
Number of hyperedges	3286	694

11.4.4 Environment Versus Trade Results

The main information concerning the ratification data of environmental agreements and UN trade agreements discussed here are summarized in Table 11.6. Not surprisingly the number of entities that have ratified the environmental and trade agreements considered here is almost the same and covers all sovereign nations that have existed in recent decades.[22] The average number of ratifications per treaty (or agreement) is twice as high for the environment than for trade. The most plausible explanation joins some crucial points of the analysis made previously:

---

[22] A more detailed analysis will have to take into account the appearance and the disappearance of States and to establish the comparisons of graphs over the same time period.

the inventory of multilateral environmental agreements made by the UN is representative of the efforts of the international community to take in consideration issues related to environmental protection, of course, with the limitations that we know. On the contrary most of the major commercial agreements are made outside the UN framework. Moreover, many trade agreements are established on a regional or interregional scale (such as the EU, NAFTA or TPP mentioned in Sect. 11.2), and not on a global scale as it is the case, for example, for major environmental conventions (in particular on climate change, biological diversity, ozone layer, etc.).

The specificity of the ratification process in the parliaments of each country should also be taken into account to explain observed differences in environmental versus trade ratification. If they are well structured, the work of analysis and the parliamentary debate run their course, and average ratification times for each agreement should be similar regardless of the area concerned. In this regard the functioning of parliamentary bureaucracy is a central variable, without forgetting that political processes are anything but linear and neutral. An opinion leader or a clever politician, depending on his political affiliation, may tip the balance to accelerate the ratification or to hinder it.[23] As it is the executive power that prepares the mandate to negotiate and signs the agreement abroad, and then it is the legislative power that ensures the process of ratification so that the head of state can ratify it, it is necessary to look more closely at the interaction of these powers and their interplay.

Considering the States as unitary and rational actors, in a utilitarian approach, a plausible hypothesis based on the work of Abbot and Snidal (2000) to explain a differentiated dynamic in environmental *versus* trade ratification, is that international obligations related to the environment are vague and often do not require delegation of authority from signatory States. The calculation of their economic impact might guide the decision to apply them at the national level but at a later stage. On the contrary obligations arising from the ratification of trade agreements are stipulated with precision and can be used by the partners regardless of the will of the application of a signatory country. This means that signatories have less control over the use of trade agreements. Now if we consider, as did Moravcsik (1997), that the national interest is the result of a recurrent balance of power between intra-national actors, environmental issues can be considered as less controversial, risky and expensive than commercial ones, or just less important among the various conflicts of interest that States have to manage. Finally, in the event of non-compliance with commercial standards, a country may be sanctioned by its trading partner or an international/regional tribunal, a situation that is unparalleled in the environmental field. States can also push for others to ratify agreements more quickly. In the trade regime, this practice is frequent, the threat of the use of economic or financial coercion coexisting with the promise of loans and other

---

[23] A research track to explore in political science would be to compare whether left-dominated parliaments vote on environmental treaties more quickly and those dominated by the liberal right, on the contrary, make trade treaties a priority. This is beyond our analytical objective and would only be useful in some countries, but probably not for the political regimes of China and Russia. Moreover, the left / right divide is no longer as clear as in the last century in the West.

types of assistance. The United States and China are two different models of the same practice. The EU is known for its practice of trying to impose rules on its trading partners.[24]

We observe that the percentage of simultaneous ratifications is more than twice as high in the field of trade (14%) than in the field of the environment (6%). Some factors contribute to this phenomenon, such as the fact that trade-related treaties are previously negotiated following concrete interests and reciprocity, whereas in the case of the environment, interests are larger, costs can be immediate and important, but the benefits are diffuse. Another explanation is that the national construction of interest (the calculation of gains/concessions) is more objective in trade agreements, and so are the lobbies from private actors.

The obvious differences in the structure of the hypergraphs associated with the environment and the trade consist of the difference of the central countries exhibited (the ten most central countries for the environmental ratifications are not the most central ones for trade ratifications) and of the heterogeneity of the communities extracted in the field of the trade, while in the field of the environment there is clearly a community of European countries that we interpret as an expression of a diplomatic leadership. The more peripheral countries in global trade ratify for three main reasons, either the hope of creating a legal framework more protective of their national economy, or because they believe that they must participate in all the multilateral mechanisms with a view to their integration into value chains or because they have been under pressure from influent trading partners. Ratifying a commercial treaty means accepting to play the game, exposing oneself to others and to international obligations. Ratifying an environmental treaty implies keeping the image of a State which makes the fair effort to contribute to the global sustainable development.

11.5 Discussion

In the research agenda of international relations there was a time when the fields of trade and the environment were treated as being hermetically separated. The former belonged to high politics, while the latter was not a priority (low politics) in multilateral agendas (Battistella 2009). Since the 1970s, the rise of transnational corporations has led to the paradigm of a complex interdependence (Keohane and Nye 1977), as asymmetric as it is inevitable. It was necessary to analyze the phenomenon of globalization and the intensification of trade flows, especially between the members of the "Triad" (Ohmae 1985) formed by Western Europe, the United States and Japan, in the context of the emergence of the latter as an industrial power during the Cold war.

---

[24]The carbon tax for commercial aviation is an interesting case of failure of this type of strategy (EU-ETS).

In reaction to the Triad, the countries of the South, named "Third World" in the bipolar order, created the G77/China to promote their right to development in organizations such as the General Assembly of the UN (UNGA), UNCTAD or UNIDO.[25] In addition, several UNGA resolutions have been voted by a majority of Third World countries to ensure their right to development. Among the most emblematic resolutions—by their content and not by their force—were those of 1974 establishing the "new international economic order" (resolutions 3201 [S-VI] and 3202 [S-VI]).

It is precisely in this context of strong economic cleavage between the North and South and ideological cleavage between the East and West that the UN has set up the Conference on the Human Environment (UNCHE), in Stockholm in 1972. In this framework, the issue was to analyze the growing role of those James Rosenau (1990) has called 'sovereignty-free actors' and their interaction with States, in a real "turbulence in international politics" articulated between macro, micro and macro-micro levels. Barely a decade later, global politics has changed completely according to a power shift from the West to Asia (Hoge 2004; Hearn 2016). The complex interdependence has deepened when the Triad and the Third World gave way to emerging countries, especially China and India. In the field of trade and finance, these countries will form the BRICs. In the climate agenda, they will form the BASIC.[26] These two groups are more or less formal alliances that were supposed ephemeral at the time of their creation. Regarding environmental talks, despite the persistence of the North/South cleavage due to obligations to finance development and technology transfers, there are no formal groups of countries comparable to those of trade. There is no regional governance, with the exception of the EU which plays a key role as a norm shaper in trade and in environmental negotiations.[27]

In this global context, our hypergraph-based analysis of the ratification of trade and environmental agreements supports the idea that their logic is different, although the key players are roughly the same. Compared to more traditional analysis of the dynamics of ratification, this approach combining modeling and International Relations theory presents three main contributions. First, it contributes to the interdisciplinary dialogue, particularly between international law and political sociology, allowing results to be compared over a long period of time. It also allow testing the supposed practices and strategies regarding the ratification of international treaties (see e. g. Chang 2016). Finally, it allows to compare the environmental logic and the trade logic (here in the UN framework) to spot the key States involved. Thanks to the analysis of the political context, we have show that the multilateral summits promoted by the UN have a considerable impact on the signing of treaties, but not necessarily on their ratification or implementation.

---

[25]United Nations Conference on Trade and Environment and the United Nations Industrial Development Organization. UNIDO, for example, is now using the platform "Inclusive and Sustainable Industrial Development". See https://isid.unido.org/index.html. Accessed 9 Feb 2018.

[26]Brazil, South Africa, India, China.

[27]See, for example, the One Planet Summit held in Paris on December 12, 2017.

11.6 Conclusion

The comparison of the dynamics of ratifications of two regimes—environment and trade—within the United Nations framework shows that they follow parallel evolution, in spite of the strengthening of their intertwining since the 1990s, notably from an institutional point of view. The UN has a central role in the environmental agenda, which explains the recurrence of multilateral summits since 1972 and the number of agreements signed and ratified by almost all members of the organization. For the trade agenda, on the contrary, the role of the United Nations is becoming less and less important, and the multilateral summits had a very limited impact, so that the economic and trading powers have strategically adopted other negotiating arenas. This explains the main outline of the results obtained from the ratification analysis using hypergraphs, with the absence of some of the major economic and commercial powers at the global level, while the countries that participate little in global trade are generally present.

Hypergraph analysis of the ratification dynamics of environmental versus trade agreements highlights the contrast between the two regimes, in particular the identification of the emerging EU community only in the first case. Is it still a "normative power" in the trade framework under the leadership of the United Nations? The mainstream of the economic policy analysis says that the EU has lost its strength since the 2008 crisis and the Chinese rise, but the assessment of the EU's role is still subject to profound divergences. In this sense, our results show that despite the fact that the UN serves as a bridge between the two regimes, it is much more effective in promoting environmental agreements than regulating global trade. Therefore the UN is at the same time central to the environment and marginal to trade agendas.[28] However in the future it would be appropriate to extend the analysis undertaken in this work by considering the treaties and agreements ratified in the WTO in relation to the G7 meetings, then G8 and G20 in order to have a second, broader analysis in the sense that it would comply more with the current global (and nevertheless fragmented) governance of commercial and environmental issues (but then without respecting the homogeneity of the sources of the data taken into account) (see also Morin et al. 2018).

Finally, the concept of sustainable development cannot be considered as a structuring principle of international relations, given that the trade regime prevails over that of the environment in practice, as demonstrated in particular by the ongoing negotiations of mega-agreements, the TTP and TTIP, and within ASEAN.

Acknowledgments Ana Flávia Barros-Platiau wishes to thank the agency CAPES (Programas Estratégicos—DRI, call 43/2013) of the Ministry of Education in Brazil and the CIRCULEX project, founded by ANR (French National Agency for Research). Pierre Mazzega conducts this

---

[28]Certainly, the creation of the World Trade Organization (WTO) outside the UN framework is a central factor in understanding the governance of global trade. But the ratifications analyzed are those of the UN for the sake of comparing two initiatives within the same system, the UN.

research as part of the project GEMA «*Gouvernance Environnementale: Modélisation et Analyse*» founded by CNRS (French National Center for Scientific Research) through the program *Défi interdisciplinaire: «InFIniti» Interfaces Interdisciplinaires Numérique et Théorique.*

References

Abbot K, Snidal D (2000) Hard and soft law in international governance. Int Organ 54(3):421–456

Barnett M, Finnemore M (2004) Rules for the word. International organizations in global politics. Cornell University Press, Ithaca

Barnett M, Finnemore M (2007) Political approaches. In: Weiss T, Daws S (eds) The Oxford handbook on the United Nations. Oxford University Press, Oxford

Battistella D (2009) Théories des Relations Internationales. Presses de Sciences Po, Paris

Biermann F, Abbott K, Andresen S, Bäckstrand K, Bernstein S, Betsill MM, Bulkeley H, Cashore B, Clapp J, Folke C, Gupta A, Gupta J, Haas PM, Jordan A, Kanie N, Kluvánkov-á-Oravská T, Lebel L, Liverman D, Meadowcroft J, Mitchell RB, Newell P, Oberthür S, Olsson L, Pattberg P, Sánchez-Rodríguez R, Schroeder H, Underdal A, Vieira SC, Vogel C, Young OR, Brock A, Zondervan R (2012) Science and government. Navigating the anthropocene: improving Earth system governance. Science 335(6074):1306–1307. https://doi.org/10.1126/science.1217255

Boulet R, Barros-Platiau AF, Mazzega P (2016) 35 years of multilateral environmental agreements ratification: a network analysis. Artif Intell Law 24:133–148. https://doi.org/10.1007/s10506-016-9180-7

Brundtland GH (1987) Notre avenir à tous. Rapport de la Commission des Nations Unies sur l'Environnement et le Développement, New York. Available via http://www.diplomatie.gouv.fr/sites/odyssee-developpement-durable/files/5/rapport_brundtland.pdf. Accessed 9 Feb 2018

Chang N (2016) Strategies of Ratification and the Paris Agreement. Available via https://nickdotchan.wordpress.com/2016/04/05/strategies-of-ratification-and-the-paris-agreement/. Accessed 9 Feb 2018

Crutzen PJ, Steffen W (2003) How long have we been in the Anthropocene Era? Clim Chang 61 (3):251–257. https://doi.org/10.1023/B:CLIM.0000004708.74871.62

de Carvalho FV (2012) The Brazilian position on forests and climate change from 1997 to 2012: from veto to proposition. Rev Bras Polít Int 55:144–169. Available via http://www.scielo.br/pdf/rbpi/v55nspe/09.pdf. Accessed 9 Feb 2018

Devin G, Smouts MC (2012) Les organisations internationales. Armand Colin, Paris

Falkner R (2015) International negotiations: towards mini-lateralism. Nat Clim Chang 5:805–806. https://doi.org/10.1038/nclimate2767

Gallo G, Longo G, Pallotino S, Nguyen S (1993) Directed hypergraphs and applications. Discret Appl Math 42:177–201

Hearn A (2016) The changing currents of transpacific integration china, the TPP, and beyond. Lynne Rienner Publishers, Bouder

Hoge JF (2004) A global power shift in the making. Foreign Affairs. Available via https://www.foreignaffairs.com/articles/united-states/2004-07-01/global-power-shift-making.   Accessed 9 Feb 2018

IISD/UNEP (2005) Environment and trade: a handbook, 2nd edn. The United Nations Environment Programme Division of Technology, Industry and Economics and Trade Branch and the International Institute for Sustainable Development, Geneva. Available via www.iisd.org/pdf/2005/envirotrade_handbook_2005.pdf. Accessed 9 Feb 2018

Karns M, Mingst K, Stiles K (2015) International organizations. The politics and processes of global governance. Lynne Rienner Publishers, Boulder

Keohane R, Nye J (1977) Power and interdependence: world politics in transition. TBS The Book Service Ltd, Colchester

Keohane R, Victor D (2010) The regime complex for climate change. Harvard Project on climate agreements, Belfer Center, Harvard. Available via https://www.belfercenter.org/publication/regime-complex-climate-change. Accessed 9 Feb 2018

Krasner S (1983) International Regimes. Cornell University Press, Ithaca

Laïdi Z (2006) La norme sans la force. L'énigme de la puissance européenne. Presses de la Fondation Nationale des Sciences Politiques, Paris

Lantis JS (2009) The life and death of international treaties. Oxford University Press, Oxford

Meadows DH, Meadows DL, Randers J, Behrens WW III (1972) The limits to growth: a report for the Club of Rome's project on the predicament of mankind. Universe Books, New York. Available via https://archive.org/details/TheLimitsToGrowth. Accessed 9 Feb 2018

Mearsheimer J (2001) The tragedy of great power politics. W.W. Norton & Company, New York

Moravcsik A (1997) Taking preferences seriously. A liberal theory of international relations. Int Organ 51(4):513–553. https://doi.org/10.1162/002081897550447

Morin JF, Dür A, Lechner L (2018) Mapping the trade and environment Nexus: insights from a new data set. Glob Environ Polit. https://doi.org/10.1162/GLEP_a_00447

Nakicenovic N, Rockström J, Gaffney O, Zimm C (2016) Global commons in the Anthropocene: world development on a stable and resilient planet. Working Paper 16-019. International Institute for Applied Systems Analysis, Laxenburg. Available via http://pure.iiasa.ac.at/14003/. Accessed 9 Feb 2018

OCDE (1982) Interdépendance économique et écologique: un rapport sur quelques problèmes posés par l'environnement et les ressources. Organisation de Coopération et de Développement Economiques, Paris

Ohmae K (1985) La Triade. Emergence d'une stratégie mondiale de l'entreprise. Flammarion, Paris

Ostrom E, Dietz T, Dolsak N, Stern PC, Stonich S, Weber E (eds) (2002) The Drama of the Commons. National Academy Press, Washington DC

Rosenau J (1990) Turbulence in world politics: a theory of change and continuity. Princeton University Press, Princeton

Shelton D, Kiss A (2007) Guide to international environmental law. Martinus Nijhoff, Leiden

Strange S (1998) States and markets, 2nd edn. Bloomsbury Academic, London

UNEP (2017a) Towards a pollution-free planet. United Nations Environment Assembly of the United Nations Environment Programme, Nairobi. Available via http://www.unep.org/assembly/backgroundreport. Accessed 9 Feb 2018

UNEP (2017b) Frontiers 2017. Emerging issues of environmental concern. United Nations Environment Programme, Nairobi. Available via https://www.unenvironment.org/. Accessed 9 Feb 2018

Viola E, Franchini M (2018) Brazil and climate change. Beyond the Amazon. Routledge, Abingdon

von Luxburg U (2007) A tutorial on spectral clustering. Stat Comput 17(4):395–416

Chapter 12
How to Compare Bundles of National Environmental and Development Indexes?

Pierre Mazzega, Claire Lajaunie, Jimmy Leblet, Ana Flávia Barros-Platiau, and Charles Chansardon

Abstract This study intends to demonstrate the value of using the partial order set theory comparing different but intertwined sets of indicators or indexes. We illustrate this approach by analysing the relative positions (partial order) of a set of countries with consideration for environmental and development indicators. Using data from 2013, the analysis mainly covers the countries with economies having a strong impact on climate change—China, the USA, the European Union (member States), India, Russian Federation, Japan, Brazil, Canada, and Mexico. The concepts of total and partial orders, linear extension or comparability are introduced and used in the analysis. The inclusion of three integrative environmental indicators and two

P. Mazzega (✉)
UMR5563 GET Geosciences Environment Toulouse, CNRS/University of Toulouse, Toulouse, France

Strathclyde Centre for Environmental Law and Governance (SCELG), University of Strathclyde, Glasgow, UK
e-mail: pierre.mazzegaciamp@get.omp.eu

C. Lajaunie
INSERM, CERIC, UMR DICE 7318, CNRS, Aix Marseille University, University of Toulon, University of Pau and Pays Adour, Aix-en-Provence, France

Strathclyde Centre for Environmental Law and Governance (SCELG), University of Strathclyde, Glasgow, UK
e-mail: claire.lajaunie@inserm.fr

J. Leblet
University of Lyon, Jean Moulin, iaelyon, Magellan Research Center, Lyon, France
e-mail: jimmy.leblet@univ-lyon3.fr

A. F. Barros-Platiau
IREL, Institute of International Relations, University of Brasilia, Brasilia DF, Brazil
e-mail: anabarros@unb.br

C. Chansardon
UMR5563 GET Geosciences Environment Toulouse, CNRS/University of Toulouse, Toulouse, France
e-mail: charles.chansardon@get.omp.fr

© Springer Nature Switzerland AG 2019
R. Boulet et al. (eds.), *Law, Public Policies and Complex Systems: Networks in Action*, Law, Governance and Technology Series 42,
https://doi.org/10.1007/978-3-030-11506-7_12

development indicators (human development index and GDP per capita) shows that in 2013 the BRICS were the worst positioned countries. In contrast, several countries in Northern Europe (Denmark, followed by Germany, Ireland, the Netherlands, Sweden and the UK) were associated with the best overall indicators. Canada is not comparable to any other country, the values of its indicators being sometimes higher and sometimes lower than those associated to any other country considered in this study. The USA, comparable to a single country, shows a similar behaviour for the same reasons.

12.1 Introduction

This study is to some extent at the junction of the interests of several disciplines that can be identified at least from the background of the authors (modelling, law, mathematics, international relations, environmental sciences). Thus, we do not deal here with the definitions underlying the use of terms such as "development", "sustainable development", "environment", terms with a broad and rather blurred semantic and pragmatic basis. On the other hand, we highlight the mathematical structure induced by the simultaneous comparison of several indicators and introduce some notions allowing a rigorous analysis to address the issue at hand, in an innovative way, apparently never used in this context.

As stated by Hammond et al. (1995), an indicator is *"something that provides a clue to a matter of larger significance or makes perceptible a trend or phenomenon that is not immediately detectable"*.[1] In this vein, the notion of environmental indicator has been promoted after the United Nations Conference on Environment and Development[2] in 1992 which put the sustainability goal at the core of international considerations together with environmental issues. Indeed, sustainable development calls for a balance between economic growth, social equity and environmental management which may involve rather complex issues, such as economic and social interconnectedness.

There are various kinds of indicators and their choice depends on the goals to pursue as well as the audience targeted (international or national decision-makers, stakeholders or the public opinion). The selection of the appropriate indicators is crucial for policy-makers and the process of indicator selection itself should be scrutinized to make sure it provides the relevant information. The choice of indicators can generate difficulties and biases (Meadows 1998).[3] Also, the creation of indicators relies on high quality data and raises the question of the geographical scale chosen (local, national, regional or global). Many questions arise from the elaboration of environmental indicators which can be used at the global level from the scale used, to the type of aggregation or the consideration of time, limit or thresholds.[4]

---

[1]In Hammond et al. (1995), p. 1.

[2]See http://www.un.org/geninfo/bp/enviro.html (accessed 20 July, 2018).

[3]In Meadows (1998), pp. 4–5.

[4]Meadows (1998), p. 12.

Some of the indicators or indexes are aggregated indicators as they gather diverse measures to give a better overview of a situation (e.g. the Human Development Index, HDI, see below). Others,—such as the Gross Domestic Product, GDP—are developed on the basis of relatively homogeneous data, should they come from the same topic area (e.g. economy), or the data used to build the indicator being expressed in a single unit (e.g. a currency like the US dollar).

After the 1992 Rio Summit, in order to assess the implementation of development policies and to inform policy-makers, the Commission on Sustainable Development was created and various indicators were produced mostly by international organizations, research centres and NGOs. However, to assess the wide-range of impacts of human activities on the environment, it became necessary to think about a framework for environmental indicators to structure sets of environmental information, to make them accessible to policy-makers, to raise public awareness and thus foster public action. At the international level, indicators are also used to report progress in the implementation of policies or commitments of the States before international organizations such as the United Nations or to compare the trends of progress of various countries regarding specific areas such as environmental management and development strategies. One good case is the transition to a low carbon economy now going on in several countries.[5]

Two warnings about the perimeter of this study must be given in this introduction. First, we do not propose an analysis of the relevance of the indicators (in general or those we use here), nor a critique of how these indicators are conceived, developed or used. However, it is important to differentiate between "indicators" and "data" that are system state variables that are empirically observed or measured (instrument measurements, survey results). The main differences reside in the three following points: (1) an indicator in general results from the composition of several empirical data or derived products of different kinds; (2) the method of composition is explicit but relatively arbitrary; it is based mainly on the knowledge of experts in a field and on their estimation that the indicator developed provides relevant and reliable information on the aggregated properties of interest to the expected users; (3) Most indicators are published without an estimate of their accuracy or associated confidence intervals. The production of this estimate is feasible (taking into account the error distributions associated with each component of the indicator and the way in which these components are used) by those who produce the indicators, but not a posteriori by the end-users.

Secondly, an analysis of the relevance of these indicators or of the areas to which they refer (here *development, environment, environmental performance*), goes far beyond the scope of this paper as well as the intent of our study. There is a priori no objective criterion for the relevance of an indicator in any field of study. An indicator is added to the instruments of a system's governance if its shared use is gradually imposed by dissemination among the organizations concerned. Moreover, the

---

[5]Conscious Uncoupling? Low Carbon Economy Index, 2015. www.pwc.co.uk/sustainability, accessed 20 July, 2018.

delimitation of the semantic field associated by a diversity of actors with a notion as broad and versatile as "environmental performance" is a political matter and if necessary stabilizes only in duration and by use. This is even more true of the notion of "development" which has been and is the subject of many analyses and criticisms (e. g. with different perspectives and 15 years of delay, Rist 2001; Monebhurrun 2016, and references cited in these works), or the notion of "sustainability" (e.g. Ness et al. 2007). More specifically, debates on the Millennium Development Goals (Fehling et al. 2013), and on the new Sustainable Development Goals and indicators to be constructed to assess the achievement of evidence-based targets (ICSU ISSC 2015) will not be discussed here. Nevertheless, the mathematical structure underlying the comparison of a bundle of indicators will necessarily be the same as that presented here, whatever the context.

It should be stressed that this mathematical structure (of partial ordered sets) necessarily results from the comparison of sets of indicators and is not an optional choice of analysis method. To our knowledge this analysis of sets of indicators has never been proposed before (though, as we shall see in the discussion, it has connections with the theory of voting).

To compare bundles of environmental and development given indexes, we will focus on national indicators. Indeed, at the national level, indicators are designed for and used in supporting decision-making, serving the monitoring and evaluation of national policies effectiveness or guiding the identification of priorities for action. Our goal is to define a method that allows comparing the relative positioning of various countries regarding different socio-economic and environmental indicators considered simultaneously. In Sect. 12.2, we present indicators used in this study and explain the choice of countries we have made. Their consideration leads to a structure of partial order presented in Sect. 12.3 where we also introduce notions of linear extension, height and width of orders as well as comparability between countries. The use of this approach is illustrated in Sect. 12.4 by the presentation of three partial orders induced by the respective integration of two socio-economic indicators and three environmental indicators or indexes, and finally the five indicators considered simultaneously. The analysis of results in Sect. 12.5 gives us the opportunity to discuss about the interest and potential of the method. We finally present our conclusions in Sect. 12.6.

12.2 Some Development and Environmental Indicators

The assessment of the evolution of the various components of the environment—mainly ecosystems and resources or media like air, water or soil for instance—but also the evaluation of the efforts undertaken by the countries to conduct public policies and develop legal tools targeting the protection or restoration of ecosystems and the sustainable management of resources, are supported by environmental indicators. The comparison of those indicators among countries is interesting in itself but it might be useful to take into account other indicators of social or economic

Table 12.1 List of indicators used, and links to databases (year 2013)

Acronym	Index	Source and link to data
EPI	Environmental Performance Index	Yale University http://epi.yale.edu/
CCPI	Climate Change Performance Index	Germanwatch http://germanwatch.org/en/home
CLIMI	Climate Laws, Institutions & Measures Index	Smith School of Enterprise and the Environment www.smithschool.ox.ac.uk/
HDI	Human Development Index	United Nations Development Program http://hdr.undp.org/en/content/human-development-index-hdi
GDP/cap	Gross Domestic Product per Capita	World Bank http://data.worldbank.org/indicator/

development. The priority given to environmental agenda over other socio-economic challenges depends on the level of development of each country, whatever definition of development we consider. We only take into account national indicators and to maintain a temporal consistency, we have gathered the values of those indicators for the year 2013. Table 12.1 presents a list of the chosen indicators and the links to the databases where values for that year are available.

At present, teams producing different indicators are working without real coordination.[6] This situation leads to indicators whose statistical independence is difficult to assess. This is all the more true given that the data included in the composition of the various indicators may be of different types but not themselves independent.[7] A priori the indicators used here could induce a form of overweight of climate performances (through CCPI and CLIMI indicators, see below) and thus create a bias in favour of countries with effective and efficient climate policies. On the other hand, the number of environmental indicators available for a large number of countries and the same year (without speaking yet about time series of indicators) is quite limited and justifies our choice. Those used here are covering a large range of information on the environment, law and policies. We now give a brief description of development (Sect. 12.2.1) and environmental (Sect. 12.2.2) indicators or indexes, and then explain our choice of a set of countries (Sect. 12.2.3).

---

[6]The international diffusion of SDGs, anticipated in recent years, probably catalyses efforts—particularly national ones—in this rapidly evolving field of research.

[7]Consider, for example, the various products providing information on environmental variables but derived on the basis of data obtained from the same sensors on board satellites and corrected according to the same standardized procedures (and themselves based on models with a limited accuracy).

12.2.1 Indexes of Development

Conventionally, the Gross Domestic Product (GDP) measures the value of all final goods and services produced in a given country in 1 year. It can be seen as an estimate of the health of a country's economy and national development level that can be compared across countries using the Purchase Power Parity dollar, i.e. an exchange rate currency. Its evaluation is based on two main approaches that should give very similar results[8]: (1) in the income approach, GDP adds up total compensation to employees, gross profits for firms, and taxes less any subsidies; (2) in the expenditure method GDP is calculated by adding total consumption, investment, government spending and net exports. The data used here are obtained from the web site of the World Bank.[9] For year 2013, the top-ten countries of your set, rank as follows (numbers in parentheses are GDP in Billions USD): (1) USA (16525,593); (2) China (8000,516); (3) Japan (6080,705); (4) Germany (3546,635); (5) France (2750,544); (6) UK (2617,375); (7) Brazil (2471,485); (8) Italy (2166,696); (9) - Russian Federation (2068,772); (10) India(1955,181). In 2013, China's population accounted for ~19% of the world population, and India's for 17.5%. Therefore, to get an idea of economic welfare at the individual level, and incorporate this information into a comparison with environmental indexes, it is better to rely on the GDP per capita which figures are given in Table 12.2. The resulting order brings up countries from Northern Europe along with the USA, Canada and Japan.

Although GDP is probably the most widely used indicator, various criticisms have been made, including recently in anticipation of the transition from the Millennium Development Goals to the Sustainable Development Goals in 2015 (United Nations 2016), which mainly point out that other dimensions of development are not taken into account or probed by this indicator to assess the progress and sustainability of our societies. Only considering the special issue "Beyond GDP" of the Human Dimensions magazine (May 2014 issue 4), human well-being (Bartelmus 2014), human and ecosystems health (Dasgupta 2014) or natural capital and human capital (Duraiappah and Fernandes 2014) in particular are nearly invisible through the GDP.

Indeed, the very concept of human development in its relations with various themes such as the environment, gender, globalization, migration, etc.—is the subject of much debate (Alkire 2010) that results are transferred to the concept of associated evaluation indexes (Kovacevic 2010). To partially fill the gap left by considering only GDP per capita as an indicator of development, we also include the human development index (HDI). This index, first published by UNDP in 1990 with the Human Development Report (UNDP 1990), is widely used in particular to capture the multidimensional nature of poverty at the national level. It constitutes an aggregation of three indicators based on health, education and standard of living. It provides a broader measure of human well-being that GDP itself but it is limited as it does not include any information regarding environmental changes. As such it

---

[8]See http://www.investopedia.com/ask/answers/199.asp (accessed 20 July, 2018).

[9]http://data.worldbank.org/indicator/NY.GDP.MKTP.CD (accessed 20 July, 2018).

Table 12.2 Top ten countries as ranked by each indicator or index, year 2013

Rank	EPI	CCPI	CLIMI	GDP/cap (USD)	HDI
1	Czech Rep. (81.47)	Denmark (72.61)	UK (0.801)	Denmark (60,368)	Netherlands (0.915)
2	Germany (80.47)	Sweden (69.37)	Finland (0.787)	Sweden (56,754)	USA (0.914)
3	Spain (79.79)	Portugal (67.81)	France (0.783)	USA (52,275)	Germany (0.911)
4	Austria (78.32)	Germany (67.54)	Spain (0.758)	Canada (50,133)	Canada (0.902)
5	Sweden (78.09)	Ireland (67.48)	Denmark (0.722)	Ireland (48,631)	Denmark (0.900)
6	Netherlands (77.75)	UK (67.33)	Sweden (0.701)	Netherlands (48,190)	Ireland (0.899)
7	UK (77.35)	Malta (67.07)	Slovenia (0.698)	Japan (47,752)	Sweden (0.898)
8	Denmark (76.92)	Hungary (66.41)	Netherlands (0.691)	Finland (45,903)	UK (0.892)
9	Slovenia (76.43)	Belgium (65.20)	Ireland (0.667)	Austria (45,663)	Korea (0.891)
10	Portugal (75.80)	Mexico (64.91)	Germany (0.665)	Belgium (44,710)	Japan (0.890)

Note that Luxembourg is ranked 1st for EPI (83.29) and GDP/cap (109,715 USD) but is not kept in our study. Indicators values (in parentheses) are dimensionless (except the GDP/cap in USD)

does not appear as an appropriate indicator of the environmental dimensions of development, a gap that is filled precisely by associating environmental indicators in our overall analysis (Sect. 12.4). Among the 10 non-European countries in our sample with the highest HDI index in 2013, we found the USA, Canada, South Korea and Japan (Table 12.2), these countries—except South Korea, also being in the top ten countries with higher GDP per capita.

12.2.2   Environmental Indicators

The Agenda 21, one of the instruments resulting from the Rio Conference, states that "indicators of sustainable development need to be developed to provide a solid basis for decision-making at all levels and to contribute to the self-regulating sustainability of integrated environment and development systems" (UNCED 1992, Chap. 40, §4). Several organizations listed environmental issues and corresponding indicators following an initial work from the OECD. The information should be organized according to a matrix of information grouping various categories of environmental issues dealing with human/environment interactions.[10] Here we have chosen three

---

[10]On the development of such matrix, see Hammond et al. (1995), pp. 13–16.

environmental indexes according to the following criteria: (a) be available for each of the countries of our list and for the year 2013; (b) be informed (identification of the original data allowing their assessment; explanations about their development mode); (c) be publicly available on the internet.

The Environmental Performance Index (EPI) is produced by a network of organizations, under the guidance of Yale University.[11] The EPI ranks countries' performance on high-priority environmental issues related to the protection of human health and the protection of ecosystems. In 2013, the EPI was constructed through the calculation and aggregation of 20 indicators reflecting national-level environmental data (Hsu et al. 2013). These indicators are combined into 9 issue categories: environment health impacts, air quality, water and sanitation, water resources, agriculture, forests, fisheries, biodiversity and habitat, climate and energy. The overall EPI framework is fully described, as well as, among others, the selection criteria for data in EPI (say relevance, performance, established scientific methodology, data quality, time series availability, completeness[12]). In the subset of 36 countries that we have selected for this study, the top-ten countries ranked on the basis of this index are all European countries, especially from Northern Europe (see Table 12.2).

The Climate Change Performance Index (CCPI) 2013 (Burck et al. 2012) is produced by Germanwatch (Bonn), a nonprofit non-governmental organization in collaboration with the Climate Action Network Europe (CAN, Brussels). Through the evaluation and comparison of the climate protection performances of 58 countries responsible for more than 90% of the energy-related CO_2 global emissions, it is an instrument supposed to enhance transparency in international climate politics. It is primarily centred on objective indicators. Eighty percent of the evaluation is based on indicators of emissions and is decomposed as 30% for emissions levels, 30% for recent development of emissions, 5% level of efficiency, 5% recent development in efficiency, 8% recent development of renewable energy and 2% share of total primary energy supply. The remaining 20% of the CCPI evaluation is based on national and international climate policy assessments (that involve more than 250 experts from the respective countries) (Burck et al. 2015). Nine of the top-ten countries ranked by this index are European ones, Mexico being at the tenth place (Table 12.2).

The "Climate Laws, Institutions and Measures Index" (CLIMI) evaluates countries' policy responses to the risk of climate change. It measures the breadth and quality of four main policies (12 constituent variables) areas in 95 countries representing 90% of the global greenhouse gas emissions (Steves and Teytelboym 2013): (1) the international co-operation: how quickly a government ratified the Kyoto Protocol and whether it developed the institutional capacity to participate in the flexible mechanisms or the Clean Development Mechanism; (2) the domestic

---

[11]Say in 2016, the Yale Center for Environmental Law & Policy and Yale Data-Driven Environmental Solutions Group at Yale University, the Center for International Earth Science Information Network at Columbia University, in collaboration with the Samuel Family Foundation, McCall MacBain Foundation, and the World Economic Forum.

[12]See https://epi.envirocenter.yale.edu/2018-epi-report/methodology (accessed 20 July, 2018).

climate framework: this includes broad climate change laws and targets, as well as the levels of institutional engagement in climate change; (3) the sectoral fiscal or regulatory measures or targets: these include targets and regulations in each of the sectors identified in the reports of the Intergovernmental Panel on Climate Change, apart from waste; (4) the cross-sectoral fiscal or regulatory measures: these include carbon taxes and emission-trading schemes. CLIMI therefore does not cover several important environmental issues.[13] However this indicator gives a large place to the evaluation of public policies implemented to fight against climate change and mitigate its effects, initiatives that affect large sectors in particular energy policy (see e.g. Jones and Warner 2016) and the oceans. Once again only European countries are in the top-ten countries ranked with this indicator.

12.2.3   The Set of Countries

We have limited our analysis to a list of 36 countries. The inclusion of all United Nations member countries would unnecessarily extend our work which aims primarily to propose a method of analysis and comparison of a set of national indicators and to allow for a partial ordering of the considered countries. Moreover environmental indicators are generally not available for all countries, their assessment requesting numerous data that are often unavailable or with too limited a reliability.

Our interest focuses first on the countries of the European Union (before the 2016 BREXIT). Whether in terms of size of the national territory, population or level of development, these countries offer a contrasted picture. However, their policies and environmental legislations are relatively harmonized (Vogler 2011), including adherence to the norms produced by the numerous environmental framework directives. The cohesion of their commitment in multilateral environmental agreements through the ratification of the major environmental conventions in particular, has given the European Union and its main economic and strategic partners (USA, Canada, Japan in particular) the leadership in the process of structuring a global environmental order over the past 40 years (Boulet et al. 2016). Note, however, that Cyprus and Luxembourg are not included in this analysis because the values of environmental indicators that we have selected (see below) are not available for these countries.

Because of their importance as climate powers (Viola and Basso 2016; Kirton and Kokotsis 2016) and as drivers of technological innovation and dissemination on the global market, we also consider the USA, Canada, Japan, South Korea and Mexico. In a nutshell, these countries were active players in multilateral negotiations since 1992 regarding environmental and development issues. Not only are they among the world's biggest GHG emitters according to the UNFCCC Secretariat, but their economies are robust and they show potential for the near future to continue on

---

[13]Such as the conservation of biodiversity, the sustainable management of marine and ocean resources or health issues in their human, animal and ecosystem dimensions.

the stage as protagonists related to the transformations in the energy and technology markets.

At the same time China became the biggest greenhouse gas emitter, ahead of the USA and the European Union, it adopted an increasingly ostentatious climate diplomacy, particularly negotiating bilaterally with the US (Shambaugh 2016). Although they failed to find a consensus on the burden sharing for the Copenhagen Conference of the Parties (CoP 15), they reached an agreement for the CoP 21 in December 2015 and ratified the Paris Agreement during the G20 Summit in Hangzhou this year.[14] Moreover China is part of a political and economic alliance, the BRICS—Brazil, Russian Federation, India, China and South Africa—which includes countries whose economic and development activities have a major impact on the overall balance of emissions (Ge et al. 2014), land use, new infrastructure and biodiversity management. Also, the global energy markets transformations are largely driven by the BRICS (Downie 2015). The indicator values and ranking of the 10 (or eleven) first countries are given in Table 12.2. Let us briefly present these five indexes or indicators.

12.3   Partial Orders and Bundle of Indexes

A partially ordered set **P** (or order) is a set V with a partial order relation denoted $<$. An order relation is an irreflexive and transitive binary relation. For example, imagine that we have a set of entities {A,B,C,...} which we compare the attractiveness. The relation "*is less attractive than*" is an order relation.[15] Indeed, it is irreflexive—we cannot say that "*A is less attractive than A*"—and transitive: if "*A is less attractive than B*" and "*B less attractive than C*" then we necessarily have that "*A is less attractive than C*". Naturally, an ordered set can be viewed as a transitive directed graph and therefore can be represented graphically.

Indeed, we consider the ordered set with vertices entities A, B, C, D and E in Fig. 12.1. The arrow going from A to B means that "*A is less attractive than B*"

Fig. 12.1 Example of a partial order set

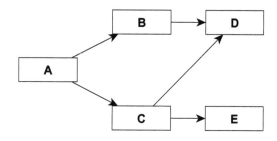

---

[15]Note that when A $<$ B holds, we can say in a general way that A is *smaller* than B.

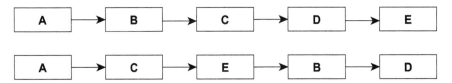

Fig. 12.2 Two distinctive linear extensions of order shown in Fig. 12.1

(or A < B). It may be noted that in this representation, all relationships are not represented. Indeed, relations induced by transitivity are not necessary in the representation and would overload the graph.

However, the transitive relations actually appear: as we have that "*A is less attractive than B*" and "*B is less attractive than D*" by transitivity we get that "*A is less attractive than D*". Graphically this means the existence of a directed path (following the arrows) ranging from A to D. Also, there is a directed path from A to E translating the fact that "*A is less attractive than E*".

Two vertices (or elements) of an ordered set are said to be **comparable** if a relationship exists between them (that is to say that one is smaller than the other). For example, in Fig. 12.1, A and B are comparable, as well as D and C. Two vertices are said to be **incomparable** if there is no relationship between them (that is to say that it is not possible to tell if one is "*smaller*" than the other). In our previous example, D and E are incomparable, as well as B and E. Graphically, two vertices are incomparable if there is no path (following the direction of the arrows) from one to the other. Orders having only elements that are comparable by pairs (i.e. having no incomparability) are called **total orders**, such as orders in Fig. 12.2. The usual orders on integer or real numbers are total orders: they can be ordered fully from the smallest to the largest elements.

The **minimal elements** of an order are the elements of this order that have no smaller elements. For example, the order in Fig. 12.1 has a single minimum which is A. Graphically this corresponds to the vertices of the graph with no arrow arriving at these vertices. Similarly, we can define the **maximal elements** of an order as the elements having no larger elements in that order. D and E are the **maximal elements** in the order of Fig. 12.1. Graphically, this corresponds to the elements having no arrow outgoing from the corresponding vertices. The height of a vertex is the maximum length of a path going from a minimum of the order to that vertex. For example, in Fig. 12.1, E has a height of 2, A has a height of 0 and C a height of 1. The **height of an order** is the maximum height of its elements. In a dual way, we define the **width of an order**. The width of an order is the maximum size of a subset of its elements such as all elements of this subset are incomparable two by two. For example, the width of the order of Fig. 12.1 is two. Indeed, if we take the set consisting of B and E, we see that these two elements are incomparable.

Then, any combinations consisting of three vertices of the order will have at least two comparable elements, so the width of the order is actually 2. As a result, a total order with n components has a height of n − 1 and width **of one**. Conversely, an order with zero heights on n elements is an order in which all elements are incomparable in pairs and has a width of n. For further details about partial orders, see Schröder's book (Schröder 2003).

Given a partial order **P**, a **linear extension L** of this order is a total order on the elements of P such that each comparability of elements in **P** is preserved in **L** (that is to say, if a vertex A is smaller than another one, say B, in **P** then A must also be smaller than B in **L**). For example, the two total orders shown in Fig. 12.2 are linear extensions of the order of Fig. 12.1. One question is whether the original order can be found from the linear extensions. First we define the intersection of two linear extensions L_1 and L_2 as the partial order **P** having the same elements as L_1 and L_2 and such that a vertex is smaller than another in **P** if it is also smaller in both L_1 and L_2. The partial order **P** is the order that respects all relations < in both L_1 and L_2. Of course two vertices A and B in **P** are incomparable if, for example, we have A < B in L_1 and B < A in L_2, that is to say, the respective relationships between A and B in the two linear extensions are opposed. For example, the intersection of the two linear extensions of Fig. 12.2 gives us exactly the partial order in Fig. 12.1. We can generalize the intersection to any number of linear extensions: a summit A will be smaller than another one B in the intersection partial order if and only if A is smaller than B in all the considered linear extensions. In particular, an order is exactly the intersection of all its linear extensions but it can also be obtained with only a subset of its linear extensions. Note that the intersection of a linear extension and its opposite (linear extension with the reverse order) is an *"empty order"*[16] say an order in which all the elements are non-comparable pairs. This shows that just by adding a linear extension to another one can go from a total order (where you can order all elements) to an empty order. For further details about linear extension of partial orders, see Trotter's book (Trotter 1992).

The five indicators presented in the previous section are linear orders on all the countries concerned and can therefore be seen as linear extensions. The partial order obtained as the intersection of these indicators then allows summarizing the whole of these indexes. Indeed, if a country is smaller than another country in the partial order so obtained, that means it is smaller than this country relatively to all indicators considered. Conversely, if country A is not comparable to country B in the order, it means that there is an indicator for which A is smaller than B (A < B) and there is another indicator showing the opposite, A larger than B (A > B).

As stated previously, usually when adding new linear extensions to the construction of the partial order, the more it approaches the "empty" order, that is to say the order where no vertices can be compared two by two. This is the reason why we decided to compose progressively partial orders from our five indicators: a first order made from the socio-economic indicators (HDI and GDP per capita), a second order made from environmental indicators (EPI, CCPI and CLIMI) and the order constituted from the five indicators. In the next section we present and comment the orders obtained.

---

[16]Let us emphasize that an *"empty order"* is not a set with no elements, but simply that its elements are not comparable in pairs.

12.4 Development and Environmental Partial Orders

Each of the five indicators presented in Sect. 12.2 defines a total order on the set of selected countries. When we combine several indicators, we consider each of them as a linear extension of a partial order that we rebuild. We now recover three partial orders: the one induced by combining HDI and GDP/capita (Sect. 12.4.1); the one resulting from the combination of the 3 environmental indexes (Sect. 12.4.2) and the one obtained with the 5 indicators (Sect. 12.4.3). The most salient results, i. e. the countries constituting the extremes of the three orders P2, P3 and P5, are presented in Table 12.3.

12.4.1 Combining Development Indexes

The graph corresponding to the partial order obtained by combining the orders induced by the HDI and GDP/capita is shown in Fig. 12.3. This partial order—which we denote **P2** below—has a height $h = 14$[17] and a width $w = 5$.

Each country is comparable to at least 27 other countries which in a way shows quite a strong consistency of the ranks induced by these two indexes. Indeed, if a country occupies a high rank with an index and on the contrary a very low rank with another index, then it is incomparable to any other country. **P2** has a unique smallest element, India, and three maximal elements, USA, Denmark and Netherlands. BRICS occupy the lower ranks, with Mexico, Bulgaria and Romania. USA, Canada and Japan are in the lead group[18] with several countries from Northern Europe (Denmark, Sweden, Netherlands and Ireland). A second group of some countries with lower ranks, includes Finland, Belgium, Austria, France, the United

Table 12.3 Lists of minimal and maximal elements of the three partial orders induced by the 2 development indicators (Fig. 12.3), by the 3 environmental indicators (see Fig. 12.4), and the 5 indicators taken all together (Fig. 12.5)

Partial order	Minimal elements	Maximal elements
Development P2	India	Denmark, Netherlands, USA
Environment P3	Brazil, Canada, China, Russian Fed., India	Czech Rep., Denmark, Germany, Spain, Sweden, UK
Development & Environment P5	Brazil, Bulgaria, Canada, China, India, Latvia, Russian Fed., South Africa	Austria, Canada, Czech Rep., Denmark, Finland, France, Germany, Netherlands, Spain, Sweden, UK, USA

---

[17]The maximum height of an order with 36 countries is 35, which would correspond to a total order.

[18]Our use of the term "country group" does not coincide with a class gathering a set of incomparable countries.

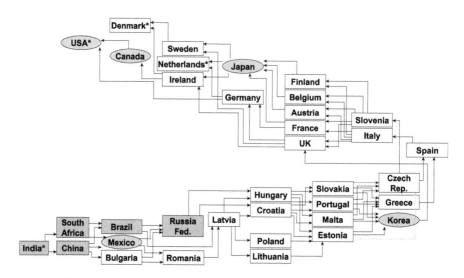

Fig. 12.3 Partial Order P2 induced by the HDI and GDP/capita. The labels of Member States of the EU are in white-rectangles. The BRICS are in grey-rectangles and labels of other countries are in blue-ellipses. Countries with the best (resp. worse) set of indexes are on the top left-side of the graph (resp. bottom left-side). The label of a maximal (resp. minimal) country is followed by a "*" (resp. a "o")

Kingdom, Slovenia, Italy and Spain. Here is the summary picture of development (economic and human) that provides a simultaneous use of the HDI and GDP per capita.

12.4.2 Combining Environmental Indexes

The relations between countries on the basis of the three environmental indexes show less regular relative positions: the obtained partial order **P3** (see the graph in Fig. 12.4) has a much lower height (here $h = 5$) and larger width ($w = 12$) that the previous order.

In other words it is more common that two countries are in reversed positions relative to each other—once "*larger*" and then "*smaller*"—when two environmental indexes are considered. We obtain five minimal elements—Brazil, Canada, China, India and Russian Federation—and six maximal elements, all European countries— Czech Republic, Denmark, Germany, Spain, Sweden and UK. In 2013 the environmental indexes of Canada, Japan, Mexico, South Korea and USA have lower values than those of most European countries.

Some countries are comparable to many others: the Russian Federation is lower than 30 countries in our set, and at the other end of the partial order—Denmark (>26 countries), Sweden (>27 countries), UK (>26 countries), have a high overall environmental quality (including policy and legal initiatives through CLIMI).

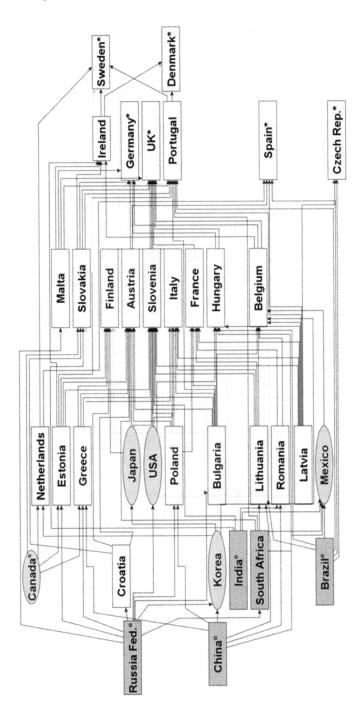

Fig. 12.4 Partial Order P3 induced by the EPI, CCPI and CLIMI environmental indexes. The labels of Member States of the EU are in white-rectangles. The BRICS are in grey-rectangles and labels of other countries are in blue-ellipses. Countries with the best (resp. worse) set of indexes are on the top (resp. bottom) of the graph. The label of a maximal (resp. minimal) country is followed by a "*" (resp. a "°")

Comparable to relatively few countries, the results for Mexico (comparable to 11 countries), Malta (comparable to 7 countries) and the Netherlands (comparable to 6 countries) have contrasted environmental performances following the environmental index considered.

12.4.3 Combining Development and Environmental Indexes

Combining the development and environmental indexes leads to the partial order **P5** shown in Fig. 12.5. With a height $h = 4$ and a width $w = 16$, this order is somewhat flattened. This also results in a high number of both minimal (8 vertices with no in-going link: Brazil, Bulgaria, Canada, China, India, Latvia, Russian Federation, South Africa) and maximal (12 vertices with no out-going link: Austria, Canada, Czech Republic, Denmark, Finland, France, Germany, Netherlands, Spain, Sweden, UK, USA) elements. Canada is not comparable to any other country (so it appears as an isolated vertex on the graph, Fig. 12.5; for the same reason it is also both a maximal and a minimal element). This is probably explained by a high ranking on development indicators (4th place on both the GDP per capita and HDI; see Table 12.2), and a position of minimal elements with the environmental indexes. The USA is comparable with one country only (the Russian Federation) for similar reasons. The Netherlands are comparable with 3 other countries. In fact, as we have noted this country is comparable to few other countries if we consider only the environmental indexes and this mixed picture is further enhanced by the inclusion by developing indexes that have high values (6th rank on the GDP/capita and HDI rank 1).

On one side of the partial order **P5**, Russia and China are comparable to many countries (24 and 21 respectively), and on the other side Denmark, Sweden and Ireland are ranked higher than 24, 23 and 22 countries respectively.[19] However, the most "politically" visible feature is probably the presence of the BRICS at the lowest level of this partial order composed of development indicators and environmental indexes.

12.5 Discussion

Once a set of indicators has been chosen to conduct an analysis, the relative position of the countries in the partial order is mathematically defined. In this sense, the method is robust and the results easily reproducible. Each indicator is a linear extension, and their simultaneous consideration induces a partial order, with some countries constituting the maximum and minimum elements and, where appropriate,

---

[19]To know the countries "higher" (resp. "lower") than a country X and their number, just follow on the graph all the paths starting from that country X following the direction (resp. the inverse direction) of the oriented links, list and count the labels of the vertices encountered.

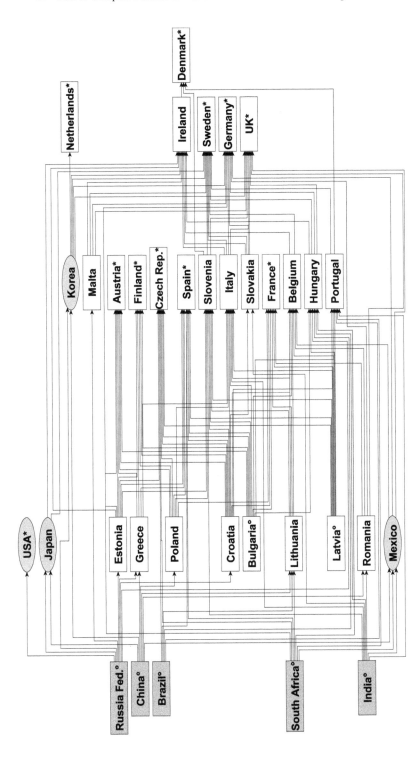

Fig. 12.5 Partial Order P5 induced by five socio-economic and environmental indexes. The labels of Member States of the European Union are in white-rectangles. The BRICS are in grey-rectangles and labels of other countries are in blue-ellipses. Note that Canada being comparable to no other country, it is disconnected from the graph (isolated vertex) and has not been represented. In this figure, countries with the best overall partial ranks are drawn at the top, those with the lowest partial ranks in the bottom. The label of a maximal (resp. minimal) country is followed by a "*" (resp. a "°")

subsets of other countries being incomparable in pairs. Usually the comparative analyses of the position of the countries, for example, as in this study, according to the developmental or environmental perspectives, are made by considering each indicator in turn and each time modulating the terms of the discourse according to the partial performances of each country. The notion of incomparability is lacking in this type of analysis. Indeed, a subset of countries that are incomparable in consideration of a set of indicators should be considered as a class of countries which is "superior" or "inferior" (in the sense of relations of order) to other subsets of countries. Within such a class, it is in turns a country or another that presents the best indicator values.

Note also that a whole body of work derived from the Social Choice Theory could be asked to continue the analysis of groups of indicators if for some reason it was necessary to produce in the end a total order of the countries whose performances are compared.[20] Indeed, voting theory was developed as early as the eighteenth century (Condorcet, de Borda) on the basis of some paradoxes like the impossibility of classifying a list of alternatives in a total order from votes casting preferences of each of the voters ("ranked ballots", in the context of a multi-candidates voting).[21] Many voting procedures were then proposed to obtain a final order which is necessary for decision-making in the political field, at the cost of abandoning at least one of the "good properties" (every two voters play equivalent roles in our voting rule; every two alternatives are treated equivalently by the rule) of the basic voting conditions (Zwicker 2016).

The approach using concepts from partial order sets theory is also ideally suited to monitoring the time-evolution of the relative positions of countries, or changes in the composition of groups of two by two incomparable countries. It is also possible to observe the impact of the introduction of a new index (a linear extension) on a partial order of countries,[22] or the effects of the composition of several partial orders as we have done here (composing **P2** and **P3** to produce **P5**).

This approach can be used to test the robustness of the partial order induced by the aggregate indexes. Another approach is to introduce random perturbations (following a chosen statistical distribution) in the values of one or more indexes. It is quite difficult to draw any dependencies between indexes resulting from a partial recovery of raw data used and even more difficult to assess the impact of these statistical dependencies on partial orders resulting from the composition of the indexes. On the other hand, what would bring an aggregation of the 5 indexes we have used here? A total order indeed, but at the cost of a loss of resolution and information. Thus the interpretation of a partial order is more detailed and relevant if it is also based on the analysis of linear extensions that compose it (here each index considered separately).

---

[20]This need does not exist a priori in the comparative analysis of country performances.

[21]In accordance with certain basic assumptions, this impossibility has been demonstrated mathematically by K. Arrow in 1951, see Saari (2001).

[22]One can also build scenarios to assess the impact of the improvement of a country index values.

In this study, four levels of information processing are actually involved (directly or indirectly): the raw data or derived basic products[23]; the set of sub-indexes or indicators relying on these data sets; the set of indexes (those presented in Sect. 12.2) obtained by aggregation; finally the partial order induced by the composition of the latter. Where do we stop the aggregation of information, and at what level should we use the approach we propose to compose a partial order on the basis of indexes? This reflection echoes the discussion engaged about the congruence between scale of legislation and the scales of the regulated ecosystems to be considered (Lajaunie and Mazzega 2017). If it does not seem possible to define in a general way an optimal level where to move from an analysis of a set of indexes to that of the partial order they induce (as linear extensions) it is certain that this choice strongly influences the conclusions drawn.[24] Therefore it has to be chosen with scrutiny considering the objectives of the analysis.

The indexes used are necessarily dependent upon matters considered and remains at the discretion of researchers. Although some degree of arbitrariness persists through this choice, conversely we note that the indexes used are designed to be robust and relevant. Indeed, these indexes usually aggregate multiple sub-indexes or indicators (themselves combining *via* an explicit method many well-identified data which quality is assessed) covering a smaller theme as we have seen in the description of the indexes in Sect. 12.2. It is therefore possible to replace an aggregate index for all the component indicators[25] and see how the resulting partial orders differ.

Concerning the choice of the indexes, the GINI index[26] (though not used here) deserves some comments. It was probably the one most used by researchers in social sciences and humanities in the last two decades, but curiously it was not taken into account by diplomats and law-makers in the main multilateral negotiations since 1992. If it were, countries showing a high level of social disparity would be comparable in a specific arena, for example, climate change. Then the North-South cleavage would make more sense, and so would the Kuznet's curve[27] and its limits. Also, it would be clearer that such a cleavage will persist because Southern countries

---

[23]In particular many products are derived from intensive processing of data supplied by sensors on board satellites, and are used to monitor multi-scales environmental changes (land use and land cover, sea level, atmospheric composition, etc.).

[24]Note that the simple aggregation of indices, producing a total order, reduces even more sharply—crushes somehow—the analysis space.

[25]As long as they are not weighted in the aggregation process as it is the case in CCPI (see Sect. 12.2).

[26]hdr.undp.org/en/content/income-gini-coefficient. Accessed on September 19, 2016. The top ten countries in the GINI rank were in 2013: Norway, Australia, Switzerland, Netherlands, USA, Germany, New Zealand, Canada, Singapore and Denmark.

[27]He found that inequality tended to decrease with robust economic growth in the 1950s. Then he had a lot of criticism afterwards because he did not consider public policy choices in his economic analysis.

have development, taken as poverty eradication, as their national priority[28] and they insist that environmental issues cannot be treated separately from the social agenda. As a consequence, international environmental commitments and compliance to international law make more sense if social vulnerability and interconnectedness, as well as risk management capacities of given countries are taken into account. In other words, social disparity makes it is harder for national public authorities to comply with international environmental obligations because constituency is far more heterogeneous. As strange as it may seem, it is the case of Greece right now. On the other hand, if we take indicators about technology and investments related to economic decarbonization then it makes no longer sense to put China in the BRICS, because it is more comparable to the US and the EU. In this sense, indicators are not new, but they lead to different results and may be useful for decision-makers seeking to deal with sustainable development issues, so they were used more frequently since 1992.

12.6   Conclusion

Our global findings so far show that there are two groups of states, the EU and the BRICS, that matter in global environmental politics and related issues, like energy, climate change, health and ocean governance. While the first group has played the role of leader in many international law-making initiatives under the UN auspices, the latter lags behind both for social and environmental indexes. As a consequence, their position in Fig. 12.5 may also bring some insights about their behaviour and their respective willingness and capacity to comply with these same initiatives. Furthermore, it is also shown that even inside these two groups there are countries much better placed than the others, notably China in the BRICS. This comes as no surprise, but it also shows that China has to make a political choice to stay in a group she does not totally belong to. The USA and Canada are key players in global governance issues, so their position in Fig. 12.5 may contribute to understanding their respective diplomatic strategies. Indeed since the USA and Canada rank high in terms of development and have rather low or medium environmental scores, they are comparable to very few countries of our set.

Several countries in northern Europe (including Denmark, Sweden, Ireland, Germany) have good scores on each index separately, which translates into a high ranking in all three partial orders **P2** (development), **P3** (environment) and **P5** (development and environment). The mixed results of the Netherlands on environmental performance—especially on the climate change index CCPI (see Table 12.2)—also place it in the group of countries comparable with very few

---

[28] According to the World Bank Development Report 2014: "more than 20 percent of the population in developing countries live on less than $1.25 a day, more than 50 percent on less than $2.50 a day and nearly 75 percent on $4 a day".

other countries. In 2013 the BRICS have the lowest scores on almost all indicators, a situation which will be interesting to follow the evolution over the years. Note, however, that the approach by partially order sets allows only monitoring the relative positioning of the country with respect to each other. The absolute improvement (resp. deterioration) of a given development or environmental performance can be masked by the simultaneous improvement (resp. degradation) of the other countries' performance. However, we insist that the results presented in this study are conditioned by the initial choice of indexes, namely the three environmental indexes EPI (Yale University et al., USA), CCPI (Germanwatch, Germany) and CLIMI (Smith School of Enterprise and the Environment, UK), and two development indexes, GDP per capita (World Bank) and the HDI (UNDP).

From a methodological point of view it is also clear that a responsible use of indicators requires a critical analysis of at least how they are developed, of the data sources and reliability, and of the meaning attributed to these aggregated indicators. In doing so it is tempting to go along with the opinion Dalal-Clayton and Bass (2002) when they write that (p. 159) "*a typical set of indicators is a mess of incompatible measurements: pollution in milligrams per litre, ecosystems conversion in hectares, species diversity in species numbers, genetic distance and population change, and so on. Combining such different indicators mixes apples and oranges.*" However how to assess the status and evolution trends of such complex systems as the environment, or the socio-ecosystems, if not by having recourse to indicators, if any valued at several spatial and temporal scales or governance levels? It seems that we have no alternative today if we adhere, however, beforehand to the idea that the measurement and comparison are useful, or that the production of evidence can assist in the design of public policies and regulations better adapted to the context of their deployment and more likely to lead to the achievement of the objectives for which they were negotiated and designed.

More generally, a broad field of study that combines mathematical and political analysis deserves to be explored in the extension of this first study. The use of indexes becomes a practice increasingly common in many policy areas, environmental issues are no exception (Surminski and Williamson 2014). Indeed, a growing number of countries is using environmental indexes (e.g. the EPI has been adopted and developed by China to evaluate its green growth priorities and policy implementations, and India launched an Environmental Sustainability Index at the state level; Hsu et al. 2016). The analysis of indicators tends to trigger the introduction of new measures to improve a particular situation in a specific field. As such the composition of a variety of indicators followed by the analysis of the comparability of countries can be useful in making international or national decision, or even for the involvement of a growing number of state or non-state actors in solving societal or environmental issues. Particularly for the achievement of the Sustainability Development Goals,[29] the possibility to consider a broad spectrum of indicators as

---

[29] See the Sustainable Development Knowledge Platform at https://sustainabledevelopment.un.org/ (accessed 20 July, 2018).

proposed in this study is an additional mathematical and representation tool to use for a comprehensive analysis of sustainable development.

Acknowledgements This study is a contribution (PM and CL) to the GEMA project "Gouvernance Environnementale: Modélisation et Analyse" funded by CNRS (Défi interdisciplinaire: «InFIniti» InterFaces Interdisciplinaires Numérique et Théorique).

References

Alkire S (2010) Human development: definitions, critiques and related concepts. OPHI Working Papers 36, University of Oxford, Oxford. http://ophi.org.uk/human-development-definitions-critiques-and-related-concepts/. Accessed 30 Nov 2017

Bartelmus P (2014) What's beyond GDP? Hum Dimens 4:8–12. http://www.ihdp.unu.edu/docs/Publications/Secretariat/Update-Dimensions/Dimensions%201-2014%20Beyond%20GDP.pdf. Accessed 30 Nov 2017

Boulet R, Barros-Platiau AF, Mazzega P (2016) 35 years of multilateral environmental agreements ratification: a network analysis. Artif Intell Law 24(2):133–148. https://doi.org/10.1007/s10506-016-9180-7

Burck J, Hermwille L, Krings L (2012) The climate change performance index - results 2013. Germanwatch - Bonn Office and CAN Climate Action Network Europe Brussels, Bonn. https://germanwatch.org/en/5698. Accessed 30 Nov 2017

Burck J, Hermwille L, Bals C (2015) The climate change performance index - background and methodology. Germanwatch - Bonn Office and CAN Climate Action Network Europe Brussels, Bonn. https://germanwatch.org/en/ccpi_bame. Accessed 30 Nov 2017

Dalal-Clayton B, Bass S (2002) Sustainable development strategies: a resource book. Earthscan, Routledge, London

Dasgupta P (2014) Health and nature in inclusive wealth. Hum Dimens 4:14–18. http://www.ihdp.unu.edu/docs/Publications/Secretariat/Update-Dimensions/Dimensions%201-2014%20Beyond%20GDP.pdf. Accessed 30 Nov 2017

Downie C (2015) Global energy governance: do the BRICS have the energy to drive reform? Int Aff 91(4):799–812. https://doi.org/10.1111/1468-2346.12338

Duraiappah A, Fernandes C (2014) GDP reexamined. Hum Dimens (4):33–36. http://www.ihdp.unu.edu/docs/Publications/Secretariat/Update-Dimensions/Dimensions%201-2014%20Beyond%20GDP.pdf. Accessed 30 Nov 2017

Fehling M, Nelson BD, Venkatapuram S (2013) Limitations of the millennium development goals: a literature review. Glob Public Health 8(10):1109–1122. https://doi.org/10.1080/17441692.2013.845676

Ge M, Johannes Friedrich J, Damassa T (2014) 6 Graphs explain the World's top 10 emitters. World Resources Institute – WRI Global Climate Program. http://www.wri.org/blog/2014/11/6-graphs-explain-world%E2%80%99s-top-10-emitters. Accessed 30 Nov 2017

Hammond AL, Adriaanse A, Rodenburg E, Bryant D, Woodward R (1995) Environmental indicators: a systematic approach to measuring and reporting on environmental policy performance in the context of sustainable development. World Resources Institute, Washington DC. http://pdf.wri.org/environmentalindicators_bw.pdf. Accessed 30 Nov 2017

Hsu A, Johnson L, Lloyd A (2013) Measuring progress: a practical guide from the developers of the Environmental Performance Index. Yale Center for Environmental Law and Policy, New Haven. http://archive.epi.yale.edu/files/ycelp_measuring_progress_manual.pdf. Accessed 30 Nov 2017

Hsu A et al (2016) 2016 Environmental Performance Index. Yale University, New Haven. https://issuu.com/rodrigovelasquezangel/docs/epi2016_final_report. Accessed 30 Nov 2017

ICSU ISSC (2015) Review of the Sustainable Development Goals: the science perspective. International Council for Science (ICSU), Paris. https://www.icsu.org/cms/2017/05/SDG-Report.pdf. Accessed 30 Nov 2017

Jones GA, Warner KJ (2016) The 21st century population-energy-climate nexus. Energy Policy 93:206–212. https://doi.org/10.1016/j.enpol.2016.02.044

Kirton J, Kokotsis E (2016) The global governance of climate change. G7, G20 and UN leadership. Routledge, Abingdon

Kovacevic M (2010) Measurement of inequality in human development – a review. UNDP – Human Dev. Rep., Res. Paper 2010/35, UNDP, New York. http://hdr.undp.org/en/content/measurement-inequality-human-development-%E2%80%93-review. Accessed 30 Nov 2017

Lajaunie C, Mazzega P (2017) Transmission, circulation et persistance des enjeux de santé dans les conventions internationales liées à la Biodiversité et Conventions de Rio. In: Maljean-Dubois S (ed) Diffusion de normes et circulations d'acteurs dans la gouvernance internationale de l'environnement, Confluence des Droits, Aix en Provence, pp 61–80. http://dice.univ-amu.fr/sites/dice.univ-amu.fr/files/public/ouvrage_circulex_2017.pdf. Accessed 30 Nov 2017

Meadows D (1998) Indicators and information systems for sustainable development. The Sustainability Institute, Hartland Four Corners. http://www.iisd.org/pdf/s_ind_2.pdf. Accessed 30 Nov 2017

Monebhurrun N (2016) La fonction du développement dans le droit international des investissements. L'Harmattan, Paris

Ness B, Urbel-Piirsalu E, Anderberg S, Olsson L (2007) Categorising tools for sustainability assessment. Ecol Econ 60(3):498–508. https://doi.org/10.1016/j.ecolecon.2006.07.023

Rist G (2001) Le développement. Histoire d'une croyance occidentale, 2ème éd. Presses de Sciences Po, Paris

Saari DG (2001) Decisions and elections. Explaining the unexpected. Cambridge University Press, Cambridge

Schröder BSW (2003) Ordered sets. An introduction. Birkhäuser Boston Inc, Boston

Shambaugh D (2016) China's future. Polity Press, Cambridge

Steves F, Teytelboym A (2013) Political economy of climate change policy. Working paper 13-06, Smith School of Enterprise and the Environment, Oxford. http://www.smithschool.ox.ac.uk/publications/wpapers/workingpaper13-06.pdf. Accessed 30 Nov 2017

Surminski S, Williamson A (2014) Policy indexes as tools for decision makers: the case of climate policy. Global Policy 5(3):275–285. https://doi.org/10.1111/1758-5899.12121

Trotter WT (1992) Combinatorics and partially ordered sets. Dimension theory. Johns Hopkins Series in the Mathematical Sciences. Johns Hopkins University Press, Baltimore

UNCED (1992) United Nations Conference on Environment & Development – Agenda 21. Rio de Janeiro.   https://sustainabledevelopment.un.org/outcomedocuments/agenda21.   Accessed 30 Nov 2017

UNDP (1990) Human development report 1990: concept and measurement of human development. United Nations Development Programme. Oxford University Press, New York. http://hdr.undp.org/en/reports/global/hdr1990. Accessed 30 Nov 2017

United Nations (2016) The sustainable development goals report 2016. UN publication issued by the Department of Economic and Social Affairs (DESA), New York. https://unstats.un.org/sdgs/report/2016/. Accessed 30 Nov 2017

Viola E, Basso L (2016) Wandering decarbonization: the BRIC countries as conservative climate powers. Rev Bras Polít Int 59(1):e001. https://doi.org/10.1590/0034-7329201600101

Vogler J (2011) The challenge of the environment, energy and climate change. In: Hill C, Smith M (eds) International relations and the European Union, 2nd edn. Oxford University Press, Oxford, pp 349–379

Zwicker WS (2016) Introduction to the theory of voting. In: Brandt F, Conitzer V, Endriss U, Lang J, Procaccia AD (eds) Handbook of computational social choice. Cambridge University Press, Cambridge, pp 23–56

Chapter 13
Network Theory and Legal Information "for" Reality: A Triple Support for Deliberation, Decision Making, and Legal Expertise

Ugo Pagallo

Abstract Work on network theory and the law has become increasingly popular over the past decade. A common feature of this work is how scholars approach the law as a matter of information. By distinguishing three different levels of analysis on legal information "as" reality, "about" reality, and "for" reality, this paper restricts the focus of the analysis to the law conceived as a set of rules or instructions for the determination of other informational objects, i.e. legal information for reality. The aim is to stress that network theory can be fruitful either as a support for the deliberation and decisions made by legislators and policy makers, or as a support for scholars and experts about what should be deemed as legally relevant. Any approach that scarcely debates, or simply ignores this facet of legal information, would simply persist in doing so at its own risk.

13.1 Introduction

Over the past decade, work on network analysis and the law has become increasingly popular among scholars. This research includes (not only but also) jurisprudence, legislation and the ways academic studies quote each other and the case law of courts. This level of abstraction represents such variants of the legal phenomenon in terms of nodes and clustering coefficients, links and diameter of the network, up to the laws according to which information is distributed and legal networks evolve as time goes by (Pagallo 2005, 2006, 2010).

A common feature of network legal analysis concerns the representation of the law and of its components, e.g. the case law of courts, legislation, and the opinion of experts, as a matter of information. Drawing on a "general definition of information" (Floridi 2009), let us present this notion here as that which is made of data, namely,

U. Pagallo (✉)
Torino Law School, University of Torino, Torino, Italy
e-mail: ugo.pagallo@unito.it

© Springer Nature Switzerland AG 2019
R. Boulet et al. (eds.), *Law, Public Policies and Complex Systems: Networks in Action*, Law, Governance and Technology Series 42,
https://doi.org/10.1007/978-3-030-11506-7_13

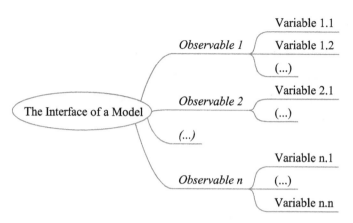

Fig. 13.1 Levels of abstraction of a model

that which is made of lack of uniformity in the real world if, and only if, such data are additionally "well formed" and "meaningful" (Floridi 2009, p. 21). Along with different types of data, such as analogue, binary, and digital data, there are multiple kinds of information. From a methodological viewpoint, it is thus necessary to set the proper level of abstraction for our analysis, i.e. to set the interface that makes possible an analysis of the legal system in terms of information and legal networks. The general idea is to define a set of features representing the observables and variables of the analysis, the result of which provides a model for the field under exam (Pagallo 2013, pp. 28–29). This methodological approach can be represented by a figure on the interface of the model, its observables and variables (see Fig. 13.1).

Significantly, Floridi has adopted different interfaces so as to discern multiple types of information: for instance, in Floridi (2009), the attention is drawn to the basic distinction between environmental information and semantic information. The former indicates "the possibility that data might be meaningful independently of an intelligent producer/informer" (*op. cit.*, 32). Think of the series of concentric rings visible in the wood of a cut tree trunk, which allows us to estimate the age of that tree. In the case of semantic information, the latter has to do with the content of the information, which can be further defined as instructional or factual. Instructional information can be environmental or semantic, and is meant to (contribute to) bring about something. As to the notion of factual information, semantic content refers to the states of the world and is "the most common way in which information is understood and also one of the most important, since information as true semantic content is a necessary condition for knowledge" (Floridi 2009, p. 36).

In another work, we find a slightly different distinction, tripartite rather than bipartite, which clearly overlaps with Floridi's previous model: indeed, "information can be viewed from three perspectives: information as reality (for example, as patterns of physical signals, which are neither true nor false), also known as ecological information; information about reality (semantic information, alethically

Fig. 13.2 A tripartite legal interface for an information society

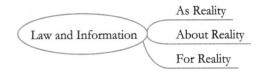

qualifiable); and information for reality (instruction, like genetic information)" (Floridi 2014, p. 560).

Since the aim of the adopted level of abstraction is to identify the set of relevant features representing the observables and variables of the investigation, i.e. the analysis of the law in terms of information, let us follow here the tripartite division. In light of the manifold ways in which the legal phenomenon has been understood throughout the centuries, this stance pinpoints three fundamental approaches to our subject matter, that is, legal information "as" reality, "about" reality, and "for" reality. This interface with its observables is illustrated by Fig. 13.2.

The next section (Sect. 13.2) explores how this tripartite approach relates to the different kinds of analysis we find in the field of network theory and the law. Against this backdrop, Sect. 13.3 dwells on that particular network approach to the law that will be dubbed as work on legal information "for" reality. Since this type of instructional information with a signalling function seems overlooked in the legal approaches of network theory,[1] some examples will illustrate why this level of analysis is however fruitful. A normative standpoint on that which should be deemed as relevant in the legal field, follows as a result in the concluding remarks of this chapter.

13.2 Networks, Information, Law, and Reality

In light of Fig. 13.2, illustrated above in the previous section, let us distinguish three different perspectives in network theory that concern legal information "as" reality, "about" reality, and "for" reality. First of all, I already mentioned that legal information "as" reality refers to data which can be meaningful independently of an intelligent "producer/informer" (Floridi 2009, p. 32). This perspective has become popular in the field of evolutionary psychology, according to which basic human concepts would be wired in our brains thus grounding cultural evolution. In addition, this stance specifies what all the variables of the natural law tradition have in common, namely the examination of being *qua* being, or its essence, so that law could be found in the nature of the individuals, of the world, of the things, i.e. the

---

[1]This is not to say, of course, that such a work does not exist yet. Consider Ashley et al. (2014): here, the network diagrams serve as visual indexes into a legal information database enabling users, such as public health officials working in field offices, to answer such questions as, "What regulations establish communications links between government public health agencies and hospitals?" (*op. cit.*, abstract).

German "Natur der Sache." Likewise, legal information "as" reality is at stake with the results of network analysis in such cases as, say, the power law distribution of information in the case law of the US Supreme Court (Fowler and Jeon 2008), of the EU Court of Justice (Malmgren 2011), or of the Italian Constitutional Court. When Tommaso Agnoloni and I started analysing the case law of the latter (Agnoloni and Pagallo 2014, 2015a, b), we were pretty confident that the result would be similar to previous work on the jurisprudence of the US Supreme Court, of the EU Court of Justice, etc. In all these cases, by fitting a power law function with the degree distribution of the network, the citation graph exhibits the properties of a scale free network. Moreover, the topological properties of the network do not change, by restricting the analysis to a specific time period so as to follow the evolution of the network. This means that a small number of cases receive a large number of citations, whereas most of the cases have few citations or none at all. This kind of legal information "as" reality means that properties and regularities were and are "out there," regardless of our awareness. Hence, the most typical and genuine of the philosophical questions: Why do the case law of the US Supreme Court, of the EU Court of Justice, of the Italian Consulta, follow the same pattern?

A possible explanation is simple and straight. Such features of complex networks, as their power laws and the presence of hubs, optimize the flow of information in the system. Interestingly, this was what Herbert Simon noted in his seminal *The Sciences of the Artificial* (1969, ed. 1996). Simon's notion of "nearly decomposable systems" proposes hierarchy as the clue for grasping the architecture of complexity, in that "most things are only weakly connected with most other things; for a tolerable description of reality only a tiny fraction of all possible interactions needs to be taken into account" (*op. cit.*) Additionally, Simon's "empty world hypothesis" can be properly grasped with the notion of hubs, for this small fraction of nodes in the network with a much higher degree of connectivity than the average, explains the clusters of dense interaction in the chart of informational exchange by offering the common connections mediating the short path lengths between the nodes of the network.

This does not mean, of course, that all legal systems should present small world-features, power laws of distribution, etc. In Boulet et al. (2010), for instance, it is argued that the French environmental code presents a small world-structure and yet, it contrasts with the reference network of all the French legal codes. Although the latter shows "a rich club of ten codes very central to the whole... system," this reference network has no small world properties at all. Eventually, we should stress the difference between human political planning and the unintentional emergence of spontaneous orders, that is, what Friedrich Hayek used to dub as the distinction between *taxis* and *kosmos* (Hayek 1982). Still, what matters here should not be the subject-matter of an ideological debate on law "as" information. Rather, the issue concerns true semantic content as a necessary condition for knowledge, namely our second level of abstraction.

Legal information "about" reality has in fact to do with matters of knowledge and concepts that frame the representation and function of a given system, and inform us about the different states of reality. This is the bread and butter of the sociological approaches to the legal phenomenon, and of some variants of legal realism as well. For example, consider the American (as opposed to the Scandinavian) legal realism and the idea that the law is a sort of prophecy of what the courts will do in fact (Holmes Oliver Jr 1963). Although this approach is mostly popular in the common law area, it does fit many instances of the civil law tradition. After all, people ask for legal information about reality every time they visit a lawyer's office or a clerk to the justices. Moreover, since they are dealing with information as semantic content, which is alethically qualifiable, what people hope is that such lawyer, clerk, or attorney, will speak the truth.

Legal information "about" reality is thus particularly relevant for the work of network theory, since this level of abstraction sheds light on the peculiarities of the system under scrutiny, notwithstanding the "family resemblances" with other legal networks. As a matter of legal information "as" reality, I already stressed the similarities of such networks as the case law of the US Supreme Court, of the EU Court of Justice, and of the Italian Constitutional Court. As a matter of legal information "about" reality, the differences between such networks can be illustrated with their semantic evolution. For instance, in their 2008 work on the US Supreme Court jurisprudence, Fowler and Jeon showed that the most authoritative cases before the American civil war involved freedom of contract, namely the contract clause, whereas, after that war and until the end of the 1930s with the New Deal, the main core became balance of power in order to regulate commercial issues in a federal system. Then, since the late 1950s, the Supreme Court shifted its focus towards civil liberties and especially, freedom of speech. In the case of such a legal network as the jurisprudence of the Italian Constitutional Court, things are necessarily different. My work with Tommaso Agnoloni has shown that over almost 60 years of evolution, the most authoritative cases of the Italian Consulta insist on two specific fields: 5 of the first 15 hubs in the network regard labour law, 3 criminal law (which become 6 if we take into account the first 25 hubs of the network). No Italian would be surprised by such results!

The final observable in Fig. 13.2 is the most usual and even important in the legal domain: the law conceived as a set of rules or instructions for the determination of other informational objects, i.e. legal information "for" reality. This is the common ground not only for every kind of positivism, normativism, or imperativism, but also for some aspects of constitutionalism, institutionalism, and the natural law tradition. Yet, this type of instructional information with a signalling function is often overlooked in the field of network theory: although network experts deal either with the norms and rules of legislators, or the decisions of some important national and international courts, i.e. all cases of legal information "for" reality, the prevailing opinion is that findings of network analysis would not aim to determine how individuals should behave in a given context. But, is it really so?

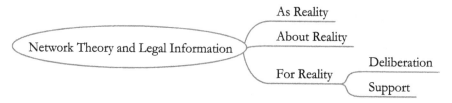

Fig. 13.3 Deliberation and support for legal information for reality

13.3 A Network Approach to Legal Information "for" Reality

The overall aim of this section is to show how the outcomes of network theory can be effective in order to (contribute to) bring about something. The topological properties of the network and the degree of complexity may indeed affect the political planning of lawmakers, the decisions of judges, and their choices.

This means, however, that we should accurately distinguish between the level of deliberation and decisions made by lawmakers and courts, and the role of network theory as a support for such deliberations and decisions. In accordance with the observables and variants of Fig. 13.3, the focus of the analysis is thus restricted to the last variant of the figure, that is support for legal information "for" reality.

At this level of abstraction, i.e. support for normative deliberation and decision, we have to further distinguish between the work of network analysis on legal information "as" reality, and "about" reality. In the first case, support for policy makers hinges on our knowledge of legal information "as" reality as a matter of strategy. In the second case, the focus is on the role that semantic information with factual content may play in this context. Here, work on legal information "about" reality may provide a twofold support for the deliberation of policy makers, e.g. preventing new hard cases, and in order to strengthen the knowledge of legal experts about what should be deemed as relevant. We can sum up this twofold level of analysis with Aristotle's classical distinction between "practical wisdom" and "theoretical knowledge" (Gadamer 1986).

So far, we have carefully distinguished three different levels of abstraction on legal information "as" reality, "about" reality, and "for" reality. Now, the time is ripe to examine how such levels of abstraction interact. The aim is to grasp a triple kind of support for deliberation and decision-making brought on by network theory in the legal domain. The new variables of the analysis are illustrated by Fig. 13.4 below.

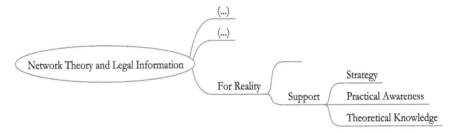

Fig. 13.4 A triple support for deliberation, decision making, and legal expertise

Each of the following parts of the current section intend to shed light on this triple kind of support.

13.3.1 Support for Policy-Makers

The first step for supporting deliberation and decision-making has to do with some key parameters of every network. These parameters are (1) the nodes of the network, (2) the average distance between nodes or diameter of the network, and (3) its clustering coefficients. This level of abstraction allows us to flesh out four different models that should make clear how fruitful a network approach to legal information "for" reality can be.

First, we may conceive a "regular network." Here, all of the nodes have the same number of links: this network has high clustering coefficients but a long diameter since the degree of separation between nodes is high.

Second, we may refer to a "random network" with opposite features: it presents low clustering coefficients but a very short diameter. The explanation is that random links exponentially reduce the degree of separation between nodes in the network.

Third, we find in between the "small world-networks": their peculiarity depends on the apparent deviation from the properties of both regular and random networks. Like regular networks, small world-networks present high clustering coefficients, but they also share with random networks a short characteristic path length, i.e. the nodes of the network need few steps in order to reach each other.

Fourth, we have "scale-free networks." As occurs in most real world networks, such as the internet (Barabási 2002), these networks grow by continuous addition of new nodes whereas the likelihood of connecting to a node would depend upon its degree of connectivity. This sort of special attachment in a growing system explains the power-law distribution of the network and why its topological properties do not change, either by restricting the analysis to specific time periods, or by following the evolution of the network. Small, tightly interlinked clusters of nodes are connected into larger, less cohesive groups through a small fraction of nodes, or hubs, with a much higher degree than the average.

Against this backdrop, we can thus appreciate how fruitful a network approach to legal information "for" reality is, once a policy maker mulls over the kind of content her law should have. Time and again, knowing the topological properties of the network with which we are dealing, turns out to be crucial. With the words of Paul Ormerod, "in a scale-free network, we know that we need to identify the well-connected individuals and to try by some means to induce them to change their behaviours. In a random network, we know that there is a critical value of the proportion of agents we need to influence in order to encourage or mitigate the spread of a particular mode of behaviour or opinion across the network. This at least gives us an idea of the scale of the effort required, and tells us that money and time which is unlikely to generate the critical mass is money and time wasted. In a small-world context, targeting our efforts is more difficult, but at least we know that it is the long-range connectors, the agents with links across different parts of the network, or who have connections into several relevant networks, who are the most fruitful to target" (Ormerod 2012, p. 275).

Work of network theory on information "as" reality can thus improve and strengthen deliberation and decision-making. We have to know first the topological properties of the network we are dealing with, e.g. terrorism or narcotics, in order to define the means to attain a given end. For example, the COPLINK program illustrated in the mid 2000s, that "narcotics networks are small-world with short average path lengths ranging from 4.5-8.5 and have scale-free degree distributions with power law exponents of 0.85 – 1.3" (Kaza et al. 2005). Correspondingly, it makes sense to target the long-range connectors of these small-world networks. Likewise, scholars have shown how the topological properties of the network may allow us to predict online extremism (Ferrara et al. 2016), or to determine the resilience of Mafia syndicates (Agreste et al. 2016). To cut to the chase, an increasing number of research has been devoted over the past years, to how policy makers and legislators could calibrate their strategy in accordance with the topological properties of the networks they aim to tackle (Lopez-Pintado and Watts 2008). Is there any other way in which network theory can improve our understanding of social interaction and the legal phenomenon?

13.3.2   The Price of Ignoring

The second way in which we can appreciate the support of network theory for decision-making and deliberation, has to do with legal information "about" reality. To make this point clear, the case law-networks mentioned above in Sect. 13.2 appear fruitful. In that occasion, the focus was on the topological properties of these networks: All the networks of the US Supreme Court, of the EU Court of Justice, and of the Italian Consulta, are scale-free and "long-tailed," i.e. characterized by the hubs of the network. The question then was why all these systems present such topological properties. Here, what is at stake concerns something different. The topological properties of the network under scrutiny help to inform us about the different states of reality, its dynamics, and evolution. Consider such informational nodes of the US Supreme Court, of the Italian Constitutional Court, etc., that we dubbed as the hubs of their jurisprudence. We may infer that it is highly likely that justices and courts will have to re-examine these "hub cases," or their variants, soon. This is the legal variant of the "rich gets richer effect," i.e. the likelihood of connecting to a node that hinges on its degree of connectivity (Barabási 2002). To make things even more complex, legislators can decide to intervene in the meanwhile. All this ends up with that, which lawyers call as their legal "hard cases," that is, cases of general disagreement that are, or become, the long-range connectors of the network. They refer to a number of different factors. Suffice it to stress here three of them:

- The intricacy of the legal matter discussed in the case. Although the legal principle(s) may be sound, or unproblematic, the complexity of the case depends on how such principle(s) are interpreted under the circumstances of a new case;
- Disagreement among jurists and even justices, so that judges and legal experts are forced to reconsider how the principles and rules of the system, vis-à-vis the case law of a given court, should be applied in the case;
- Lawmakers' activism that compel both courts and legal experts to discuss the ways in which the subject matter should be interpreted in accordance with the constitutional principles of the system.

What these different scenarios have in common is the level of abstraction that reflects on the law as legal information "about" reality, i.e. matters of knowledge and concepts that frame the representation and function of a given system. On the basis of the information about the topological properties of the network under investigation, we can pinpoint the set of rules, or instructions, for the determination of other informational objects, that are under pressure in the system. The result of this approach is both to flesh out a problem, and the ways we should tackle it. Going back to the support of network theory for the deliberation of policy makers, such as the variant (c) mentioned above, the focus shall be on the hubs or large connectors of the network. First, network theory has to attest this kind of variant (c) of the analysis, i.e. lawmakers perpetrating or triggering a set of legal hard cases. Next, we have to ascertain whether the impact of a clumsy lawmaker ended up with variants of the (b)-type, i.e. disagreement among jurists and justices. Then, regardless of variant (a), it seems fair to affirm that whenever lawmakers should decide to intervene again in this specific domain, they have to know the subject matter they intend to govern, e.g. the topological properties and network effects of the issue under examination. Although the proviso may appear as a truism, this is the bread and butter of scholars focusing on the regulation of the internet (Murray 2007); making laws for cyberspace (Reed 2012); proposing new economic models for the online world (Cerf et al. 2014), and more. The price of ignoring semantic information with factual content seems to fatally end up with the making of further contentious cases. This is what Tommaso and I showed with the network representation of the Italian Consulta's case law apropos of legal transplants and their rejection (Agnoloni and Pagallo 2014).[2]

---

[2]Suffice it to mention that, on 22 September 1988, Italy adopted a new code of criminal procedure. It was a case of legal transplant, according to the formula of Watson (1993), since the aim was to substitute the previous inquisitorial system with an adversarial system, typical of the common law tradition. Yet, a number of the new provisions on the role of the parties and their powers, on the notion of procedural truth, etc., contrasted with some principles of the Italian constitution and the

13.3.3   The Price of Ignoring 2.0

There is a second way in which we can appreciate the support of network theory for decision-making and deliberation, as a matter of legal information "about" reality. Going back to Tommaso's and my own work on the case law of the Italian Constitutional Court, this research has been complemented with the analysis of scholarly work on the rulings of the Consulta. One of the interesting outcomes of this research does not only concern the "scale free" features of the net of scholarly opinions, but the fact that some rulings of the Court with some relevant average degree are not commented by scholars and experts at all. More precisely, this is what occurred with three out of the first 30 top rank cases from the 2011 case law of the Court of Rome; five out of the first 30 in 2012; four out of the first 30 in 2013; etc. (Agnoloni and Pagallo 2015b). This sort of oblivion may be explained by the small world properties of the web of scholarly contributions and their in-degree values. Since most of the Italian experts seem to publish on a restricted number of constitutional rulings, no surprise then to find out this kind of silence.

However, scholars who shall proceed ignoring such cases, face a dire fortune. The higher a case is ranked in the citation network of a court, the higher the probability that scholars will have to reflect on such case soon. The probability that a case will gain attention from scholars can be computed as the joint probability that a case has high ranking in the network of the court, and a low ranking in the web of scholarly opinions. As proposed with Tommaso (Agnoloni and Pagallo 2015b), this interplay can also be approximated in terms of incoming citations respectively from court cases and from scholars, as:

$$P_{\text{SCHOLAR}} = (\text{CaseIndeg}/\text{MaxCaseIndeg})(1 - \text{ScholarIndeg}/\text{MaxScholarIndeg})$$

Admittedly, further work is needed so as to test the consistency of this conjecture. Yet, the relevance of the topics in the case law of the court suggests that either the complexity of the case, or new disagreement among justices, or the drawbacks of a clumsy lawmaker, will induce the courts to re-examine such cases with their variants. By putting a legal case in the spotlight, complexity, jurisprudential disagreement, and political activism may thus turn the cases of scholarly oblivion into the next "it" of legal journals, namely, a new hub in the network of academic opinions. Whereas, in the previous Sect. 13.3.2, the attention was drawn to the awareness of policy makers and legislators about semantic information with factual content, i.e. legal information "about" reality, this section has focused on the theoretical knowledge that scholars should have at this level of abstraction. The time is ripe for the conclusions of this chapter.

---

legal culture of this country. Our network analysis casts light on this rejection in a twofold way, that is, by pinpointing the hubs of the case law that show the fields of the system under pressure, and how the latter evolves and varies throughout the decades (Agnoloni and Pagallo 2014).

13.4 Conclusions

The chapter has stressed the threefold ways in which work on network theory may tackle the complexity of legal information. First, the law can be grasped in terms of legal information "as" reality, namely data that can be meaningful regardless of any smart producer, or informer. Although we had to wait until the mid-2000s, in order to start understanding the laws according to which information flows in some relevant networks of jurisprudence, it seems fair to affirm that such laws were over there, notwithstanding our awareness. In more general terms, these properties of the law can reasonably be traced back to Friedrich Hayek's classical distinction between *kosmos* and *taxis*, namely between the emergence of spontaneous orders and human political planning, or "constructivism." In other words, work of network theory on legal information "as" reality revolves around the *kosmos* side of the law and the emergence of unintentional orders (Pagallo 2010, 2015).

Second, we dwelt on legal information "about" reality and work of network theory on legal knowledge and concepts that frame the representation and function of a given system. By informing us about the different states of reality, this perspective casts light on the semantic peculiarities of the system under scrutiny. At times, such a viewpoint on legal information "about" reality converges with the outcomes of network analysis on legal information "as" reality. For example, in our research on the case law of the Italian Constitutional Court (Agnoloni and Pagallo 2014, 2015a, b), we have examined several cases that are extensively commented by scholars and well connected in the citation network of the Court in Rome. This convergence suggests that both stances reinforce each other in determining whether a legal case should be conceived of as relevant. And yet, legal information "as" reality expands our comprehension of the knowledge and concepts that frame the representation and function of a given system, i.e. legal information "about" reality, by fleshing out e.g. cases with some relevant average degree in the case law of a court that, nevertheless, are not commented by scholars and experts. Such outlook introduces the final way in which network theory can improve our understanding of the legal phenomenon.

The final part of the paper concerned in fact the most common and even important information in the legal domain, that is, legal information "for" reality as a set of rules or instructions for the determination of other informational objects in the system. Here, three levels of analysis were distinguished:

- To start with, legal information "for" reality and that which Hayek used to call the *taxis* side of the law, or legal constructivism;
- Then, the attention was drawn to the rules passed by lawmakers and the decisions of the courts, to pinpoint the laws, according to which information flows in the system, i.e. legal information "as" reality, and the semantic content of the system as legal information "about" reality;
- Finally, the focus was on the results of network analysis on legal information "as" reality, and "about" reality, that can effectively support political deliberation and decision making.

Against this backdrop, three different ways in which network theory can support deliberation, law-making, and legal expertise were illustrated. Section 13.3.1 examined work on legal information "as" reality and how this research helps the strategy of legislators, mulling over the content or the type of their laws, and the means to achieve certain aims. Section 13.3.2 scrutinized the role that work on legal information "about" reality plays for political planning, and the risk that legislators run for ignoring semantic information with factual content, e.g. new hard cases for the legal system. Section 13.3.3 analysed the role of legal information "about" reality for legal scholars and experts. Here, the example was given by scholars simply ignoring at their own risk, some cases of the Courts. Three cases of legal relevance were thus mentioned: (1) the aforementioned convergence between cases that are extensively commented by scholars and well connected in the citation network of a court; (2) the semantic information with factual content that lawmakers ignore at their own risk; and, (3) the semantic information with factual content that scholars and legal experts should take into account, lest the case law of the high courts and even the pressure of public opinion force them to do so. In light of this overall picture, my conclusion is twofold.

On the one hand, network theory as a support for the deliberation and decisions of policy makers and legislators has increasingly become the bread and butter of work on information "as" reality and the topological properties of the network under scrutiny: see above Sect. 13.3.1. Still, few work on legal information "for" reality and what should be considered as legally relevant has been discussed so far. An aim of this paper has thus been to show how the topological properties of the network under investigation can improve our comprehension of that which is legally relevant, in order to prevent further hard cases (Sect. 13.3.2), or cases of scholarly oblivion that may turn it into the next "it" of the legal journals (Sect. 13.3.3). On the other hand, this sort of oblivion of scholars and legal experts depends on that which Hayek used to call *taxis*, or legal constructivism. This perspective, once properly set the level of abstraction, makes of course a lot of sense, e.g. Herbert Simon's *The Sciences of the Artificial* mentioned above in Sect. 13.2. Yet, legal scholars forget most of the time the *kosmos* side of the law, so that the result is a partial picture of the phenomenon. Network analysis on legal information "as" reality, or "about" reality, appears crucial, in order to fill the gap. This level of abstraction does not only enhance our understanding of the relevance of the legal cases, but ground them on the laws according to which the legal phenomenon evolves. Whilst public order officers, intelligence services, or anti-corruption task forces seem to really have grasped this point, academic research plods along. As stressed time and again in this paper, this lack of attention is critical, for any legal approach that scarcely debates, or simply ignores this facet of legal information and furthermore, how legal information "about," or "as" reality, impact legal expertise, would simply persist in doing so at its own risk.

References

Agnoloni T, Pagallo U (2014) The case law of the Italian constitutional court between network theory and philosophy of information. In: Winkels R, Lettieri N (eds) 2d International Workshop on Network Analysis in Law (with JURIX 2014), Krakow, December 2014, pp 26–38. http://www.leibnizcenter.org/~winkels/NAiL2014-pre-proceedings.pdf. Accessed 30 Nov 2017

Agnoloni T, Pagallo U (2015a) The case law of the Italian constitutional court, its power laws, and the web of scholarly opinions. In: ICAIL'15 proceedings of the 15th international conference on artificial intelligence and law. ACM Digital Library, New York, pp 151–155. https://dl.acm.org/citation.cfm?id=2746108

Agnoloni T, Pagallo U (2015b) The power laws of the Italian constitutional court, and their relevance for legal scholars. In: Rotolo A (ed) Legal knowledge and information systems - JURIX 2015: the twenty-eighth annual conference. IOS Press, Amsterdam, pp 1–10

Agreste S, Catanese S, De Meo P, Ferrara E, Fiumara G (2016) Network structure and resilience of Mafia syndicates. Inf Sci 351:30–47. https://doi.org/10.1016/j.ins.2016.02.027

Ashley K, Ferrell Bjerke E, Potter M, Guclu H, Savelkaand J, Grabmair M (2014) Statutory network analysis plus information retrieval. In: Winkels R, Lettieri N (eds) 2d International Workshop on Network Analysis in Law (with JURIX 2014), Krakow, December 2014, pp 9–15

Barabási A-L (2002) Linked: the new science of networks. Basic Books, New York

Boulet R, Mazzega P, Bourcier D (2010) Network analysis of the French environment code. In: Casanovas P, Pagallo U, Sartor G, Ajani G (eds) AI approaches to the complexity of legal systems, complex systems, the semantic web, ontologies, argumentation, and dialogue. Springer, Berlin, pp 39–53

Cerf V, Ryan P, Senges M (2014) Internet governance is our shared responsibility. J Law Policy Inf Soc 10(1):1–41. http://moritzlaw.osu.edu/students/groups/is/files/2014/08/5-Cerf-Ryan-Senges.pdf. Accessed 30 Nov 2017

Ferrara E, Wang W-Q, Varol O, Flammini A, Galstyan A (2016) Predicting online extremism, content adopters, and interaction reciprocity. In: Spiro E, Ahn YY (eds) Social informatics. SocInfo 2016. Lecture notes in computer science, vol 10047. Springer, Cham, pp 22–39. https://doi.org/10.1007/978-3-319-47874-6_3

Floridi L (2009) Information: a very short introduction. Oxford University Press, Oxford

Floridi L (2014) The fourth revolution. How the infosphere is reshaping human reality. Oxford University Press, Oxford

Fowler JH, Jeon S (2008) The authority of Supreme Court precedent. Soc Netw 30(1):16–30. https://doi.org/10.1016/j.socnet.2007.05.001

Gadamer HG (1986) The idea of the good in Platonic-Aristotelian Philosophy (trans: Smith PC). Yale University Press, New Haven

Hayek FA (1982) Law, legislation and liberty. A new statement of the liberal principles of justice and political economy. University of Chicago Press, Chicago

Holmes Oliver W Jr (1963) In: De Wolfe Howe M (ed) The common law. Little, Brown, Boston

Kaza S, Xu J, Marshall B, Chen H (2005) Topological analysis of criminal activity networks in multiple jurisdictions, dg.o '05 Proceedings of the 2005 National Conference on Digital Government Research, pp 251–252. https://dl.acm.org/citation.cfm?id=1065307. Accessed 30 Nov 2017

Lopez-Pintado D, Watts D-J (2008) Social influence, binary decisions and collective dynamics. Rationality Soc 20(4):399–443

Malmgren S (2011) Towards a theory of jurisprudential relevance ranking: using link analysis on EU case law. Master of Laws degree under the supervision of C. Magnusson Sjöberg. Stockholm University, Stockholm

Murray AD (2007) The regulation of cyberspace: control in the online environment. Routledge-Cavendish, New York

Ormerod P (2012) Positive linking - how networks can revolutionize the world. Faber and Faber, London

Pagallo U (2005) Introduzione, in privacy digitale. Giuristi e informatici a confronto. Giappichelli Ed, Torino, pp 3–12

Pagallo U (2006) Teoria giuridica della complessità. Giappichelli Ed, Torino

Pagallo U (2010) As law goes by: topology, ontology, evolution. In: Casanovas P, Pagallo U, Sartor G, Ajani G (eds) AI approaches to the complexity of legal systems, complex systems, the semantic web, ontologies, argumentation, and dialogue. Springer, Berlin, pp 12–26

Pagallo U (2013) The laws of robots: crimes, contracts, and torts. Springer, Dordrecht

Pagallo U (2015) Good onlife governance: on law, spontaneous orders, and design. In: Floridi L (ed) The onlife manifesto: being human in a hyperconnected era. Springer, Dordrecht, pp 161–177

Reed C (2012) Making laws for cyberspace. Oxford University Press, Oxford

Simon HA (1996) The sciences of the artificial. MIT Press, Cambridge

Watson A (1993) Legal transplants: an approach to comparative law, 2nd edn. University of Georgia Press, Athens

CPSIA information can be obtained
at www.ICGtesting.com
Printed in the USA
LVHW021941050222
710366LV00004B/174